CW00520868

The Bristol and Gloucestershire Archaeological Society
Gloucestershire Record Series

Hon. General Editor
C. R. Elrington, M.A., F.S.A., F.R.Hist.S.

Volume 15

Registers of Llanthony Priory, 1457–66, 1501–25

A CALENDAR
OF THE REGISTERS OF
THE PRIORY OF LLANTHONY
BY GLOUCESTER
1457–1466, 1501–1525

Edited by John Rhodes, M.A., F.M.A.

The Bristol and Gloucestershire Archaeological Society

2002

The Bristol and Gloucestershire Archaeological Society
Gloucestershire Record Series

© The Bristol and Gloucestershire Archaeological Society 2002

ISBN 0 900197 56 0

The moral rights of the editor have been asserted

British Library Cataloguing in Publication Data.
A catalogue record for this book is available from the British Library.

Printed in Great Britain by J. W. Arrowsmith Ltd., Winterstoke Road, Bristol BS3 2NT

CONTENTS

ACKNOWLEDGEMENTS

The Bristol and Gloucestershire Archaeological Society is grateful to the Public Record Office, Kew, to the Bodleian Library, Oxford, and to the Gloucestershire Record Office for permission to publish this edition of manuscripts in their care. The edition has been compiled from microfilm in the Gloucestershire Record Office except the notes of Prior Deane's register, which are taken from a photocopy in Gloucester Library, and the appendices, which are drawn from original manuscripts in the Gloucestershire Record Office and the Public Record Office. The elevation of the priory gatehouse is drawn by Philip Moss and reproduced by courtesy of Gloucester City Council.

I began the edition twelve years ago when managing the site of Llanthony Priory within the museum service of Gloucester City Council. David Smith, then serving simultaneously as evening-class tutor, county archivist, general editor of the record series and secretary of the society, obtained the microfilm and kindly taught me to read and edit it. Other archivists at Gloucester, including the present county archivist, have been equally helpful and Christopher Elrington, the present general editor, has been tireless in bringing the work to its present form. My former colleagues and successors at the museum, notably Linda Coode and Malcolm Watkins, courteously allowed me to continue to use the museum's facilities after my retirement. It has been a pleasure to exploit the excellent record offices and public libraries in Gloucester, Kew, Hereford, Newport and Birmingham, the Gloucester Cathedral Library and the society's own library at the University of Gloucestershire. David Walker read through the text and made helpful suggestions. In addition to the people and institutions already named I should like to thank, for help with the topics and activities indicated: Carole Berry (Llantrisant), Rosalind Caird (Hereford cathedral muniments), B. J. Cook (coins of Edward IV), Angela Craft (monastic bookbinding), Christopher Dyer (sheephouses), Martin Ecclestone (Haresfield), Beryl Elliott (Prestbury), Ann Geddes (the priory cartularies), Michael Greet (Lady chapel choirs and canons of Cirencester), Joe Hillaby (Herefordshire), Bridgett Jones (Newark House), Nancy Lockwood (the Arnold and Porter families), John Malden (Henry Deane), Michael Oakeshott (South Cerney), Nicholas Orme (priory schoolmasters), Yvonne Stafford (Gloucester Abbey), Elaine Talbot (Bishop Booth's register), Nigel Cox and Julia Knight (scanning) and Crystal Harrison, David Rice and Sylvia Smith (word-processing). For errors I am responsible.

Gloucester, July 2002   John Rhodes

TABLES

ILLUSTRATIONS

LIST OF PRINCIPAL SOURCES AND ABBREVIATIONS

Austin, *Crypt School*	R. Austin, *The Crypt School, Gloucester, 1539–1939* (Gloucester, 1939)
B.C.L.	Bachelor of Civil Law
B.Cn.L.	Bachelor of Canon Law
B.G.A.S.	Bristol and Gloucestershire Archaeological Society
B.L.	British Library
B.Th.	Bachelor of Theology
Barrow, *Hereford Episcopal Acta*	Julia Barrow, *English Episcopal Acta VII: Hereford 1079–1234* (British Academy, 1993)
Bigland, *Glos.*	Ralph Bigland, *Historical, Monumental and Genealogical Collections relative to the County of Gloucester* (originally published 1791 and later; reprinted in 4 vols., B.G.A.S., Glos. Record Ser. ii, iii, v and viii, 1989–95)
Bradney, *Mon.*	J. A. Bradney, *History of Monmouthshire* (4 vols. in 9, London, 1904–32)
Cal. Charter R.	*Calendar of Charter Rolls in the P.R.O.* (H.M.S.O. 1903–27)
Cal. Close	*Calendar of Close Rolls in the P.R.O.* (H.M.S.O. 1892–1963)
Cal. Fine R.	*Calendar of Fine Rolls in the P.R.O.* (H.M.S.O. 1911–62)
Cal. Inq. Misc.	*Calendar of Inquisitions Miscellaneous (Chancery) in the P.R.O.* (H.M.S.O. 1916–68)
Cal. Inq. p.m.	*Calendar of Inquisitions post mortem in the P.R.O.* (H.M.S.O. 1904–74)
Cal. Inq. p.m. Hen. VII	*Calendar of Inquisitions post mortem, Henry VII* (H.M.S.O. 1898–1955)
Cal. Liberate R.	*Calendar of Liberate Rolls in the P.R.O.* (H.M.S.O. 1917–64)
Cal. Papal Letters	*Calendar of Entries in the Papal Registers relating to Great Britain and Ireland, Papal Letters* (H.M.S.O. 1894–1961)
Cal. Pat.	*Calendar of Patent Rolls in the P.R.O.* (H.M.S.O. 1891–1982)
Camd. Misc. xxii	*Camden Miscellany*, xxii (Camden 4th Ser. i), including 'Charters of the Earldom of Hereford, 1095–1201'
Ciren.	Cirencester
Close Rolls	*Close Rolls of the Reign of Henry III in the P.R.O.* (H.M.S.O. 1902–75)
Complete Peerage	G. E. Cokayne and others, *Complete Peerage* (2nd edn. 13 vols. 1910–59)
D.C.L.	Doctor of Civil Law
D.Cn.L.	Doctor of Canon Law
D.N.B.	*Dictionary of National Biography*
Dugdale, *Mon.*	W. Dugdale, *Monasticon Anglicanum*, ed. J. Caley and others (6 vols. 1817–30)

Duncumb, *Herefs.* i–iii	John Duncumb, *Collections towards the History and Antiquities of the County of Hereford* (2 vols. Hereford, 1804–12; continued as vol. iii by W. H. Cooke, London, 1882)
Duncumb, *Herefs.*, Hundred of Grimsworth	W. H. Cooke, *Collections towards the History and Antiquities of the County of Hereford in continuation of Duncumb's History, Hundred of Grimsworth* (London, 1892)
Emden, *Biog. Reg. Oxon.*	A. B. Emden, *Biographical Register of the University of Oxford to 1500* (Oxford, 1957–9); *1501–40* (Oxford, 1974)
Feudal Aids	*Inquisitions and Assessments relating to Feudal Aids in the P.R.O.* (H.M.S.O. 1899–1920)
Fosbrooke, *Glos.*	T. D. Fosbrooke, *Abstracts of Records and Manuscripts respecting the County of Gloucester, formed into a History* (2 vols. Gloucester, 1807)
Fosbrooke, *Glouc.*	T. D. Fosbrooke, *Original History of the City of Gloucester* (London, 1819)
Glos. R.O.	Gloucestershire Record Office
Glos. R.O. GBR/J5/3	Rental of property in Gloucester belonging to the mayor and burgesses, A.D. 1509
Glos. R.O. GBR/J5/4	Rental of property in Gloucester belonging to the priory of Llanthony-by-Gloucester, A.D. 1535
Glouc.	Gloucester
Glouc. Corp. Rec.	*Calendar of Records of the Corporation of Gloucester*, ed. W. H. Stevenson (Gloucester, 1893)
Glouc. Rental 1455	*Rental of all the Houses in Gloucester A.D. 1455 compiled by Robert Cole, Canon of Llanthony*, ed. W. H. Stevenson (Gloucester, 1890)
Hereford Probates 1407–1581	*Calendar of Probate and Administration Acts 1407–1541 and Abstracts of Wills 1541–81 in the Court Books of the Bishop of Hereford*, ed. M. A. Faraday and E. J. L. Cole (British Record Society, Index Library, Microfiche Ser. ii, 1989)
Herefs. Field-Name Survey, Llanwarne	*Herefordshire Field-Name Survey, Llanwarne & Llandinabo* (Woolhope N.F.C., Hereford, n.d.), 'Llanwarne'
Hist. & Cart. Mon. Glouc. (Rolls Ser.)	*Historia et Cartularium Monasterii Sancti Petri Gloucestrie*, ed. W. H. Hart (Rolls Ser. 3 vols. 1863–87)
Hist. of Parl., Biographies 1439–1509	*History of Parliament, Biographies of Members of the Commons House 1439–1509*, ed. J. C. Wedgwood (H.M.S.O. 1936)
Hist. of Parl., Commons 1386–1421	*History of Parliament, House of Commons 1386–1421*, ed. J. S. Roskell (4 vols. Stroud, 1992)
Hist. of Parl., Commons 1509–58	*History of Parliament, House of Commons 1509–58*, ed. S. T. Bindoff (3 vols. London, 1982)
Hockaday Abs.	'Hockaday Abstracts', being abstracts of ecclesiastical records relating to Gloucestershire, compiled by F. S. Hockaday, 1908–24, transferred from Gloucester Library to Glos. Record Office

Irish Cart. Llanth.	*Irish Cartularies of Llanthony Prima and Secunda*, ed. E. St. J. Brooks (Dublin, 1953)
J. Soc. Archiv.	*Journal of the Society of Archivists*
Knowles, *Religious Orders*	David Knowles, *The Religious Orders in England* (3 vols. Cambridge, 1948–59)
L. & P. Hen. VIII	*Letters and Papers, Foreign and Domestic, of the Reign of Henry VIII* (H.M.S.O. 1864–1932)
Le Neve, *Fasti*	J. Le Neve, *Fasti Ecclesiae Anglicanae* (revised edn. issued by the Institute of Historical Research, 1962–99)
Leech, *Topog. Bristol*, i	R. H. Leech, *Topography of Medieval and Early Modern Bristol*, Part i (Bristol Record Soc. xlviii, 1997)
Military Survey of Glos. 1522	*Military Survey of Gloucestershire, 1522*, ed. R. W. Hoyle (B.G.A.S., Glos. Record Ser. vi, 1993)
Mr.	'Magister', i.e. graduate
O.E.D.	*Oxford English Dictionary*
P.R.O.	Public Record Office
P.R.O. C 115/73 (see note on p. xii)	Terrier of property in Gloucester belonging to the priory of Llanthony-by-Gloucester, A.D. 1442 (formerly C 115/A13 or C 115/K1/6678; Glos. R.O. microfilm 1100)
P.R.O. C 115/77, 75 (see note on p. xii)	Great Cartulary (*Magnum Registrum*) of the priory of Llanthony-by-Gloucester, *c.* A.D. 1350 with later additions (2 vols., formerly C 115/A1–2 or C 115/K2/6683 and C 115/K1/6681; Glos. R.O. microfilms 1104, 1101)
P.R.O. C 115/83, 81 (see note on p. xii)	Another similar, A.D. 1449–50 (2 vols., formerly C 115/A4–5 or C 115/L1/6689 and 6687; Glos. R.O. microfilms 1105–6)
P.R.O. C 115/84 (see note on p. xii)	Cartulary of property in Gloucester belonging to the priory of Llanthony-by-Gloucester, A.D. 1441 (formerly C 115/A6 or C 115/L2/6690; Glos. R.O. microfilm 1106)
Pantin, *Chapters of Black Monks*	W. A. Pantin, *Documents illustrating the Activities of the General Chapters of the English Black Monks 1215–1540* (3 vols. Camden 3rd Ser. xlv, xlvii and liv, 1931–7)
Rec. Com.	Record Commission
Reg. Bourgchier	*Registrum Thome Bourgchier, Cantuariensis Archiepiscopi 1454–86*, ed. F. R. H. Du Boulay (Cant. & York Soc. 1957)
Reg. Bothe	*Registrum Caroli Bothe, Episcopi Herefordensis 1516–35*, ed. A. T. Bannister (Cant. & York Soc. 1921)
Reg. Brockworth (see note on p. xii)	Register of Simon Brockworth, prior of Llanthony-by-Gloucester 1362–76, P.R.O. C 115/82 (formerly C 115/A12 or C 115/L1/6688; Glos. R.O. microfilm 1103)
Reg. Chirton (see note on p. xii)	Register of William Chirton, prior of Llanthony-by-Gloucester 1376–1401, P.R.O. C 115/78 (formerly C 115/A7 or C 115/K2/6684; Glos. R.O. microfilm 1103)
Reg. Forest (see note on p. xii)	The MS. edited here, P.R.O. C 115/85 (formerly C 115/A14 or C 115/L2/6691; Glos. R.O. microfilm 1103)
Reg. Hayward (see note on p. xii)	The MS. edited here, P.R.O. C 115/79 (formerly C 115/A11 or C 115/K2/6685; Glos. R.O. microfilm 1103)

Reg. Mayew	*Registrum Ricardi Mayew, Episcopi Herefordensis 1504–16,* ed. A. T. Bannister (Cant. & York Soc. 1921)
Reg. Morton	*Register of John Morton, Archbishop of Canterbury 1486–1500,* ed. C. Harper-Bill (2 vols. Cant. & York Soc. 1991)
Reg. Myllyng	*Registrum Thome Myllyng, Episcopi Herefordensis 1474–92,* ed. A. T. Bannister (Cant. & York Soc. 1920)
Reg. Stanbury	*Registrum Johannis Stanbury, Episcopi Herefordensis 1453–74,* ed. A. T. Bannister (Cant. & York Soc. 1919)
Reg. Swinfield	*Registrum Ricardi de Swinfield, Episcopi Herefordensis 1283–1317,* ed. W. W. Capes (Cant. & York Soc. 1909)
Reg. Trefnant	*Registrum Johannis Trefnant, Episcopi Herefordensis 1389–1404,* ed. W. W. Capes (Cant. & York Soc. 1916)
Reg. Wyche (see note below)	Register of John Wyche, prior of Llanthony-by-Gloucester 1408–36, P.R.O. C 115/76 (formerly C 115/A3 or C 115/K2/6682; Glos. R.O. microfilms 1102–3)
Rudder, *Glos.*	S. Rudder, *A New History of Gloucestershire* (Cirencester, 1779)
S.T.P.	'Sancte Theologie Professor', i.e. Doctor of Theology
Salter, *Chapt. Augustin.*	H. E. Salter, *Chapters of the Augustinian Canons* (Cant. & York Soc. 1922)
Tax. Eccl. (Rec. Com.)	*Taxatio Ecclesiastica Anglie et Wallie auctoritate P. Nicholai IV circa A.D. 1291,* ed. S. Ayscough and J. Caley (Rec. Com. 1802)
Trans. B.G.A.S.	*Transactions of the Bristol and Gloucestershire Archaeological Society*
Trans. Woolhope N.F.C.	*Transactions of the Woolhope Naturalists' Field Club*
V.C.H.	*Victoria County History*
Valor Eccl. (Rec. Com.)	*Valor Ecclesiasticus temp. Hen. VIII auctoritate Regia Institutus,* ed. J. Caley and J. Hunter (Rec. Com. 6 vols. 1810–34)
Visit. Glos. 1623	*Visitation of the County of Gloucester, 1623,* ed. J. Maclean and W. C. Heane (Harleian Soc. xxi, 1885)
Visit. Herefs. 1569	*Visitation of Herefordshire in 1569,* ed. F. W. Weaver (Exeter, 1886)
Wilkins, *Concilia*	David Wilkins, *Concilia Magnae Britanniae et Hiberniae* (4 vols. London, 1737)

In references to the MS. cartularies and registers of Llanthony Priory (P.R.O. C 115) the original folio numbers, where they exist, are preferred to the modern folio numbers. For the terrier C 115/73 the modern numbers are added in brackets as many of the original numbers are illegible.

INTRODUCTION

THE PRIORY AND ITS REGISTERS

Monastic Registers

Registers or letter-books, containing copies of the current documents which came before monastic heads and their chapters, were compiled from the late 13th century in response to episcopal injunctions such as that addressed to Gloucester Abbey by Archbishop Winchelsey in 1301. Winchelsey ordered that all writings issued under the conventual seal should be transcribed by the abbot's chaplain into a register kept in the abbey treasury. Such a volume served both as a record of current rights and obligations and a formulary. In England one or more registers have survived for seven cathedral priories and twelve greater Benedictine abbeys (including Gloucester Abbey for the period 1500–38), but otherwise only fourteen are known.[1] Six of them are registers of the Augustinian priory of Llanthony-by-Gloucester, as follows:

Letters, dietaries and a rental of the time of Prior William of Ashwell, *c.* 1270: Corpus Christi College, Oxford, MS. 154, ff. 1–4, 386–93, 403–34.

Register of Prior Simon Brockworth, 1362–76: P.R.O. C 115/82.

Register of Prior William Chirton, 1376–1401: P.R.O. C 115/78.

Register of Prior John Wyche, 1408–36: P.R.O. C 115/76.

Register of Prior John Hayward, 1457–66: P.R.O. C 115/79, calendared below.

Register of Prior Edmund Forest, 1501–25: P.R.O. C 115/85, calendared below.

Like others of their kind these registers document the community, its servants, its fraternity, its churches, manors and estates and its dealings with bishops and the Crown. Unusually, they also contain narrative memoranda,[2] incoming letters[3] and important reference material both current and historic.[4] For instance, 14th-century tax assessments for Gloucestershire missing from the Subsidy Rolls have been supplied from Prior Wyche's register,[5] and Cardinal Wolsey's citation to the last chapter of the Augustinian order in England, printed below,[6] is preserved nowhere else.

In the last 200 years the priory registers have been drawn upon for histories of Llanthony Priory and the borough of Gloucester by Richard Furney,[7] Richard Holt[8] and Ann Geddes,[9] and more generally by the authors of the *Victoria County History of*

---

[1] W. A Pantin, 'English Monastic Letter-Books' in *Historical Essays in Honour of James Tait*, ed. J. G. Edwards, V. H. Galbraith and E. F. Jacob (Manchester, 1933), 201–22; cf. Gloucester Cathedral Library, Registers C, D, E.

[2] e.g. below, **7–37, 84, 215–221, 226**.

[3] e.g. below, **230–1, 233, 380, 382, 385, 390–1**.

[4] e.g. below, **41–2, 62, 66, 80, 83, 298, 338–9**.

[5] *Feudal Aids*, ii. 244–58, 292–5.

[6] Below, **386**.

[7] Bodleian Library, MSS. Top. Gloucs. c. 4–5; Glos. R.O. D327; cf. below, **101–12**.

[8] 'Gloucester in the Century after the Black Death', *Trans. B.G.A.S.* ciii. 149–61.

[9] 'The Priory of Llanthony by Gloucester: an Augustinian House in an English Town, 1136–1401', Ph.D. dissertation, Johns Hopkins University, Baltimore, Maryland, 1997: copy in Glos. R.O.

Gloucestershire. Because their original tables of contents are missing or incomplete the two registers published here have been used the least.

Resources of the Priory

Before it was dissolved in 1538 Llanthony-by-Gloucester[1] was arguably the richest Augustinian house in England and the third richest monastery in Gloucestershire. Its English and Welsh possessions were valued in 1535 at £737 a year.[2] In addition its Irish property yielded £597 gross, £514 net to the king's receiver for 18 months in 1536–7, a sum greater than the aggregate revenue of all other Irish property then confiscated from English monasteries and equivalent to £343 annually.[3] The combined annual total of £1,080 puts it slightly ahead of its nearest Augustinian rival, Cirencester Abbey (£1,051), and ahead of all other monasteries in Gloucestershire except the abbeys of Tewkesbury (£1,598) and Gloucester (£1,430). At the surrender it mustered 24 canons, a number exceeded among Augustinian houses only by Nostell, Yorks. (29), Thornton, Lincs. (28), Leicester (26), Bridlington, Yorks. (26) and Guisborough, Yorks. (25).[4]

Its unusual wealth arose from its unusual history as a double foundation. After small beginnings as a hermitage, the church of Llanthony St. John the Baptist was founded in 1108 by Hugh de Lacy in his Welsh lordship of Ewyas, north of Abergavenny, and became an Augustinian priory in about 1118. During a Welsh rising in 1136 it was overwhelmed with refugees and half the canons fled, including the prior. For them Miles of Gloucester, sheriff of Gloucestershire, founded the priory of Llanthony St. Mary in 1136 in the plain below his Gloucester castle. By papal bull Llanthony-by-Gloucester was a cell of Llanthony-in-Wales, but when peace returned successive priors controversially remained seated in Gloucester,[5] leading to a separation of the two priories by deed in 1205–11.[6] By that time, owing mainly to gifts from the two founders' kin, the priory estate already approached its final extent of 115 churches and chapels and 41 principal manors in England, Wales and Ireland.[7] The partition between the two priories generally followed the boundary between Gloucestershire and Herefordshire but the Gloucester house kept half the Irish property together with Kington (Herefs.), Llantrisant and Caldicot (Mon.).[8]

In the early 15th century the fortunes of the two priories diverged. From the time of Prior Chirton (1377–1401) Llanthony-by-Gloucester prospered and invested heavily in

---

[1] The modern name Llanthony Secunda lacks medieval authority, although Llanthony Prima was a medieval name for Llanthony-in-Wales.

[2] *Trans. B.G.A.S.* lxxvi. 105–6, correcting *Valor Eccl.* (Rec. Com.), ii. 430, where the total £649 conflicts with the accompanying schedule.

[3] For the gross, *L. & P. Hen. VIII*, xii (2), p. 461; for deductions, ibid. p. 465.

[4] Comparative totals of income and communities are conveniently tabulated in D. M. Robinson, *The Geography of Augustinian Settlement in England and Wales* (British Archaeological Reports, British Ser. lxxx, 1980), Appendices, and *Trans. B.G.A.S.* lxxvi, tables opp. p. 114.

[5] Dugdale, *Mon.* vi. 128–134.

[6] Below, **37** and n.

[7] Below, pp. xxv–xxxi.

[8] P.R.O. C 115/75, s. xxvii no. 11. Properties held by the Gloucester house between 1350 and 1450 are listed in the tables which preface P.R.O. C 115/75, C 115/77 and C 115/83.

its parish churches, manor houses and barns.[1] Llanthony-in-Wales, however, was held and plundered by the followers of Owain Glyndwr in 1402–6[2] and shared thereafter in the general impoverishment of the principality. Meanwhile the patronage of the Gloucester house passed to the Crown in 1421 by agreement with Anne countess of Stafford[3] and the patronage of the Welsh house followed suit in 1461 on the accession of the earl of March as Edward IV.[4] In 1481, when the community of Llanthony-in-Wales numbered only five, the king united it to the priory of Llanthony-by-Gloucester at the instance of the latter's prior, Henry Deane.[5] John Hayward was among the last priors at Gloucester before the union.

PRIORS HAYWARD AND SHOYER, 1457–67

John Hayward, Prior 1457–66

John Hayward was elected prior in succession to the late John Garland on 18 October 1457. He was born in 1423 the son of the elder John and Margaret Hayward, who married about 1417.[6] The family home, at no. 108 Southgate Street, covered two burgage plots at the south corner of St. Owen's Lane, less than half a mile from the priory church. It had been built by Margaret's previous husband John Foliot. The elder John Hayward held it in fee from Llanthony Priory together with a croft at nos. 157–171 Southgate Street and a tannery at no. 205 Westgate Street;[7] his career suggests that he also had a country estate. In 1450 he was trustee of a settlement of the manor of Hardwicke.[8] He was escheator of Gloucestershire and the Marches in 1450 and 1453, J.P. for the county 1452–8 and commissioner of array for raising archers there in 1457.[9] He served the abbot of Gloucester until 1460 as auditor of accounts, auditor of servants and understeward of courts and hundreds; he was also steward of St. Oswald's Priory, Gloucester, from 1454 to 1464.[10]

In both the latter offices the elder John was succeeded by his son Thomas.[11] John's daughter Catherine, the prior's sister, married Thomas Porter of Newent and was mother[12] of William Porter S.T.P., warden of New College, Oxford, 1494–1520, prebendary of Lincoln 1489–1519, vicar of Newent to 1524 and precentor and prebendary of Hereford 1515–24.[13] She was also mother of a legal adviser to the priory, Roger Porter (d. 1523), and grandmother of its understeward Arthur Porter, J.P., M.P.,

---

[1] *Trans. B.G.A.S.* lxiii. 97.

[2] *Cal. Pat.* 1405–8, 53.

[3] *Rotuli Parliamentorum* (London, 1783), iv. 136; *Cal. Close* 1500–9, p. 173 contradicting *Trans. B.G.A.S.* lxiii. 96.

[4] Dugdale, *Mon.* vi. 139.

[5] Ibid.

[6] Below, **3**.

[7] P.R.O. C 115/73, f. 7 (5)v. no. 8; f. 12 (10)v. nos. 20–2; f. 48 (46)v. no. 95; *Glouc. Rental 1455*, 64. For the postal addresses cf. below, p. xlii.

[8] *Cal. Close* 1447–54, 181.

[9] *Cal. Fine R.* 1445–52, 187; 1452–61, 74; *Cal. Pat.* 1452–61, 408, 666.

[10] Below, **80**; *Trans. B.G.A.S.* xliii. 120.

[11] Below, **80**; *Trans. B.G.A.S.* xliii. 121.

[12] *Visit. Glos. 1623*, 127.

[13] Emden, *Biog. Reg. Oxon. to 1500.*

who purchased the priory at the Dissolution.[1] On the monuments of William and Roger the arms of Porter are quartered with those of Hayward: *Three bars, over all three hanks of cord.*[2]

Born within sound of the priory bells and bred to monastic administration, the younger John Hayward professed vows at age 19, was ordained priest at 21 and was already cellarer of the priory when elected prior at age 34.[3] His administrative skill, or that of his lawyers, is best demonstrated by his defence of the priory fish-weir at Cokeyn. Although the weir was more than 300 years old it stood in the Severn at the approach to Gloucester quay and fell foul of a general prohibition in *Magna Carta.* When attached in 1459 for possession of this and other weirs Prior Hayward was able to obtain a pardon,[4] but in 1464 he had to defend it at an Admiralty court before a jury containing several mariners. Impressed by the good condition of the weir, and no doubt by good advocacy, the jury refused to condemn it and it survived until 1535.[5]

In 1465 or 1466 he excommunicated Canon Thomas Alford for being absent from the priory without leave. This was among his last registered acts as prior. It may be that Alford, a later treasurer of the priory,[6] returned with an official visitor who deprived Hayward or caused him to resign. The events that followed suggest that tension between the priory and the borough contributed to his fall.

Relations with the borough

Prior Hayward's register contains memoranda for arbitrators in a dispute which arose in the time of his predecessor John Garland. Garland and his canons sheltered two debtors whom the Gloucester bailiffs' officers wished to arrest.[7] The bailiffs evidently reacted by claiming a right of entry into the priory similar to that which they had obtained at Gloucester Abbey in 1429, and cited in support a controversial perambulation of 1377–8.[8] Cleverly, Prior Garland counterclaimed jurisdiction over the south suburb of Gloucester for his quasi-manorial court of St. Owen, and referred the whole matter in 1456 to the arbitration of six eminent lawyers[9] who failed to agree. Both sides seem to have fallen back upon an agreed perambulation of 1370, which put most of the south suburb inside the borough liberty and Llanthony outside it, until the borough jurisdiction was extended by royal charter in 1483.[10] At about the time of Hayward's election in 1457 the parties aired their mutual grievances at a loveday similar to that which ended their last serious dispute in 1392.[11]

The author of the memoranda claimed that the burgesses had trampled on the priory's rights when its ablest canons died in the Black Death. He delighted to see the borough

---

[1] Below, **120** and pp. xxxi–xxxii.
[2] *Dictionary of Arms, Medieval Ordinary*, i (Soc. of Antiquaries, 1992), 71.
[3] Below, **3**.
[4] Below, **56–7**.
[5] Below, **68–9**; cf. *L. &. P. Hen. VIII*, ix, pp. 50, 166; xiv (1), p. 60.
[6] Below, **95–6, 109**.
[7] Below, **7–32, 33**(a).
[8] *V.C.H. Glos.* iv. 61; below, **8**.
[9] Below, **8, 10, 40**.
[10] Below, **83**; *V.C.H. Glos.* iv. 54.
[11] Below, **33, 38**; Reg. Chirton, f. 159v.

market undermined by illicit trading at Llanthony.[1] He was probably the former town renter Canon Robert Cole whose terrier of the priory's 160 properties in Gloucester, compiled in 1442, is a catalogue of frauds allegedly perpetrated against the priory by the borough and its burgesses in the previous 90 years. He even accused the elder John Hayward of denying due suit to the court of St. Owen, and the Haywards' wedding guest Thomas Bisley of failing to surrender six properties which should have passed to the priory under a 14th-century will.[2] Some of Cole's claims were repeated at the loveday in 1457 but nearly all were open to challenge and remained unresolved in 1535.[3] It was by avoiding litigation, by purchase and by building that the priors ultimately developed an urban estate worth £73 a year, more valuable than that of any other Augustinian house outside London.[4] Paradoxically, Cole cultivated the burgesses' goodwill by compiling a landgavel rental for them in 1455.[5] Nevertheless, his accusations hampered relations not only with the borough but with fellow-canons who weighed the chances of litigation against the likely reaction of an urban mob. In 1449 a mob, displeased at the participation of Abbot Boulers of Gloucester in an embassy to Aachen, ransacked his residence at Over Vineyard in Highnam and poured his vintage into the ground. In 1463 another mob pursued the borough bailiff John Dodyng into the abbey infirmary, polluted the abbey church with his blood and killed him at the high cross of the town.[6] It was probably a threat of similar violence that caused Canon Bisege alias Bristowe of Llanthony, a former hosteler, to fear for his life and move to Combwell Priory in Kent.[7] Such were the circumstances when Prior Hayward left office.

John Shoyer, Prior 1466–7

The Shoyer family of Alvington and Awre is discussed below in connection with the later prior Edmund Shoyer alias Forest. A contemporary Gloucester annalist described the tumultuous priorate of John Shoyer as follows:

On St. Augustine's day [28 Aug.] before the Beheading of St. John the Baptist in the year 146[...] there was great discord between John Shoyer, prior of Llanthony, and John Hayward, late prior. As a result, foresters rose in armed force on Shoyer's side to reinforce his party. On the other side the people of Gloucester and neighbouring gentry supported John Hayward. Many blows were struck on both sides. When the foresters and the Gloucester people met at Llanthony many of both were wounded and many killed, as it was said. Canons of the house, greatly afraid, abandoned the priory and fled to the earl of Warwick, taking the goods of the house with them. They stayed for eight months at Hanley Castle, performing religious duties and divine service there and not daring to return home through fear of the foresters of their prior, John Shoyer. But afterwards Prior Shoyer was urged to return home by King Edward IV. So, after

[1] Below, **15, 21, 25**.
[2] P.R.O. C 115/73, ff. 12 (10)v., 41 (39); cf. below, **3** n.
[3] Below, **38** (d–n); Glos. R.O. GBR/J5/4.
[4] Below, **117, 462** n; *Valor Eccl.* (Rec. Com.), ii. 430; for comparative values, D. M. Robinson, *The Geography of Augustinian Settlement in Medieval England and Wales* (British Archaeological Reports lxxx, 1980), 338.
[5] *Glouc. Rental 1455*, 2.
[6] C. L. Kingsford, *English Historical Literature in the Fifteenth Century* (Oxford, 1913), 161–2, 355–6, extracts of Latin annals which are translated in *Glevensis* xxxv (forthcoming).
[7] Below, **53–4**.

long wrangling between him and ex-prior Hayward and after spending great sums of money, the canons of the house came together again and returned home with their belongings. But Shoyer, persisting in his malice, imprisoned some of the canons a second time. Then, through fear of the people, who disliked and reviled him, he plundered the monastery and carried its goods away with him.[1]

The annalist's Gloucester bias must be taken into account. If Prior Shoyer employed a guard of foresters to defend the priory he was following the prudent example of Abbot Boulers, who protected Gloucester Abbey similarly in 1449.[2] The attacking mob of Gloucestrians is more likely to have driven the canons from the priory and delayed their return. In his final flight Prior Shoyer again acted prudently by protecting the community's assets from his opponents.

Recent historians,[3] relying on the illegible final digit of the date, have argued that these events took place during an interval of Hayward's priorate in 1460–1 or 1461–2, just as Shoyer's contemporary Thomas Sutton interrupted the abbacy of Walter Newbury at Bristol.[4] The annals, however, clearly refer to a time when Shoyer was rightful prior and Hayward a turbulent ex-prior. A further hypothesis, that ff. 26–52 of Prior Hayward's register recorded Prior Shoyer's acts and were torn out on Hayward's return,[5] is even less likely. If re-elected, Prior Hayward would have been obliged to honour the acts of his canonically appointed predecessor and to register a record of his re-election as detailed as that of his election. Canon Hayward died in 1487.[6]

HENRY DEANE, PRIOR 1467–1501

The prior is called Deane by modern biographers but Dene at Llanthony and on his monument;[7] the alternative Denny[8] suggests that the final vowel was sounded. His register, now lost, apparently contained evidence that he was born near Gloucester, that he was elected prior in July 1467 and that he obtained the degree of D.D.[9] He was indeed the priory's scholar at Oxford in 1457 and rented rooms at Exeter College 1473–88. Oxford University has no record of awarding him a degree but its records are incomplete.[10]

During his term as prior of Llanthony-by-Gloucester he was proprietor of the priory of Llanthony-in-Wales 1481–1501,[11] J.P for Gloucestershire 1493–9,[12] privy councillor, chancellor of Ireland 1494–6, lord deputy there 1496, bishop of Bangor in Wales 1496–1500, bishop of Salisbury 1500–1 and keeper of the great seal 1500–2. As chancellor to Sir Edward Poynyngs he gave an address to the Irish parliament on 1 December 1496

---

[1] British Library, Cotton MS. Domitian A iv, f. 256, printed in the original Latin in Kingsford, op. cit. 357.
[2] Ibid. 356.
[3] Ibid. 355; J. N. Langston in *Trans. B.G.A.S.* lxiii. 121–2.
[4] *Trans. B.G.A.S.* xiv. 129.
[5] Ian Jack in *J. Soc. Archiv.* iv. 373–4.
[6] *Trans. B.G.A.S.* lxiii. 122.
[7] Below, **120**, **215**, **217–21**; *Archaeological Journal*, xviii. 256 n.
[8] Below, **102**.
[9] Ibid.
[10] Below, **3(f)**; Emden, *Biog. Reg. Oxon. to 1500*.
[11] Below, **107**; for details of his priorate, *Trans. B.G.A.S.* lxiii. 122–32.
[12] *Cal. Pat.* 1485–94, 487; 1494–1509, 640.

which persuaded the Irish to renounce Perkin Warbeck's rebellion and cede their legislative powers to Westminster.[1] As bishop of Bangor he exercised in person his fishing rights in the Skerries and defeated a challenge by the principal tenant of the islands.[2]

Henry VII issued letters, writs and commissions as Deane's guest at Llanthony-by-Gloucester between 18 and 29 December 1500, between 29 May and 4 June 1501 and between 7 and 21 August 1501.[3] Meanwhile, on 26 April, Deane was elected to the archbishopric of Canterbury, for which the king served the grant of temporalities to him at Llanthony on 7 August.[4] On becoming archbishop he resigned the priorate. The convent apparently elected a new prior in the presence of the king and the archbishop without obtaining the correct form of *congé d' élire*, an omission which it was to regret.[5] In 1502 Archbishop Deane negotiated a marriage alliance and a peace treaty between England and Scotland. He died in 1503.[6]

Prior Deane's Buildings

The outer gatehouse of the Gloucester priory, pinnacled, crenellated and faced with oolite ashlar, was built by Prior Deane on the evidence of a sculpted shield there which was formerly legible as bearing the same personal arms as the sinister side of his archiepiscopal seal: *A chevron between three choughs.*[7] Bricks of a distinctive sandy fabric were used both to line this gatehouse and to build the precinct wall adjacent on the

THE GATEHOUSE FROM THE WEST. *Drawing by Philip Moss*

[1] *D.N.B.*; *Archaeological Journal* xviii. 256–67.
[2] Browne Willis, *Survey of the Cathedral Church of Bangor* (London, 1721), 244–5.
[3] *Cal. Pat.* 1494–1509, 240–1, 244, 249, 639, 641; *Cal. Close* 1500–9, 20; *Cal. Fine R.* 1485–1509, pp. 306–7, 313–14, 316.
[4] Le Neve, *Fasti 1300–1541, Monastic Cathedrals*; *Cal. Pat.* 1494–1509, 240.
[5] Below, **215**.
[6] *D.N.B.*
[7] Below, **110** n.; W. de G. Birch, *Catalogue of Seals in the British Museum* (London, 1887–1900), no. 1258. There is no evidence for Bazeley's suggestion that Deane first acquired these arms as bishop of Bangor: *Trans. B.G.A.S.* xxvi. 47.

south, which is crenellated in oolite and ornamented with vitrified headers. They were also used, with oolite dressings and an upper storey of close studding, to enlarge the south and west ranges of the service court of the priory into an L-shaped block altogether 500 ft. long and 30 ft. wide.[1] The enlarged ranges, similar in cross-section to medieval stables in the outer court of Gloucester Abbey,[2] may have been intended to house the servants and mounts of Henry VII's court during the king's visits in 1500 and 1501.

Deane's principal work at Llanthony-by-Gloucester was the rebuilding of the priory church, for which he received bequests of five gads of iron from Richard Roger of Littledean in 1493 and 100s. from John Eliottes of Gloucester in 1497.[3] This work was continued by Prior Forest and its final appearance is discussed below. Deane probably employed the same master mason for the church at Hempsted, where a small mitred figure labelled with his initials in stained glass[4] evidently portrayed him as donor of the chancel and of the tower above it.[5] Three sides of the tower are ingeniously suspended over the clear space of the chancel on intersecting arches which concentrate the weight upon responds with ogee bracket capitals.[6] Since capitals of the same form appear in the nave arcades at Painswick and at St. Mary de Crypt in Gloucester it seems likely that the prior, as patron of the latter churches,[7] recommended the same mason for employment by the parishioners there. Such capitals also appear at Painswick in the north chancel arcade, built by the parishioners as proprietors of St. Peter's chapel, and in the sanctuary arch which was built by the prior as rector or by his vicar.[8] Although the priors had quarrying rights in the demesne of Matson at Pope's wood near Prinknash,[9] Prior Deane rented a quarry at Painswick for some or all of these works.[10]

EDMUND FOREST, PRIOR 1501–25

Edmund Forest, called Shoyer, was prior by 15 September 1501.[11] His family, of yeoman stock, was long associated with the priory. John Shoyer had been prior in 1466–7.[12] Elizabeth Schoyar of Littledean (d. 1480) named Prior Deane as her executor.[13] Richard Shoyer held benefices in the prior's gift at Painswick from 1507, at

---

[1] Most of the block survives in ruins. For a plan and a drawing of the north extremity, demolished in the 19th century, cf. John Clarke, *Llanthony* (Gloucester, 1853), 35 and fig.

[2] At nos. 10–13 College Green: Suzanne Eward, *No Fine but a Glass of Wine* (Salisbury, 1985), 317–18.

[3] Hockaday Abs. ccxx, 1497; cclx, 1493.

[4] Browne Willis, *Survey of the Cathedral Church of Bangor* (London, 1721), 244–5; below, **110**.

[5] Illustrated in Bigland, *Glos.* ii. 712.

[6] *Trans. B.G.A.S.* xiii. 53 and figs.

[7] *V.C.H. Glos.* iv. 300; xi. 80.

[8] W. St. C. Baddeley, *History of the Church of St. Mary at Painswick* (Exeter, 1902), 11, 26; *V.C.H. Glos.* xi. 82.

[9] P.R.O. C 115/75, s. xxii no. 2; cf. *V.C.H. Glos.* iv. 438.

[10] *V.C.H. Glos.* xi. 78; W. St. C. Baddeley, *A Cotteswold Manor, Painswick* (2nd edn. London and Gloucester, 1929), 126, rental dated 1496.

[11] Will of Mr. Thomas Steward, P.R.O. PROB 11/13, f. 38, copied in Hockaday Abs. ccxvi, 1501. For the prior's alias, **222** below.

[12] See above.

[13] *Hereford Probates 1407–1581*, 90.

Gloucester All Saints from 1509 to 1511 and at Gloucester St. Mary de Crypt from *c.* 1509 to 1517, exploiting them to finance his studies at Oxford and to obtain pensions.[1] Philip Shoyer held office in 1515 and Edward Shoyer 1517–35 as bailiff of one or both of the prior's manors of Alvington and Aylburton, Edward living at Alvington where he and a namesake owned goods worth £12.[2] John Shiar farmed the prior's rectory of Awre in 1535; he and one Philip were the richest lay inhabitants of that parish in 1522, together owning goods worth £27 and freehold land worth £3 a year.[3] Thomas Shoyer, gentleman, who attended the prior at Hempsted in 1515, may be the Thomas (d. 1540) who left Awre to become a citizen and goldsmith of London.[4] Alternatively he may be the Thomas who rented Prior Hayward's birthplace at no. 108 Southgate Street from the priory in 1535, the castle orchard (now the site of Gloucester docks) from the priory in 1538 and a length of town ditch from the borough of Gloucester in 1544.[5]

In 1498, while studying as the priory's scholar at St. Mary's College, Oxford, the future prior was ordained deacon in the adjacent diocese of Salisbury and priest at Osney Abbey.[6] He was still an undergraduate and among the youngest members of the community when elected prior and appointed J.P. for Gloucestershire, an office which he held from 1502 to 1508.[7] He attended Archbishop Deane when the latter surrendered the great seal at Lambeth in 1502.[8] One of his first duties was to provide for the retirement of Deane's old administrators.[9] His own administration was tested when the earl of Kildare, as lord deputy, seized two thirds of the priory's property in Ireland under an ordinance against absentees. Prior Deane had obtained exemption in 1496 but the patent was lost and the registered copy was not discovered until 1515. Prior Forest recovered the property in 1503–4 by meeting the earl in person, by offering him gifts and by legal sophistry.[10] In the same year a royal escheator seized the former property of the priory of Llanthony-in-Wales and denied Prior Forest's title to it on the grounds that the Welsh house was not mentioned in his *congé d' élire*, a finding which the king's council confirmed. Local gentry also challenged the priory's title to estates at Newent, Quedgeley, Haresfield and elsewhere.[11] The lost property was recovered between 1504 and 1507 through the efforts of the prior and William Greville of Arle in Cheltenham, later a justice of common pleas. Greville's son-in-law Robert Wye became steward of the priory in 1510 and oversaw an unprecedented volume of business in the next five years.[12]

[1] Below, **177** and n., **191** and n., **351** and n.
[2] Below, **336, 360**; *Valor Eccl.* (Rec. Com.), ii. 425–6; *Military Survey of Glos. 1522*, 64.
[3] *Valor Eccl.* (Rec. Com.), ii. 429; *Military Survey of Glos. 1522*, 65.
[4] Below, **335**; P.R.O. PROB 11/28, f. 33.
[5] Glos. R.O. GBR/B2/2, f. 31; GBR/J5/4; *L. & P. Hen. VIII*, xiv (1), p. 590.
[6] Emden, *Biog. Reg. Oxon. to 1500.*
[7] *Cal. Pat.* 1494–1509, 640–1.
[8] *Cal. Close* 1500–9, p. 48.
[9] Below, **119, 120**.
[10] Below, **216, 326–7**.
[11] Below, **215, 217–19**; *Cal. Close* 1500–9, p. 173.
[12] Below, **203, 215** n., **217** and Table V (p. xli).

Resuming his studies at St. Mary's College, Prior Forest obtained a dispensation towards the degree of B.Th. by glazing two windows of the Congregation House at the church of St. Mary the Virgin. He qualified as B.Th. and B.A. in 1509 and as S.T.P. in 1514.[1]

Prior Forest's Buildings

The continuing expense of rebuilding the conventual church qualified the priory for a tax rebate in 1518.[2] Many of the principal priory buildings of this time, including the church and a tower, survived in domestic use until 1643 when an eye-witness said that they were 'built in the same manner as the cloisters of the cathedral', i.e. fan-vaulted, 'at least two storeys high and covered with lead on the top'.[3] It was probably for the priory church that Prior Forest commissioned a heraldic tile pavement incorporating his personal grant of arms: *Per pale azure and purpure, on a chevron between three trees argent a pink* (otherwise *a rose*) *gules seeded or between two marigolds gules all stalked vert.*[4] In four-tile patterns which survive dismembered in Gloucester cathedral, the British Museum[5] and elsewhere the pavement depicted Prior Forest's arms encircled by the motto *Timentibus Deum nichill deest,*[6] Archbishop Deane's arms encircled by the motto *Letabor in misericordia et sethera*[7] and what was probably a Tudor rose encircled by the words *Deo gracias.*[8] It also depicted the Bohun arms[9] and unidentified arms which may be those of the priory: *A bend between six trees.*[10]

Prior Forest also commissioned at least six copies of his arms and nine copies of his badge in stained glass for his manor house at Quedgeley, whence they were removed to Bromsberrow about 1800. The badge is *A hand sinister, issuant a manche azure, holding an oak tree erased or,* behind a scroll bearing his motto.[11] The glass probably identified him as builder of a wing at Quedgeley containing an upper parlour in which he held court in 1524. The prior's manor place there was distinguished in 1538 from a newly built house called the farmer's place, which was evidently also built by Prior Forest and

[1] *Trans. B.G.A.S.* lxiii. 132; Emden, *Biog. Reg. Oxon. to 1500.*

[2] Below, **426**.

[3] John Washbourn, *Bibliotheca Gloucestrensis* (Gloucester, 1825), pp. xlii, 372.

[4] For the grant, *Archaeologia* lxix. 93; cf. *Dictionary of British Arms, Medieval Ordinary,* ii (Soc. of Antiquaries, 1996), 486.

[5] E. S. Eames, *Catalogue of Medieval Lead-glazed Earthenware Tiles in the British Museum* (London, 1980), i. 255–6; ii, illustrated patterns as numbered below, notes 6–10. Four-tile patterns incompletely represented there can be completed from unpublished tiles in the Lady chapel floor at the cathedral.

[6] 'They that fear God lack nothing' from Psalm xxxiv. 9; cf. below, **222** n. The pattern includes Eames's nos. 1496–7.

[7] 'I will rejoice in thy mercy' from Psalm xxxi. 8, *et sethera* being an attempt at *et cetera.* The pattern includes Eames's no. 1498.

[8] 'Thanks be to God'; Eames's no. 1439.

[9] Including Eames's nos. 1704–5.

[10] Including Eames's no. 1706.

[11] Thomas Niblet, 'On the arms of Llanthony' (*recte* the arms of Prior Forest), appendix to G. Roberts, *Llanthony Priory, Monmouthshire* (1847 edn.), 46–7 and pl.; cf. John Bellows, *A Week's Holiday in the Forest of Dean* (Gloucester, 1959 edn.), 36. For photographs (including examples at Flaxley and Bristol) and text likewise mistaking Forest's arms for those of the priory, *Trans. B.G.A.S.* xlvii. 298, 314 and figs. 36–7; xlix. 305 and pl. 1.

let for the first time in 1522. One or both of these properties partly survive in the present Quedgeley Manor Farm, a house of 16th-century timber framing with close studs, moulded beams and carved roof brackets.[1]

At Great Barrington Prior Forest as lord of the manor was largely responsible for building the clerestoried nave of the church, dated 1511 on its panelled timber ceiling.[2] At St. Mary de Crypt in Gloucester the clerestoried chancel, although commissioned by his client the rector, was doubtless constructed by his master mason; it is dated to the 1520s by a primary wall painting[3] and is a daring structure in which the arcade piers are suspended over voids in openwork screens. A floor-tile seen there by Richard Furney, bearing Archbishop Deane's arms,[4] clearly belonged to the series described above.

St. Mary's College, Oxford

In 1509 the Augustinian general chapter appointed Prior Forest as its visitor in the dioceses of Worcester, Hereford and St. David's. His fellow-visitor, the prior of Haverfordwest, never made any visits, and the chapter to which they were to report did not meet until 1518.[5] Nevertheless, in May 1511 the presidents of the order commanded him to set out immediately, to collect contributions and fines from delinquent houses and to pay the proceeds within two months to the prior of the Augustinian college of St. Mary at Oxford, which was too ruinous to accommodate students. He responded by visiting Studley Priory (Warws.), which owed no fines, and Cirencester Abbey which owed £15.[6]

Forty-four Augustinian houses were required each to support a student at university by order of the general chapter of 1443. St. Mary's College, on the site of the present Frewin Hall in New Inn Hall Street, was founded in 1435 to accommodate those sent to the university of Oxford, its first buildings being a 12th-century merchant's house and a chapel with a library over.[7] At convocation in 1502 Archbishop Deane, the former prior of Llanthony, persuaded the order to finance further buildings there with an annual levy which was set in 1506 at 2d. in the £. The levy was suspended at the general chapter of 1509 because William Salyng, collector and bursar of the building fund, failed to submit accounts,[8] and the mandate cited above shows that Salyng's buildings were left incomplete.

At the next general chapter, which met under Prior Forest's presidency in 1518, Cardinal Wolsey undertook to resume collecting the levy and to build a college (at St. Mary's, as he later confirmed) for the order's use.[9] Ultimately the college included a vaulted gatehouse which survives as a ruin, timber-framed lodgings which survive in

---

[1] Below, **456, 465**, cf. **329**; *V.C.H. Glos.* x. 218.
[2] *V.C.H. Glos.* vi. 25; for his quarry there cf. below, **318** n.
[3] *V.C.H. Glos.* iv. 301; illus. in D. A. Brazington and others, *St. Mary de Crypt, Gloucester* (Gloucester, 1995), 10.
[4] Below, **110**.
[5] Salter, *Chapt. Augustin.* pp. xxxv, 130, 139–40.
[6] Below, **230–4, 236–8**.
[7] *Oxoniensia*, xliii. 65.
[8] Salter, *Chapt. Augustin.* 125, 128, 139.
[9] Ibid. 131–5; below, **376–7, 382**.

part as nos. 22–4 New Inn Hall Street and a chapel of which the hammerbeam roof, seven bays long, was re-erected at Brasenose College in 1658–9.[1]

As a teaching institution, however, the college was in terminal decline. The young Edmund Forest had studied there under Richard Charnock, prior of students *c.* 1496–*c.* 1501, who taught Erasmus.[2] Charnock's successors John Hagbourne and William Wall were student graduates who left on obtaining higher degrees, while Hugh Witwicke, prior in 1518, never graduated.[3] The college had no royal charter, as the general chapter reminded Wolsey in 1518,[4] and no teaching endowment. When Wolsey procured such an endowment in 1524–5 he applied it not to St. Mary's but to his secular foundation of Cardinal College.[5] Although the Augustinian priory of Bruton (Som.) had five graduates at the Dissolution, Llanthony Priory no longer supported a student at Oxford in 1519 and Prior Forest was the last member of his community to obtain a university degree.[6]

Cardinal Wolsey's Attempted Reform

In 1518, to judge by its registers, Llanthony Priory was more prosperous and efficiently run than ever before. Yet when Prior Forest took his seat as joint president of the Augustinian general chapter on 13 June that year he was told that the whole Augustinian order faced imminent ruin. Delinquent canons, for instance, threatened to obtain a writ of *Praemunire*, leading to confiscation of assets, if the chapter exacted disciplinary penalties according to its papally approved rules, and the order no longer enjoyed the goodwill to avert such a catastrophe. The obvious remedy was to adopt new rules, but some argued for a stricter regime while others, quoting the doctors of the church, argued against. The chapter adjourned debate for three years and weakly asked Cardinal Wolsey, as Lord Chancellor, not to let a harmful writ pass his Chancery.[7]

In response to this crisis Wolsey obtained papal authority in August 1518 and June 1519 to reform all the British monastic orders. He devised new rules of monastic life, which he laid before Prior Forest and other leading Augustinians, Benedictines and Cistercians at York Place on 12 November 1519 and before simultaneous general chapters of the Augustinians and Benedictines which he ordered to meet on 26 February 1520.[8] The Benedictines, meeting at York Place, rejected the rules as too strict.[9] The Augustinians, summoned to St. Bartholomew's Priory in Smithfield, also failed to adopt them, since Wolsey reissued rules for the order under legatine authority on 22 March 1520 for a trial period ending at Trinity 1521, when he hoped to get them approved

---

[1] *Oxoniensia*, xliii. 78–92.

[2] Knowles, *Religious Orders*, iii. 152; Emden, *Biog. Reg. Oxon. to 1500*, s.v. Richard Charnock.

[3] Below, **231** n., **232** n., **379** n.; cf. **380**.

[4] Below, **377**.

[5] *V.C.H. Oxon.* iii. 228, 234.

[6] *V.C.H. Som.* ii. 138; below, **380**; *Trans. B.G.A.S.* xlix. 92–3. Prior Hart, listed at the last of those references as a graduate, did not attend university and has been confused with a namesake: cf. Emden, *Biog. Reg. Oxon. 1501–40*, s.v. Richard Harte.

[7] Salter, *Chapt. Augustin.* 133, 137–8; below, **377**, cf. **376**.

[8] Below, **386** and nn.

[9] Pantin, *Chapters of Black Monks*, iii. 123–4.

at a legatine council.[1] In the event, if the silence of our sources can be relied upon, the legatine council never met, nor did the Augustinian general chapter ever meet again. The monasteries remained unreformed until Thomas Cromwell's visitors reformed them by injunction, without consultation, in 1535–6.[2]

Prior Forest's Fall

Early in 1524 Cardinal Wolsey's agent Dr. John Allen took the surrender of five Augustinian priories to provide endowments for Cardinal College. Another five were treated similarly including St. Frideswide's at Oxford, of which Allen appropriated the revenues early in 1525.[3] After the deaths of Prior Spires of Guisborough in 1519 and Prior Salyng of Merton in 1520 Prior Forest was the only surviving president and spokesman of the Augustinian order and was probably foremost among the critics against whom Wolsey had to defend Allen before the king on 5 February 1525.[4] Shortly afterwards, on 5 March, Wolsey ordered Allen to visit Prior Forest, whom he accused of failing to regulate the conduct of his canons and servants.[5] Since the notice of this visitation is among the last entries in Prior Forest's register it may be concluded that Allen silenced Forest by depriving him of office. Before the next prior, Richard Hart, was installed Wolsey forbade the ordinary from intermeddling in the priory and thereby took direct control.[6]

ADMINISTRATION UP TO THE DISSOLUTION

Ecclesiastical Administration

Obedientiaries managed the almonry, infirmary, domestic offices and conventual church of the priory.[7] Canon proctors based at Duleek (Meath) managed its 59 parish churches and chapels in Ireland.[8] The priors, on the evidence of their registers, were more personally concerned with the priory's general ecclesiastical business in England and Wales, in which they were probably assisted by their chaplains; for instance William Chaddesley, Prior Forest's chaplain in 1515, was his proctor for the churches of Kington (Herefs.), Caldicot (Mon.) and Barton Stacey (Hants.).[9]

Canon and civil lawyers of the secular church also played a large part. Some examined the priory as visitors on behalf of the bishop, the archbishop or the cardinal legate.[10] Four

---

[1] Wilkins, *Concilia*, iii. 683–8; cf. *L. & P. Hen. VIII*, iii, p. 231. The summons to meet at St. Bartholomew's Priory is attested only in **386** below and is unknown to previous historians such as Knowles, whose otherwise helpful discussion of the matter also assigns wrong dates to both meetings at York Place: *Religious Orders*, iii. 158–9.

[2] *L. & P. Hen. VIII*, iv, p. 2558; Knowles, *Religious Orders*, iii. 268–90.

[3] *L. & P. Hen. VIII*, iv, pp. 435, 501–2; Knowles, *Religious Orders*, iii. 161–2, 470.

[4] Below, **378** and nn., cf. **386** n.; *L. & P. Hen. VIII*, iv, p. 464.

[5] Below, **479**.

[6] John Rylands Library, Rylands Charter 1762, final gloss.

[7] For obedientiaries cf. below, 3(f); for a lay refectorer, **460**.

[8] Below, **65, 121, 235, 324, 353**. The churches and chapels numbered 33 before union with Llanthony-in-Wales: *Glevensis*, xxiii. 21–3. For Irish business cf. below, **470–4**.

[9] Below, **300, 319, 328, 336**.

[10] Below, **161, 276, 427, 435, 479**.

or five attended Hayward's election to the priorate, including William Vauce, who as conciliator procured a unanimous vote.[1] Some, again including Mr. Vauce, took the prior's place at convocation or synod[2] or helped to administer his more remote churches: John Allen and Nicholas Hillington in Ireland, Henry Martyn in the diocese of Hereford, Dr. Thomas Myllyng and three others at Barton Stacey (Hants.) and Robert Stinchcombe and Hugh Green at Kington (Herefs.), where the prior had testamentary jurisdiction.[3] In 1521 Robert Stinchcombe, Dr. William Burghill and nine notaries took more general responsibility for the priory.[4]

Such lawyers were needed even to draft routine documents, as Prior Salyng reminded Prior Forest.[5] Their part in preparing business for the priory chapter can be seen most clearly in the changing forms of proxies. A proxy to attend convocation as used in 1460 was redrafted in 1502 and again in 1515, each new draft being more concise than the last.[6] A proxy to act in Ireland as used in 1464 was redrafted in 1501 with a gloss *Vide ut hec generalia verba semper deveniantur in omnibus aliis procuratoriis vestris futuris*, 'See that these general words always occur in all your future proxies'; nevertheless the draft of 1464 was chosen in 1511 and 1515, augmented with an additional proviso.[7] A proxy to act for the church of Chirton (Wilts.) was also used at Stanton Lacy (Salop.) and was adapted to deal with a problem at Caldicot (Mon.).[8]

The priors were patrons of 49 churches and chapels in England and seven in Wales.[9] They retained their ecclesiastical lawyers by presenting Mr. Vauce to benefices at Colesbourne and Painswick, Mr. Martyn at Llanwarne (Herefs.), Dr. Burghill at Eardisley (Herefs.) and Mr. Stinchcombe at Brockworth, Gloucester All Saints, Gloucester St. Mary de Crypt and Tytherington.[10] Most of the priory's lawyers already held high office elsewhere but Mr. Stinchcombe never received another preferment. Indeed Prior Forest promoted him from benefice to benefice as he promoted surprisingly few others of the priory's client incumbents.[11] Many of those whom the priors presented may have been recommended by influential men such as the courtier Sir William Kingston, who intervened at Harescombe.[12] Prior Forest granted to laymen a turn of the advowson of Weobley (Herefs.) in 1525, probably to raise money for taxes; Prior Hart followed suit at Tillington (Herefs.), Doynton, Elmore, Gloucester St. Mary de Crypt,

---

[1] Below, 3(f).

[2] Below, **59, 76, 334**.

[3] Below, **121, 148, 300, 328**.

[4] Below, **434**.

[5] Below, **385**.

[6] Below, **59, 114** (cf. **302**), **334**.

[7] Below, **65, 121, 229, 235, 324**.

[8] Below, **130, 285, 319**, cf. **214**.

[9] Before union with Llanthony-in-Wales 28 churches and chapels in England and 2 in Wales: P.R.O. C 115/75, C 115/77. For the final total the list in *Glevensis* xxiii. 16–21 has to be amended by adding Colesbourne, Doynton, Pitchcombe, Brilley (Herefs.), Canon Frome (Herefs.) and Tillington (Herefs.): below, **39, 127, 134, 226, 257, 300**.

[10] Below, **3** n., **300** n., **347, 374**.

[11] Below, **317** n. and possibly **144** n; for contrary examples cf. **46** n., **48** n., **113** n., **134** n., **138** n., **212** n.

[12] Through the lord of Harescombe, who had the right of nomination: below, **439**, cf. **256** n.

Painswick and Tytherington.[1] At Ballingham, Llancillo, Rowlstone and Tillington (all in Herefs.) and at Elmore and Hempsted the priors recruited curates outside episcopal control, whom they appointed not by presentation but by lease or grant.[2]

The priors controlled recruitment to the priesthood by granting title, namely a testimonial or guarantee which qualified a candidate for ordination.[3] Surprisingly, only two of the 24 recipients of title named in these registers subsequently obtained a benefice from the priory, and only three or four others are recorded as obtaining any benefice, chaplaincy or chantry priesthood in Gloucestershire.[4] Only one was a graduate, although two supplicated unsuccessfully for degrees.[5] Prior Forest, who had ceased to record this practice by 1519, normally attached such titles to the priory's hospital of Dudstone (St. Mary Magdalene, Gloucester), thereby limiting the guarantee.

Administration of Property

At Llanthony-by-Gloucester the prior kept in hand a demesne of 392 acres stocked with cattle and sheep and incorporating a cheese dairy, a rabbit warren and one or more fish-weirs.[6] He kept similar demesnes of 438 acres at Llanthony-in-Wales and of 215 acres at Duleek (Meath).[7] He had residences with parks at Great Barrington and Brockworth, lodgings at Newark and Podsmead in Hempsted, at Alvington and at Quedgeley and rights of lodging at Rea in Hempsted, Prestbury and South Cerney.[8] His superintendent of sheep managed pastures in the Cotswolds at Great Barrington, Windrush, Aylworth in Naunton, Sevenhampton and Colesbourne, with facilities at Barrington for the shearing and sale of wool.[9] Some quarries and parochial tithes were also in hand.[10]

With these exceptions the priory's estates and tithes were let to tenants, chiefly under the superintendence of the cellarer, the steward and the understeward. A subcellarer assisted in 1511 and 1516.[11] Lay lawyers trained at the Inns of Court were required for this work. William (later Sir William) Nottingham, steward of the priory's manors, lands and tenements in Gloucestershire and Wiltshire from 1465 to 1483, rose to become Chief Baron of the Exchequer. Robert Wye, holder of the same office from 1510 to 1538, was a son-in-law and protegé of William Greville, justice of Common Pleas, who undertook Prior Forest's legal business both personally and through his servant John Chadwell.[12]

[1] Below, **39** n., **441** n., **481**, cf. **226**; *Reg. Bothe*, 343; Hockaday Abs. ccxvi, 1538; ccclxxxii, 1549; *V.C.H. Glos.* xi. 81.
[2] Below, **113, 147, 157, 274, 441, 464, 466**, cf. **155**.
[3] e.g. below, **132**; cf. R. N. Swanson, 'Titles to orders in medieval English episcopal registers' in *Studies in Medieval History presented to R. H. C. Davis*, ed. Henry Mayr-Harting and R. I. Moore (London, 1985), 240–1. Ann Geddes supplied this reference.
[4] Below, **146, 175, 182, 304, 363, 464, 466–7**, cf. **260**.
[5] Below, **172, 189, 304**.
[6] *Valor Eccl.* (Rec. Com.), ii. 430; below, **69, 385** n., **461**.
[7] *Valor Eccl.* (Rec. Com.), ii. 431; *Irish Cart. Llanth.* pp. 291–2.
[8] Below, **314, 343** and Tables I and II (pp. xxix–xxx).
[9] Below, **314, 321, 329**; *V.C.H. Glos.* vi. 181; ix. 179.
[10] e.g. **484** n. (quarries), *Valor Eccl.* (Rec. Com.), ii. 424 (tithes).
[11] Below, Tables I and II (pp. xxix–xxx); **252, 355**.
[12] Below, **94, 117, 203, 215** n., **217–18**, cf. **184, 404, 477**.

Understewards are not named explicitly in the registers, but John Carwent of Newent held this or a similar position until 1502 and Thomas Symes of Quedgeley in 1513;[1] the career of Arthur Porter, understeward at the Dissolution, is discussed below. Although Prior Deane audited an account personally in 1486 the office of auditor was performed or held by John Carwent in 1482–3, William Lawrence in 1515 and William Morgan in 1535.[2] Outside Gloucestershire and Wiltshire, Prior Forest retained John Chadwell as his lay lawyer at Kington (Herefs.) and Roger Porter at Caldicot (Mon.).[3]

At the priory of Llanthony-in-Wales David ap Gwilym Morgan was appointed steward of the Honddu valley (Honddu Slade) before the union of the two houses in 1481 and remained in office until 1524. A conditional grant of that stewardship to Lord Herbert did not take effect, as William Vaughan held it in 1535. The steward of Honddu Slade exercised part of the prior's jurisdiction as a marcher lord and was assisted by a lieutenant, two serjeants and a constable gaoler.[4] Other local stewards held office at manors in Herefordshire and Shropshire formerly belonging to the priory of Llanthony-in-Wales, such as a steward whom the lessees of Stanton Lacy (Salop.) were required to find in 1508.[5] Thus Sir Roger Mynors was steward at Llanwarne (Herefs.) and John (later Sir John) Scudamore at Fawley (Herefs.) in 1535. Prior Forest probably received similar service from the lawyers John Breynton and John Warnecombe in Herefordshire, and from Edmund Goldyng in Ireland.[6]

Manorial demesnes, mills, fish-weirs and rectorial tithes were let at term by leases sealed in the priory chapter house, for which the lessees paid rent directly to the priory exchequer.[7] Normally a demesne was let as a single unit together with any manor house, but the demesnes of Hempsted, Brockworth, Alvington[8] and Monkton in Llanwarne (Herefs.) were split, that at Llanwarne being divided into nine or more leaseholds.[9] When a lease expired it was granted either to the prospective lessee who offered the highest entry fine or to one who qualified by service to the priory. Occasionally the fine was advanced by a third party.[10] Other parcels of land were held from the priory by hereditary free tenure dating from the 13th century, the largest including the Netheridge estate in Quedgeley and two estates in Aylburton for which Prior Forest accepted homage in 1511, 1515 and 1524.[11]

The priory supervised the rest of its free tenants, copyholders and tenants-at-will through manor courts and collected their rents through manorial bailiffs (Table I). For administrative convenience some manors, like Redgrove in Cheltenham, incorporated

---

[1] Below, **117, 119, 370**, cf. **369, 415, 456–7**.
[2] Below, **335, 484, 487, 489**; *Valor Eccl.* (Rec. Com.), ii. 430.
[3] Below, **142, 319**.
[4] Below, **269, 309**; *Valor Eccl.* (Rec. Com.), ii. 431.
[5] Below, Table II (p. xxx); **196**.
[6] *Valor Eccl.* (Rec. Com.), ii. 426; below, **210, 311, 459**.
[7] e.g. below, **314, 484**.
[8] *Valor Eccl.* (Rec. Com.), ii. 423–4, 426.
[9] The nine are below, **170, 173, 178, 180, 201** (with **278, 444**), **202** (with **458**), **296, 373, 422**.
[10] Below, **180, 278, 311, 370, 444, 477**, cf. **293, 295**.
[11] Below, **239, 335–6, 465**.

TABLE I: *Manors in England and Wales administered from and anciently belonging to the priory of Llanthony-by-Gloucester*

Manor	Prior's residence	Hospitality for cellarer, steward and understeward	Bailiff in 1535	Ref. in Registers
Llanthony demesne	The Newark[1]	—	John Hunt	—
Alvington	Alvington Court[2]	Not known	Edward Shiar	cf. **414**
Aylburton	—	(no manor house)	Edward Shiar	—
Barrington, Great	Barrington Park	at Barrington Park	Ric. Monyngton	**314**
Barton Stacey, Hants.	—	as required	—	**185**
Brockworth	Brockworth Court	as required	Richard Reve	**343**
Caldicot, Mon.	—	(no manor house)	Wm. Morgan	cf. **248**, **266**
Cerney, South	1–2 days a year	in steward's chamber	Walter Barnard	**292, 477**
Chirton, Wilts.	—	as required	John Nicols	**50, 252**
Cirencester	—	(no manor house)	Thomas ap Ellin	—
Colesbourne	—	as required	John Kenelocke	**329**
Gloucester borough	—	—	James Cady	—
Haresfield	—	—	Thomas Rollys	**126**
Hempsted	Podsmead[3]	—	David Johns	**287**
Henlow, Beds.	—	4 days a year	Michael Cooper	**354**
Kington, Herefs.	—	(no manor house)	James Vaughan	cf. **270**
Llantrisant, Mon.	—	(manor ho. ruinous)	Thos. ap Phelip	**249**
Okle in Newent	—	1 day a year	Walter Cocks	**359**
Painswick	—	(no manor house)	Thomas Cooke	—
Prestbury	1–2 days a year	as required	Robert Atwell	**78, 325, 430**
Quedgeley	Manor Farm[4]	—	Chris. Rogers	cf. **456**
Redgrove in Cheltenham	—	(no manor house)	Giles Roberts	cf. **184**
Turkdean	—	2 days a year	Wm. Haukyns	**145**
Tytherington	—	(no manor house)	John Webbe	cf. **416**
Westbury-on-Severn	—	(no manor house)	Humph. Calowe	—

Gloucester, Haresfield, Hempsted and Quedgeley are within 5 miles of the priory; cf. below, **10, 12**. For the presence or absence of manor houses and the names of bailiffs: *Valor Eccl.* (Rec. Com.), ii. 423–30.

[1] Below, **217** n.
[2] *Cal. Pat.* 1485–94, 97.
[3] The prior also reserved a right of residence in a fish-house at Rea: below, **253**.
[4] Above, p. xxii.

scattered holdings in several parishes; thus the miller of Mordiford owed suit to the court of Fawley (Herefs.) and the bailiff of Prestbury collected revenue in Southam, Charlton Kings and Leckhampton.[1] At ten manor houses in Gloucestershire and Wiltshire, as the table shows, the cellarer, the steward and the understeward were entertained with their servants and horses when they came to supervise the manors or to hold courts. They probably had similar facilities at Alvington and at four Herefordshire manors for which information is lacking. At Great Barrington an inner court and at South Cerney a steward's chamber were reserved for their use. When visiting Stanton Lacy (Salop.) they were accommodated at Ludlow or, from 1519, in

TABLE II: *Other manors of the Priory*

Manors formerly of Llanthony-in-Wales, administered after 1481 from Llanthony-by-Gloucester; with the names of the bailiffs in 1535

Burghill, Herefs.	Richard Bowgham
Canon Frome, Herefs.	John Bowgham
Fawley in Fownhope, Herefs.	John ap Ellin
Llanwarne, Herefs.	John ap Ellin
Stanton Lacy, Salop.	William Haynes
Widemarsh Moor in Hereford	Richard Warnecombe

When visiting Stanton Lacy the cellarer, the steward and the understeward received hospitality at Ludlow or, from 1519, at the rectory: below, **196, 454**. They probably had similar facilities at Burghill, Canon Frome, Fawley and Widemarsh Moor in manor houses of the priory which are attested in the main source: *Valor Eccl.* (Rec Com.), ii. 426, 428.

Manors administered from Llanthony-in-Wales, with the names of the bailiffs in 1535

Honddu Slade. i.e. Llanthony, Cwmyoy and Oldcastle, Mon.	James Nicolls
Ewyas, i.e. Clodock and Longtown, Herefs.	Thomas ap Rosser
Foxley in Yazor, Herefs.	Philip Hoggs
Newton, Herefs.	Thomas Jenkyns
Stanton in Llanvihangel Crucorney, Mon.	Robert Philippe

All except Foxley are within six miles of the Welsh priory. Source: *Valor Eccl.* (Rec. Com.), ii. 431.

Manors administered from Duleek, with references to surveys in Irish Cart. Llanth.

Duleek, Meath	pp. 289–95
Ballybin in Cookstown, Meath	pp. 191–2
Colp, Meath	pp. 178–80
Lougher in Duleek, Meath	pp. 300–1
Mullingar, Westmeath	pp. 303–4

Ballybin and Colp were administered until 1481 from a cell of the priory of Llanthony-in-Wales at Colp.

---

[1] Below, **135, 184** n., **485**.

the rectory.[1] Courts for Hempsted, Quedgeley and Haresfield, however, were held at the priory.[2] The prior's urban tenants in Gloucester owed suit to a court at St. Owen's church and were supervised not by the cellarer but by the canon renter, an office held by Thomas Colsey in 1457, by Robert Cole in 1481–2 and by David Matthew in 1535.[3]

Although Robert Cone, cellarer in 1515, commanded respect, Cardinal Wolsey's rules show that even when the cellarer attended manorial courts a steward presided. The stewardship of men like Sir William Nottingham at Llanthony Priory and Sir Robert Poyntz at Bristol and Kingwood Abbeys was more than a professional duty, since both made wills attesting their faith in monastic intercessory prayer.[4]

The Surrender, 17 March 1538

Local support for monasteries was put in doubt in 1536 when a reformist preacher called Benet, chaplain to Bishop Latimer of Worcester, declared in Gloucester that intercessory prayer was useless to departed souls.[5] A preacher of similar views, Hugh Rawlings, was deprived of the curacy of Holy Trinity in 1537 after complaints from the mayor Thomas Bell, a traditionalist. Rawlings's reformist supporters nevertheless secured his reinstatement. Ominously, they included John Arnold (d. 1545), the steward of Gloucester Abbey, his son Nicholas (1509–80) and his son-in-law Arthur Porter (1505–59), understeward of Llanthony Priory.[6] Since 1524 these three had shared chambers at Lincoln's Inn, where John was a bencher.[7] Richard Hart, prior of Llanthony since 1525, was of the same family, as was the late Prior Hayward.[8]

By 1535 the priory steward Robert Wye had so distanced himself from the priory that he drew no fee.[9] The chief understeward Sir David Owen, uncle to the king, died in that year.[10] The administration of the priory's property therefore fell to the understeward Arthur Porter, who was escheator of Gloucestershire in 1526–7 and J.P. for the county 1537–47. From his father Roger (d. 1523), one of the prior's attorneys, he had inherited Porter's Place and Boulsdon Manor at Newent, but by 1535 he was living mainly at Quedgeley as lessee of the priory's manor and tithes. He also held the priory's sheep

[1] Below, **196, 292, 314, 454**.

[2] Below, **12**.

[3] Below, 3(f) and n., **10, 250, 384, 429**; Glos. R.O. GBR/J5/4.

[4] Below, **94** n., **240, 336** and n.; Wilkins, *Concilia*, iii. 688.

[5] *L. & P. Hen. VIII*, x, p. 463.

[6] Ibid. xii (1), pp. 139, 313, 366; xii (2), p. 484. For Thomas Bell and John Arnold cf. below, **239, 462**. For Nicholas Arnold and Arthur Porter cf. *Hist. of Parl., Commons 1509–58; Visit. Glos. 1623*, 4–5, 127; *Valor Eccl.* (Rec. Com.), ii. 430.

[7] *Records of Lincoln's Inn, the Black Books* (London, 1897), i. 208.

[8] *L. & P. Hen. VIII*, xiv (1), p. 248; above, p. xv.

[9] Below, **203**; *Valor Eccl.* (Rec. Com.), ii. 430.

[10] Of Cowdray in Easebourne, Sussex, 1459–1535, understeward by 1522: *Valor Eccl.* (Rec. Com.), ii. 430; *Military Survey of Glos. 1522*, 191; R. A. Griffiths, *Making of the Tudor Dynasty* (Gloucester, 1985), 191–2, with date corrected by I. Nairn and N. Pevsner, *Buildings of England, Sussex* (Harmondsworth, 1965), 212.

pasture at Colesbourne and, from 1537, its estate at Alvington Court.[1] On 4 March 1537 Prior Hart despatched him to Thomas Cromwell, the king's vicar general, with a proposal to dissolve the priory of Llanthony-in-Wales and apply the revenue to compensating the priory at Gloucester for seizure of its property in Ireland. Porter returned with a counter-proposal involving the dissolution of both priories and refined it by mutual consent into an agreement or 'book' to which both Cromwell and the prior subscribed.[2] Thus the priory chapter had already signed a deed of surrender a week before the commissioners Dr. John Tregonwell, Dr. William Petre and John Freman asked for it on 17 March 1538.[3]

Under the first part of the agreement, implemented on 18 May 1538, ex-prior Hart received a pension of £100 a year, fuel from Buckholt Wood and a residence at Brockworth Court, where he lived (latterly within a manor granted to John Guise) until shortly before his death in 1545.[4] The second part took effect in 1540 when Arthur Porter purchased for £723 the priory of Llanthony-by-Gloucester with its local demesne of 392 acres and its freehold title to his estate at Alvington.[5] During the interval he had acquired Crown leases in 1538 of the late priory's tithes at Great and Little Barrington, Hempsted and Painswick and of its rents-in-kind at Brockworth, Hempsted and Quedgeley;[6] he was receiver of the late priory's revenues from 12 August 1539 and lessee of the priory site from 31 October 1539.[7] Making his residence at Llanthony, he became sheriff of Gloucestershire in 1548–9, M.P. for the county in 1554 and M.P. for Gloucester in 1555.[8] The third part of the agreement was implemented on 23 May 1546 when the priory of Llanthony-in-Wales, with its property in Honddu Slade (Mon.) and Ewyas (Herefs.), was sold to Nicholas Arnold, later to become Sir Nicholas, M.P. and lord justice of Ireland.[9] Writing to Cromwell in 1539, the former prior commended the honourable conduct of his understeward Porter, by whom he and his brethren had been ordered in these matters.[10]

COMPILATION, PRODUCTION AND SURVIVAL OF THE REGISTERS
Transmission of the Registers

Having used the priory registers as working documents in the posts of understeward and receiver before and after the surrender, Arthur Porter retained them as muniments of title in 1540 when he acquired the priory site and its local manor or demesne.[11] Most of the registers descended with the manor until 1820, passing on Arthur Porter's death in

---

[1] *Hist. of Parl., Commons 1509–58*; Bigland, *Glos.* iii. 999; *Valor Eccl.* (Rec. Com.), ii. 423, 425; *V.C.H. Glos.* v. 9; x. 217; cf. vii. 187; below, **120** and n.

[2] *L. & P. Hen. VIII*, xii (1), p. 264; xiv (1), pp. 60, 248.

[3] Ibid. xiii (1), pp. 176, 197.

[4] *Trans. B.G.A.S.* lxiii. 142; lii. 284–7; cf. *L. & P. Hen. VIII*, xv, p. 411.

[5] P.R.O. C 66/700, mm. 41–2; cf. *L. & P. Hen. VIII*, xvi, pp. 383–4; for the acreage, *Valor Eccl.* (Rec. Com.), ii. 430.

[6] Hockaday Abs. under 1538 in vols. cxiii, cxxv, ccxl, cccix, cccxix.

[7] Ibid. ccxxiv, 1539; *L. & P. Hen. VIII*, xiv (1), p. 607.

[8] *Hist. of Parl., Commons 1509–58.*

[9] Ibid.; *L. & P. Hen. VIII*, xxi (1), p. 576.

[10] *L. & P. Hen. VIII*, xiv (1), pp. 60, 248.

[11] Above, this page.

1559 to his son Sir Thomas (d. 1597) and thence to his grandson Arthur, later Sir Arthur (d. 1630).[1] They were kept within the manor at the Newark, a former prior's residence, in 1575 when Sir Thomas supplied certified copies of entries nos. **239** and **465,** and they were still there in about 1600 when the younger Arthur allowed a visiting antiquary to copy nos. **1, 7, 23, 57** and **62**.[2] The mutilation of Prior Forest's register, which resulted in the loss of all entries concerning Alvington, may have occurred in 1599 when Arthur sold the former priory's Alvington Court estate.[3]

On the death of Sir Arthur's widow Anne the inheritance passed to their daughter Elizabeth and her husband John first Viscount Scudamore (1601–71), who removed the registers to his family seat at Holme Lacy (Herefs.). They remained there in the possession of John second viscount (d. 1697), James third viscount (1684–1716), the latter's daughter Frances (1711–38), Frances's daughter also called Frances (1750–1820) and the latter's husband Charles (Howard) duke of Norfolk (1746–1815).[4] During this period John Prinn of Charlton Kings (1662–1735) obtained a copy of part of Prior Wyche's register,[5] and he or another procured a copy of Prior Chirton's register which later passed to Sir Thomas Phillipps.[6] Richard Furney borrowed the registers of Priors Brockworth, Chirton, Wyche, Hayward and Forest from Holme Lacy in 1746 and used them to compile a manuscript history of the priory which became a standard source for the next 200 years. He referred to Hayward's and Forest's registers by their Holme Lacy press-marks A.11 and A.14.[7] Prior Deane's register he discovered among the records of Gloucester City Council, whence it was subsequently lost.[8]

In 1816, to protect the interests of the widowed, childless and lunatic duchess of Norfolk, the Lord Chancellor ordered the muniments at Holme Lacy to be listed. Prior Hayward's register was accordingly numbered 6685 in box K.2 and Prior Forest's register 6691 in box L.2. In 1817 they were removed to the office of John Springett Harvey, Master in Chancery, and they remained Chancery Masters' exhibits after the duchess's death when her estate was divided. They passed to the Public Record Office in 1881, a transfer formally confirmed in 1910–11. Within class C 115, comprising the duchess of Norfolk's deeds, the office originally listed the registers by Holme Lacy press-marks, but in the 1970s it reverted to the numbers assigned in 1816 and in 1996 it recatalogued them, Prior Hayward's register becoming C 115/79 and Prior Forest's register C 115/85.[9]

---

[1] *V.C.H. Glos.* iv. 395; *Inquisitions post mortem for Glos.* 1625–36 (Index Lib. 1893), 128.

[2] John Rylands Library, Rylands Charter 1762; B.L. Harleian MS. 6079 (55–6), ff. 101–4. For the Newark cf. below, **217** and n.

[3] *V.C.H. Glos.* v. 9.

[4] R. Ian Jack, 'An archival case history: the cartularies and registers of Llanthony Priory in Glos.' *J. Soc. Archiv.* iv. 370–83, esp. 371; *Complete Peerage*, s.v. Scudamore.

[5] Cf. Fosbrooke, *Glouc.* 147 n.

[6] Cardiff Central Library, MSS. 2/98–100, cited in *J. Soc. Archiv.* iv. 382; cf. I. Gray, *Antiquaries of Glos. and Bristol* (B.G.A.S. 1981), 53–6.

[7] *J. Soc. Archiv.* iv. 380; Bodleian Library, MS. Top. Gloucs. c. 5; *Trans. B.G.A.S.* lxiii. 7–8 n.

[8] Cf. below, **101–12**.

[9] *J. Soc. Archiv.* iv. 370–3; P.R.O. TS. catalogue of C 115.

TABLE III: *Quires and hands in Prior Hayward's Register*

Quires	Leaves	Lost leaves	Entries	Hands
A, 3 sheets[1]	Fly-leaf	—		
	—	3 leaves[2]		
	blank leaf	—		
B, 4 sheets	ff. 1–8	—	**1–6**	Hand 2
C, 2 sheets and 2 half-sheets (ff. 9–10)	ff. 9–14	f. 15[3]	**7–37**	Hand 1
D, 4 sheets	ff. 16–23	—	**38–40**	Hand 6
			41–43	Hand 3
			44–part of **59**	Hand 6
E, 4 sheets	ff. 24–5	ff. 26–31	part of **59–61**	Hand 6
			62	Hand 3
			63	Hand 6
F, 4 sheets	—	ff. 32–9	(Lost)	(Lost)
G, 4 sheets	—	ff. 40–7	(Lost)	(Lost)
H, 4 sheets	ff. 53–5	ff. 48–52[4]	**64–5**	Hand 5
			66	Hand 6
			67	Hand 4
			68–9	Hand 6
I, 4 sheets	ff. 56–61	—	**70–2**	Hand 4
			73	Hand 6
			74–80	Hand 4
			81	Hand 5
			82	Hand 6
			83	Hand 4
			84–7	Hand 6
			88–9	Hand 2
J, 4 sheets and 1 half-sheet (f. 64)[5]	f. 62 (blank) ff. 63–9	—		
			90	Hand 3
			91	Hand 6
			92–3	Hand 4
			94	Hand 6
			95–6	Hand 4
			97–8	Hand 5
			99–100	Hand 7

[1] The first half-sheet is pasted to the cover.
[2] Probably originally containing or intended to contain an index, but surviving only as narrow stubs.
[3] If f. 15 existed it was the other half of one of the half-sheets f. 9 or f. 10.
[4] ff. 26–31, 32–9 and 48–52 survive as diagonally cut stubs.
[5] The final half-sheet is pasted to the cover.

Binding[1]

Prior Hayward's register is in a medieval binding which measures 12½ by 9 in. (315 by 230 mm.). Its covers are of thin split hide (possibly oil tanned sheep) over wooden boards and its spine has pronounced spine bands. Its parchment leaves are trimmed to 12¼ by 8¾ in. (310 by 225 mm.) with the loss of some marginalia.[2]

Prior Forest's register was rebound in 1983 but fragmentary remains of its medieval binding are preserved: a cover of limp vellum, tackets (i.e. tied loops) of rolled parchment and a spine lining of parchment pierced as for unstaggered tacketing.[3] Its parchment leaves are trimmed to 9¾ by 9½ in. (245 by 240 mm.) with the loss of marginal flourishes.[4]

Two quires of Prior Hayward's register seem to have existed separately (cf. Table III). Quire B, which covers the prior's election, is written in hand 2 while quire C, which covers the history of the priory site, is written in hand 1 and quire D begins with a further change to hand 6; quire B contains an explicit cross-reference to the first leaf of the quire (*primo folio huius quaterni*).[5] In Prior Forest's register (cf. Table IV) quire I is partly a replacement, since the end of entry no. **240** is written in hand 12 at the end of that quire but repeated in hand 9 at the beginning of quire J. As the writing of Prior Hayward's register also proceeds further into the gutter than would be possible within the present binding, the register books were clearly not bound up blank but were written quire by quire unbound, as was common practice in the middle ages,[6] or in limp temporary bindings. Thus for instance the record of Prior Forest's election, which is now absent from his register, may have been written in a quire which was discarded (before the leaves were numbered) when the election proved to have been defective.[7]

The quires of Prior Forest's register, although heavily repaired and rebound in 1983, are pierced for a medieval binding which may relate to the holes in its preserved spine lining. Prior Hayward's register, however, shows more sewing holes than are used in its present medieval binding and was therefore bound more than once in the middle ages. Its piercings suggest a pattern seen more clearly in the registers of Priors Chirton and Wyche and in the accessible parts of Prior Brockworth's register, whereby used or disused holes or holes of both kinds seem to be paired at head and tail in the manner of tacket holes. Originally, therefore, it may have had a temporary binding made by tacketing individual quires directly onto a limp vellum cover, a method which was

[1] This section is based, by kind permission, on unpublished research in a TS. by Angela Craft, 'A comparative study of library and archive bindings on books from Llanthony-by-Gloucester, with reference to their production, use, storage and status in the thirteenth to sixteenth centuries': copy in P.R.O. library.
[2] e.g. at f. 9v.
[3] P.R.O. C 115/85/2. The date of rebinding appears on a label inside the new cover.
[4] e.g. at ff. 33v., 96v.
[5] Below, **3**(c).
[6] N. Denholm-Young, *Handwriting in England and Wales* (Cardiff, 1954), 55.
[7] Cf. below, **215**.

TABLE IV: *Quires and hands in Prior Forest's Register*

Quires	Leaves	Lost leaves	Entries	Hands
(Gathering sheet)[1]	Fly-leaf		The prior's initials	Illuminator
A: 1 sheet and 1 half-sheet	3 prefatory leaves	—	Title and index	Hand 21
B: 2 half-sheets	ff. 1–2	—	113–part of **120**	Hand 10
C: 3 sheets	ff. 3–8	—	part of **120**–**141**	Hand 10
(Gathering sheet)	f. 9		**142**–**5**	Hand 10
D: 4 sheets	ff. 10, 17	ff. 11–16	**146**–**8**	Hand 10
			161–part of **163**	Hand 9
E: 2 sheets	ff. 18–21	—	part of **163**–**174**	Hand 9
F: 2 sheets and 1 half-sheet (f. 22)	ff. 22–6	—	**175**–**98**	Hand 9
G: 4 sheets and 2 half-sheets (ff. 27–8)	ff. 27–36	—	**199**–part of **222**	Hand 10
H: 2 sheets and 1 half-sheet (f. 39)	ff. 37–41	—	part of **222**–**229**	Hand 10
			230–part of **231**	Hand 11
I: 2 sheets and 1 half-sheet (f. 42)[2]	ff. 42–6	—	part of **231**–**234**	Hand 11
			235–**40**	Hand 12
J: 6 sheets	ff. 47–58	—	**241**–**50**	Hand 9
			251–**5**	Hand 11
			256–part of **279**	Hand 12
K: 6 sheets	ff. 59–70	—	part of **279**–**297**	Hand 12
			298	Hand 8
			299–**304**	Hand 12
			305–part ot **315**	Hand 17
L: 4 sheets	ff. 71–8	—	part of **315**–**329**	Hand 17
M: 4 sheets	ff. 79–86	—	**330**–**50**	Hand 17
N: 5 sheets	ff. 87–9, 94–6	ff. 90–3	**351**–part of **379**	Hand 17
O: 4 sheets	ff. 97–104	—	part of **379**–**396**	Hand 17
			397–**401**	Hand 18
P: 5 sheets	—	ff. 105–14	**402**–part of **417**	(Originals lost)
Q: 3 sheets	ff. 115–20	—	part of **417**–**422**	Hand 19
			423–**5**	Hand 13
			426	Hand 14
R: 3 sheets and 3 half-sheets (ff. 121–2, 124)	f. 121–9	—	**427**–**37**	Hand 13
			438–**9**	Hand 15
			440–**3**	Hand 14
			444–**7**	Hand 15
S: 1 sheet	ff. 130–1	—	**448**–**50**	Hand 15
T: 3 sheets and 1 half-sheet (f. 134)	ff. 132–3, 135–8	f. 134	**451**	Hand 16
			452–**8**	Hand 15
			459–**63**	Hand 14
			part of **464**	Hand 20
U: 4 sheets and 1 half-sheet (f. 148)	ff. 139–40, 142–8	—	part of **464**–**467**	Hand 20
			468	Hand 16
			469–**83**	Hand 14

[1] The gathering sheet enfolds quires A–C and recurs as f. 9.

[2] A discontinuity between nos. **240** and **241** (qq.v.) shows that quire I is partly a replacement.

common from the late 13th to the middle of the 17th century[1] and was adopted for the modern rebinding of Prior Forest's register. Within such a binding quires could be added progressively provided that the fore-edge flap was wide enough, and a register could be tailored, as the registers of Llanthony Priory are tailored, to the length of a priorate. Permanent binding could be deferred until a prior's resignation or death.

The Handwriting of Prior Hayward's Register

A parchment label pasted to the back cover of the register bears a title in contemporary bastard[2] hand: *Registrum Iohannis Heyward prioris Lanthonie: nota hic de libertatibus nostris.*[3] On the fly-leaf *Registrum Iohannis Heywarde* is repeated in 16th-century secretary hand. The book is written entirely in black ink. Foliation is in roman numerals and is uniform throughout.[4] Headings appear only at nos. **38, 64, 67, 83–7, 99** and **100**. Seven original original hands can be distinguished as in Table III, where they are numbered in order of letter forms from gothic book hand (hand 1) through increasingly free varieties of splayed bastard hand (hands 2–6) to a precursor of secretary hand (hand 7). The writers of hands 2–6 begin each entry with a tall bold initial more or less ornamented with flourishes. The most elaborate initial is the P of no. **65**, by hand 5, of which the bow is a scroll bearing a pattern as of bonded brickwork. Marginalia such as *Verte folium* and *Nota diligenter*[5] occur both in original and secondary hands and are ignored in this edition. The reverse of the final leaf contains trials of penmanship including an I ornamented with a bearded face in profile.

The Handwriting of Prior Forest's Register

The cover, now damaged, bears no title and bore none in 1575 when the volume was identified[6] only by three letters which still survive on the fly-leaf: *E F P* for *Edmundus Forest Prior*. These are large square capitals in red (*E* and *P*) and blue (*F*).[7] On the next three leaves red is used for the initial of the title *Registrum* (a square capital ornamented with foliate scrolls within a square frame) and for names of countries and places in the index. Foliation is also in red up to f. 20. The rest of the manuscript is written in black. Foliation, which is in roman numerals, is in large square capitals with or without Lombardic serifs up to f. 30; it is continued in a free hand up to f. 119 and in another free hand thereafter.[8] Headings appear throughout except before bonds and at nos. **208, 221, 338–9, 388–9, 423** and **465–7**. They are written with a wider pen than the text and were added afterwards, as demonstrated at no. **202** where a false start to

---

[1] e.g. Exchequer accounts of 1300 and 1487, P.R.O. E 101/9/20, E 101/55/20.

[2] For terminology cf. L. C. Hector, *Handwriting of English Documents* (London, 1966), 54–62.

[3] 'The register of John Heyward, prior of Llanthony: note here concerning our liberties.' A press-mark A.11 in an 18th-century hand appears on the back of the front cover.

[4] There is also a modern arabic foliation in pencil.

[5] 'Turn the leaf' and 'Note carefully.'

[6] John Rylands Library, Rylands Charter 1762, gloss.

[7] A press-mark A.14 in 18th-century hand also appears on the fly-leaf.

[8] There is also a modern arabic foliation in pencil.

the text lacks a heading. Fourteen original hands can be distinguished as numbered 8–21 in Table IV, the letter forms being as follows:

8:	gothic book hand.
9:	bastard book hand.
10–16:	splayed bastard hands.
17–20:	splayed bastard free hands.

The number of scribes may be less than the number of hands as demonstrated at the top of f. 140, where the writer of no. **467** has written lines 1–2 and 8–11 in a formal upright hand and lines 3–7, without change of pen, in a free sloping hand. Each entry begins with a tall initial more or less ornamented with flourishes, many of the flourishes being interlaced. Some initials in hands 9–12 and 18 are ornamented additionally with oak leaves and cusped fringes and bound with scrolls, inscribed scrolls being found on capitals at nos. **222–3** and on intermediate letters at nos. **114** and **124** (qq. v.). The initial of no. **133** is ornamented with a face and that of no. **400** with a fish. A notary's sign appears at no. **281**.

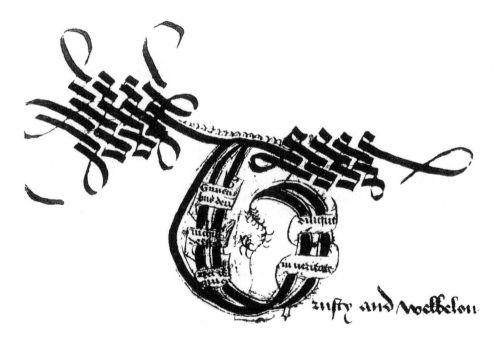

INITIAL LETTER T FROM PRIOR FOREST'S REGISTER (see below, p. 90, note 1)
By courtesy of the Gloucestershire Record Office

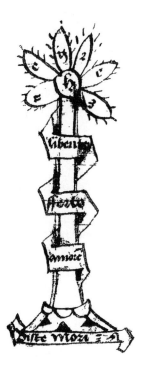

HUGH GRENE'S NOTARIAL SIGN (see p. 111, note 1)
By courtesy of the Gloucestershire Record Office

Compilation and Chronology

There is little evidence to show how the unknown compilers of the registers set about their task. Some sequences of ecclesiastical business[1] are in strict chronological order and so could have been copied directly from original documents before the documents left the priory, this being the procedure enjoined upon Gloucester Abbey.[2] But some documents issued by the priory[3] were registered so late that the registrar must have worked from intermediate copies, including at least one copy made under extreme pressure at Prior Forest's lodging in London.[4] Incoming correspondence, indentures of appointment and indentures of lease are not in chronological order and evidently accumulated to be registered at leisure.

Table V (p. xli) shows the number of documents registered yearly, including registrations in arrear from previous years. The listed arrears include historic documents brought forward to support current claims,[5] and the earlier part of a registered bundle

---

[1] e.g. below, **127–134, 187–194, 254–63**.
[2] Above, p. xiii.
[3] e.g. below, **54, 121, 140–2, 211–4, 417–21**.
[4] Below, **419**, cf. **390**.
[5] e.g. below, **91–2, 298, 424**, cf. **93, 299, 425**.

recording three years' litigation with the prior of Mullingar.[1] They also include several leases.[2] Leases were sealed in the priory chapter-house and were immediately effective in naming the date from which rent was due. Frequently, perhaps normally, a lessee furnished a performance bond within a few days.[3] But a lessee at Prestbury took three months to obtain his bond, a lessee at Bishop's Frome (Herefs.) took four months and a lessee at Stanton Lacy (Salop.) obtained two years' grace. A lease of land at Brockworth, sealed in 1513, was not registered until it was supported with a bond three years later.[4] Late registration of other leases may be explained similarly.

Some entries contain manifest errors of fact[5] or date.[6] Others are backdated or postdated for reasons which are not always apparent, so that for instance a letter dated at Llanthony on 10 January reached Taunton (Som.) on 9 January[7] and a file of correspondence conducted across 30 miles of hills between Llanthony and Bradenstoke (Wilts.) is dated 20 July throughout.[8] A lease of the rectory at Stanton Lacy (Salop.), registered in 1508, named William Cheyne as joint lessee; owing to his death or incapacity it was registered again without his name in 1513 but still bore the date 1508 so as to render the remaining lessees liable for arrears.[9]

EDITORIAL METHOD

The manuscripts are written in Latin and English. In this edition English entries are transcribed except nos. **62, 66, 312** and part of **472** which are calendared; Latin entries are calendared except the most important which are transcribed, as are specimens of common forms in both languages as follows:

A citation to a visitation, with a certificate: **165–6**

Proxies to attend convocation: **59, 114, 334**

Proxies to act for churches in England and Wales: **130, 142**

A proxy to act for the prior in Ireland: **65**

A presentation to, and a resignation from, a living: **39, 46**

A grant of title for the purpose of ordination: **132**

Letters of fraternity to laity and clergy: **128, 254**

Indentures of appointment: **80, 125, 169, 225, 289, 461**

Leases: **167, 196, 198, 253, 287, 311, 323, 357, 458**

An inventory of stock: **288**

A bond: **197**

A quittance: **44**

A manumission: **164**

Transcripts and quotations from the manuscripts are printed in italic. Editorial interpolations and editorial cross-references are enclosed in square brackets, the

---

[1] Below, **470–4**.

[2] e.g. below, **145, 253, 287**.

[3] e.g. below, **52, 98, 136, 197, 262, 267, 356, 401, 433, 452**.

[4] Below, **246, 343, 345, 431, 455**.

[5] e.g. below, **177**.

[6] e.g. below, **91** or **92**; **176, 214, 236, 272, 287, 376**.

[7] Below, **387**, cf. **390, 419**.

[8] Below, **232–4**; for other possible examples cf. **122, 349, 442**.

[9] Below, **286**, cf. **196**.

TABLE V: *Chronology*

Year	Entries	Same year	Previous years	Undated	Total
1457	**1–42**	7	3	32	42
1458	**43–5**	2	1	—	3
1459	**46–56**	11	—	—	11
1460	**57–62**	6	—	—	6
1461	**63**	1	—	—	1
1464	**64–70**	6	1	—	7
1465	**71–80**	8	2	—	10
1466	**81–98**	8	8	2	18
1501	**113**	1	—	—	1
1502	**114–25**	11	1	—	12
1503	**126–8**	3	—	—	3
1504	**129–33**	5	—	—	5
1505	**134–7**	2	2	—	4
1506	**138–47**	4	5	1	10
1507	**148–78**	14	4	13	31
1508	**179–86**	8	—	—	8
1509	**187–91**	5	—	—	5
1510	**192–206**	9	6	—	15
1511	**207–55**	39	7	3	49
1512	**256–67**	12	—	—	12
1513	**268–99**	24	8	—	32
1514	**300–12**	13	—	—	13
1515	**313–40**	23	3	1	27
1516	**341–50**	8	2	—	10
1517	**351–70**	3	7	10	20
1518	—	—	—	—	—
1519	**371–86**	12	4	—	16
1520	**387–423**	15	7	15	37
1521	**424–37**	9	5	—	14
1522	**438–41, 444–51**	9	3	—	12
1523	**452–8**	2	5	—	7
1524	**442–3, 459–76**	14	5	1	20
1525	**477–83**	5	1	1	7

symbol [   ] denoting a blank. Folio numbers in the text, as in the footnotes, are taken from the original rather than the modern foliations. Counties and parishes are referred to as defined *c.* 1850. Places named are in Gloucestershire unless specified otherwise.

In transcripts punctuation and the use of capital letters are modernised and roman numerals are replaced with arabic; the manuscripts use arabic numerals only at nos. **377**, **453** and **468**. In Latin transcripts I or J is printed as I but the manuscript usage of c and t, which is clearer, is followed. In summaries and calendared entries the spelling of place-names and forenames is modernised, the term 'prior and convent' is commonly shortened to 'prior', financial accounts are converted from continuous to tabular layout and where the priory or the prior is party to a transaction only the other party is named. Manuscript place-names which are not homophones of the modern names are added in transcript. Calendared leases are abbreviated by omitting quarter days, default clauses, sealing clauses and a standard prohibition against assignment without leave.

Tenements in Gloucester are identified in the notes and in the introduction by reference to postal addresses as numbered in *Smart's Gloucester Directories* (1927–36) and on Ordnance Survey 1:1250 and 1:2500 maps SO 8218 and 8318 (1955 edn.). Few of those addresses are still current, as medieval tenement boundaries have been lost since 1955 through demolition and rebuilding on different lines.

THE REGISTER OF JOHN HAYWARD
PRIOR OF LLANTHONY BY GLOUCESTER 1457–66

Public Record Office C 115/79

1. [f. 1] The king's instruction to the bishop of Worcester to proceed with the election of a prior. Chertsey Abbey [Surrey], 7 Oct. 1457.

Henry bi the grace of God king of Engelond & of Fraunce and lord of Irelond to the right reverent fadre in God John [Carpenter] *bisshop of Worcester gretyng. We lete you wite that the supprior and convent of our monastery of Lanthony of youre diocise have shewed unto us by Seer John Heyward oon of theer brethren how that oure seid priorye standeth now destitute and viduate of an heede & governor by the deth of Sir John Garlond last prior of the same, humbly beseching us that hit myght please us to graunt unto them oure licence to procede to thellection of a newe prior there. Wherefore we not willyng eny hurt or damage to growe unto oure seid priory by the longe avoidance thereof have of oure special grace & favour graunted unto thaym oure licence to procede to the seide election, whereupon we desire & wille yow that ye doo herein that that longeth to your office pastorall in that behalve. Geven undre oure signet of oure Duchy of Lancastre at oure monastery of Chortesey the 7 day of Octobre the yere of oure regne 36.*

2. Another letter from the king to John [Carpenter] bishop of Worcester. Being informed by William Saundres, sub-prior of Llanthony, that the canons have unanimously elected John Hayward as prior, the king consents thereto so that the bishop may perform his pastoral duty. Given under the seal of the Duchy of Lancaster at Westminster Palace on 24 Oct. 36 Hen.VI [1457].

3. [f. 1v.] Letters patent from John [Carpenter] bishop of Worcester about proceedings for confirmation of John Hayward's election held before Mr. Reginald Mile B.Cn.L., commissary general, in St. Owen's church, Gloucester, on 7 Nov. 1457 according to the bishop's commission to Mile and to Thomas Mordon, rector of Fladbury [Worcs.],[1] [f. 2] given at Bredon Manor [Worcs.] on 3 Nov. 1457.

Mr. William Vauce,[2] archdeacon of Worcester, appeared as the priory's proctor according to the priory's proxy to Vauce and to fellow-canon William Hooke

---

[1] d. 1458; B.C.L. and papal notary, rector of Fladbury 1428–58, treasurer of St. Paul's, London, and prebendary of Hereford 1433–58: Emden, *Biog. Reg. Oxon. to 1500.*

[2] Alias Vaws, d. 1479; B.Cn. & C.L., vicar general of Worcester diocese from 1448, archdeacon of Worcester 1452–67, vicar of Marshfield 1457–8, prebendary of St. Mary's, Warwick, 1458–79, dean of Westbury-on-Trym 1459–79, precentor of Lichfield 1472–9, prebendary of Hereford 1476–9 and holder of many other parochial benefices including those in the prior's gift at Colesbourne 1465–72 and Painswick 1472–3: Emden, *Biog. Reg. Oxon. to 1500*; below, **73.**

[f. 2v.] dated 30 Oct. 1457. Vauce exhibited the following, of which (a), (b), (e) and (f) are recited.

(a) The bishop's mandate to the archdeacon of Gloucester and others to cite any objectors to the election to appear at that time and place, given at Bredon Manor on 18 Oct.

(b) [f. 3] A letter from Thomas Smalcombe[1] to the bishop, certifying that he received the above mandate on 24 October and issued the citation accordingly in Llanthony priory church on 25 October; given under the archdeacon's seal at Gloucester on 5 Nov.

(c) The king's letter as above [2] (*ut superius in primo folio huius quaterni*).

(d) A letter under the signet of an eagle which he caused Mr. Edmund Hecker, notary public, to read out.

(e) Vauce's article asking the commissary to confirm the election.

(f) [f. 3v.] An instrument subscribed by Mr. Thomas Eggecomb, B.Cn. & C.L., general proctor of the court of Canterbury, clerk of Exeter diocese and notary public,[2] containing the decree of election in the following terms. On 18 October 1457 William Saunders sub-prior,[3] John Heyhampsted warden of the order and sacrist, William Grene, John Carpenter refectorer, Robert Cole,[4] John Frompton precentor,[5] John Lawrence, John Eliot, Thomas Colsey renter,[6] William Hook treasurer, John Bat kitchener, John Hayward cellarer, John Deverose infirmarer, Robert Herford, Robert Laus, Walter Banknot subsacrist,[7] Henry Dene scholar, Walter Steward undertreasurer, Thomas Alford and John Tulby canons in holy orders and John Payneswike and John Mersfeld canons in minor orders, [f. 4] after

---

[1] Deputising for Archdeacon Polton: cf. below, **6**.

[2] d. 1485; vicar of Henbury 1458–85, prebendary of Westbury-on-Trym from 1460, rector of Colesbourne 1461–5, master of St. John's Hospital, Cirencester, from 1462 and prebendary of St. Asaph to 1467: Emden, *Biog. Reg. Oxon. to 1500*. Warden of St. Oswald's Priory, Gloucester, from 1466: *Trans. B.G.A.S.* xliii.122.

[3] Infirmarer in 1442; probably a kinsman of his namesake the brewer, bailiff of Gloucester in 1445, who lived in Eastgate Street and held nos. 4 and 39–55 Longsmith Street as tenant of St. Oswald's Priory, Llanthony Priory and Winchcombe Abbey: P.R.O. C 115/73, f. 6 (4)v. no. 6, f. 31 (29)v. no. 64; *Glouc. Rental 1455*, 16b, 20–2, 96b; *V.C.H. Glos.* iv. 34.

[4] Born 1398, tonsured 1418, according to an autobiographical note of 1458: Bodleian Library, MS. Phillipps-Robinson c. 201. Prior's chaplain 1424–5: Bodleian Library, MS. Top. Gloucs. c. 5, p. 667, from Reg. Wyche. Proctor in Ireland 1425–8, 1433–42: *Cal. Pat. 1422–9*, 319, cf. 477; 1429–36, 251; 1436–41, 35. Renter in 1442 when he compiled a terrier (P.R.O. C 115/73) and in 1455 when he compiled a landgavel rental: *Glouc. Rental 1455*, pp. vi, 2. Renter again in 1481–2: below, **106**.

[5] Almoner in 1442: P.R.O. C 115/73, f. 7 (5) no.7.

[6] Probably a kinsman of Walter Colsey, proctor of St. Owen's church, Gloucester, in 1442, who held at will from Llanthony Priory the second tenement in Lower Southgate Street south of the corner of Parliament Street: P.R.O. C 115/73, f. 15 (13) no. 29, f. 18 (16) no. 34.

[7] Probably a kinsman of his namesake the mercer, bailiff of Gloucester in 1440, who lived at no. 10 Westgate Street and held no. 12 adjacent in fee from Llanthony Priory: *V.C.H. Glos.* iv. 374; *Glouc. Rental 1455*, 28b; P.R.O. C 115/73, f. 61 (59)v. no. 122.

celebrating a mass of the Holy Ghost at the high altar of the priory church, met in chapter in Eggecomb's presence. William Hooke exhibited (i) the chapter's mandate, dated 9 October, to William Hoke and Owen Bredeshawe to hold an election at that time and place [f. 4v.] and (ii) Bredeshawe's certificate that he fixed the mandate to the door of the priory church on 10 October, the certificate being dated 17 October under the archdeacon of Gloucester's seal. The sub-prior caused Mr. Edmund Hecker, notary public, to read out the certificate and a list of canons entitled to vote, [f. 5] and also caused the king's letter as above [1] to be read. After Hooke had excluded strangers, [f. 5v.] the chapter adopted Mr. William Vauce archdeacon of Worcester as director and conciliator, Mr. Henry Pantrye B.Cn.L.,[1] Thomas Wych and Edmund Hecker notary public as witnesses and Thomas Eggecomb notary public as clerk (*scribam*) of the election. Vauce read out the constitution of the general council beginning *Quia propter* and explained the method of election, after which the canons sang the hymns *Veni Creator Spiritus* and *Deus qui corda.* Then the sub-prior chose John Hayward as prior, the other brothers confirmed his election and William Hooke declared him elected. [f. 6] All sang the hymn *Te deum laudamus* and caused Hayward to be led to the high altar of the priory church. There, after an address by the sub-prior, Robert Cole announced the election in the vernacular to the clergy and people who were present in a copious multitude. Returning to the chapter house, the chapter appointed as its proctors William Hooke and Thomas Colsey, who went with Hayward to the infirmary chapel and there in Eggecombe's presence asked him urgently and repeatedly to consent to his election. He asked for time to consider his reply. [f. 6v.] Shortly afterwards they returned to the chapel and Hayward gave his formal consent.

Testifying before the commissary, Canon Robert Cole [f. 7] said that he saw Hayward profess the order of St. Augustine in the priory church before Prior Garland on the feast of the Annunciation [25 Mar.] 1442. Canon Thomas Colsey said that he saw him ordained priest by [Thomas Spofford] bishop of Hereford in the episcopal chapel at Hereford on Easter eve [14 Apr.] 1444. Hayward's father John Hayward, gentleman, said that he married Hayward's mother Margaret Foliet in St. Owen's church about 40 years ago and that Hayward was now 34 years old. Thomas Bisley, gentleman,[2] said that he attended the wedding. After inviting objections, [f. 7v.] the commissary formally confirmed the election [f. 8] and ordered Hayward to be inducted by the archdeacon of Gloucester and assigned his place in the priory church and chapter house. The bishop grants these letters at Hayward's request. Bredon Manor, 24 Nov. 1457.

4. Note of Thomas Eggecomb, B.Cn. & C.L., general proctor of the court of Canterbury, clerk of Exeter diocese and notary public, being engaged as clerk

---

[1] d. 1475; rector of Stow-on-the-Wold 1452–72 and of Hanbury, Worcs., 1465–75: Emden, *Biog. Reg. Oxon. to 1500.*

[2] d. by 1463. M.P. for Gloucester 1429, owning property in Gloucester and Hazleton: *Trans. B.G.A.S.* lxxiv. 73; *Cal. Close* 1461–8, 180. Resident in the Mercery at no. 8 Westgate Street: *Glouc. Rental 1455*, 28b.

(*scriba*) by Commissary Mr. Reginald [Mile], that he witnessed all these things and caused them to be written out on six pieces of parchment.[1]

5. [f. 8v.] Letter of John [Carpenter] bishop of Worcester granting to Hayward the spiritualities and temporalities of the priory. 7 Nov. 1457.

6. Letters patent of Philip [Polton][2] archdeacon of Gloucester. As mandated today by the bishop of Worcester, he has today caused John Hayward to be inducted and installed as prior by Mr. Henry Pantry B.Cn.L. 7 Nov. 1457.

7–32. Memoranda of evidence that Llanthony and the adjacent suburb are outside the borough of Gloucester.[3]

7. [f. 9] On the founders' gifts of land outside the south gate of Gloucester.
    Shortly after the conquest of England Roger [de Pîtres], lord of Gloucester,[4] founded two prebends in St. Owen's church, the first prebendaries being Roger of Toc[ken]ham and Richard of Quedgeley. Roger's son Walter of Gloucester, lord of Gloucester and constable of all England, built Gloucester castle, which has never been part of the town liberty. In his time Shipster's Lane extended from the south gate near St. Kyneburgh's chapel to the castle ditch and was flanked by houses on his property in the Hide including the house of one of the prebendaries. There were six houses between this dwelling and the Severn and another six between it and the south gate, each having a named tenant. At the end of the lane towards the Severn were Walter's hay barns and stables and his dog kennel. Walter's son Miles, lord of Gloucester and constable of England and later earl of Hereford, founded Llanthony Priory on his own land on 25 May 1136. At the dedication of the priory church and cemetery on 10 September 1137 he endowed it[5] with his Hide at Gloucester in free alms and with St. Owen's church and its possessions including the chapel within the castle, a small piece of land on the bank of the Severn, St. Kyneburgh's chapel, the parish of the constable's land inside and outside the south gate and all the land which the prebendaries had held inside and outside the south gate. Miles's son and

---

[1] Not a description of the registered copy, which is written on a quire of four sheets making eight leaves ff. 1–8.
[2] Archdeacon 1428–61: Le Neve, *Fasti 1300–1541, Monastic Cathedrals.*
[3] Apparently as submitted to arbitration by Prior Garland in 1456: below, **40**. These and the associated memoranda **33–7** fill a quire comprising ff. 9–14.
[4] d. before 1086: *Hist. & Cart. Mon. Glouc.* (Rolls Ser.), i, p. lxxvi. He and his descendants Walter (d. *c.* 1126), Miles (d. 1143) and Roger (d. 1155) of Gloucester are discussed by David Walker in 'Miles of Gloucester, earl of Hereford', *Trans. B.G.A.S.* lxxvii. 66–84; 'The Honours of the earls of Hereford in the twelfth century', ibid. lxxix. 174–211; and 'Charters of the earldom of Hereford', *Camd. Misc.* xxii. 1–11.
[5] Dugdale, *Mon.* vi. 136.

heir Roger confirmed the gift,[1] adding the prebendaries' land below the castle. King Henry II confirmed these gifts[2] and added the rights belonging to them inside and outside the borough. *Cokeyn* fish weir and the castle fish weir were also given by the priory's founders.[3] The almoner's and the renter's curtilages next to New Lane and Frogmarsh,[4] and all the tenements in Severn Street, Sudbrook Street, the high street outside the south gate, Small Lane and St. Owen's Lane[5] (except those that are of the liberty of King's Barton) are part of the Hide and of the prebends.

Memorandum quod tempore conquestus Anglie quidam Algarus stallarius, comes Essex' et dominus de Plesset, fuit constabularius Anglie.[6] Post quem de voluntate et consensu regis et nobilium regni quidam Walterus de Gloucestria, filius Rogeri de Gloucestria, constabularius fuit tocius Anglie ac constabulariam tenuit sibi et heredibus suis imperpetuum. Dictus Rogerus de Gloucestria, pater Walteri de Gloucestria, de genere Saxonico, paulo ante conquestum Anglie fuit dominus ville Gloucestrie. Hic Rogerus primo fecit et ordinavit duas prebendas canonicorum secularium in ecclesia Sancti Audoeni Gloucestrie, in quibus institui fecit quemdam Rogerum de Tocham et Ricardum de Quedesley.

Tandem obiit dictus Rogerus apud Phalesiam etc. Post cuius mortem predictus Walterus, filius eiusdem Rogeri et dominus ville Gloucestrie, fieri fecit castrum de Gloucestria in solo suo proprio, quod quidem castrum numquam fuit nec est de libertate nec infra libertatem ville Gloucestrie. Et sciendum quod post edificacionem eiusdem castri dictus Walterus habitabat et hospicium suum tenebat in eodem. Et adtunc erat quedam venella vocata Shipstereslane extendens se a fossato dicti castri usque ad portam australem ville Gloucestrie, et in dicta venella et prope fuit mansio unius prebendariorum Sancti Audoeni.[7] Et a dicta mansione versus Sabrinam in dicta venella fuerunt sex mansure et sex tenentes in eisdem manentes. Videlicet

[1] *Camd. Misc.* xxii. 16–19.
[2] P.R.O. C 115/75, f. 229 nos. 4, 5.
[3] *Camd. Misc.* xxii. 18, 48, 61. For *Cokeyn* weir cf. below, **68**. For the castle weir, which incorporated a mill until the 1260s, cf. *Cal. Inq Misc.* i, pp. 115, 126; *Trans. B.G.A.S.* lxii. 144.
[4] The almoner's and the renter's curtilages lay between Severn Street on the N., New Lane on the S. and a ditch called Frogmarsh by the Severn on the W.: P.R.O. C 115/73, ff. 3–5 (1–3). New Lane therefore coincided with the present eastern stretch of Llanthony Road.
[5] Severn Street, Sudbrook Street and Small Lane are plotted in *V.C.H. Glos.* iv. 68 fig. 4, which also shows St. Owen's Lane running E. from St. Owen's church: cf. ibid. 367; C 115/73, ff. 5–6v., 13 (3–4v., 11).
[6] The author confuses an officer of Edward the Confessor's reign with the much later Geoffrey de Mandeville (d. 1144) who was earl of Essex, lord of Pleshey and constable of the Tower of London: cf. *Complete Peerage.* His source is a memorandum in Reg. Chirton, f. 1.
[7] Details of early property in Shipster's lane are taken from a memorandum which was copied from an old martyrology into the surviving cartulary P.R.O. C 115/84, f. 16v. The memorandum adds that Seulf and Aldwyn were tenants of St. Owen's and that the prebendal house was occupied successively by Robert the chaplain, Master William and Roger of Tockenham. It flanked St. Owen's churchyard and, like the other dwellings mentioned, lay south of the lane: P.R.O. C 115/73, ff. 14–15 (12–13).

primam mansuram tenuit quidam faber nomine Seulfi, secundam mansuram tenuit Aldewynus, terciam mansuram tenuit Walterus de la Fenne, quartam tenuit Willelmus Butor, quintam Goldewynus filius Frye, et sextam mansuram tenuit Turkill. Et omnes isti tenuerunt dictas mansuras de dicto domino Waltero constabulario, et quattuor eorum fuerunt cum dicto Waltero in servicio. Et ex alia parte mansionis dicti prebendarii versus portam australem iuxta ecclesiam sive capellam Sancte Kyneburge fuerunt alie sex mansure, quarum primam tenuit Ricardus Pyncun,[1] secundam tenuit senex Wihtric, terciam Sebricht, quartam Milet pater Richeri, quintam Baldewynus Wenecok, sextam Froda cursor Walteri constabularii. Et omnes dicte mansure erant in Hida et de proprio dominio dicti domini Walteri etc. Et in fine dicte venelle versus Sabrinam dictus Walterus constabularius habuit horrea sua pro feno et stabula pro equis et quoddam canile pro suis canibus. Et dictus Walterus inter alia per cartam suam[2] dedit capellanis suis deo servientibus capellam Sancte Kyneburge et terrulas [f. 9v.] in perpetuam elemosinam etc.

Postea dictus Walterus mundo valefaciens filium suum reliquit heredem nomine Milonem, cum dominio ville et castri Gloucestrie ac constabularia tocius Anglie iure hereditario, qui vocabatur Milo de Gloucestria. Cui propter probitatem suam Rex Henricus Primus dedit sibi et heredibus dominium foreste de Dene et fecit eum comitem Herefordie.[3] Hic Milo desponsavit Sibillam filiam et heredem Bernardi de Novo Mercato cum dominio de Brekenok etc. Hic Milo dominus ville de Gloucestria et manerii de Heyhampsted ac aliorum maneriorum in comitatu Gloucestrie et alibi octavo Kalendarum Iunii, videlicet vicesimo quinto die mensis Maii in festo Sancti Aldelmi anno ab incarnacione Domini millesimo centesimo tricesimo sexto et anno regni Regis Stephani primo, super solum suum proprium[4] ecclesiam et monasterium sive prioratum Lanthonie iuxta Gloucestriam de novo fundavit, cuius anime propicietur Deus. Amen. Et anno sequenti post fundacionem, videlicet quarto Idus Septembris, videlicet decimo die mensis eiusdem, dedicata fuit ecclesia et cimiterium eiusdem monasterii sive prioratus per dominum Robertum [de Béthune] Herefordie episcopum, domino Milone dicti loci fundatore tunc ibidem presente cum copiosa multitudine populorum. Quo die dictus Milo de Gloucestria fundator dicti loci inter cetera dona sua magnifica per manum dicti Roberti Herefordie episcopi ut pro gleba primaria eiusdem monasterii sive prioratus dedit deo et Beate Marie et canonicis eiusdem ecclesie Lanthonie in perpetuam elemosinam Hidam suam iuxta Gloucestriam liberam et quietam ab omni servicio [et] ecclesiam Sancti Audoeni extra portam australem Gloucestrie cum capellis et omnibus terris pertinentibus ad eandem specificatis et nominatis in carta sua primaria, videlicet inter cetera capella

---

[1] Alias Richard of Quedgeley, the other prebendary: *Camd. Misc.* xxii. 6 n. 4.

[2] *Camd. Misc.* xxii. 37–8.

[3] Copied from a genealogy of the founders: Dugdale, *Mon.* vi. 134. The alleged grant of Dean Forest is discussed by W. E. Wightman, *The Lacy Family in England and Normandy* (Oxford, 1966), 181. Miles received the earldom from the Empress Matilda in 1141: *Complete Peerage.*

[4] The words *et parochiam et manerium de Heyhampsted* are erased here.

infra castrum Gloucestrie, terrula super ripam Sabrine, capella Sancte Kyneburge et tota parochia terre constabularii infra portam de South et tota parochia que est extra portam eandem et tota terra quam Rogerus de Tocham et Ricardus de Quedesley prebendarii Sancti Audoeni nuper tenuerunt infra portam australem et extra, prout in carta dicti Milonis plenius continetur que sic incipit: Milo constabularius, etc.

Et post mortem dicti Milonis dominus Rogerus filius et heres predicti domini Milonis comes Herefordie et constabularius Anglie per cartam suam donacionem patris sui Milonis ratificavit et confirmavit prefatis canonicis superaddendo terras prebendarum ecclesie Sancti Audoeni predictarum sub castello Gloucestrie cum omnibus hominibus in eis habitantibus, liberas et quietas ab omni servicio de geldo et de assisa et de cuiuslibet exactionis auxiliis etc. Et Rex [f. 10] Henricus Secundus filius Imperatricis per diversas cartas suas sive dationes dedit et confirmavit prefatis canonis predictas donaciones addendo de iure suo regio libertates, rectitudines et consuetudines ad easdem pertinentes infra burgum et extra. Quarum auctoritate prior primus adtunc, videlicet Robertus Bracy, et canonici seisiti fuerunt per longum tempus de donacionibus et libertatibus predictis etc. De gorto sive gurgite in Sabrina vocato 'le Cokeynwere' cum pertinentibus et de gorto sive gurgite vocato 'Castelwere' iuxta castellum, per fundatores et patronos nostros nobis datis et confirmatis, carte eorundem manifeste testantur. Et memorandum quod duo curtilagia videlicet elimosinarii et rentarii iuxta Novam Venellam et Frogmerssh ac omnia alia edificia, tenementa, cotagia et curtilagia cum pertinenciis existencia in vicis Sabrine, Sudbroke, alto vico extra portam australe, Parva Venella et Viculo Sancti Audoeni (exceptis quibusdam tenementis que sunt de libertate Bertone Regis iuxta Gloucestriam) sunt de Hida et prebendis Sancti Audoeni et fuerunt dominica vera predicti Milonis cum omnibus libertatibus, serviciis et liberis consuetudinibus tempore primarie fundacionis Lanthonie. Que omnia supradicta per donaciones fundatorum nostrorum ad manus predecessorum nostrorum et nostras devenerunt etc.

8. The prior held view of frankpledge[1] over all the founder's land inside and outside the south gate until he was unjustly dispossessed of this right by the town bailiffs. In 1377–8 the bailiffs John Compton and Robert Pope made a perambulation of the town liberty which took no account of the liberties of King's Barton or of the prior.[2] Robert More archdeacon of Llandaff was appointed by Henry Wakefield bishop of Worcester to arbitrate between the prior and the bailiffs. He met the parties at Llanthony before dawn on Sunday 20 June 1378, when the bailiffs agreed to cease their perambulation and to make no new claim by it.

---

[1] In *Quo warranto* proceedings of 1287 the prior of Llanthony did not claim to hold view of frankpledge for his Gloucester tenants although he claimed it for his tenants in Hempsted and 11 other vills of Glos., Wilts. and Beds.: *Placita de Quo Warranto* (Rec. Com.), 20, 244, 800.

[2] An earlier perambulation, by the bailiffs of 1369–70, partitioned the disputed area: below, **83**.

Et sciendum quod post fundacionem Lanthonie predictam per longum tempus priores Lanthonie, predecessores prioris nunc, seisiti et possessionati fuerunt libere, quiete et pacifice de libertatibus et franchesiis quibuscumque ad visum franciplegii spectantibus in Hida iuxta Gloucestriam et in omnibus terris constabulario et prebendariis Sancti Audoeni spectantibus infra portam de South et extra, quousque per ballivos Gloucestrie et eorum servientes disseisiti fuerunt iniuste et contra consienciam et directe contra tenorem cartarum fundatorum nostrorum et contra privilegia paparum, episcoporum et regum dicto priori et canonicis concessa, non obstante quod contravenientes, impedientes et perturbatores eorundem incurrunt graves et terribiles sensuras ecclesiasticas contra eosdem latas etc. Et memorandum quod post mortem Regis Edwardi Tercii, videlicet primo anno Ricardi Secundi, Iohannes Compton et Robertus Pope ballivi ville Gloucestrie cum sibi adherentibus ex malicia precogitata, sine aliqua commissione seu litteris regis super hoc obtentis, fecerunt quandam perambulacionem circa procinctum libertatis ville Gloucestrie ut asseruerunt, nichil ponderantes de libertate Bertone domini regis nec de libertate prioris Lanthonie. Unde aliqualis materia questionis et dissensionis inter dominum priorem Lanthonie et dictos ballivos fuit exerta etc. Demum [f. 10v.] reverendus in Christo pater Henricus Wakefeld episcopus Wygornie zelator pacis hoc audiens per assensum et concensum utriusque partis assignavit et deputavit Robertum More clericum archidiaconum Landavensem ad tractandas et finiendas litem et materiam predictas. Qui quidem Magister Robertus More die dominica proxima ante festum Sancti Iohannis Baptiste anno Domini 1378 et anno regni Regis Ricardi Secundi primo misit pro ballivis[1] cum aliis comburgensibus ad numerum 12 personarum qui eadem dominica ante horam diei primam venerunt Lanthoniam, et in presencia predicti prioris et quinque fratrum suorum ac ballivorum et 12 comburgensium suorum Gloucestrie, dicta materia ibidem recitata et exposita per dictum Robertum[2] More etc., responsum fuit ex parte dicti prioris quod non fuit nec est voluntatis sue neque intencionis aliqualiter impedire ballivos Gloucestrie qui pro tempore fuerunt exercere iurisdiccionem suam temporalem qua usi fuerunt legitime ipsi et ipsorum antecessores a tempore cuius contrarii memoria hominum non existit; quod quidem responsum placuit ballivis et suis comburgensibus etc. Qui quidem ballivi et burgenses gratanter et expresse promiserunt quod qualicumque tali perambulacione facienda decetero cessabunt omnino et quod nulla nova et inusitata dictis priori et conventui preiudicialia vendicabunt, attemptabunt aut exercebunt quovismodo per que gravamina vel molestie eisdem priori et conventui ac ipsorum prioratui Lanthonie supradicto inferri, parari aut contingere poterunt in futurum, nec per dictam perambulacionem nichil usurpabunt quod ante non habuerunt etc. Et sic facta est pax.

9. In Shipster's Lane, where the town ditch is now, there were tenants in the time of Henry III, namely Adam Blome, Geoffrey Bakon, Robert Frome,[3] William of

---

[1] MS. *misit per ballivos*; apparently a rendering of the English usage 'sent for'.

[2] MS. *Reverendum.*

[3] Vicar of St. Owen's, who lost his vicarage there: *Trans. B.G.A.S.* lxiii. 44–5.

Cheltenham,[1] Roger l'Enveysé[2] and Miles of Cowley, as appears in rentals. In 1265–6 the bailiffs and community of Gloucester destroyed the tenements[3] and dug a ditch[4] where the lane had been. The priory has lost rent thereby, although the borough is receiving rent from curtilages and gardens there.[5]

Item notandum quod in predicta venella vocata Shepstereslane de qua prius fit mentio, ubi nunc est fossatum ville Gloucestrie, diu post fundacionem videlicet tempore Henrici Tercii fuerunt tenentes ibidem in dicta venella Adam Blome, Galfridus Bakon, Robertus Frome, Willelmus de Cheltenham, Rogerus l'Enveyse et Milo[6] de Cowley, ut patet in rentalibus etc. Et anno quinquagesimo Regis Henrici Tercii tenementa nostra in dicta venella destructa fuerunt et deposita per ballivos et communitatem Gloucestrie et ubi adtunc fuit venella foderunt, levaverunt et fecerunt fossatum, per quod predecessores prioris nunc ac ipsemet prior amiserunt et amittunt redditum suum, non obstante quod ballivi et senescalli Gloucestrie percipiunt redditum ibidem annuatim de curtilagiis et gardinis ibidem occupatis ad grave dampnum dicti prioris.

10. For a long time after the founding of the priory there were no bailiffs in Gloucester but only reeves who had no liberty there, as appears in the borough charter.[7] The priory's founders the earls of Hereford used to hold a court for their Gloucestershire out-tenants on the day after the county court, sitting in Gloucester in token of their ancient lordship at the church of St. Mary in the South. Likewise the priors, through their stewards and their town renters, have always held court in St. Owen's church[8] on the day after the county court for their town tenants, especially for those of the constables' land both inside the town and outside the south gate in

---

[1] Town bailiff at least six times between 1255 and 1269: *V.C.H. Glos.* iv. 372. Resident in Longsmith Street: *Landboc de Winchelcumba*, ed. D. Royce (Exeter, 1892), i. 116–20.
[2] Alias Roger le Wyse, town bailiff 1244 and 1258: *Glouc. Corp. Rec.* p. 188 n.; *V.C.H. Glos.* iv. 372.
[3] It was Prince Edward who 'destrued al then toun' after outwitting the adherents of Simon de Montfort: *Metrical Chronicle of Robert of Gloucester* (Rolls Ser.), 746, line 11305. This was in 1264: *V.C.H. Glos.* iv. 20.
[4] By the king's orders: *Close Rolls* 1264–8, 343, 414; *Trans. B.G.A.S.* cii. 92–3.
[5] E. of St. Owen's churchyard Shipster's Lane veered southwards away from the town ditch. In 1509 its E. end was said to be blocked by the S. side of Edmund Young's house (earlier Thomas Young's, approximating to no. 96 Southgate Street) while a closed length between there and the churchyard was let by the borough to the owner of an adjacent garden: Glos. R.O. GBR/J5/3; cf. P.R.O. C 115/73, f. 14 (12).
[6] MS. *Milis.*
[7] *Glouc. Corp. Rec.* pp. 7–8; *V.C.H. Glos.* iv. 29. The borough charter of 1200 awarded the right to elect local magistrates but gave the magistrates the title of reeves (*prepositi*) previously used by royal officials rather than the title of bailiffs used later.
[8] Except from 1298 to 1340 when the court of St. Owen was superseded by the borough court, by the priory chapter and by meetings of burgesses at the priory: Glos. R.O. Library: A. M. Geddes, 'The Priory of Llanthony by Gloucester 1136–1401' (Ph.D. thesis for Johns Hopkins University, 1997), 331–6, 397.

the Hide and the prebends of St. Owen. The priory's liberties in the Hide and elsewhere were confirmed by Richard I and Henry II.[1]

Item memorandum quod tempore fundacionis nostre et diu post non fuerunt ballivi in [f. 11] *Gloucestria sed prepositi non habentes libertatem, ut patet in carta primaria eorundem etc. Et in crastino comitatus Gloucestrie comites Herefordie, constabularii Anglie, fundatores nostri et patroni semper habuerunt et tenuerunt curias suas de tenentibus suis forincecis infra comitatum predictum in supradicta villa Gloucestrie in signum dominacionis antique, que curie tenentur in ecclesia Beate Marie in Austro unde prior et conventus Lanthonie sunt veri patroni. Et sicut predicti comites curias suas tenuerunt[2] ut premittitur in die et loco predictis de tenentibus suis forincecis, sic consimiliter priores Lanthonie qui fuerunt et qui nunc est a tempore fundacionis sue hucusque pacifice et continue pro libito suo per senescallos et rentarios suos dicte ville habuerunt et tenuerunt curias suas in crastino comitatus predicti in ecclesia Sancti Audoeni Gloucestrie de tenentibus eorum dicte ville, et specialiter de hiis qui fuerunt et sunt infra dictam villam de constabularia et similiter de hiis qui sunt extra portam australem qui sunt et fuerunt de Hida et prebenda Sancti Audoeni, qui omnes fuerunt de constabularia etc. Et de libertatibus nostris in Hida et alibi habemus confirmacionem Domini Ricardi et Henrici filii Imperatricis.*

11. When the priory's founders were lords of Gloucester they addressed charters[3] to their town reeve.

Item in cartis fundatorum nostrorum quando fuerunt domini ville Gloucestrie scribunt preposito suo de Gloucestria etc.

12. The cellarers and stewards have always held courts and leets in the guests' hall or in the barn[4] or elsewhere within the Llanthony precinct for tenants, offences and matters pertaining to the view of frankpledge in Hempsted, Quedgeley, Rea and Haresfield,[5] these being the constables' lands. These proceedings take place outside the liberty of Gloucester, and the priory has all judicial instruments for punishing offenders.

Item continue a tempore fundacionis nostre hucusque cellerarii et senescalli qui pro tempore fuerunt in aula hospitum sive in grangia sive in alio loco infra procinctum Lanthonie ad eorum libitum curias et letas nostras tenuerunt manifeste et pacifice absque alia interrupcione de tenentibus nostris et de aliis transgressionibus et de materiis pertinentibus ad visum franciplegii, videlicet de feloniis, weyff, streyff, sooke, sake, toll, tem, infangenthef, owtefangenthef, effusione sanguinis, assisa panis

---

[1] P.R.O. C 115/75, ff. 239–41 nos. 4, 22.

[2] MS. *tenent.*

[3] *Camd. Misc.* xxii. 14, 29.

[4] The barn still stands.

[5] The prior made similar claims in 1287 for Hempsted only: *Placita de Quo Warranto* (Rec. Com.), 244.

et cervisie, ut de tenentibus nostris de Heyhampsted, Quedesley, Ree et Harsfeld qui sunt de constabularia Anglie. Que quidem loca ubi curie et lete nostre tenentur sunt infra libertatem et franchesiam,[1] non infra libertatem ville Gloucestrie. Et [infra] dictam libertatem de Heihampsted habemus omnia instrumenta iudicialia pro transgressoribus et malefactoribus ac iura offendentibus puniendis competencia et conveniencia prout iura volunt.

13. Parliament granted a poll tax to Richard II at Northampton in the quindene of Michaelmas 1380.[2] Accordingly on 9 May 1381 Walter Leycetre the king's serjeant[-at-arms], [John of Neubold], clerk, and William Heyberer sat in Gloucester as royal commissioners[3] to inquire into the tax for Gloucestershire, and John Asshelworth and Richard Coffre were appointed collectors for Gloucester town. Coming to Llanthony, the collectors demanded tax both from the Llanthony servants and from the servants of the countess of Buckingham who was there at the time.[4] Answer was given that the Llanthony servants being within the hundred of Dudstone would pay the current tax, like the last four years' taxes, to the collectors of Hempsted. The collectors retired abashed and excused themselves before the commissioners, asserting that the collectors of Hempsted should answer for the tax of the Llanthony community and servants.

Memorandum quod in parliamento tento apud Northampton anno quarto Ricardi Regis Secundi, in subsidium et relevamen guerre dicti domini regis et ob specialem favorem domini Thome comitis Buck' in Britannia tunc existentis, commune terre Anglie concesserunt [f. 11v.] de singulis domibus pro viro et uxore 12d. ac viri ecclesiastici videlicet singuli sacerdotes tam seculares quam religiosi fratribus exceptis 6s. 8d., clerici vero inferioris gradus 12d. Et post finem parliamenti, videlicet nono die mensis Maii anno superiore, Walterus Leycetre sarjiantus domini regis et quidam clericus cum eo ac Willelmus Heyberer virtute commissionis regie sederunt Gloucestrie ad inquirendum ibidem et in toto comitatu de dicto subsidio nuper regi concesso, videlicet in quindena Michaelis apud Northampton, videlicet de singulis domibus pro viro et uxore 12d. Virtute cuius commissionis assigni fuerunt duo collectores pro villa Gloucestrie et omnibus habitantibus infra libertatem et franchesiam eiusdem ville, videlicet Iohannes Asshelworth et Ricardus Coffre, ad levandum et recipiendum dictum subsidium. Qui quidem collectores venerunt Lanthoniam et pecierunt dictum subsidium de servientibus Lanthonie et

[1] The words *de Heyhampsted* are erased here.

[2] On 6 Dec. in the parliament which convened on 8 Nov. 1380: *Rotuli Parliamentorum* (London, 1783), iii. 90, ss. 15–16; C. C. Fenwick, *The Poll Taxes of 1377, 1379 and 1381* (Oxford, 1998), p. xvi.

[3] Appointed as reassessment commissioners on 16 Mar. 1381: *Cal. Fine R. 1377–83*, 249. Heyberer (d. 1390) was J.P. for Glos. from 1380 and seven times bailiff of Gloucester, eight times M.P. for the borough and four times M.P. for Glos. between 1361 and 1390: *Hist. of Parl., Commons 1386–1421*; N. Saul, *Knights and Esquires* (Oxford, 1981), 127, 146; *Cal. Pat. 1388–92*, 407.

[4] As patroness: *Trans. B.G.A.S.* lxiii. 95.

non solum de servientibus Lanthonie sed eciam de servientibus domine comitisse
Buck' tunc ibidem existentis. Quibus responsum fuit quod servientes Lanthonie
solverunt subsidium per quattuor annos elapsos, videlicet quelibet persona 4s.
domino regi concessos, collectoribus de Heyhampsted eo quod sunt infra hundredum
de Duddeston, et quoad subsidium nunc domino regi concessum, respondebunt dictis
collectoribus de Heyhampsted etc. Et sic predicti collectores de Gloucestria quasi
confusi cum pudore recesserunt et coram predictis inquisitoribus pro subsidio ville
Gloucestrie responderunt. Et de subsidio famulie et serviencium Lanthonie se
ibidem excusaverunt, asserantes quod collectores villate de Heihampsted de famulia
et serviencibus Lanthonie colligere et pro eisdem respondere debent pro eo quod
sunt infra hundredum de Duddeston etc.

14. Servants of Llanthony who have no homes elsewhere have never paid tax with
the Gloucester burgesses.

Item memorandum quod servientes Lanthonie qui non habent alia domicilia nisi
ibidem nunquam fuerunt contributores cum burgensibus Gloucestrie ad solucionem
decime domino regi concesse neque aliquod aliud subsidium.

15. Merchants from all parts of England, Wales and Ireland and those who are afraid
to use the Gloucester market because of its unjust charges constantly sell their
merchandise at Llanthony without challenge or fee.[1]

Item mercatores ex quibuscumque partibus Anglie, Wallie et Hibernie venerunt et
continue veniunt Lanthoniam et ibidem vendunt diversa mercimonia quibuscumque
personis absque interrupcione ballivorum Gloucestrie. Et plures qui timent vendere
sua mercimonia in villa Gloucestrie propter iniustas prestaciones et exacciones
veniunt Lanthoniam et ibidem vendunt libere sua mercimonia quibuscumque
personis absque aliquo fine seu amerciamento etc.

16. Llanthony is a parish[2] in its own right for the community and its servants. The
parish includes Gloucester castle, in which the prior collects tithes, oblations and
mortuary payments.

Item memorandum quod in Lanthonia est parochia per se pro famulia et servientibus
ibidem et ubi percipiunt sacramenta et sacramentalia, infra quam parochiam
situatur castellum Gloucestrie. [f. 12] *In quo quidem castello prior Lanthonie habet*
et recipit decimas, oblaciones et mortuaria etc.

---

[1] A market and a fair were entered as yielding no income in 1539 in the bailiff's accounts
for what had been the prior's adjacent manor of Hempsted: *V.C.H. Glos.* iv. 426. But the
author may mean merely that vendors such as Welsh drovers (below, **25**) were being
forestalled near Llanthony.

[2] Long Madleaze, a part of the priory demesne, was said to be in Llanthony parish in 1542,
but in 1396 the demesne fish weirs were said to be in the parish of St. Owen: *L & P. Hen.*
VIII, xvii, p. 488; *Trans. B.G.A.S.* lxii. 148.

17. Servants of Llanthony who have no homes elsewhere are not burgesses or portmen of Gloucester and have never paid the borough taxes or made suit to the borough courts.

Item servientes Lanthonie non habentes[1] alia domicilia non sunt burgenses Gloucestrie neque portmenni nec sunt contributores ad onera burgensibus dicte ville incumbencia, nec unquam fecerunt nec faciunt aliquam sectam ad curiam sive letam eorundem.

18. In Edward II's *Nomina Villarum* of 1316 one finds 'In the hundred of Gloucester is the borough of Gloucester and no other town besides.'

Virtute brevis Domini Edwardi dei gracia regis Anglie ad cerciorandum de civitatibus, hundredis, burgis et villis in comitatu Gloucestrie anno regni sui nono inter alia compertum est: In hundredo Gloucestrie est burgus Gloucestrie et non est aliqua alia villa in eodem hundredo.[2]

19. In 1381–2 an eleven year old servant girl of Simon Baker of Gloucester fell and drowned in the Severn and was found at Cokeyn.[3] The body was viewed by the local coroner and taken to Llanthony for burial.

Item memorandum quod quedam parvula ancilla etatis 11 annorum, serviens Symonis Baker de Gloucestria, periclitata fuit et submersa in Sabrina, et postea inventa apud 'le Cokeyn' et visa per coronatorem patrie. Et postea deportata fuit Lanthoniam et ibidem sepulta, anno quinto Regis Ricardi Secundi.

20. On 13 July 1381, after defeating and pacifying those who were disturbing the peace in Essex and after killing 500 commoners, Thomas [of Woodstock] earl of Buckingham came to Llanthony with 200 knights and men under arms. The next day, Sunday 14th, the prior and convent in chapter received the earl, his wife Eleanor, his six knights and their squires and pages into spiritual fraternity, and letters came from the king revoking the concessions he had made to the commons in London about serfdom and pardon. On Monday the earl with his soldiers held a court in Gloucester, attended by almost all the townspeople, to discover the identity of rebels. On Tuesday the earl held another court in Sudmeadow with Gilbert [Lord] Talbot, John Harleston and many other knights and their retinues, attended by commoners of all the hundreds of Gloucestershire. On the earl's instructions John Harleston described the perils of the kingdom. Those attending took an oath of loyalty and were commanded, under threat of severe punishment, to continue to fulfil their obligations as serfs and as customary tenants. At the same time some men of Gloucester who had previously spoken carelessly and seditiously were arrested and brought before the earl and his council at Llanthony, namely Thomas Biseley and his son, Thomas son of John Compton, Thomas Loude, smith, and John Kent.

[1] MS. *habentibus.*
[2] *Feudal Aids*, ii. 264 copied in Reg. Wyche, f. 261v.
[3] See below, **68.**

Unable to excuse themselves of rebellion, they were condemned to prison by the earl and his council and were sent to Gloucester castle. Significantly, they were not put into the custody of the Gloucester bailiffs.[1]

Terciodecimo die mensis Iulii anno regni Regis Ricardi Secundi quinto Dominus Thomas Buckingham, peragratis et superatis per eum et suos in manu valida in partibus Essex circumquaque pacis perturbatoribus et occisis per partes 500 de comunibus, et tandem cum Dei adiutorio pacificatis et ad propria reversis, licenciatus a rege venit Lanthoniam cum militibus et aliis armatis ad numerum 200 etc.

In crastino vero videlicet die Dominica in festo Reliquiarum dictus dominus comes cum Alianora uxore sua et 6 militibus, armigeris et domicellis recepti fuerunt in spiritualem fraternitatem domus nostre Lanthonie hora et loco capitulari, presentibus ibidem priore et toto conventu etc. Et eodem die venerunt Lanthoniam nuncii domini regis cum litteris patentibus dicto domino comiti directis de revocacione cuiusdam concessionis domini regis nuper communibus facte apud Londinium de manumissione et omni bondagio etc. ac de perdonacione feloniarum predictarum, transgressionum et extorsionum etc. In crastino videlicet die Lune dictus comes cum suis armatis sedebat in Gloucestria pro stabilitate et conservacione pacis, ubi coram eo comparuerunt quasi omnes tocius ville, et fecit inquisicionem si qui forent rebelles et insurgentes contra pacem. Et in crastino videlicet die Martis dominus Thomas comes predictus, dominus Gilbertus Talbot, dominus Iohannes Harleston et plerique alii milites cum eorum familia sederunt in prato nostro de Southmede, ubi omnes communes omnium hundredorum comitatus Gloucestrie comparuerunt coram se. Quibus exposita fuerunt per dictum Iohannem Harleston, per mandatum dicti comitis, pericula regni etc. Et iuratis et examinatis omnibus promiserunt per levacionem et extencionem manuum suarum, et sic [f. 12v.] in pace recesserunt singuli et universi ad propria etc. Quibus fuerat proclamatum et iniunctum ex parte domini regis quod singuli tenentes tam nativi quam tenentes secundum consuetudinem manerii facerent de cetero opera sua et custumas ut semper per prius facere et operari consueverunt, et hoc sub pena gravi et punicione etc.

Quo tempore quidam de Gloucestria qui non posuerunt custodiam ori suo et eciam quidam de patria qui prius contumaciter et cum rebellione verba perversa persuflassaent capti fuerunt et coram domino comiti et consilio suo Lanthoniam adducti, videlicet Thomas Biseley cum filio suo, Thomas filius Iohannis Compton, Thomas Loude faber et Iohannes Kent, qui omnes fuerunt de Gloucestria. Et examinati coram domino comiti et consilio suo nescierunt excusare se de rebellione, quapropter in continenti per dictum comitem et consilium suum adiudicati fuerunt prisone et missi fuerunt ad castellum Gloucestrie in arta custodia custodiendi sine manucapcione quovismodo etc. Et sic nota quod non fuerunt missi ballivis Gloucestrie ad custodiendum. Ideo etc.

---

[1] Printed and discussed by Richard Holt in 'Thomas of Woodstock and events at Gloucester in 1381': *Bulletin of the Institute of Historical Research*, lviii (no. 138), 237–42.

21. In 1349 nineteen professed canons of Llanthony died, leaving only eleven alive. After this the bailiffs of Gloucester made many improper claims, because those who died were the abler and wiser members of the convent, while the survivors had no knowledge of its muniments and liberties. Thus the error grew.

Memorandum quod anno Domini 1349 obierunt in Lanthonia novemdecim canonici et professi et sic remanebant tantum viventes undecim. Post quorum mortem ballivi Gloucestrie capitose et per usurpacionem multa inconveniencia fecerunt et vendicabant ea que numquam prius habuerunt, pro eo quod valenciores et scienciores conventus fuerunt mortui et qui remanebant vivi fuerunt innocentes non habentes noticiam munimentorum et privilegiorum Lanthonie. Et sic intumuit et crescebat error quem Deus pacificet, anno regni Regis Edwardi Tercii post conquestum Anglie vicesimo secundo.

22. After the French captured the Isle of Wight in 1377 the burgesses of Gloucester flooded the ditch under the Black Friars' wall and widened it by 12 ft. to the harm of the prior of Llanthony,[1] cutting down elm and ash trees on the bank and in St. Kyneburgh's churchyard. The prior met the bailiffs in the castle orchard and they agreed that he should have and dispose of the trees.[2]

Item anno primo Regis Ricardi Secundi Franci ceperunt insulam Vectam in manu forti et armata, Hugone Tirell capitaneo eiusdem existente. Qui quidem Hugo cum aliis inhabitantibus vi coacti dederunt Francigenis pro tributo mille marcas etc. Qua de causa timor et tremor invasit plures in Anglia et paraverunt se contra Francos. Unde burgenses Gloucestrie cum sibi coadherentibus fossatum sub muro Fratrum Predicatorum inundaverunt et multum dilataverunt plus solito ad quantitatem 12 pedum in decrimentum prioris Lanthonie, ac arbores videlicet ulmos et fraxinos in ripa et in cimiterio Sancte Kyneburge succiderunt et fossatum ibidem elargaverunt in exheredacionem ecclesie Lanthonie. Quapropter materia litis suborta fuit, et tandem assignato die convenerunt simul in 'le castel orchard', videlicet prior Lanthonie cum paucis et ballivi cum magna [f. 13] multitudine, et materia declarata ex utraque parte concesserunt predicti ballivi pro bono pacis quod predictus prior haberet predictas arbores et disponeret eas ad libitum suum. Et sic quievit lis pro tempore.

23. When parliament met in Gloucester in 1378 [John of Gaunt] duke of Lancaster lodged at Llanthony with his household while the King's Bench was sitting in the town. One of the duke's grooms killed another. The bailiffs of Gloucester John Rusebye and William Crooke, with their coroners Gilbert Clive and John Butte,

---

[1] To minimise encroachment on the prior's property they made this ditch encroach on the line of the Roman town wall opposite: *Trans. B.G.A.S.* cii. 113 & fig. 5.

[2] In 1391 Prior Chirton sued the bailiffs of 1377–8 for this intrusion on a writ of *ad quod damnum*. He pleaded that it was an armed assault in which his servants were wounded and abused, a stone wall thrown down and earth and trees to the value of £50 carried away: Reg. Chirton, ff. 145, 152–5.

came to Llanthony to hold an inquest, but the king's justices forbade them to infringe the liberty of Llanthony church on pain of £100. Three days after the death, by order of the king's justices, the king's coroner John Shardelowe and the local coroner Nicholas Vey came to Llanthony and sat and performed their duty and the homicide was hanged.

Item tempore parliamenti tenti Gloucestrie anno secundo Regis Ricardi dux Lancastrie cum sua familia hospitabatur in Lanthonia sedente in Gloucestria adtunc communi banco domini regis. Quo tempore unus garcio dicti ducis de stabulo occidit socium suum. Quo mortuo ballivi Gloucestrie videlicet Iohannes Rusebye et Willelmus Crooke cum coronatoribus suis videlicet Gilberto Clive et Iohanne Butte et aliis multis venerunt Lanthoniam ut ibi sederent super visum corporis et inquisicionem caperent super morte predicta etc. Unde iusticiarii domini regis hoc audientes inhibuerunt eisdem sub pena centum librarum ne sic facerent in preiudicium libertatis ecclesie Lanthonie. Unde tercio die post mortem dicti garcionis venerunt Lanthoniam hac de causa Iohannes Shardelowe coronator domini regis et Nicholaus Vey coronator de patria cum pluribus aliis et de precepto iusticiariorum domini regis sederunt et officium suum exercuerunt etc. et homicida suspensus fuit etc.

24. During that parliament [of 1378] a bridge was made over the land between Gloucester castle and Llanthony as a way for the king and his men. The priory has the king's letters patent[1] that nobody may claim this bridge as a king's highway, and has a similar letter from Queen Eleanor[2] about an [earlier] bridge and a way by the castle.

Item tempore parliamenti predicti factus fuit unus pons super terram inter castellum Gloucestrie et Lanthoniam pro aisiamento et via domini regis et suorum. De quo ponte habemus litteras patentes dicti domini regis ne quis postea vendicaret dictam viam quasi regiam. Consimiles litteras habemus de Alianora Regina de ponte et de via iuxta castellum etc.

25. English and Welsh merchants have always sold sheep, cattle and merchandise at Llanthony to all comers without paying toll to the Gloucester bailiffs.

Memorandum quod mercatores ex omnibus partibus Anglie et Wallie ab antiquo venerunt et continue veniunt Lanthoniam et vendunt oves et boves ac alia

---

[1] From Richard II in 1378: *Cal. Pat.* 1377–81, 285, copied in Reg. Chirton, f. 25 and P.R.O. C 115/83, f. 192v.

[2] From Eleanor of Provence in 1277: P.R.O. C 115/75, f. 233v. no. 28 = C 115/83, f. 192, translated in *Trans. B.G.A.S.* lxiii. 54.

quecumque mercimonia quibuscumque personis absque aliqua interrupcione ballivorum[1] Gloucestrie seu theloneo solvendo eisdem.

26. A man from Nantwich [Ches.] killed two men, his master Lakyn and another, in Eastgate Street when they were in Gloucester with two from Shrewsbury for business at Wotton. The killer fled, came to Llanthony and entered the church with his dagger in his hand unsheathed and bloody. Because he would not admit his offence nor seek the coroner, he was taken to Gloucester castle, and not into the custody of the bailiffs, after dinner on the same day and soon afterwards was hanged.

Item quidam [   ] de Nantwyche occidit duos viros videlicet magistrum suum [   ] Lakyn et unum alium apud Gloucestriam in Ailesyatestrete, qui fuerunt Gloucestrie cum duo Salop' pro materia de Wotton etc. Et ipse occisor fugit et venit Lanthoniam et intravit ecclesiam cum daggaro suo nudo et sanguinolento in manu sua. Et eodem die post prandium dictus felo, pro eo quod nollet confiteri feloniam predictam nec petere coronatorem, cariatus fuit ad castellum Gloucestrie et non ad custodiam ballivorum Gloucestrie, et cito post suspensus fuit. Post cuius mortem veniebat Lanthoniam [   ] clericus elimosinarius domini regis et peciit dictum daggarum vel precium eiusdem quasi deodandum, pro eo quod ballivi [f. 13v.] Gloucestrie non habebant iurisdiccionem apud Lanthoniam.

27. In 1424–5 Henry Croke, Esq., was arrested at Llanthony by virtue of the king's writ at the suit[2] of Anne countess of Stafford. He was taken not into the custody of the bailiffs but to Gloucester castle, where he died.

Item memorandum quod anno regni Regis Henrici Sexti tercio Henricus Croke armiger arestatus fuit apud Lanthoniam virtute brevis regis ad sectam domine Anne comitesse Stafford et ductus ad castellum Gloucestrie, et non ad custodiam ballivorum, et in dicto castello obiit.

28. There are at Llanthony nearly 80 laymen who receive Easter communion. They have never made suit or service to the bailiffs of Gloucester and are not answerable to their summons.

Item memorandum quod in Lanthonia sunt fere 80 persone seculares qui recipiunt communionem in die Pasche, qui numquam fecerunt nec faciunt aliquam sectam seu servicium ballivis Gloucestrie nec sunt infra summonicionem eorundem.

---

[1] MS. *ballivi.*
[2] Probably concerning Olveston, where Roger Crook held a manor in 1327, where Henry Croke owed 100s. to the vicar in 1407 and where the lords Stafford held a manor by 1521: Rudder, *Glos.* 587; *Cal. Pat.* 1405–8, 254.

29. The priory's possessions were confirmed by popes and kings.

Item memorandum quod omnes possessiones nostre confirmate sunt per auctoritatem Celestini, Eugenii, Adriani, Alexandri paporum[1] et per litteras patentes Henrici II, Ricardi, Iohannis,[2] Henrici,[3] Edwardi,[4] Edwardi, Edwardi et Ricardi[5] regum Anglie.

30. Miles gave Castle Mead, of 60 acres,[6] in exchange for which Henry III gave meadow at Sudmeadow and Walham. To this day the Gloucester bailiffs have no jurisdiction over it.

Memorandum quod 'le Castelmede' datum fuit priori et canonicis Lanthonie per Milonem fundatorem eiusdem loci prout liquet in carta primaria dicti Milonis etc.,[7] quod quidem pratum continebat in se sexaginta acras. Pro quo quidem prato Henricus Rex Tercius dedit nobis in escambium pratum suum in Southmede et Waleham et alias terras prout patet in carta dicti regis etc. In quo quidem prato ballivi Gloucestrie usque in hodiernum diem non habent aliquam iurisdictionem etc.

31. They claim jurisdiction in Oxleaze although Oxleaze is farther from the town than Castle Mead.

Memorandum quod pretendunt habere iurisdictionem in 'le Oxlese' iacente iuxtam predictum pratum non obstante quod 'le Oxlese' est remocior a predicta villa quam 'le Castelmede'.

---

[1] By Celestine III in 1191, Eugenius III in 1147, Adrian IV in 1158 and Alexander III in 1162: P.R.O. C 115/75, ff. 214–7 nos. 23, 25–7.

[2] By Hen. II: P.R.O. C 115/75, f. 228 no. 1 = C 115/83, f. 187. By Ric. I in 1198: P.R.O. C 115/75, f. 231 no. 22. By John in 1199: *Rotuli Chartarum* (Rec. Com.), 7, copied in P.R.O. C 115/75, f. 232 no. 23.

[3] Hen. III confirmed them only to Llanthony Prima: *Cal. Chart. R.* 1226–57, 186.

[4] No confirmation by Edw. I is recorded.

[5] By Edw. II in 1309: *Cal. Charter R.* 1300–26, 128, copied in P.R.O. C 115/75, f. 234 no. 33. By Edw. III in 1340: *Cal. Charter R.* 1327–41, 470, copied in P.R.O. C 115/75, f. 237 no. 42. By Ric. II in 1378: *Cal. Pat.* 1377–81, 216, copied in P.R.O. C 115/83, f. 189.

[6] Although Castle Meads survived into the 20th century as a 60-acre meadow (Ordnance Survey 1:2500 sheet Glos. xxv. 14, 1901 edn.), it attained that size only by encroachment on Prestham; indeed Henry III called it Prestham when taking the 60 acres from Llanthony in 1265: below, **32**. The encroachment took place when Miles cut a ditch across Prestham, an ancient possession of Gloucester Abbey, and although his son Roger promised to restore the severed portion to the abbey in 1154 his other sons Henry and Mahel gave it to Llanthony in 1160–5, a gift for which the abbey received compensation in 1192: *Hist. & Cart. Mon. Glouc.* (Rolls Ser.), ii. 7–8, 85; *Camd. Misc.* xxii. 48, 50. After 1265 Castle Meads became a perquisite of the castle constable: *V.C.H. Glos.* iv. 245. The residue of Prestham west of Miles's ditch survived into the 20th century as Oxleaze: Ordnance Survey, op. cit. A deed of 1518 which equates Oxleaze with Nunham and Port Ham with Prestham is inconsistent with other evidence: *Glouc. Corp. Rec.* p. 426.

[7] Dugdale, *Mon.* vi. 136.

32. Henry [III]'s grant[1] of 44½ acres in Sudmeadow and 16 acres in Walham[2] in exchange for 60 acres in Prestham.[3] [20 May 1265.]

Henricus dei gracia rex Anglie, dominus Hibernie et dux Aquitanie archiepiscopis, episcopis, abbatibus, prioribus, comitibus, baronibus, justiciariis, vicecomitibus, prepositis, ministris et omnibus ballivis et fidelibus suis salutem. Sciatis quod pro prato prioris et conventus de Lanthonia subtus castrum nostrum Gloucestrie quod vocatur Prestenham continens in se sexaginta acras per perticam nostram etc. dedimus et concessimus et hac carta nostra confirmavimus eisdem priori et conventui in escambium pratum nostrum de Southmede iacens extra situm dicti prioratus quod continet in se quadraginta et quatuor acras et dimidium per eandem perticam etc., et similiter pratum nostrum quod vocatur Walleham extra Gloucestriam continens in se sexdecim acras per eandem perticam etc.

33. *Thees ben the complay[n]tes of the bailiffs of Glouc' ayenst the prior of Lanthony.*

[a] *First, where oon Roger Colmon, prest, sued an accion ayenst Ric' Vanner and* [f. 14] *William Martyn of Glouc', and so process continued til he had jugement to recover and thereupon a 'capias ad satisfaciendum' directed unto the ministres of the seid bailiffs, by fors off whech the seid officers arrested the seid William Martyn at Lanthony withyn the procincte of the liberte of the towne of Glouc', and thei were recorsed* [i.e. rescued].

[b] *Item, thei complayneth that the seid prior occupieth and loppeth certayne withies by the Cokeyn upon Sevarn banke.*

[c] *Item, they complayneth that the seid prior accrocheth unto hym certayn ground of the comon dich of the seid towne by Seint Kyneborugh and thereof makyn certayn gardeynes to grete availe of the seid prior and hurt to the seid towne etc.[4]*

[d] *Item, they complayneth hem that the chapell of Seynt Kyneborugh aforesaid is edified upon the comon grownd of the seid towne.[5]*

[e] *Item, they complayneth hem of a dore next to the seid towne diche being out of the seid chapell, the whiche in cas of trouble might be cause of the lost of the seid town.[6]*

[f] *Item, thei complayneth hem that the seid prior hath bild a shuyre* [i.e. shed] *to*

---

[1] Abbreviated from the charter which is summarised in *Cal. Charter R.* 1257–1300, 55, copied in P.R.O. C 115/75, f. 233 no. 26 and discussed in *Trans. B.G.A.S.* lxiii. 51.

[2] Sudmeadow of *c.* 180 a. and Walham of *c.* 100 a. were common meadows held in strips: *V.C.H. Glos.* iv. 404. This grant, worth £6 4s. a year, was taken from the manor of King's Barton: *Cal. Liberate R.* 1267–72, p. 116.

[3] See above, **30** n.

[4] A counterclaim to **38**(d) below.

[5] Richard II ratified the prior's title to the chapel site in 1390: *Cal. Pat.* 1388–92, 285.

[6] The south door of St. Kyneburgh's chapel had been obstructed by the digging of the town ditch in 1263–5: *Cal. Inq. Misc.* i, no. 338. In 1391, however, the burgesses complained to the marshal of the Marshalsea that thieves, fugitives and priors of Llanthony had been entering and leaving the town by it for the last 30 years, and in 1392 they complained to the prior that people were using it to evade toll and customs at the town gate: Reg. Chirton, ff. 144v., 159v.

the walle of Seint Michellchurche, the whiche R. Blake, glover, holdeth of the seid prior, the whiche is bild upon the comon grownd of the seid towne.[1]

[g] *Item, they complayneth hem of 6d. of rent withdrawe by the seid prior going out of a shop, the whiche oon John Pole holdith of the seid prior beside Seint Michellchurch aforesayd.*[2]

[h] *Item, they complayneth hem of an howse to be set uppon the comon grownd of the seid towne by a lone ycalled Smale Lane etc.*

34. On St. Kyneburgh's[3] father Penda, king of Mercia, from Higden's *Polychronicon.*

Memorandum quod anno gracie 626[4] *Penda rex Merciorum paganus cepit regnare super Mercios et regnavit 30 annos. Hic duos reges Northumbrie, Edwynum et Oswaldum, et tres reges Estanglorum, Sigebertum, Egricum et Annam,*[5] *bello extinxit. Cui regina sua Kyneswyda peperit quinque filios, Wolferum, Etheldredum, Merewaldum, Mercellinum et Wedam, et duas filias, Sanctam Kyneburgam et Sanctam Kyneswydam.*[6] *Libro quinto Polic[hronici] ante medium.*[7]

Et Anno Domini 655 Rex Penda decessit cum 30 ducibus suis extinctis iuxta Eboracum iuxta flumen Wynwed, ab Oswy rege interfectus. Qui quidem Penda venerat ad partes Northumbranas ut Regem Oswy deleret sicut [f. 14v.] *fratrem suum Oswaldum dudum deleverat.*[8]

35. In the present year 1455–6 Llanthony Priory has existed for 319 and St. Kyneburgh's chapel for 919 years.

Memorandum quod prioratus Lanthonie fundatus fuit per 319 annos elapsos etc.

---

[1] A shed at the extreme corner of Southgate and Eastgate Streets, the site of which measured 11 ft. 9 in. by 8 ft. 1 in. in the 13th century and was recovered by Prior Wyche in 1416–7. It was rebuilt by Robert Blake after 1442: P.R.O. C 115/73, f. 26 (24)v. no. 51; C 115/84, ff. 36–7 nos. 112–13; Reg. Wyche, ff. 15, 20, 75, 104; *Glouc. Rental 1455*, 2b.

[2] The second shop east of the church entrance under the north wall of St. Michael's church in Eastgate Street, a shop which was 13 ft. 10 in. wide and 10 ft. 9 in. deep in 1363 and in which John Pole lived as the prior's tenant. The prior owed 12d. a year to the bailiffs for a purpresture of a stall in front: P.R.O. C 115/73, f. 63 (61)v. no. 115; C 115/75, f. 125v. no. 187; *Glouc. Rental 1455*, 103b.

[3] Kyneburgh daughter of Penda was foundress and abbess of a convent at Castor (Northants.), whence her bones were translated later to Peterborough and Thorney. The author evidently confuses her with a namesake buried in St. Kyneburgh's chapel at Gloucester: *Oxford Dictionary of Saints*, s. v. Cyniburg.

[4] MS. *625*. Corrections are from the Rolls Series edition of the *Polychronicon.*

[5] MS. *Amnam.*

[6] The MS. has spellings *Ethelredum* and *Marwaldum*, the latter being also found in MS. B at Caius College, Cambridge. Other sources confirm Penda's issue as including Wulfhere, Ethelred, Peada and Cyneburh but not Merewald, Mercelm or Cynewise: *Handbook of British Chronology*, ed. E. B. Fryde and others (London, 1986), 15–16.

[7] *Polychronicon Ranulphi Higden* (Rolls Ser.), v. 440–2.

[8] Ibid. vi. 80–2.

Scriptum fuit hoc memorandum anno Henrici VI 34. Et memorandum quod capella sive ecclesia Sancte Kyneburge fuit edificata ante fundacionem Lanthonie per 600[1] annos.

36. Priors of Llanthony in each reign.[2]
Notandum quod Rex Stephanus regnavit viginti quatuor[3] annos, quibus annis fuerunt priores Clemens Doctor Sacre Theologie, Rogerus de Norfolk et Galfridus medicus. Rex Ricardus Primus regnavit 9 annos, quibus annis fuerunt priores Gaufridus et Martinus. Rex Iohannes regnavit 18 annos, quibus annis fuerunt priores Walterus de Monemoth et Gilbertus Cornubiensis.[4] Rex Henricus Tercius regnavit 56 annos, quibus annis fuerunt priores Iohannes et Iohannes dictus de Heihampsted et Godfridus de Bannebury. Rex Edwardus Primus regnavit 35 annos, quibus annis fuerunt priores predictus Godfridus 12 annis[5] et Willelmus Asshwell et Walterus Markeley. Rex Edwardus II regnavit 19 annos, quibus annis fuerunt priores Iohannes Chaundos et Willelmus Pendebury. Rex Edwardus Tercius regnavit 51 annos, quibus annis fuerunt priores predictus Willelmus Pendebury 37 annis et Simon Brockeworth. Rex Ricardus II regnavit 22 annos, quibus annis fuit prior Dominus Willelmus de Chiriton. Rex Henricus IV regnavit 13 annos, quibus annis fuerunt priores dictus Willelmus de Chiriton 1 anno et dimidio et Dominus Iohannes Lymnor fere 7 annis et Iohannes Wiche annis inde residuis. Rex Henricus Quintus regnavit 9 annos et dimidium, quibus annis predictus Iohannes Wiche solus fuit prior. Rex Henricus VI regnavit [unfinished].

37. The property of the two Llanthonys was divided by composition[6] in 1211.
Nota quod anno ab incarnacione Domini 1211 composicio facta fuit inter Lanthoniam in Wallia et Lanthoniam iuxta Gloucestriam de particione ecclesiarum et aliarum possessionum eisdem[7] datarum et concessarum etc.

[If f. 15 existed it survives here as one of two stubs in the binding which retain ff. 9 and 10 in the previous quire and are trimmed with a single cut.]

---

[1] Apparently an error for *c.* 500.
[2] Compare B.L. Harleian MS. 6079 (60) f. 106, which omits Martin and Walter of Monmouth but adds later priors up to Henry Dene; and D. Knowles, C. N. L. Brooke and V. C. M. London, *Heads of Religious Houses 940–1216* (Cambridge, 1972), 172–3.
[3] Stephen reigned only for 19 years. Henry II, who is not mentioned, ruled for 35.
[4] Knowles, Brooke and London confirm the sequence of these two priors, which is reversed in *V.C.H. Glos.* ii. 91 and *Trans. B.G.A.S.* lxiii. 37.
[5] Godfrey of Banbury was replaced in Henry III's reign. William of Ashwell was the prior who resigned in 12 Edw. I: *Trans. B.G.A.S.* lxiii. 50, 61.
[6] A composition dividing Irish property: *Irish Cart. Llanth.* p. 75 no. 59. English and Welsh property was divided by agreement in 1205: P.R.O. C 115/75, s. xxvii no. 11.
[7] MS. *eiusdem.*

38. [f. 16] Injuries inflicted on the priory.

De gravaminibus illatis priori et conventui Lanthonie etc.

(a) The bailiffs and stewards of Gloucester lately closed a common lane under the wall of Gloucester abbey to the detriment of the prior's tenement.[1]

De eo quod ballivi et senescalli Gloucestrie nuper claudere fecerunt quandam venellam communem subtus murum abbatie ad grave nocumentum liberi tenementi predicti prioris.

(b) They allow anyone to commit nuisance and to dump filth in Sheep Lane to the detriment of the prior's tenements adjacent.[2]

Item de eo quod ballivi et senescalli permittunt quoscumque cacare et proicere fimum et multa alia vilia et inhonesta in quandam venellam vocatam 'Shepes Lane' per que tenementa dicti prioris iuxta dictam venellam multum deteriorantur et peiorantur ad grave dampnum dicti prioris.

(c) They exercise their offices outside the south gate of Gloucester contrary to the prior's privileges.[3]

Item de eo quod dicti ballivi et eorum servientes exercent officia sua in diversis locis extra Southgate Gloucestrie contra cartas et privilegia dicti prioris.

(d) They unjustly occupy the prior's land outside the south gate extending westwards from St. Kyneburgh's chapel to the castle ditch, land from which former priors received 42s. 4d. yearly rent.[4]

Item de eo quod ballivi et senescalli sine iusto titulo occupant terram dicti prioris extra Southgate extendentem se a capella Sancte Kyneburge a parte orientali usque ad fossatum castelli ex parte occidentali, que quidem terra est de feodo prioris Lanthonie. De qua quidem terra predecessores predicti nunc prioris solebant recipere annuum redditum videlicet 42s. 4d.

---

[1] The lane under the south wall of the abbey precinct flanked the prior of Llanthony's tenements at nos. 28–30 Westgate Street and on the west side of College Court: P.R.O. C 115/73, ff. 56–9 (54–7) nos. 107, 114–6; *Glouc. Rental 1455*, 32b, 36b. The borough won from the abbey the right to enclose and appropriate it by an arbitrator's award of 1429, and still owned parts of it in 1826: Glos. R.O. GBR/B2/1, f. 195v.; GBR/J4/12, plans 18–21.

[2] Sheep Lane ran behind the prior's tenements nos. 53–65 Southgate Street south of St. Mary de Crypt: P.R.O. C 115/73, ff. 22–3 (20–1) nos. 40–1; *Glouc. Rental 1455*, 12b. The borough licensed closure of part of it in 1307 and in 1414 let the south end of it to Thomas More of the George, no. 67 Southgate Street, whose successor in title John Caple had a privy there in 1509: Glos. R.O. GBR/J1/778–9, 1073; J5/3. The borough still owned part of the lane in 1826: ibid. J4/12, plan 32.

[3] Pursuant to their perambulation of 1370: below, **83.**

[4] The borough collected 20d. rent in 1509 from a garden by the town ditch west of the south gate, a garden of which the limits are here disputed by both parties: Glos. R.O. J5/3; above, **33**(c). For the alleged loss of 42s. 4d. see below, **38**(g) n.

(e) They occupy parcels of the prior's land at Rikenel Stile for which he used to receive 9s. 9d. rent.[1]

Item de eo quod predicti ballivi et senescalli occupant diversas parcellas terre dicti prioris apud 'Rynellestile' pro quibus idem prior et predecessores sui solebant recipere certum redditum videlicet 9s. 9d.

(f) In 1404–5 they built a plastered wall outside the south gate between the highway and Thomas Yonge's house, impeding access to St. Kyneburgh's chapel.[2]

Item de eo quod anno 6 Henrici Quarti ballivi et senescalli Gloucestrie erexerunt quendam murum plastratum extra Southgate inter viam communem et domum Thome Yonge, occasione cuius muri liber exitus et introitus ad capellam Sancte Kyneburge impeditur ad grave dampnum prioris predicti.

(g) They occupy lands and tenements in and near Bareland from which former priors received 78s. 6d. yearly rent.[3]

Item de eo quod dicti ballivi et senescalli tenent et occcupant diversas terras et tenementa in 'le Barelond' et iuxta, de quibus predecessores predicti nunc prioris solebant recipere de annuo redditu 78s. 6d.

(h) They demised to John Derehurst vacant land in the prior's fee next to the rectory of St. Mary in the South, and are keeping the rent from it.[4]

---

[1] A strip of land at the south corner of Parliament Street and Brunswick Road, used for archery butts and a dunghill from the reign of Richard II: P.R.O. C 115/73, ff. 16–17 (14–15). It was plotted as the Butts in 1611 and was called Long Butts in 1629 when the borough let it, as a former gravel pit, to a tenant who was to lay a bowling green there: J. Speed, *Theatre of the Empire of Great Britain* (London, 1611), map of Glos; Glos. R.O. GBR/J3/1, f. 239; GBR/J4/1, plan 18.

[2] Thomas Yonge's house adjoined the town ditch immediately south west of the south gate: P.R.O. C 115/73, f. 14 (12) no. 28. A wall built there blocked the access objected to in **33**(e) above.

[3] After Prince Edward 'destrued then toun' in 1264 (above, **9** n.) an inquisition of 1267 found that the prior of Llanthony had lost annual rents of 31s. 10d. owing to the pulling down of houses in front of the castle and of 42s. 4d. owing to the making of a ditch about the town: *Cal. Inq. Misc.* i, no. 338. A priory terrier of 1442 argued that the 31s. 10d. referred to houses on the south side of the castle in Shipster's Lane and the 42s. 4d. to those on the north side in the Bareland: P.R.O. C 115/73, ff. 45–6 (43–4). The author of **38**(d) and (g) interprets the figures the other way round and double-counts the annual value of houses in the Bareland by adding 31s. 10d. to 46s. 8d., the latter being a total calculated from priory deeds and rentals for houses lost to the Bareland in Longsmith Street, Castle (Upper Quay) Street and Walkers' Lane (Lower Quay Street) and on the Severn bank. The Bareland was never recovered by its original owners but was appropriated by the borough, which in 1442 collected rents throughout an area extending northwards from the present Bearland, Quay Street and Quay to the rear boundaries of tenements in Westgate and Berkeley Streets: P.R.O. C 115/73, ff. 45–7 (43–5).

[4] At nos. 37–43 Southgate Street, south of St. Mary de Crypt. The prior sold this property rent free in 1360 to Sir Thomas Berkeley for the use of the Grey Friars, who conveyed it to the borough in 1402; the borough still owned it in 1826: P.R.O. C 115/84, f. 27 no. 85; *Cal. Pat.* 1358–61, 257; Glos. R.O. GBR/J1/1050; J4/12, plans 32–5. John Derehurst the elder, who built five tenements there as the borough's first lessee, was a J.P. from 1389, escheator in 1410 and justice of gaol delivery in 1407: *Glouc. Rental 1455*, 12b; N. Saul, *Knights and Esquires* (Oxford, 1981), 163.

Item de eo quod ballivi et senescalli Gloucestrie nuper dimiserunt Iohanni Derehurst vacuam terram de feodo prioris Lanthonie iuxta rectoriam Sancte Marie in Austro Gloucestrie, de qua predecessores prioris nunc solebant recipere certum redditum, qui quidem redditus detinetur per ballivos et senescallos ad dampnum dicti prioris.

(i) The prior seeks repayment for the past, and discharge for the future, of 7s. 9½d. and half a farthing of landgavel which he has paid under duress for property which he does not hold.[1]

Item predictus prior petit allocacionem de 7s. 9d. ob. di. q. de redditu per ipsum soluto per cohercionem ad longabulum pro diversis terris et tenementis que non sunt in manibus suis nec in possessione. Unde petit resolucionem et satisfaccionem de denariis iniuste per prius receptis et imposterum petit exonerari a solucione eiusdem summe.

(j) They occupy a shop in the prior's fee within the south gate and pay no rent for it.[2]

Item de eo quod ballivi et senescalli occupant unam seldam de feodo prioris Lanthonie infra portam australem Gloucestrie et nichil inde reddunt dicto priori ad grave dampnum ipsius etc.

(k) They occupy tenements in the prior's fee between the property of St. Mary in the South and the gate of Blackfriars and pay no rent for them.[3]

Item de eo quod predicti ballivi et senescalli occupant et tenent diversa tenementa iacentia et situata inter terram rectoris Beate Marie in Austro ex una parte et portam Fratrum Predicatorum ex altera, que quidem tenementa sunt de feodo prioris Lanthonie, et nichil reddunt eidem ad grave dampnum ipsius.

(l) They occupy land by St. Owen's churchyard which was given to Llanthony Priory at its foundation and pay no rent for it.[4]

Item de eo quod ballivi et senescalli Gloucestrie tenent et occupant diversas parcellas terre iuxta cimiterium Sancti Audoeni sine titulo, nichil inde reddendo.

---

[1] In landgavel, a chief annual rent on burgages held from the king, the prior was paying altogether 19s. 0¾d. and half a farthing. In 1455 the priory renter, Canon Robert Cole, submitted an itemised claim for a rebate on alienated properties of 8s. 2d.: *Glouc. Rental 1455*, 114. The present claim reflects two or three corrected assessments.

[2] At no. 76 Southgate Street, north of Kimbrose Lane. The prior had granted in fee the whole property at this address in the reign of Henry III but only the rear tenement reverted into his hands, the front passing into the hands of the borough which employed a carpenter to rebuild it as two shops later united into one measuring 13 ft. 8 in. wide by 14 ft. 7 in. deep. The borough, perhaps as trustee, held title deeds dated 1369–71 in the names of two burgesses: P.R.O. C 115/73, f. 21 (19)v. no. 39; C 115/84, f. 21v. no. 67; Glos. R.O. GBR/J1/993, 1934e; *Glouc. Rental 1455*, 16.

[3] At nos. 52–4 Southgate Street, south of Blackfriars entry, where the borough had paid rent as the prior's tenant in fee from the reign of Richard I at least until 1442: P.R.O. C 115/73, f. 24 (22) no. 45; *Glouc. Rental 1445*, 12. The borough, perhaps as trustee, held title deeds dated 1248–9 and 1348 in the names of two burgess families, and still owned the property in 1826: Glos. R.O. GBR/J1/374, 941; J4/12 plan 29.

[4] Apparently a repeat of the claim **38**(d) above.

Que quidem parcelle date fuerunt priori Lanthonie et successoribus suis in eorum fundacione.

(m) [f. 16v.] They occupy stalls by All Saints' church and by the gable of St. Michael's from which the prior used to receive rents of 13s. 6d.[1]

Item de eo quod predicti ballivi et senescalli tenent et occupant diversas seldas iuxta ecclesiam Omnium Sanctorum Gloucestrie et iuxta gabelam ecclesie Sancti Michelis de quibus predictus prior et conventus habuerant annuatim 13s. 6d., qui quidem denarii detinentur per dictos ballivos ad grave dampnum ipsius prioris.

(n) They occupy the prior's vacant land outside the Alvin Gate.[2]

Item de eo quod predicti ballivi et senescalli occupant certas parcellas terre vacantis prioris predicti extra 'Alvynyate' ad dampnum dicti prioris etc.

(o) Prior Chirton was awarded £50 against the bailiffs by the king's justices in 1391,[3] a sum for which the bailiffs have yet to answer.

Item de eo quod Willelmus Chiriton nuper prior Lanthonie predecessor prioris nunc coram Roberto de Chorleton et Iohanne Cassy iusticiariis domini regis recuperavit quinquaginta libras versus ballivos et communitatem Gloucestrie anno regni Regis Ricardi Secundi 13 etc., unde predictus prior petit quod ballivi et communitas Gloucestrie respondeant eidem de dicta summa.

39. Presentation of Thomas Wolley, chaplain, to the rectory of Doynton.[4] 29 June 1457.

Reverendo in Christo patri ac divino domino Iohanni [Carpenter] dei gratia Wigorniensi episcopo, eiusve vicario in spiritualibus generali, vestri si placet humiles et devoti [Iohannes Garland] prior monasterii sive prioratus Lanthonie iuxta Gloucestriam ordinis Sancti Augustini Wigorniensis diocesis et eiusdem loci conventus obedienciam et reverenciam tanto patri debitas cum honore. Ad rectoriam ecclesie pariochialis de Doyngton vestre dicte diocesis vacantem et ad nostram presentacionem spectantem dilectum nobis in Christo dominum Thomam Wolley capellanum vestre paternitati, reverende, presentamus, humiliter supplicantes et

---

[1] A speculative claim based on two enigmatic early deeds whereby the priors granted a stall under All Saints' church for 3s. 6d. rent and were granted a rentcharge of 9s., misread as 10s., on stalls by the small door of St. Michael's. Although they could not find receipts for these amounts in their rentals nor reconcile these deeds with other early records of priory property there (see **33**(f), **169**) the canons argued that they referred to adjacent stalls belonging to the borough: P.R.O. C 115/73, ff. 62–3 (60–1); C 115/84, f. 174v. nos. 434–5; *Glouc. Rental 1455*, 2–4.

[2] On the west side of Skinner Street, used for a dunghill from the reign of Edward II: P.R.O. C 115/73, f. 78 (76) no.150.

[3] By writ of 11 May 1391, in damages for dispossessing the prior of a recluse's house east of St. Kyneburgh's chapel. The prior was unable to claim the damages at the time owing to a temporary escheat and apparently waived them at a loveday on 10 Jan. 1392: Reg. Chirton, ff. 144–6, 151v., 159, cf. 163; P.R.O. C 115/73, ff. 19–20 (17–18) no. 35.

[4] Given to the priory before 1191: P.R.O. C 115/75, f. 217v. no.37; C115/77, s. xiii nos. 20, 23. It retained the advowson in 1531 when Prior Hart granted the next presentation to Thomas Bell and others: Hockaday Abs. clxxxii; Glos. R.O. GDR/D1/100.

devote quatinus dictum dominum Thomam ad dictam rectoriam admittere et ipsum in eadem canonice instituere velitis intuitu caritatis, porcionibus, pensionibus, percepcionibus ac iuribus nostris quibuscumque nobis et prioratui nostro antedicto in dicta ecclesia debitis et consuetis in omnibus semper salvis. Data in domo nostro capitulari Lanthonie predicte sub sigillo nostro conventuali vicesimo nono[1] die mensis Iunii anno Domini 1457.

40. [f. 17] Bond of John Kilray,[2] fishmonger of Gloucester, and John Aspyon, baker of Gloucester, in £100 that William Eldesfeld and Richard Skidmore, bailiffs of Gloucester, will observe the arbitrators' decision in the bailiffs' dispute with Prior [Garland] by the octave [30 May] of Trinity next. The arbitrators are William Notingham,[3] Thomas Bisley[4] and John Andreaux[5] for the bailiffs and Thomas Mille,[6] John Edward[7] and John Hayward[8] for the prior, and if they cannot decide by that date Thomas [Sebroke] abbot of Gloucester is to decide by the feast of the Assumption [15 Aug.]. 10 Apr. 34 Hen. VI [1456].

41. [f. 17v.] Record of an assize[9] to try whether John Hamelyn and John Luke, bailiffs, and the community of Gloucester have unjustly disseised Stephen [Myle], prior of St. Bartholemew's Hospital, Gloucester, of a messuage, two shops and a garden 15 yd. long and 17 yd. wide. The bailiffs, through their attorney Thomas Henster, say that they hold the property as parcel of the borough fee farm by royal letters patent and that the justices should first consult the king. The suit is adjourned to the Gloucester assizes of Thursday after St. James [30 July 1434].

---

[1] MS. *tricesimo nono.*

[2] Bailiff in 1456–7: *V.C.H. Glos.* iv. 374.

[3] d. 1483: below, **94**.

[4] d. by 1463: above, **3**(f) n.

[5] d. 1460; Esquire and lawyer, M.P. for Gloucester 1437, 1449–51 and 1455 and bailiff of the borough 1450, owning land in Gloucester and Southam: *Trans. B.G.A.S.* lxxiv. 70; *Hist. of Parl., Biographies 1439–1509.* Resident outside the north gate at no. 3 London Road: *Glouc. Rental 1455*, 102.

[6] d. 1460; escheator of Glos. 1430–1, M.P. for the county 1435, 1439–40 and 1449, sheriff of Herefs. 1435–6 and 1455–6, J.P. for Glos. 1437–60 and a member of all Glos. commissions 1440–59: *Hist. of Parl., Biographies 1439–1509.* Lord of Harescombe and Duntisbourne Rous, of Chalford in Bisley and of Avenbury, Allensmore and Tregate (in Llanrothal) in Herefs., attainted posthumously as a Lancastrian: *Calendarium Inquisitionum post mortem* (Rec. Com.), iv. 319; *V.C.H. Glos.* xi. 18; below, **239** n.

[7] d. 1461; gentleman and lawyer, M.P. for Gloucester 1429, J.P. for Glos. 1435–60, lord of Rodmarton and owner of land in Gloucester and Staverton: *Trans. B.G.A.S.* lxxiv. 83; *Cal. Pat.* 1429–36 and later vols., Commissions of the Peace; *V.C.H. Glos.* iv. 37; viii. 92; xi. 236. Resident in Lower Westgate Street: *Glouc. Rental 1455*, 52.

[8] The future prior's father: above, p. xv.

[9] On 5 Feb. 1434 the king appointed William Westbury and Thomas Rolf to hear this assize: *Glouc. Corp. Rec.* p. 57 no.52.

42. The king's mandate to the justices of assize in Glos. [f. 18] to proceed with the above assize and to consult him before giving judgement. Westminster, 11 July 12 Hen. VI [1434].

43. The king's general pardon to John, prior, and the convent of Llanthony for offences committed before 7 December last [f. 18v.] and for dues incurred before 1 September 33 Hen. VI [1454]. [f. 19] Westminster, 1 Oct. 37 Hen. VI [1458].

44. Quittance to the abbot of Kingswood for 20s. of 40s. annual pension owed at Culkerton and Hazleton [in Rodmarton].[1] 12 Apr. 1458.

Pateat universis per presentes quod nos Iohannes prior Lanthonie iuxta Gloucestriam recepimus de abbate de Kyngeswode viginta solidos argenti in quibus idem abbas nobis tenebatur de termino Annunciacionis Beate Marie proxime preterito in partem solucionis quadraginta solidorum annue pensionis de predicto abbate apud Colkerton et Haselden nobis debite, de quibus quidem viginti solidis predictum abbatem et successores suos acquietamus per presentes sigillo nostro signatas. Data Lanthonie predicte 12 die mensis Aprilis anno regni Regis Henrici Sexti post conquestum Anglie tricesimo sexto.

45. Resignation of Richard Mey as vicar of Hempsted (*Heyhampstede*), delivered in St. Owen's church, Gloucester [f. 19v.] in the presence of Canon Thomas Colsey, William Nayler literate (*litterato*) of Worcester diocese and a notary public.[2] 10 Dec. 1457.

46. Resignation of Edmund Benne[3] as vicar of Kington [Herefs.], delivered in the canonical residence of Mr. Richard Pede D.Cn.L., canon of Hereford,[4] in the presence of Pede himself, John Jones notary and John Dyny chaplain and recorded by William Pede, clerk of Hereford diocese and imperial notary public. 31 July 1459.

In Dei nomine Amen. Per presens publicum instrumentum cunctis appareat evidenter quod anno ab incarnacione Domini secundum cursum et computacionem ecclesie Anglicane 1459, indiccione septima, pontificatus sanctissimi in Christo patris et domini nostri Domini Pii divina providencia pape Secundi anno primo, mense Iulii, die vero ultima, infra mansum canonicalem Magistri Ricardi Peede decretorum doctoris ac canonici[5] ecclesie cathedralis Herefordie, in mei notarii

---

[1] In composition for tithes: *V.C.H. Glos.* xi. 244; *Trans. B.G.A.S.* lxxiii. 147, 179.

[2] Space is left on f. 19v. for the notary's attestation, which is missing.

[3] Vicar of Foy (Herefs.) until 1456, of Kington 1456–9 and of Stockton-on-Teme (Worcs.) 1462–7: *Reg. Stanbury*, 174, 178, 184, 190.

[4] d. 1480; Prebendary of Ledbury 1450–62, residentiary canon of Hereford 1452–60, prebendary there 1452–80, rector of Stoke-on-Trent (Staffs.) 1454–80, vicar general of Hereford diocese 1457–72, prebendary of Lichfield 1457–80, chancellor there 1458–70 and dean of Hereford 1463–80: Emden, *Biog. Reg. Oxon. to 1500.*

[5] MS. *canonice.*

publici[1] *et testium subscriptorum presencia, personaliter constitutus discretus vir Dominus Edmundus Benne, vicarius perpetuus ecclesie parochialis de Kyngton Herefordiensis diocesis, ut asseruit, quandam resignacionem seu renunciacionem ipsius vicarie in scripta redactam publice legit, non vi coactus neque metu ductus sed pura sponte et absolute ex certa sua scientia resignavit sub hac forma verborum.*

In Dei nomine Amen. Coram vobis auctentica persona et testibus hic presentibus fidedignis ego Dominus Edmundus Benne, vicarius perpetuus ecclesie parochialis de Kyngton Herefordiensis diocesis, volens et affectans ex certis causis veris et legitimis me ad hoc moventibus a cura et regimine ipsius vicarie [f. 20] *exonerari, predictam vicariam cum suis iuribus et pertinenciis universis in sacras et venerabiles manus reverendi in Christo patris et domini Domini Iohannis [Stanbury] Dei gracia Herefordiensis episcopi, seu alterius cuiuscumque huiusmodi resignacionem seu renunciacionem admittendi potestatem habentis, pura sponte, libere et absolute in his scriptis resigno.*

Acta sunt hec prout suprascribuntur et recitantur sub anno Domini, indiccione, pontificatu, mense, die et loco predictis, presentibus tunc ibidem discretis viris Magistro Ricardo Pede decretorum doctore, Iohanne Jones auctoritate apostolica notario et Domino Iohanne Dyny capellano dicti diocesis ad premissa vocatis specialiter et rogatis.

Et ego Willelmus Pede, clericus Herefordiensis diocesis, publicus auctoritate imperiali notarius, premissis omnibus et singulis dum sic ut premittitur agerentur et fierent sub anno Domini, indiccione, pontificatu, mense, loco et die predictis una cum prenominatis testibus presens personaliter interfui, eaque omnia et singula sic fieri vidi et audivi, scripsi, publicavi et in hanc publicam formam redegi, signoque et nomine meis solitis et consuetis signavi rogatus et requisitus in fidem et testimonium omnium premissorum.

47. Letter from Richard Pede, as official of the consistory of Hereford,[2] reporting the above resignation. Hereford, 31 July 1459.

48. Presentation of John ap Howell[3] to the vicarage of Kington [Herefs.] vacant by the resignation of Edmund Benne. 6 Aug. 37 Hen. VI [1459].

49. [f. 20v.] Bond of John ap Howell, clerk of Kington, in £20. [Condition not stated.] 7 Aug. 37 Hen. VI [1459].

50. Lease to Robert White *alias* Crowcher of Conock [in Chirton], Wilts., of the manor and tithes of Chirton (*Churton*)[4] except rents, fines, tallage, wards, marriages,

---

[1] MS. *publice.*
[2] Holder of this office 1456–60: *Reg. Stanbury*, 35, 57.
[3] Alias ap Holl ap Redenegh, alias Fermour, instituted 30 Aug.; vicar of Foy (Herefs.) 1456–9, of Kington 1459–65, of Llanafanfawr (Brecknock) 1465 and of English Bicknor 1465–72: *Reg. Stanbury*, 174, 178, 180, 182, 187, 190; below, **85**.
[4] Farmed from no. 61 High Street, Chirton: *V.C.H. Wilts.* x. 62, 69.

reliefs, escheats, heriots and the tithes of Conock, for 12 years at £10 6s. 8d. The lessee will:

(a) render 1 lb. of pepper yearly to the abbess of St. Mary in Winchester;

(b) feed the cellarer and the steward, their servants, the prior's servants and their horses whenever they come to superintend the manor or to hold courts or leets;

(c) maintain a dovecot and houses, walls and enclosures including earthen walls (*muris terreis*) and roofs;

(d) leave the lands at the end of the term seasoned, manured, fallowed, thrice ploughed and sown (*seisionatas, compostatas, warectatas et rebinatas ac de eisdem generibus bladorum seminatas*), the hay garnered and the stock as currently valued;

(e) carry materials and feed craftsmen and workmen if the prior erects or repairs buildings in the manor. [f. 21] St. James 37 Hen. VI [25 July 1459].

51. Stock delivered by John Barton to the above lessee, to be restored (or its value repaid, at the prior's choice) at the end of the lease. St. James 37 Hen. VI [25 July 1459].

In the granary: 1 qr. 4 bu. wheat (of which 8 bu. are heaped), 2 qr. barley malt (alternate bushels heaped).

In the fields: 9 a. 3 r. sown with wheat, 42 a. sown with barley (of which 24 a. are in *Lez Sondez*), 7½ a. of peas, 13 a. sown with vetch. Also 11 a. of well seasoned fallow (*terre bene seisionate et warecte*) of which 1 a. is thrice ploughed (*rebinata*), 5 a. are manured by folding and 3 a. by cart.

Live and dead stock: 9 geese (including a gander and 4 young birds), 12 capons, a cock, 5 hens, 5 pullets; a plough with a ploughshare, a cable (*cabillam*), an iron chain for a plough, 2 timber-chains (*cathenas ligneas*) with iron rings and clasps (*claspis*), 2 ox yokes with bows (*arcubus*), 2 horse harrows (*hercias equinas*) with sufficient iron rings, 2 pairs of hemp *akerstringes* to pull the harrows, with hames (*hamis*), a cart saddle with thill-hames (*cellam carectalem cum thilhamis*), a cart rope (*cordam carectalem*), 3 leather collars (*coleria*), 3 pairs of traces (*tractatorum*) suitable for a cart, a serviceable *dungpot*, an iron-bound shovel (*tribulam*), 2 iron dung forks, a sheaf fork (*furcam garbalem*), 2 trestle tables with two pairs of trestles, 2 benches (*formulas*), an iron-bound *bushell*, a corn-basket (*sportam pro blado portando*), a canvas winnowing-fan (*ventilabrum*), 2 canvas sacks (*saccas*), 2 sieves (*cribra*), a riddle (*ridellum*), a seed-lip (*semilionem*), an iron-bound *boket* with a cord and an iron windlass (*cum cordula et manutencione ferrea*) for drawing water, an iron *tripod* worth 6d., a *payll*, a *cowll*, 6 dishes (*discos*), 3 plates (*platellas*), 6 wooden *saucers*, a standing salt (*stond pro sale imponendo*), 30 sheep-hurdles (*clatas pro faldis*) and 6 locks fitted to doors, of which one is on the dovecote.

All the hay produced from the demesne meadows.

52. Bond of Robert White alias Crowcher, *husbandman* of Conock, in £30. [Condition not stated.] [f. 21v.] 30 July 37 Hen. VI [1459].

53. Letter from Henry [Cranebroke],[1] prior of Combwell [Kent]. As Hayward has licensed his canon Robert Bisege alias Bristowe[2] to change his profession and profess to [Cranebroke], [Cranebroke] has admitted him canon of Combwell. Combwell, 2 Aug. 1459.

54. Letter to Canon Robert Bisege alias Bristowe. Since, for reasonable and lawful causes, Bristowe cannot remain at Llanthony without great harm and bodily danger, Hayward licenses Bristowe to profess to the prior of Combwell and discharges him from his profession to himself. 22 July 1459.

Iohannes, prior prioratus sive ecclesie conventualis de Lanthonia ordinis Sancti Augustini Wigorniensis diocesis, dilecto nobis in Christo Fratri Roberto Bisege alias Bristowe, canonico et confratri nostro in dicto nostro prioratu ordinem Sancti Augustini expresse professo, salutem in omnium salvatore. Cum ex certis causis racionabilibus et legitimis per nos approbatis absque magno detrimento corporisque periculo non possis in dicto nostro prioratu pacifice remanere, ac dilectus nobis in Christo prior prioratus de Combewell dicti ordinis Sancti Augustini te in confratrem suum et prioratus predicti admittere ac tuam obedienciam recipere voluerit, ut credibiliter informamur, eapropter tibi tenore presencium concedimus facultatem ut liceat tibi mutare professionem tuam priori prioratus de Combewell predicto et eidem facere obedienciam iuxta regulares observancias ordinis predicti, ac te ex nunc prout extunc a[3] professione et obedientia nostris dimittimus et absolvimus per presentes, ita quod nos de admissione et recepcione tuis in prioratu de Combewell predicto ac de obediencia priori eiusdem per te facta[4] cum omni celeritate certificari procures. In cuius rei testimonium sigillum nostrum presentibus duximus apponendum. Data in prioratu nostro predicto 22 die mensis Iulii anno Domini 1459.

55. Quittance to the abbot of Kingswood for 20s. [as **44** above]. [f. 22] 4 Nov. 38 Hen. VI [1459].

56. Mandate from Henry [Holland] duke of Exeter and admiral of England, Ireland and Aquitaine to all bailiffs, sheriffs etc. and to Richard Ryse and his marshal Richard a Pole to attach the abbot of Gloucester and the prior of Llanthony. On the fifteenth day after attachment they are to appear before the duke or his commissioner on the English coast to answer certain articles and interrogatories concerning maritime law.[5] 1 Sept. 38 Hen. VI [1459].

---

[1] *V.C.H. Kent*, ii. 161.
[2] Hosteler of Llanthony in 1442: P.R.O. C 115/73, f. 8 (6) no.9.
[3] MS. *ac.*
[4] The MS. repeats *nos* here.
[5] As appears in **68–9** below, the admiral was here applying in tidal waters the statutes against constructing fish weirs on navigable rivers: 9 Hen. III c. 23; 25 Edw. III stat. 4 c. 4; 45 Edw. III c. 2; 21 Ric. II c. 19; 1 Hen. IV c. 12; 1 Hen. V c. 2.

57. Henry duke of Exeter's pardon to John prior of Llanthony for offences rashly committed (*transgressiones temerarie factas*) within the admiralty's jurisdiction. 6 Feb. 38 Hen. VI [1460].

58. [f. 22v.] Mandate from John [Carpenter] bishop of Worcester to the archdeacon of Gloucester, reciting the following.

(a) Henry VI's mandate to Thomas [Bourgchier] archbishop of Canterbury to call a convocation of his province with all speed. Westminster, 12 Feb. 38 Hen. VI [1460].

(b) Mandate from Thomas archbishop of Canterbury to Thomas [Kempe] bishop of London to cite fellow-bishops and suffragans or their vicars general, the dean or the prior and one of the chapter of each cathedral church, archdeacons, abbots or priors of convents and two clerks from each diocese to appear in St. Paul's Cathedral, London, on Tuesday [6 May] after the Invention of Holy Cross.[1] [f. 23] He was to certify the names of those cited. Mortlake Manor [Surrey], 28 Feb. 1459[/60].

(c) Mandate from Thomas bishop of London to John bishop of Worcester to cite the clergy of his diocese accordingly. Given at his palace in London on 13 Mar. 1459[/60] and received at Westbury College [in Westbury-on-Trym] on 7 Apr.

The archdeacon is to cite the clergy of his archdeaconry accordingly and certify the names of those cited by St. Philip and St. James [1 May]. [f. 23v.] 8 Apr. 1460.

59. Proxy to Mr. John Stokes, D.C.L.,[2] and Mr. William Vauce, B.Cn. & C.L., to attend the above convocation. 30 Apr. 1460.

Pateat universis per presentes quod nos Iohannes, prior monasterii sive prioratus Beate Marie de Lanthonia iuxta Gloucestriam ordinis Sancti Augustini Wygorniensis diocesis, dilectos nobis in Christo Magistrum Iohannem Stokes Legum Doctorem et Magistrum Willelmum Vauce Utriusque Iuris Bacallarium coniunctim et divisim et utrumque eorum per se et in solidum, ita quod non sit melior condicio occupantis set quod unus eorum inceperit alter eorum per se prosequi valeat, mediare pariter et finire, nostros veros et legitimos procuratores negociorumque gestores ac nuncios speciales ordinamus, facimus et constituimus per presentes, dantes et concedentes eisdem procuratoribus nostris ac eorum utrique potestatem et mandatum speciale pro nobis et nomine nostro coram reverendissimo in Christo patre ac domino Domino Thoma [Bourgchier] Dei [gracia] Cantuariensi archiepiscopo, tocius Anglie primate et apostolice sedis legato, vel suis in hac parte commissario, in ecclesia cathedrali Sancti Pauli London' sexto die mensis Maii proxime futuri una cum aliis prelatis et clero tocius provincie Cantuariensis comparendi, necnon cum ipso reverendissimo prelato una cum aliis prelatis et clero predicto, cum continuacione et prorogacione dierum extunc sequencium (si

---

[1] Dissolved on 15 July 1461: below, **67**.

[2] d. 1466; vicar general of Worcester diocese from 1435, rector of St. Peter's, Worcester, 1441–66, prebendary of Chichester from 1444, archdeacon of Ely 1445–66, prebendary of Hereford 1449–66 and precentor of Salisbury 1457–66: Emden, *Biog. Reg. Oxon. to 1500*.

oporteat) et locorum, de et super nonnullis arduis et urgentibus negociis ecclesiam Anglicanam et clerum eiusdem, necnon illustrissimum regem nostrum et regnum suum Anglie eorumque defencionem et salvacionem concernentibus ibidem ceriosius exponendi, tractandi suaque consilia et auxilia super eis impendendi ac hiis que ibidem ex deliberacione communi ad honorem [Dei] et ecclesie sue utilitatem regnique predicti et tocius rei publice concorditer ordinari contigerint consenciendi, iniurias et gravamina nobis et ecclesie Anglicane illata allegandi, proponendi et probandi ac super eis iusticie complementum fieri petendi et obtinendi, nosque a personali comparacione excusandi, causam et causas absencie nostre allegandi et eam seu eas (si necesse fuerit) in forma iuris proponendi et probandi, faciendique ulterius et recipiendi quod huiusmodi negocii qualitas et natura in se exigunt et requirunt, necnon insuper quodcumque iuramentum licitum et commodocum in animam nostram prestandi et iurandi, necnon[1] in integram[2] restitucionem tam principaliter quam incidenter a quibusdam suspensionis, excommunicacionis, sequestracionis et interdiccionis sentenciis a iure vel ab homine in personam nostram latis (quod absit) seu ferendis relaxacionis et absolucionis beneficium a dicto reverendissomo prelate aut ipsius commissario petendi, recipiendi et obtinendi, ac de stando et parendo iuribus, mandatis ecclesie et iudiciis cuiuslibet competentis, eciam arbitrio boni viri, iuramentum corporale ac sacra Dei evangelia prestandi, moniciones, iniuncciones et mandata licita, salubria et honesta humiliter subeundi et dimittendi et aliis hiis contrariis contradicendi, alium seu alios procuratorem seu procuratores loco suo substituendi, substitutum seu substitutos ab eisdem vel eorum altero revocandi procuratorisque officium in se vel eorum alterum reassumendi quociens et quando eis vel eorum alteri melius videbitur expedire, ac generaliter omnia alia et singula faciendi, exercendi ac expediendi que per veros et legittimos procuratores [f. 24] fieri poterunt seu expediri, eciam si mandatum magis exigant speciale.

Pro dictis vero procuratoribus nostris vel eorum altero, substituto vel substitutis, substituendo vel substituendis ab eisdem vel eorum altero rem ratam haberi, iudicio sisti ac iudicatum solvi sub ypotheca et obligacione rerum nostrarum promittimus et exponimus cauciones per presentes. In cuius rei testimonium sigillum nostrum ad causas presentibus apposuimus. Date in monasterio[3] nostro predicto ultimo die mensis Aprilis anno Domini 1460.

60–1. Two quittances to the abbot of Kingswood for 20s. each [as **44** above]. 9 June 38 Hen. VI [1460] and 11 Nov. 39 Hen. VI [1460].

62. The king's order to the sheriff of Gloucester to proclaim an accord of parliament,[4] which is recited in English, whereby Richard Plantagenet duke of York

---

[1] In the MS. *necnon* is misplaced eight words later after *incidenter.*
[2] MS. *integrum.*
[3] MS. *manerio.*
[4] Dated 16 Oct.; printed in *Rotuli Parliamentorum* (Rec. Com.), v. 378.

[ff. 24v., 25] is next heir to the kingdoms of England and France and the lordship of Ireland. [f. 25v.] Westminster, 8 Nov. 39 Hen. VI [1460]; [signed] Fryston.

63. Acknowledgement by the abbot of Kingswood to Martin Chyverton undersheriff of Glos. of the receipt of a commission from John [Carpenter] bishop of Worcester, given under the bishop's seal outside the *barre* of the New Temple[1] in London on 11 Dec. 1461, to collect in the archdeaconry of Gloucester a tenth which was granted to the king at the last convocation.[2] The undersheriff showed the abbot a tally, dated 13 Aug. 1 Edw. IV [1461], given to the archdeacon for receipt at the Exchequer at Westminster of £47 4s. 9d., being a moiety of the tenth which was advanced to the king by the bishop and is now to be received by the bishop. Kingswood, Tuesday after St. Thomas, 1 Edw. IV [22 Dec. 1461].

[ff. 26–52 have been cut out, the cut starting diagonally so as to leave the lower corners of 19 leaves still sewn to the binding and ff. 24–5 and 53–5 as fragments of mutilated quires.]

64. [f. 53] Lease to Walter Lane of Gloucester of the tithes of corn and hay of Longford (*Langford*)[3] previously held by Andrew Wye, for 24 years at 53s. 4d. a year. The Annunciation 4 Edw. IV [25 Mar. 1464].

65. Proxy to fellow canons Thomas Colsey and John Playsted to act for the prior in Ireland. 18 July 1464.

Pateat universis per presentes quod nos Frater Iohannes, prior prioratus Lanthonie iuxta Gloucestriam ordinis Sancti Augustini Wigorniensis diocesis, et eiusdem loci conventus, in omnibus causis, litibus et querelis ac negociis quibuscumque in terra Hibernie nos seu prioratum nostrum Lanthonie predicte necnon ecclesiam nostram de Dyvelek[4] cum suis iuribus et pertinenciis universis ac omnes ecclesias nostras, domos et possessiones in dicta terra Hibernie qualitercumque directe vel indirecte contingentibus tam ex officio quam eciam ad instanciam partis cuiuscumque contra nos seu pro nobis contra quoscumque adversarios nostros coram quibuscumque iudicibus, ordinariis, delegatis, subdelegatis vel eorum commissariis, arbitris, arbitratoribus, amicabilibus, compositoribus ac privilegiorum quorumcumque

---

[1] At the bishop of Worcester's inn in the Strand, which was demolished in 1549 to make way for Somerset House. It lay west of Temple Bar and the New Temple, so called because the Templars moved there from Holborn in 1184: John Stow, *Survey of London* (Everyman edn., 1956), 354, 390, 395.

[2] Granted on 15 July 1461: cf. below, **67**.

[3] The tithes of Walter of Gloucester's demesne in Longford, sometimes called a portion of the parish of St. Mary de Lode, were given to St. Owen's church in 1086 × 95 and to Llanthony Priory in 1137: *Camd. Misc.* xxii. 38; Dugdale, *Mon.* vi. 136; cf. *Tax. Eccl.* (Rec. Com.), 224. The tithed land lay dispersed in Longford and Kingsholm: P.R.O. C 115/77, f. 313v.

[4] At the priory's cell of St. Michael, Duleek (Meath): *Irish Cart. Llanth.* pp. 289–91.

conservatoribus quamcumque iurisdiccionem, ne[gocia]cionem seu ministerium habentibus aut eciam habituris motis vel movendis, dilectos nobis in Christo Fratres Thomam Colsey et Iohannem Playsted, salve concanonicos et confratres nostros domus nostre Lanthonie predicte, coniunctim et divisim nostros facimus, ordinamus et constituimus procuratores, yconomos, actores, defensores et negociorum gestores ac nuncios speciales, et utrumque eorum in solidum, ita quod non sit melior condicio occupantis, sed quod unus eorum inceperit alter eorum prosequi valeat, mediare et finire; dantes et concedentes eisdem procuratoribus nostris et eorum alteri nomine nostro et prioratus nostri predicti, racione ecclesiarum ac rerum monasterii huius sic in Hibernia, ut premittitur, existencium, potestatem plenam et specialem et mandatum generale ad agendum et defendendum, litem contestandum, pensiones quascumque, porciones ac iura et debita quecumque nobis qualitercumque competencia ibidem petendum, prosequendum, recipiendum, provocandum et appellandum; provocacionum et appropriacionum causas prosequendum ac officiandum; ecclesias nostras possessionemque corporalem earum vice et nomine nostris optinendum, conservandum [et] continuandum; et curam ipsarum ecclesiarum et personarum et pariochianorum ibidem existencium per se et suos deputatos seu deputandos ac eisdem ecclesiis ac parochianis earundem nomine nostro in omnibus et singulis que ad rectores earundem sive ad nos pertinere noscimus gerendum, faciendum, expediendum et exercendum; fructusque, redditus et proventus, iura et obvenciones ipsarum exigendum, recipiendum, colligendum, recuperandum et obtinendum et de eis libere disponendum pro nobis; in sinodis, consistoriis et in convocacionibus cleri quibuscumque ac in capitulis et visitacionibus quorumcumque ordinariorum comperendum, interessendum [et] tractandum; testes et instrumenta, acta, litteras et munimenta producendum et exhibendum; ac in eleccionibus episcoporum Midie cum eas fieri contigerit nomine nostro interessendum, eligendum, postulandum, consenciendum, contradicendum, excipiendum, repplicandum, reconveniendum, transigendum et in arbitros compromittendum; in manus nostras tam de calumpnia quam de veritate [f. 53v.] dicendum, iurandum et omne aliud genus liciti sacramenti prestandum [et] ponendum; posicionibus respondendum; expensas, dampna et interesse et iudicata statusque nostri reformacionem et ab omni sentencia excommunicacionis, suspensionis et interdiccionis quociens opus fuerit in forma iuris relaxionem et absolucionis beneficium simpliciter et ad cautelam petendum, optinendum et recipiendum, et integrum restitucionis beneficium tam principaliter quam incidentaliter implorandum; ac de stando mandatis ecclesie iuramentum prestandum; crimina et defectus obiciendum; et prebenda naniciscendum, ingrediendum, adquirendum, optinendum et custodiendum; quoscumque redditus, exitus et proventus, necnon emolumenta, debita et commoda quecumque spiritualia et temporalia in dicta terra Hibernie nobis et ecclesie nostre Lanthonie antedicte qualitercumque pertinencia [recipiendum]; ad vicarias ecclesiarum ad nostram presentacionem spectantes et ad rectoriam nostram de Kilwylagh,[1] cum eas vel earum aliquam vacare contigerit, personas ydoneas loci diocesano presentandum;

---

[1] Killulagh rectory, co. Westmeath, in dispute since *c.* 1240: ibid. p. 305.

necnon de hominibus nostris Hibernie in curia cuiuscumque domini ibidem curie nostre petendum et eandem de hominibus nostris tenendum; cum sibi vel eorum alteri videbitur expedire, procuratorem alium seu alios loco eorum seu alterius eorum substituendum et eundem seu eosdem revocandum, procuratorisque officium cum eisdem seu eorum alteri videbitur expedire in se et eorum alterum reassumendum; et omnia alia et singula pro nobis seu nomine nostro faciendum, procurandum et expediendum que ad officium spectant veri procuratoris et que facere possemus si ibi personaliter interessemus, eciam si mandatum exigant in se speciale.

Pro eisdem eciam procuratoribus nostris et eorum altero et ab eisdem substituto seu ab altero eorum substituto rem ratam haberi, iudicio sisti et iudicatum solvi sub ypotheca rerum nostrarum et dicti prioratus nostri omnium promittimus et exponimus cauciones per presentes, omnia alia procuratoria et omnes litteras tam generales quam speciales, quacumque concipiantur forma verborum, que et quas aliquibus personis in Hibernia ante presens procuratorium fecimus, omnino revocantes. In cuius rei testimonium sigillum nostrum commune fecimus hiis apponi. Data in domo nostra capitulari Lanthonie predicte decimo octavo die mensis Iulii anno Domini millesimo quadringensimo sexagesimo quarto.

66. The king's mandate to the sheriff of Gloucester to make a proclamation, which is recited in English,[1] that silver bullion will henceforth be received at the Tower of London mint at 33s. instead of 29s. a lb. [f. 54] and that from 15 days hence the gold noble will be worth 8s. 4d. instead of 6s. 8d. [f. 54v.] Reading, 29 Sept. 4 Edw. IV [1464]; by writ of the privy seal, [signed] Moreland.

67. The prior's account as collector, appointed by episcopal letters patent, in the archdeaconry of Hereford[2] of a tenth which was granted to the king at a convocation of Canterbury province in St. Paul's cathedral, London, on 15 July 1 Edw. IV [1461],[3] of which half was payable on the feast of the Annunciation following [25 Mar. 1462] and the other half on St. Martin in winter 2 Edw. IV [11 Nov. 1462]. The account is rendered in Easter term 3 Edw. IV [1463].

A tenth from the spiritualities and temporalities of the archdeaconry is given in the detailed Exchequer roll as £350 2s. 7d. This sum excludes small benefices worth less than 6 marks [a year]. It includes 13s. 4d. from the church of Sutton St. Michael[4]

---

[1] Printed, slightly abridged, in *Cal. Close* 1461–8, 216. An order to the mint on 13 Aug. 1464, implementing this proclamation, was superseded by another on 16 Apr. 1465 which instituted the ryal or rose noble worth 6s. 8d.: *Cal. Pat.* 1461–7, 370–1; R. Ruding, *Annals of the Coinage of Great Britain*, i (London, 1840), 282–3; *New History of the Royal Mint*, ed. C. E. Challis (Cambridge, 1992), 190–2. References supplied by Dr. B. J. Cook.

[2] Places named in this entry are in Herefs. unless described otherwise.

[3] Originally assembled on 6 May 1460: Wilkins, *Concilia*, iii. 577; *Reg. Bourgchier*, 77; cf. above, **58, 63**.

[4] Included for accounting purposes but exempted *per contra* under 'Hospitallers of Dinmore' below.

which is taxed at 10 marks and appropriated to the priory of St. John of Jerusalem, but in accordance with the King's Remembrancer's roll 47 of Michaelmas 1 Edw. IV [1461] it excludes £49 16s. from 72 unappropriated benefices with resident incumbents which are worth 12 marks a year or less [f. 55] and are so enrolled at the exchequer and certified by the bishop.[1]

	£	s.	d.
Five Exchequer tallies	189	0	0

Allowances:

	£	s.	d.
The collector's expenses, as in previous rolls	4	15	0
The bishop of Hereford's spiritualities and temporalities	47	18	9
Winchester College [Hants.]:[2] spiritualities and temporalities		40	5
Thomas Pryk of Mitcheldean, Glos., yeoman: Mitcheldean church[3]		13	4
[Much] Dewchurch vicarage		8	0
Westbury[-on-Severn] church, Glos.		106	8
King's Pyon vicarage[4]		8	10¾
Sheen Charterhouse [Surrey]:[5] spiritualities and temporalities	11	12	5¾

Allowances for benefices and possessions belonging to monks, nuns and other ecclesiastics who are poor or impoverished by flood, fire, ruin, war or other misfortunes, as exempted in the King's Remembrancer's records of Michaelmas 1 Edw. IV [1461]:

	£	s.	d.
Limebrook Nunnery: Stoke Bliss (*Stokblez*)			
church		13	4
temporalities		15	4
Aconbury Nunnery: churches of Wulferlow, Bridge Sollers and Mansell Lacy (*Wulfrelawe, Brugge-solers et Malmeshullacy*)		56	0
temporalities		7	2

[1] In response to an Exchequer writ of 28 July 1461 Bishop Stanbury of Hereford had certified the prior of Llanthony's appointment as collector, the names of 11 poor religious houses holding property in the archdeaconry (as here below) and the names of 80 unappropriated benefices in the archdeaconry which had resident incumbents and were worth 12 marks a year or less. He recited the writ, which gave more categories of exemptions: *Reg. Stanbury*, 61–7.

[2] Exempted specifically: ibid. 62.

[3] An error for Littledean chapel, which the inhabitants held from St. Bartholomew's Hospital, Gloucester: *V.C.H. Glos.* v. 169. It was exempted from the clerical tenth as being taxed in the lay subsidy: *Reg. Stanbury*, 63.

[4] Westbury church and the vicarages of Much Dewchurch and King's Pyon were included in Bishop Stanbury's list of 80 exempt benefices (see above) and were evidently additional to the Exchequer list of 72. The appropriated rectory of King's Pyon was taxed separately from the vicarage and is exempted under Wormsley Priory below.

[5] Exempted specifically: *Reg. Stanbury*, 62. For its spiritualities in Herefs., *Trans. Woolhope N.F.C.* 1900–2, 153.

	£	s	d
Ledbury Hospital: Weston [Beggard], Yarkhill and Kempley [Glos.] churches		34	8
temporalities		7	4
Clifford Priory: Clifford church		60	0
Dorstone (*Dorsynton*) church		40	0
portions in Dorstone and Staunton-on-Wye (*Standon*) churches		7	4
temporalities		41	3¾
Monmouth Priory [Mon]: churches of Monmouth, Tarrington, Dixton [Mon.], Goodrich, Stretton Grandison with Ashperton, Llanrothal and Longhope [Glos.] (*Monemuta, Tadyngton, Dukeston, Castro Godrici, Stratton et Asperton, Lanrothall, Langehope*)	4	17	4
Dore Abbey: Bacton and Avenbury churches		30	0
temporalities	6	11	6
Wormsley Priory: [churches of] Dilwyn, King's Pyon, Wormsley, Almeley and Lyonshall (*Dylewe, Pionia, Wormesley, Almaly, Lenhales*)		109	9¼
Hospitallers of Dinmore: Sutton St. Michael church		13	4
Wroxall Nunnery [Warws.]: a portion in St. Michael's church, Hereford		2	8
Cook Hill Nunnery [Worcs.]: temporalities			9½
St. Bartholomew's Hospital, Gloucester: Newnham [Glos.] church		20	0
Sum[1]	43	9	4¼
[f. 55v.] Two Exchequer tallies	27	0	0
Allowance for Fotheringhay College [Northants.]:[2] spiritualities and temporalities	10	12	6¼
Now paid into the Exchequer[3]	6	17	7
Total	**350**	**2**	**7**

'And he [the prior] is quit.'

68. Mandate from Alexander Cely, clerk of the Admiralty and royal conservator and searcher of the Severn stream from *le marke de Silly* [Sully, Glam.] to Worcester

---

[1] £43 9s. 5¼d. if other figures are correct.

[2] Evidently the prior was unable to reach Fotheringhay and left this contribution to be collected by royal officials, as the writ permitted: *Reg. Stanbury*, 63.

[3] Overpaid by 6d. if the subtotal of allowances is £43 9s. 4¼d. as stated, or 7d given the actual sum of those allowances as detailed.

bridge,[1] to John Priddon. Priddon is to summon a jury of 24 merchants, mariners and other trustworthy men to come before Cely or his deputy at a place near *Cogan Were*[2] [Gloucester] on 4 June to make inquiry and presentment of certain articles and circumstances touching Admiralty jurisdiction.[3] 30 May 4 Edw. IV [1464].

69. Record of a royal inquisition held at *Lanthoney Key*[4] beside the Severn on 4 June 4 Edw. IV [1464] before Alexander Cely, clerk of the Admiralty. Llanthony Priory holds *Cogan Were* on the Severn, a weir which is well maintained and of the same width as the priory has had it built from time out of mind, so that the king's people can pass with vessels and merchandise without danger. Jurors: Nicholas Hert, Robert Hardyng, John Huntley, William Boteman, John Wodewell, Richard Hull, John Hayle, Robert Coke, Thomas Coke, John Pipar, John Elyot the younger, John Kent, John Yelff, John Hyman, Thomas Whitby, John Beryman, Richard Whitby, William Bullok, William Coke,[5] John Gosling.

70. [f. 56] Quittance to the abbot of Kingswood for 20s. 4 Dec. 4 Edw. IV [1464]. [Abstract in MS.; cf. **44**]

71. Mandate from John [Carpenter] bishop of Worcester to the archdeacon of Gloucester. Although the clergy of the diocese, assembled by the king's order[6] in Worcester cathedral, granted to the pope a subsidy of 4d. in the £ payable at St. Peter *ad vincula* last [1 Aug. 1464] for defence against the Turk, many have refused to pay and the king has ordered the bishop to call a new synod to grant 6d. in the £. The archdeacon is to cite the clergy of his archdeaconry to appear accordingly in Worcester cathedral on Tuesday before Whitsun [28 May], and certify to the bishop the names of those cited. Westbury College, 27 Apr. 1465.

---

[1] Appointed to these offices in 1461. Yeoman of the chamber 1461–76, king's serjeant 1476–83 and M.P. for Gloucester 1472–5 and 1478: *Hist of Parl.: Biographies 1439–1509*. In 1509 he or a namesake lived near Gloucester quay: Glos. R.O. GBR/J5/3.

[2] Cogan, Cocan or Cokeyn fish weir was given to the priory in 1143 × 55: *Camd. Misc.* xxii. 18; cf. above, **7**, **19**. It was enlarged or rebuilt before 1276: *Rotuli Hundredorum* (Rec. Com.), i. 178. It lay on the north side of the priory precinct near the present Llanthony navigation weir, since the intervening field was called Cogings in 1799 when it still belonged to the Llanthony estate: Glos R.O. Q/RI 70.

[3] As above, **56**.

[4] Llanthony Quay was still known by that name in 1693 when it was used for unloading tiles for the rebuilding of Newark House: B.L. Add. MS. 11046/vi, f. 37. It can be identified with a quay mentioned in 1370 which lay at the end of the medieval Severn Street, west of the modern dry dock of Gloucester Docks: below, **83**. This was still in use in 1811–2 when it was called Naight Wharf: David Bick, *The Gloucester and Cheltenham Tramroad* (Headington, 1987), 19–21.

[5] Robert Coke was master of the carvel *St. Peter* of Worcester in 1463: *Cal. Pat.* 1461–7, 302. John Pypar, master of the *George* of Brightlingsea, Essex, and William Koke, master of the *Mary* of 'Undyrscofft', were carrying between London and Calais in 1478: *The Cely Papers*, ed. H. E. Malden (Camden 3rd ser. i, 1900), 194–7.

[6] Of 17 May 1464: Wilkins, *Concilia*, iii. 594–5.

72. Quittance to the abbot of Kingswood for 20s. 26 May 5 Edw. IV [1465]. [Abstract in MS.; cf. **44**]

73. [f. 56v.] Presentation of Mr. William Vauce to the rectory of Colesbourne. 28 Feb. 1464[/5]. [Abstract in MS.; cf. **39**]

74. Acknowledgement by Richard Frensh of Gloucester of liability for the rent of a tenement in Northgate Street, Gloucester.

Frensh holds of the prior of Llanthony for 9s. 4d. a year a tenement formerly held by John Biseley and before him by Robert Butte on the west side of the North Street of Gloucester,[1] abutting on the north in front another tenement of the prior of Llanthony,[2] on the south in front a tenement of the prior of St. Margaret's [Hospital], Gloucester,[3] on the north at the back the abbot of Gloucester's tenement inhabited by John Hilley,[4] on the south at the back the abbot of Gloucester's tenement inhabited by John Porter, mercer[5] and on the west William Estynton's tenement.[6] Although he contested the rent previously he has now paid it with arrears, and he and his heirs will do so in perpetuity. 6 May 5 Edw. IV [1465].

75. [f. 57] Appeal to Pope Paul II and the court of Canterbury to take the priory into their protection in case anyone tries to prevent its receiving the tithes of

[1] No. 3 Northgate Street. Frensh's tenement was in three parts, a division which is shown on a map of 1852 and survived until 1970: Glos. R.O. GBR/L10/1/2; *Glevensis* vi. 2–4. The front part, a shop 13 ft. wide and 21 ft. deep, was held not from Llanthony Priory but in two moieties from Gloucester Abbey; although John Bisley held it in 1442, Frensh was the first to use it as the main entrance in lieu of an entry on the north side of no. 5 Northgate Street, and perhaps the first to occupy it after rebuilding as a jettied building of three storeys. The central part, a principal tenement roughly 50 ft. square, was assembled in the 13th and 14th centuries from land which Osbert the cellarer gave to Llanthony Priory and land to which the priory had no title; although Nicholas Bursy, tenant in fee in the time of Edward III, paid 9s. 4d. rent to the priory his successors in title refused to do so. The rear part, measuring about 30 ft. by 20 ft., yielded additional rent to the priory as an orchard from the time of Henry III, when Adam Keyl demolished a stone chamber there, to the time of Richard II, when Robert Butte built a kitchen there: P.R.O. C 115/73, ff. 66–7 (64–5) nos. 126–7, cf. nos. 124, 128; *Glouc. Rental 1455*, 68b–72b. Robert Butte was five times bailiff between 1399 and 1413: *V.C.H. Glos.* iv. 373. Despite Frensh's acknowledgement the rent was in dispute in 1535, when the property was called the Bull: Glos. R.O. GBR/J5/4.
[2] The south part of no. 5 Northgate Street: P.R.O. C 115/73, f. 66 (64) no. 125.
[3] The north part of no. 1 Northgate Street: ibid. no. 124.
[4] No. 11 Northgate Street, whither John Hilley moved from no. 23 Northgate Street after 1455 in succession to Philip Monger: ibid. f. 67 (65)v. no. 128; *Glouc. Rental 1455*, 72b–74b.
[5] No. 2 Westgate Street, rebuilt in 1454: *Glouc. Rental 1455*, 26b; plan, Glos. R.O. D1740/P23.
[6] Nos. 6–8 Westgate Street, part of an estate purchased by William Estynton from Thomas Toky: *Glouc. Rental 1455*, 28b; cf. ibid. 72b; cf. P.R.O. C 115/73, f. 62 (60) no. 123.

Southam demesne in the parish of Bishop's Cleeve (*Cliva*).[1] The appeal is delivered in the priory church on 16 May 1465 [f. 57v.] in the presence of William Naylard, chaplain, and William Somerford,[2] literate (*litterato*) of Worcester diocese, and recorded by of John Mill,[3] clerk and notary public of Worcester diocese.

76. Proxy to Mr. Robert Slymbrigge, B.Cn.L.,[4] to attend a diocesan synod in Worcester cathedral on Tuesday [28 May] before Whitsun 1465.

77. [f. 58] Lease to Richard Smith alias Tochet of Southam of a barn (*grangiam*)[5] by the gate of Prestbury rectory or manor and the tithes and oblations belonging to the rectory,[6] formerly held by John Baderon, for 12 years at 20 marks a year. St. John the Baptist, 5 Edw. IV [4 June 1465].

78. [f. 58v.] Lease to Richard Smith, as above, of Prestbury manor with buildings and a dovecot on the manor site[7] and demesne land, meadow and pasture in

---

[1] Tithes of Walter of Gloucester's manor of Southam were given to St. Owen's church in 1086 × 95 and to Llanthony Priory in 1137: *Camd. Misc.* xxii. 38; Dugdale, *Mon.* vi. 136; *V.C.H. Glos.* viii. 13. By 1150 they were limited to the demesne excluding Sapleton, and from 1234 they also excluded 'Moketon' and one third of demesne assarts: P.R.O. C 115/77, s. vi nos. 62–3. Prior Hayward's dispute evidently involved one of seven successive farmers of the tithes who owed arrears in 1482–6, the seventh being Robert Stevenes to whom they were demised in 1480 for 53s. 4d. a year: below, **485–6**.

[2] A receiver of priory rents in 1483: below, **487**.

[3] d. 1474; B.Cn. & C.L., vicar of Stonehouse 1435–74 and prebendary of Lichfield 1457–74: Emden, *Biog. Reg. Oxon. to 1500*. Warden of St. Oswald's Priory, Gloucester, 1456–66: *Trans. B.G.A.S.* xliii. 121–2.

[4] d. 1505; notary public 1466, B.C.L. (Oxon.) by 1467, D.Cn.L. (Bologna) 1474; rector of Upton-on-Severn (Worcs.) 1465–74, prebendary of St. Asaph from 1467, rector of Bredon (Worcs.) 1470–1505, dean of Westbury-on-Trym from 1474 and precentor of Lichfield 1488–1505: Emden, *Biog. Reg. Oxon.*

[5] The tithe barn, which is to be distinguished from the demesne barn, was ruinous in 1481–6 but rebuilt by 1515: below, **325, 484, 487, 489**. As a 'tithe grange situate near the gate of the rectory' it was still included in the title of the rectory when sold to James Agg in 1833 and when mortgaged by his sons in 1841–3 and 1885: Glos. R.O. D855/T9. Nevertheless it ceased to be a tangible asset before 1838 when the tithe map shows that the lay rector, W. J. Agg, had no real estate in the village and that the vicar John Edwards, who owned the former rectory site in his private capacity, had no building by the gate: Glos. R.O. P254/SD2.

[6] Cf. *V.C.H. Glos.* viii. 72, 78.

[7] The manor house, now called the Priory, still stands on the south side of the church, incorporating a 14th-century hall of four bays, with a 17th-century dovecot adjacent: *V.C.H. Glos.* viii. 72–3.

Prestbury[1] and Cheltenham,[2] now held by John Baderon, for 12 years from Michaelmas next [29 Sept.], rendering annually £4 and 12 geese and 12 capons or 6s, at the prior's choice. The lessee will

(a) acquit the prior and his tenants of manorial services except 12d. a year payable to the lord of Southam,

(b) feed the cellarer, the steward and the understeward and their men when they come to hold court and to superintend,

(c) live on site and

(d) entertain the prior, his men and his horses overnight once or twice a year.

St. John the Baptist, 5 Edw. IV [4 June 1465].

79. [f. 59] Record[3] of a court of Cheltenham hundred, held by a precept dated Monday after the feast of the Conception 4 Edw. IV [10 Dec. 1464], to hear a plea by John prior of Llanthony against John Higgons alleging unjust taking of amercements.

The abbess [of Syon, Mdx.][4] and her predecessors in title have never been seised of homage, fealty or any suit from the prior of Llanthony in Cheltenham manor and hundred.[5] The plaintiff is to receive 20 marks for damages and 40s. for court costs and is to have the amercements returned. Jurors: John Alre, Thomas Goderych, Walter Spencer, William Halle, Richard Milleyn, Richard Lonyar, Richard Cook, John Higgys,[6] Walter Hawthorn, Walter Mochegros, William Clerk and John

[1] The priory's demesne in Prestbury was distinguished by deed of Prior Geoffrey of Henlow (c. 1185–1203) as the only part of the parish where all tithes were reserved to the prior as rector: P.R.O. C 115/77, s. vi no. 72. Later rectors alienated the demesne but kept the whole tithes of it, still known in 1874 as the Llanthony tithes, and it was mapped in 1838 as 8 scattered parcels totalling 44 a., the largest being High Breach of 13 a. at SO 984238: Glos. R.O. GDR/T1/143, schedule 3.

[2] i.e. Prior's Farm at SO 970229 in Oakley, an assart in the fee of Cheltenham given before 1160: *Camd. Misc.* xxii. 44, 46–7; *Cheltenham Local Hist. Soc. Journal* vi. 7–8, where the quoted area of 8 a. is an error.

[3] Beginning with an incomplete sentence about a previous hearing: *continuabatur usque proximam ex assensu presencium* ('it was adjourned until the next [court] by agreement of those present').

[4] Lady from 1443 of the hundreds and manors of Cheltenham and Slaughter: Gwen Hart, *History of Cheltenham* (Leicester, 1965), 40–2; cf. *V.C.H. Glos.* vi. 4, 130.

[5] But an inquest of 1274–6 found that the prior owed suit, and he was fined for not rendering it in 1333: Hart, *History of Cheltenham*, 21, 28.

[6] About 1450 Goderych was the abbess's free tenant at Bafford in Charlton Kings, Cook her free tenant at Bellman's Place in Cheltenham and Lonyar and Higgys her customary tenants at Sandford in Cheltenham: Glos. R.O. D855/M68, ff. 39v., 42–3.

Maunsell. Witnessed and sealed by John Grevel, Kt.,[1] steward of the manor and hundred.

80. Appointment by the abbot, Richard [Hanley],[2] and convent of Gloucester of Thomas Hayward as auditor of accounts, auditor of servants and understeward of courts and hundreds from the time when Thomas' father John ceases to hold these offices, receiving:

(a) 100s. annual pension, paid quarterly,

(b) an abbey esquire's cloth whenever such are issued,

(c) for his servant, 2½ yd. of striped cloth and 2 yd. of plain coloured cloth annually for an abbey groom's suit,

(d) the chamber now occupied by John Hayward in the abbey by the abbey gate,

(e) every week, seven white manchet loaves,

(f) every quarter, 3s. 4d. for ale,

(g) outside Lent every Sunday and every Tuesday or Wednesday, a meat dish from the first course as much as is put before two monks,

(h) in Lent every Sunday and Wednesday, as much fish similarly and

(i) a stable, hay and litter within the abbey for two horses.

Thomas binds himself by oath to perform the offices. When he becomes too infirm to do so he will receive:

(a) the chamber, the loaves and the cloths as above, like John Hayward,

(b) 40s. annual pension,

(c) every day, a dish of as much meat or fish as is put before one monk,

(d) every quarter, 8s. 6d. for ale,[3]

(e) for his boy, a groom's loaf daily,

(f) two wagon-loads or 200 shides [i.e. 200 units of ½ cu. ft.] of firewood and 8 lb. of candles.

Gloucester Abbey chapter house, 22 July 1460.

---

[1] Of Milcote by Stratford-on-Avon (Warws.), d. 1480: Worcs. R.O., Reg. of Worcester wills i, f. 44. Succeeded his father John Grevel Esq. in 1444: *Cal. Close* 1441–7, 262, 323. J.P. for Warws. 1460–80 and for Glos. 1468–75: *Cal. Pat.* 1452–61 and later vols., Commissions of the Peace. Sheriff of Glos. 1460 and 1467, sheriff of Warws. and Leics. 1461 and 1469–70 and a knight by 1463: *Cal. Fine R.* 1452–61, 289; 1461–71, 9, 61, 99, 209, 254, 268. Lord of Ashley in Charlton Kings and owner of other property there and in Cheltenham: *Trans. B.G.A.S.* liv. 157; *Charlton Kings Local Hist. Soc. Bulletin* viii. 8–9. Ultimately lord of Tetbury, Lasborough, Great Rissington, Sezincote and Weston-on-Avon and of 12 manors in Bucks., Derb., Surrey, Sussex, Warws., Wilts. and Worcs.: *Calendarium Inquisitionum post mortem* (Rec. Com.), iv. 401; *Cal. Close* 1476–85, 181; *V.C.H. Glos.* vi. 100, xi. 265, 287.

[2] Or Hauley, abbot 1457–72: *V.C.H. Glos.* ii. 61.

[3] When on duty the understeward received food and drink from monastic tenants for himself and his servant: cf. below, **145**, **185**, **196** etc. On retirement he lost some of the servant's allowances but received more from the abbey for himself.

Omnibus Christo fidelibus hoc presens scriptum indentatum visuris vel audituris Ricardus permissione divina abbas monasterii Sancti Petri Gloucestrie et eiusdem loci conventus salutem in deo sempiternam. Noveritis quod nos prenominatus abbas et conventus unanimis nostris assensu, concensu et voluntate ex fidelitate, circumspectione et industria dilecti nobis in Christo Thome Hayward plenius confidentes dedimus et concessimus eidem Thome pro bono et fideli servicio suo in officiis auditoris compotorum et ministrorum nostrorum ac subsenescalli sive subsenescallie curiarum et hundredorum nostrorum nobis et successoribus nostris impetendis[1] et exercendis sicut Iohannes Hayward, pater dicti Thome, ea iam occupat et exercet seu occupavit et exercuit, cum eadem officia per impotenciam corporalem aut aliam causam ex parte eiusdem Iohannis vacari contigerint, et dum idem Thomas ad hoc eciam potens fuerit, unam annuam pensionem centum solidorum annuatim ad festa Natale Domini, Pasche, Nativitatis Sancti Iohannis Baptiste et Sancti Michelis archangeli per equales porciones de monasterio nostro predicto percipiendam.

Concessimus eciam eidem Thome ad terminum vite sue liberacionem panni tociens et tantum quociens et quantum aliquis esquierius familiaris et domesticus abbatis monasterii predicti qui pro tempore fuerit percipiet de eodem. Concessimus similiter eidem Thome pro famulo suo annuatim ad terminum vite eiusdem Thome erga festum Natale Domini duas virgas et dimidiam panni stragulati et duas virgas panni unius coloris plani de secta palefridariorum nostrorum.

Concessimus eciam eidem Thome ad terminum vite sue unam cameram in abbatia nostra situatam quam dictus Iohannes Heyward modo occupat et occupavit iuxta portam abbatie predicte, et eciam qualibet septimana septem panes albos vocatos 'myches', et quolibet quarterio anni pro cervisia sibi providenda tres solidos et quatuor [f. 59v.] denarios sterlingorum de monasterio nostro supradicto, et qualibet die Dominica extra tempus quadragesimale tantum ferculum carnium de primo cursu quantum eodem die coram duobus monachis apponetur, et quolibet die Martis dum esus carnium habetur legittimus aut die Mercurii extra dictum tempus quadragesimale tantum ferculum carnium quantum erit ferculum supradictum, et qualibet die Dominica in quadragesima tantum de piscibus de primo cursu quantum duobus monachis dicti loci ministratur, et quolibet die Mercurii in quadragesima tantum de piscibus quantum sibi in dicta die Dominica quadragesimali ministrari continget.

Et concessimus insuper eidem Thome stabulum, fenum et literam pro duobus equis suis infra abbatiam nostram predictam per totum tempus quo ipsum dicta officia personaliter exercere continget.

Habendo et percipiendo dictam annuam pensionem centum solidorum et dictos tres solidos et quatuor denarios pro cervisia sibi providenda et dictum corodium carnium et piscium eidem Thome, ut prefertur, annuatim dum predicta officia exercebit in potencia corporali et non ulterius. Et insuper habendo et percipiendo dictam cameram, liberacionem panni, dictos panes albos eidem Thome ad terminum vite sue, ut superius est expressum et prout dictus Iohannes ea omnia et singula habet et percipit.

[1] MS. *impetiendis.*

Et ego vero predictus Thomas ad omnia et singula predicta duo officia debite concernencia sacramentum corporale prefato domino abbati et conventui prestiti bene et fideliter per me facienda, et eciam pro attendencia mea in dictis officiis debitis temporibus habenda et aliis in eisdem ex[s]equendis et expediendis iuxta posse meum obligo me fidi firmiter prefato domino abbati et conventui et eorum successoribus per presentes.

Cum autem contigerit prefatum Thomam ad impotenciam devenire corporalem quominus dicta officia valebit personaliter exercere comode prout debet, dedimus et concessimus eidem Thome pro bono servicio nobis prius impenso unam annuam pensionem quadraginta solidorum de monasterio nostro predicto percipiendam annuatim ad terminum vite eiusdem Thome ad terminos supradictos per equales porciones, et eciam qualibet die carnium tale et tantum ferculum de carnibus qualem et quantum uni monacho dicte domus contigerit exhiberi, et qualibet die piscium tale et tantum ferculum de piscibus quale et quantum uni monacho dicte domus continget apponi, et similiter quolibet quarterio anni octo solidos et sex denarios sterlingorum pro cervisia sibi providenda, et pro suo garcione quolibet die unum panem palefridariorum nostrorum. Et concessimus eciam predicto Thome durante dicta impotencia sua corporali duas plaustratas focalium aut duo centena buchie vocate 'staffe shydes' et octo libras candelarum unacum camera, liberacione panni et septem panibus albis predictis ad terminum vite sue percipiendis modo et forma supradictis.

In cuius rei testimonium uni parti huius scripti indentati penes prefatum dominum abbatem et conventum remanenti ego dictus Thomas sigillum meum apposui, alteri vero parti eiusdem scripti indentati penes predictum Thomam remanenti nos prefatus abbas et conventus sigillum nostrum commune apposuimus. Datum in domo nostra capitulari Gloucestrie in festo Sancte Marie Magdalene, anno regni Regis Henrici Sexti post conquestum tricesimo octavo.

81. Quittance to the abbot of Kingswood for 20s. 20 Feb. 5 Edw. IV [1466]. [Abstract in MS.; cf. **44**]

82. Title (for the purpose of ordination) granted to Richard Wolfe, clerk. 13 Feb. 1465[/6]. [Abstract in MS.; cf. **132**]

83. [f. 60] Perambulation of the borough liberties of Gloucester by Thomas Styward and John of Elmore, bailiffs, on the advice and in the presence of the burgesses Thomas of Bisley, John of Anlep,[1] William James fishmonger, Richard Zavan spurrier, William Heyberer, John of Monmouth,[2] Walter of Marcle, Ralph at

[1] *Alias* John Head (d. 1382), draper and bailiff in 1367: *V.C.H. Glos.* iv. 41–2, 373.
[2] Merchant, bailiff in 1371 and lessee of the demesne of Elmstone Hardwicke from 1373: ibid.

Feld and many others. Wednesday after St. James the apostle, 44 Edw. III [13 July 1370].[1]

From the west gate to a cross in the middle of the west bridge, excluding the meadows and pastures of the abbot and convent of St. Peter of Gloucester on either side of the bridge. Then from the Great Severn within a little gate,[2] continuing eastwards between the archdeacon's meadow and the garden of St. Bartholemew's Hospital to the Little Severn. Along the Little Severn to *Tullewelle* Brook, over which stands a bridge with iron bars. Along the king's highway to the gate of the monks' garden [Monkleighton]; by *Fete Lone* to *Newlond* to metes and bounds, as appears at the stones fixed there (*ibidem ad lapid' fix'*).[3] Then from the south gate to the boundaries in the same street, excluding the inn there[4] and the houses and lands opposite, in the lawyers' view. Within *Rygle Style*[5] to the tenement of the abbot of Gloucester,[6] then to Severn Street and the quay at the end of that lane upon the Severn, reserving to the king the king's castle and meadow together with the orchard (*prat' cum pomerio*)[7] because the castle is of the hundred of King's Barton, as appears by an extent in the king's Exchequer.

The burgesses also find that the borough stands within the hundred of Dudstone and comes in front at all assizes.

84. On Gloucester and the hundred of Dudstone.

In 6 Hen. VI [1427–8] when William Botiler and Thomas Huwes were bailiffs of Gloucester, and when the assizes were held over for want of jurors, the justices of assize John Hals and Thomas Rolfe asked the bailiffs in what hundred the town of Gloucester stood. They replied that Gloucester was a hundred of itself. The justices denied this and said that Gloucester was of the hundred of Dudstone, standing as it

[1] Printed in the original Latin in *Hist. & Cart Mon. Glouc.* (Rolls Ser.), iii. 256–7. Most of the landmarks mentioned are plotted in *V.C.H. Glos.* iv. 68 fig. 4 together with the borough boundary as perambulated from the 16th century to 1835, which, however, varies from that described here: cf. ibid. 56–7, 145–6, 191.

[2] A postern gate opposite nos. 223–7 Westgate Street, piercing a wall demolished in 1702 which ran along the north side of the street from the west gate to a ditch on the west side of St. Bartholomew's Hospital: *Glouc. Rental 1455*, 68; Glos. R.O. GBR/B3/8, p. 70. The perambulation excludes a little meadow, later called Pen Meadow, behind the wall: cf. *V.C.H. Glos.* iv. 67.

[3] The context requires expansion to *lapides fixos* rather than *lapidem fixum* as in *Hist. & Cart. Mon. Glouc.*

[4] Apparently the George, later called the Talbot, at no. 67 Southgate Street within the gate: *Glouc. Rental 1455*, 12b.

[5] Immediately south of the junction of Parliament Street and Brunswick Road: P.R.O. C 115/73, f. 17 (15); cf. above, **38**(e). After diverting to the south gate the perambulation continues clockwise as before.

[6] At nos. 105–19 Southgate Street, south of the junction with Norfolk Street: ibid. ff. 7–8 (5–6). Nos. 75–103 Southgate Street, excluded in post-medieval perambulations, are included here.

[7] The castle orchard is omitted in the text of *Hist. & Cart. Mon. Glouc.* For it see P.R.O. C 115/73, ff. 5, 15 (3, 13); *L. & P. Hen. VIII*, xiv (1), p. 590.

does in the midst of that hundred.[1] Extracted from the register of John Marwent, abbot of Gloucester.

85. [f. 60v.] Note of John Waldebeff, archdeacon of Brecon and commissary of Robert [Tully] bishop of St. David's, that John ap Holl ap Redenegh has resigned from the vicarage of Kington (Herefs.), and been inducted to the vicarage of Llanafanfawr (*Llanhavanvawre*)[2] [Brec.]. Brecon, 30 Sept. 1465.

86. Presentation of David Yeuans[3] to the vicarage of Kington [Herefs.]. 28 Feb. 1465[/6].

87. [f. 61] David Yeuans's bond to the priory in £20. [Condition not stated.] 28 Feb. 5 Edw. IV [1466].

88. Resignation of John Hawton as vicar of Henlow [Beds.], delivered in Ampthill church [Beds.] in the presence of John Goldesmyth rector of Ampthill and William Aleyn chaplain of Lincoln diocese [f 61v.] and recorded by John May, clerk of York diocese and papal and imperial notary public. 6 Feb. 1465[/6].

89. Presentation of Robert Colby, chaplain, to the vicarage of Henlow [Beds.] vacant by the resignation of John Hawton. 2 Apr. 1466.

[f. 62 is blank, being part of a sheet which is sewn into the next quire and pasted to the back cover.]

90. [ff. 63–5] The king's letters patent ordering that the tenants of the duchy of Lancaster of the inheritance of the earls of Hereford in Haresfield and elsewhere be permitted to enjoy their liberties and customs. Westminster, 8 Jan. 5 Edw. IV [1466], [signed] Neuhous.

91. [f. 65v.] John Joce's feoffment to Thomas Heyward, Thomas Smalcombe, Thomas Porter, William Burnell, Thomas Burnell and their heirs of lands, tenements, rents, reversions and services in Coleford, Westbury-on-Severn,[4]

[1] Contradicting **18** above.
[2] Of which the bishop of St. David's was patron by 1491: *Episcopal Registers of the Diocese of St. David's*, i, 1397–1518 (Cymmodorion Rec. Ser. vi, 1917), p. 283. David Walker supplied this reference. The link with Kington here and in **281** below seems coincidental.
[3] Instituted 16 Mar.: *Reg. Stanbury*, 182. d. in office 1484: *Reg. Myllyng*, 200.
[4] Possibly the manor of Sellars or Cellars in Westbury, which is recorded as property of the priory from this time; cf. *Valor Eccl.* (Rec. Com.), ii. 425; *V.C.H. Glos.* x. 88; P.R.O. SC 6/Hen. VIII/1224, m. 5d.

Blaisdon, Minsterworth (*Colford, Wessebury, Blechedon, Mynstreworth*) and the Forest of Dean except those which he holds by right of his wife Elizabeth. Witnesses: Thomas Mull Esq., Thomas Baynam Esq.,[1] John Anne, Thomas Wodeward of Mitcheldean and William Moton. 9 Jan. 34 Hen. VI [1456].

92. John Joce's endowment of a chantry in the priory by way of a condition to the above feoffment, which is here recited [f. 66] with (different) date 9 Jan. 38 Hen. VI [1460]. The feoffees are to create a legal title to the property, except the property in Coleford, for the prior and convent, [f. 66v.] who have granted as follows.

(a) An Augustinian priest will celebrate mass daily at the ninth hour at the altar of All Saints in the priory church for the souls of John and Elizabeth Joce, John's parents John and Joan, Robert Joce, Richard Joce, all their family and friends and all the faithful dead, receiving from the prior 12d. a week.

(b) The sacrist will provide bread, wine, wax and vestments at the altar for the masses, receiving from the prior 6s. 8d. a year.

(c) The prior and convent will hold an obit annually on the anniversary of John Joce's death, receiving from the prior 6s. 8d. among them.

(d) The almoner will give 6s. 8d. to the poor at the anniversary and at other times to pray for the said souls.

Residual income from the property may remain for the use of the priory. The grant is not to take effect during the lifetimes of John and Elizabeth Joce or John's brother Richard.

93. [f. 67] Quitclaim by John's brother Richard Joce to Thomas Smalcombe, Thomas Porter, William Burnell and Thomas Burnell of lands, tenements, rents, reversions and services in Westbury[-on-Severn], Blaisdon, Minsterworth and the Forest of Dean formerly belonging to his father John, except the property in Coleford. Witnesses: James Hyot, Thomas Grey, Richard Wynter, Robert Wynter and Richard Gryffyth. 8 Feb. 5 Edw. IV [1466].

---

[1] 1422–1500. Escheator of Glos. 1451 and J.P. for the county 1471–1500: *Cal. Pat.* 1446–52, 414; 1467–77 and later vols., Commissions of the Peace. Sheriff of Glos. 1476, warden of Dean Forest and constable of St. Briavel's castle 1478–83; ultimately lord of Abenhall and Mitcheldean, of Clearwell in Newland, of Hathaways in Ruardean and of Aston Ingham, Putley and 'Bykerton' (Herefs.) and mortgagee of seven manors in Somerset: *Trans. B.G.A.S.* vi. 131–2, 146–9, 184; *V.C.H. Glos.* v. 95, 180, 211, 237, 414; *Cal. Close* 1485–1500, 174 no. 604.

94. [f.67v.] Appointment of William Notyngham[1] as steward of manors, lands and tenements in Glos. and Wilts., receiving annually a fee of 40s., cloth for a gown and a reward of 20s., in default of which he may distrain upon the manor of Brockworth. 6 Dec. 5 Edw. IV [1465].

95. Citation of Canon Thomas Alford, who has absented himself from the priory against the rule, to appear in the chapter house one week hence. [No date.]

96. [f. 68] Declaration that Canon Thomas Alford, having been cited and failed to appear at the appointed time, has incurred sentence of the greater excommunication. [No date.]

97. [f. 68v.] Lease to Robert Panell of a tithe barn within the site of Henlow manor [Beds.][2] and tithes of corn belonging to Henlow rectory for nine years at £8. St. Luke 5 Edw. IV [18 Oct. 1465].

98. Bond of Robert Panell of 'Clare', Henry Bromeham of Clifton [Beds.] and William Daye of Henlow [Beds.] in 50 marks to perform the covenants of the above lease. 22 Oct. 5 Edw. IV [1465].

[**99** and **100** are additions in a 16th century hand.]

99. [f. 69] [Recipe for] *oxymell* [a medicinal syrup].

Take lyme stones and ley them in a potell of clene water, and when the stones beth molte, stere the stonys and the water togedir and then powre out the clere wotter from the stones. And then take 12 races [i.e. roots] of gynger and put them into the clere water and let them ly therein 24 howres. And then take them oute of the water and waysshe the races clene. And then kutte every rase in 2 or 3 partes. And then put them into a potte with a quarte of hony and boyle them over the fire till they be browne, and alwey skome [i.e. skim] awey the skome clene as they boylith. And then

---

[1] d. 1483. Born in Cirencester, where his father William d. 1427: *Trans. B.G.A.S.* 1. 185. Steward of the bishop of Worcester's estates 1450–70: Christopher Dyer, *Lords and Peasants in a Changing Society* (Cambridge, 1980), 380. Justice of gaol delivery and J.P. for Glos. 1445–83, J.P. for Wilts. 1457–8 and 1475 and for 12 other counties between 1472 and 1483; escheator of Glos. and the Welsh March 1446–7, 1471–2; bailiff of Gloucester 1449, M.P. for the borough 1449–50 and for Glos. 1453–4; attorney general 1452–83, Baron 1461–79 and Chief Baron 1479–83 of the Exchequer, Privy Councillor by 1465, knighted 1480: *Hist. of Parl., Biographies 1439–1509*, 642–3. Resident on the north side of Eastgate Street, Gloucester: *Gloucester Rental 1455*, 90b. Lord of Wiggold in Cirencester and purchaser of the manors of Matson in 1458, of Sapperton in 1463 and 1480, of Elmbridge in Hucclecote in 1467, of Coates with Trewsbury in 1467–77 and of Great Rissington in 1481; founder of St. Thomas' Hospital in Cirencester: *Trans. B.G.A.S.* 1. 185–200; *V.C.H. Glos.* iv. 433, 443; vi. 100; xi. 91.

[2] Henlow Llanthony, one of several manors in the parish: *V.C.H. Beds.* ii. 281, 285; P.R.O. C 115/77 s. xx.

b[u]y a penyworth of notemygge and a penyworth of longe peper and make them into powdir. And then take it fro the fire and take a penyworth of treacle and put therto. And drynke thereof at mornynge half a sponefull and as muche at nyght when ye goe to bedde.

100. [Another medicinal recipe] *for all maner of ache in a mannes body, of scabbes.*

Take wyld tansy and boyle it in clene water over the fire till it be softe. And then streyne them thorogh a clothe and put thereto a halfpenyworth of white sope, and boyle all togedre over the fire. And then take it fro the fire and put thereto as muche rede vyneacre as the 3rd parte of the other likour. And herewith waysshe thereas the sore is downewarde.

Notes from
THE REGISTER OF HENRY DEANE
PRIOR OF LLANTHONY BY GLOUCESTER 1467–81
and after union with Llanthony in Wales
PRIOR OF LLANTHONY 1481–1501

rearranged in chronological order from Richard Furney's manuscript
'The Monastery of Lanthony near Gloucester'
Bodleian Library MS. Top. Gloucs. c. 5[1]

101. [p. 657] *The register belonging to Prior Dene, wrote on vellum in folio and containing 103 leaves, is now among the records belonging to the city of Gloucester,[2] and in it are contain'd many of the particulars relateing to this prior in this account of him. This in their records is commonly [called] the Red Book on account of its binding, but now it is bound in leather of a different colour.*

---

[1] Richard Furney M.A. (1694–1753) was rector of Doynton 1720–7, master of the Crypt School, Gloucester, *c.* 1720–4 and archdeacon of Surrey 1725–53: Irvine Gray, *Antiquaries of Glos. and Bristol* (B.G.A.S. 1981), 59–61.

[2] Now lost, but in 1720 among the borough records and catalogued by Furney as follows (Glos. R.O. GBR/I1/41 ff. 17–8): *An old ledger book belonging formerly to Lanthony Priory wherein among other remarkable & valuable records relating to several places in the county of Gloucester and elsewhere are* (*viz.*)

[a] *several presentations of that priory to the churches of All Saints, St. Mary de Crypt, St. Owen's & the chappel of St. Kineburg,*

[b] *the copy of Pope Gregory's bull confirming the church of St. Nicholas to St. Bartholomew's Hospitall and granting them sixpence to be paid after day by the priory according to their agreement, page 12,*

[c] *an agreement between the priory and hospital about the said alms, an exemplification thereof and a letter from the prince to the priory concerning them,*

[d] *an exchange made by the priory of Lanthony with the hospital of two acres of meadow in Wallham for two acres in Sudmead* [in 1476: *Glouc. Corp. Rec.* p. 410 no. 1165],

[e] *the perambulation of the town of Gloucester made 44th Edw. III (1370).*

The presentations [a] were drawn upon by Furney for lists of incumbents published in Fosbrooke, *Glouc.* 163, 189. The bull [b] of Gregory IX (1227–43), in whose time St. Nicholas's changed hands (*V.C.H. Glos.* iv. 308), was exhibited at an episcopal visitation in 1477: *Glouc. Corp. Rec.* p. 411 no. 1167. Another copy of the perambulation [e] is in Prior Hayward's register: above, **83**. Prior Deane's register also disclosed the following.

[f] *In 1474 the abbess of Sion* [Mdx.] *granted, for £110 rent, the manors and hundreds of Cheltenham and Slaughter to farm, for seven years, to the priory of Lanthony*: Fosbrooke, *Glos.* ii. 373.

[g] *The poor people of* [St. Mary Magdalene's hospital] *assigned two loaves a day, a load of hay and a tree for fewel yearly, with the pasturage of a cow and some other lands, for the maintenance of their priest*: Rudder, *Glos.* 187.

102. *Henry Dene or Dean or Denny or Deene, D.D., a canon of the priory born near this town, and at Prior Heyward's election call'd the scholar (concerning which see* [   ] *[above,* **3**(f) *in this edition]), succeeded in July 1467.*

103. [p. 663] *William Hook, cellarer, is met with in 1468 and John Batte, sub-prior, in 1476.*

104. [p. 658] *King Edward 4th, in consideration of the priory's great want of fuel, by his charter dated at Westminster in the 20 of May in the seventeenth year of his reign* [1477],[1] *granted thereto so much wood as three horses could carry from his wood and lands at Buckwold,*[2] *part of the lordship of Brimpsfield, to their priory or their mannor of Brockworth every day. And for this grant the priory paid twenty marks, and was oblig'd to perform certain offices and to keep up an obit yearly for the king.*

105. *Cecily dutches of York, King Edward the Fourth's mother, 14 of June 17th Edward 4th* [1477], *gave to the priory for her life, for the obit yearly to be kept in the month of January, out of the Buckholt Wood, so many trees to be burnt in the priory, and in their mannor of Brockworth, as four horses could carry in a day from the same to these places.*[3]

106. [p. 664] *Walter Banknot, sacrist, and William Hooke, treasurer, are met with in 1480.* [p. 666] *Robert Cole, rentar, is met with in 21st Edward 4th* [1481–2].[4]

107. [p. 659] [Prior Deane] *was at great trouble and expence to get the priory of Lanthony St. John Baptist appropriated, united and incorporated to this priory. King Edward 4th, having receiv'd three hundred marks, did on the 10th of May in the 21st year of his reign* [1481], *upon the surrender and ill government of John Adams the prior, by his letter patents*[5] *give authority and licence to unite them, and this is said to be confirm'd by the pope's seal*[6] *and the seal of the chapter of St. David's. But this union seems to have been disputed or not finally consented to in all particulars till the time of the person who succeeded him in this priory.*[7]

Tho' the said King Edward 4th in another charter dated on the 26 of October[8] *in the 21st year of his reign* [1481], [and] *the bishop of St. David's on the 17th of November 1483, say the priory of Lanthony the First with his possessions was appropriated and united to Lanthony the Second. And A14* [below, **133** *in this*

---

[1] Granted to Prior Deane as the king's chaplain: *Cal. Pat.* 1476–85, 44.

[2] Buckholt in Cranham: *V.C.H. Glos.* vii. 200.

[3] A confirmation and variation of grant **104** above, issued by the duchess (d. 1495) as life tenant of the royal manors of Brimpsfield and Bisley: *V.C.H. Glos.* vii. 203; xi. 13.

[4] P.R.O. C 115/73, gloss to f. 16 (14) no. 30.

[5] *Cal. Pat.* 1476–85, 284; transcript in Dugdale, *Mon.* vi. 139.

[6] By Sixtus IV in 1482: *Cal. Papal Letters,* 1474–84, 912.

[7] Below, **215.**

[8] *Recte* 22 Oct: *Cal. Pat.* 1476–85, 246.

edition] *by virtue of this appropriation, as 'tis expressly said, the prior and convent of Lanthony the Second being proprietors of Lanthony the First presented to the bishop of Hereford on the 28 of October 1504 a clerk for institution to the church, rectory or free chapel of Cuyshope* [i.e. Cusop] *in the diocese of Hereford.*

108. [p. 642] *John Byconyll[1] being a special benefactor obtain'd letters of fraternity from the priory 1492.*

109. [p. 663] *John Marsfeld sub-prior and* [p. 664] *Thomas Alford treasurer are met with in 1493 and John Sodbury 'custos ordinis' in 1494.* [p. 663] *John Marsfeld sub-prior,* [p. 664] *John Sodbury 'custos ordinis', John Brown sacrist,* [p. 665] *Walter Cheltnam precentor, Richard Newente succentor and William of Awre infirmarer are met with in 1497.[2]*

110. [p. 659] *While he was prior he was a great benefactor hereto. His arms, viz. a chevron charged with three pastoral staffs, are over the gate at the west end.[3] 'Tis probable he built the chancels or churches or was a great benefactor to St. Mary de Crypt and Hempsted, which belong'd to the priory until its dissolution. For his arms impaled with the see of Canterbury are on a brick toward the east end of the first;[4]*

---

[1] Kt., d. 1501; customer of London 1455, M.P. for Shaftesbury 1455–6, Som. 1472–5 and Dorset 1491–2, escheator of Devon 1456–7, member of all Som. commissions 1459–94, J.P. for Devon 1468–70, Som. 1472–1501 and Dorset 1497–1501, sheriff of Som. and Dorset 1472–3, knighted at Bosworth 1485: *Hist. of Parl., Biographies 1439–1509.* Commissioner for gaol delivery at Ilchester (Som.) 1487–98 and Bristol and Dorchester 1492: *Cal. Pat.* 1485–94, 212, 391–2; 1494–1509, 146, 161. Lord of North Perrott with Pipplepen (Som.) and owner of much other land in Som., Dorset and Devon: *Cal. Inq. p.m. Hen. VII,* ii, pp. 439–40, 554–5; *Som. Medieval Wills 1501–30* (Som. Record Soc., 1903), 6–9. Buried at Glastonbury Abbey, to which he bequeathed three manors: *Proc. Som. Archaeol. and Nat. Hist. Soc.* xl. 209–25; *Cal. Pat.* 1494–1509, p. 275.

[2] At a visitation by Archbishop Morton in 1498, after the death or transfer of Walter Cheltnam, the list of canons was certified as John Mersfeld sub-prior, John Sodbury *custos ordinis,* Thomas Alford, John Brown sacrist, Walter Keylok and Thomas Siscestre proctors in Ireland, John Gloucestre, John Chestre, William of Aure infirmarer, William Notingham almoner, Richard Newent precentor, Richard Deene subcellarer, John Combe, Philip Bristowe, Edmund Forest scholar, Thomas Hale refectorer, John Halynton, Thomas Lylliston and Robert Cone: *Reg. Morton,* ii. 129–30.

[3] Furney may here confuse variants of Deane's arms. Those over the west gatehouse, now defaced, were drawn by Lysons and read by Bazeley as *a chevron between three choughs:* Samuel Lysons, *Collection of Gloucestershire Antiquities* (London, 1803), pl. 18; *Trans. B.G.A.S.* xxvi. 47; *Dictionary of British Arms: Medieval Ordinary,* ii (Soc. of Antiquaries, 1996), 304, cf. 458.

[4] Although this floor-tile, lost in a 19th-century restoration, belonged to a series commissioned by Prior Forest there is other evidence connecting the nave of St. Mary de Crypt with Prior Deane: above, pp. xxii–xxiii.

*the initial letters of his name are in the windows of the second, and [he] being then
attired with a mitre and pastoral staff.[1] He was then bishop of Bangor or Salisbury.*

111. [p. 657] *In 1495* [Prior Deane] *was made chancellor of Ireland.[2]* [p. 658] *And
being signally serviceable to King Henry 7th, that king constituted him deputy of
that kingdom.[3] Some time after he was recall'd. In 1496 he was preferr'd to the
bishoprick of Bangor,[4] where he rebuilt the choir[5] and laid out a great deal of money
on his ruin'd palace[6] and several other uses. And by the king being esteem'd as a
wise and industrious man, in 1500 he was translated to the bishoprick of Salisbury,[7]
but held both his bishopricks successively with this priory. Within few months after
this he obtain'd the archiepiscopal see of Canterbury,[8] and then left his priorship.
Until the dissolution an anniversary was constantly kept for him in this priory.*

112. [A summary of **205** below.]

---

[1] Of Deane's cipher and figure in stained glass only a small mitred head survives in the
chancel at Hempsted: *V.C.H. Glos.* iv. 428.
[2] Appointed initially on 13 Sept. 1494, when he was called a king's councillor, but
reappointed 20 Nov. 1495: *Cal. Pat.* 1494–1509, 15, 38.
[3] On 1 Jan 1496: ibid. 64.
[4] Initially granted custody of temporalities 13 Apr. 1494, provided 4 July 1494 and
consecrated 20 Nov. 1495; provided again 21 July 1496, granted temporalities 6 Oct. 1496:
Le Neve, *Fasti 1300–1541, Welsh Dioceses.*
[5] The choir was probably reroofed before Deane's appointment: M. L. Clarke, *Bangor
Cathedral* (Cardiff, 1969), 16. The tradition that he rebuilt it is derived from W. Camden,
Britannia (London, 1586), 387–8 through Browne Willis, *Survey of the Cathedral Church of
Bangor* (London, 1721), 95.
[6] The timber framed palace in which the bishops lived until 1899 was begun by Deane on
the evidence of Humphrey Humphreys, bishop 1689–1701: Clarke, *Bangor Cathedral*, 91
quoting Anthony Wood, *Athenae Oxonienses* (ed. Bliss, Oxford, 1813), col. 742.
[7] Translated 8 Jan. 1500, granted temporalities 22 Mar.: Le Neve, *Fasti 1300–1541,
Salisbury.*
[8] Elected 26 Apr. 1501, translated 26 May, granted the pallium 20 July and temporalities 2
Aug.: Le Neve, *Fasti 1300–1541, Monastic Cathedrals.*

THE REGISTER OF EDMUND FOREST
[ALIAS SHYAR] PRIOR OF LLANTHONY 1501–25

Public Record Office C 115/85

'Register or copy of all indentures, proxies, presentations, charters, corrodies, mandates, certificates, titles, letters, bonds, quittances, manumissions, resignations and other instruments made in the days of Edmund Forest S.T.P., prior of Llanthony-by-Gloucester, beginning from 17 Hen. VII [1501].'

[The MS. has below the title an *index locorum* to ff. 1–119. The index occupies three unnumbered leaves and is arranged in simple alphabetical order under three headings for England, Wales and Ireland. Llanwarne and Pencoyd (Herefs.) appear incorrectly, and Kington (now in Herefs.) correctly, under Wales.]

113. [f. 1] Lease to Hugh Martyn,[1] chaplain, of the greater and lesser tithes, oblations and revenues of the rectory of Ballingham (*Balyniam*) in Archenfield [Herefs.] for life at 27s. 8d. a year. He or his deputy will administer the sacraments and celebrate divine service in Ballingham church, pay dues and maintain the chancel.[2] Christmas 17 Hen. VII [25 Dec. 1501].

114. Proxy to [   ] to attend a convocation of Canterbury province in St. Paul's cathedral, London, on 14 Feb.[3] 9 Feb. 1501[/2].
Pateat universis per presentes quod nos Edmundus, permissione Divina prior monasterii sive prioratus Lanthonie iuxta Gloucestriam ordinis Sancti Augustini Wigorniensis diocesis, ad comperendum pro nobis et nomine nostro coram reverendissimo in Christo patre ac domino Domino Henrico [Deane] Dei gracia Cantuariensi archiepiscopo, tocius Anglie primati et apostolice sedis legato, suisve in hac parte locum tenentibus aut commissariis quibuscumque, ad interessendum in concilio dicti reverendissimi in Christo patris una cum episcopis et suffraganeis suis ac eciam clero sue provincie Cantuariensis in ecclesia Sancti Pauli London' 14 die mensis Februarii modo instantis cum continuacione et prorogacione dierum tum sequencium et locorum celebrandorum, discretos viros [   ] coniunctim et divisim et quemlibet eorum in solidum et per[4] se nostros veros et legittimos procuratores

---

[1] d. 1514, vicar of Avenbury (Herefs.) 1510–14: *Reg. Mayew*, 277, 282.
[2] Ballingham church was given to the priory by Hugh de Lacy (d. *c.* 1115) as a chapel of Llanwarne, so the cure remained a chaplaincy: P.R.O. C 115/75, f. 217 no. 26.
[3] Cf. Wilkins, *Concilia*, iii. 646.
[4] MS. *pro.* The stroke of *p* descends into the lower margin and is bound with a scroll bearing the motto *Timentibus Deum nichil deest*: cf. below, **223** n.

absencieque nostre excusatores facimus, [f. 1v.] *ordinamus et constituimus per presentes, dantes et concedentes eisdem procuratoribus nostris coniunctim et divisim et cuilibet eorum, ut premittitur, in solidum et per se potestatem generalem et mandatum speciale nomine nostro ad tractandum ibidem et audiendum, quecumque ibidem expediendum communem ecclesie et regni Anglicani statum, utilitatem et necessitatem concernencia, episcopisque*[1] *concilia et auxilia in hac parte impendendum, et consenciendum pro nobis hiis que ibidem ex deliberacione communi ad honorem Dei et ecclesie sue contigerint ordinari, aliumque procuratorem loco eorum et cuiuslibet ipsorum substituendum, aliaque omnia et singula faciendum et recipiendum que ipsum sacrum concilium duxerit ordinanda et que in premissis vel circa ea necessaria fuerint vel eciam oportuna, eciam si mandatum exigant in se speciale, ratum et gratum habituri sub ypotheca dicti prioratus nostri quicquid per dictos procuratores nostros seu aliquem subsituendum, vel ab eisdem*[2] *seu ipsorum aliquo, actum seu gestum fuerit in premissis. In cuius rei testimonium sigillum nostrum presentibus est appensum. Date nono die mensis Februarii anno Domini millesimo quingentesimo primo.*

115. Presentation of Ralph Grymschawe, chaplain,[3] to the vicarage of Stanton Lacy [Salop.][4] vacant by the death of Thomas Kenley.[5] 29 Jan. 1501[/2].

116. Grant of a corrody to Thomas Hawkyns[6] of Littledean and his wife Joan, sister of Archbishop Henry [Deane], for Joan's lifetime, comprising every week seven manchet loaves (*miches*), four cheaper brown loaves (*broun loves*) and seven gallons of better ale and every day a dish of meat or fish such as [f. 2] is served to one brother of the convent. 28 Mar. 17 Hen. VII [1502].

117. Feoffment by John Carwent, lately of Newent, to Thomas and Joan Hawkyns of Littledean of a tenement and curtilage between the bridges of Gloucester held by Carwent with the late John Hilley, alderman of Gloucester,[7] of the feoffment of John

---

[1] MS. *episcoporumque.*
[2] MS. *eiusdem.*
[3] Formerly vicar of Hughley (Salop.) 1486–9 and of Sidbury (Salop.) from 1491: *Reg. Myllyng,* 195, 197–8.
[4] Given to the priory by Hugh de Lacy (d. *c.* 1115): P.R.O. C 115/75, f. 217 no. 26.
[5] Vicar since 1484: *Reg. Myllyng,* 200.
[6] d. 1503, resident at Littledean and also occupying chambers at Llanthony and Brockworth: P.R.O. PROB 11/13, f. 202v. copied in Hockaday Abs. cclx, 1503.
[7] d. 1494; wiredrawer and owner of 600 sheep, resident at no. 23 Northgate Street in 1455, at no. 11 Northgate Street in 1465 and on the west side of Lower Southgate Street at his death: P.R.O. PROB 11/10, f. 110, copied in Hockaday Abs. ccxxi, 1494; above, **74** & n.; Glos. R.O. GBR/J5/3. Town bailiff 1457, M.P. for Gloucester 1467–8 and mayor 1487: *V.C.H. Glos.* iv. 374–5; *Hist. of Parl., Biographies 1439–1509.* Prior Deane was his executor: P.R.O. op. cit.

Monmouth of Gloucester.[1] After the Hawkynses' death the property will remain to Robert Coof chaplain,[2] John Chadwell[3] lately of Stow-on-the-Wold (*Stowe Sancti Edwardi*), Richard Pere lately of Bridge Sollers [Herefs.] and their heirs. Witnesses: John Coke mayor, William Hanshawe and John Hawkyns sheriffs and John Caple and Thomas Hert aldermen of Gloucester. 28 Mar. 17 Hen. VII [1502].

118. Presentation of Richard Aleyn, chaplain,[4] to the vicarage of Great Barrington (*Bernynton Magna*) vacant by the death of William Massenger. 23 May 1502.

119. [f. 2v.] Quitclaim to the priory's servant John Carwent, lately of Newent,[5] and his heirs of any suit against them. Michaelmas morrow 18 Hen. VII [30 Sep. 1502].

120. Grant to Richard and Elizabeth Chapmon and their son John, at the instance of Archbishop Henry Dene, of property in Quedgeley for their lives as follows.[6]

(a) A messuage, half a yardland and 7 a. of demesne land in South Field[7] and Westhill Field[8] lately held by John White, neif, and now Richard's copyhold at 8s. 8d. a year.

(b) Groveacre Croft and Little Croft lately held by William Nowe and now Richard's copyhold at 3s. a year.

(c) 4½ a. of land at Sockesworthe, Ninche,[9] Theeblake in Alder Mead and Acrey (the latter lately held by Henry Garon) together with Small Mead between

---

[1] Bailiff in 1371: above, **83** n. John of Monmouth's house, at nos. 172–4 Westgate Street immediately north-west of the Foreign Bridge, was in other hands in 1455 (*Glouc. Rental 1455*, 52b) but yielded 26s. 6d. rent to the priory in 1535: Glos. R.O. GBR/J5/4. Presumably it was acquired by Prior Deane, vested temporarily in the successive feoffees named here and appropriated in mortmain in 1509 under the pardon **222** below. It passed in 1542 to Thomas Bell, in 1562 to St. Kyneburgh's hospital and in 1603 to the borough, which let it from 1630 as a tenement measuring 34 ft. in front, 279 ft. on the west, 285 ft. on the east and 49 ft. on the north: *L. & P. Hen. VIII*, xvii, p. 265 no. 64; Hockaday Abs. ccxxiii; *V.C.H. Glos.* iv. 354–5; Glos. R.O. GBR/J3/3, f. 23. A glasshouse was built there by 1672 and remained accessible by boat through the Foreign Bridge until 1743: Glos. R.O. GBR/J5/7; GBR/F4/7, p. 76; GBR/F4/9, pp. 398, 404; GBR/J4/12, plan 23.

[2] Vicar of Holy Trinity, Gloucester: *Reg. Morton*, ii. 136.

[3] Servant in 1501 of the lawyer William Greville: *Trans. B.G.A.S.* lxxvi. 172; cf. below, **184.**

[4] d. 1505: below, **138.** One of the name was fellow of Magdalen College, Oxford, 1486–7 and vicar of Chipping Norton, Oxon., from 1487: Emden, *Biog. Reg. Oxon. to 1500.*

[5] Formerly auditor and feoffee of the priory: **117, 484–90.** The quitclaim evidently marks his retirement.

[6] Since Chapmon was a receiver of priory rents in 1481–2 (below, **484**) Deane's purpose was evidently to reward him for good service.

[7] At SO 807152 east of Lower Rea, later bisected by a canal. Fields in Quedgeley are located in tithe and inclosure maps of 1839: Glos. R.O. GDR/T1/144; Q/RI/144.

[8] Alias West Field: A. H. Smith, *Place-Names of Glos.* (Eng. Place-Name Soc.), ii. 189. At SO 819146, now the site of Holmleigh Park in Tuffley.

[9] At SO 817133 SE. of Manor Farm.

Harsebroke[1] and Catteland,[2] all now held by Richard at will for (specified) rents totalling 12s. a year.

During his lifetime Richard will render a red rose annually, due services and heriots on the deaths of Elizabeth and John. After Richard's death the survivors will resume payment of the above rents totalling 33s. 8d., suit of court and other customary services. The prior's attorneys Roger Porter[3] and John Chadwell will deliver seisin. 1 Mar. 1502.

Carta concessa Ricardo Chapmon, uxori sue et uni filio ad instanciam Reverendissimi Patris Domini Henrici Dene Cantuariensis Archiepiscopi.

Omnibus Christo fidelibus ad quos presens scriptum indentatum pervenerit Edmundus permissione divina prior domus et ecclesie Beate Marie de Lanthonia iuxta Gloucestriam et eiusdem loci conventus salutem in Domino sempiternam. Noveritis nos, prefatum priorem et conventum dedisse, concessisse et per hoc presens scriptum nostrum indentatum confirmasse Ricardo Chapmon de Quedesley et Elizabethe uxori eius ac Iohanni filio eorum unum messuagium et dimidium virgate terre nostre in Quedesley ac unam acram terre dominice iacentem in 'le Southfelde' et sex acras terre dominice iacentes in certis locis in campo vocato 'le Westhyll' nuper in tenura Iohannis White nativi nostri et modo in tenura dicti Ricardi Chapmon per rotulum curie sub redditu octodecim solidorum et octo denariorum per annum.

Noveritis eciam nos, priorem et conventum dedisse, concessisse et per hoc presens scriptum nostrum indentatum confirmasse predicto Ricardo et Elizabethe ac Iohanni filio eorum duo crofta terre nostre in Quedesley predicta unde unum vocatur Groveacre et alterum vocatur Lytelcroft nuper in tenura Willelmi Nowe et modo in tenura eiusdem Ricardi per rotulum curie sub redditu trium solidorum per annum.

Noveritis insuper nos prefatum priorem et conventum dedisse, concessisse et per hoc presens scriptum indentatum confirmasse predicto Ricardo et Elizabethe ac Iohanni filio eorum diversa parcella terre et prati in Quedesley predicta prius in tenura eiusdem Ricardi ad voluntatem nostram, videlicet unam acram terre nostre in Sockesworthe sub redditu duodecim denariorum per annum, unam aliam acram terre arrentate iacentem in 'le Ninche' sub redditu decem denariorum per annum ac dimidium acre terre vocatum 'le Theeblake' 'forwardys' in medio campo apud

---

[1] At SO 822130 N. of Nass Farm, later bisected by a railway.

[2] At SO 822142, now the site of Chatsworth Avenue in Tuffley.

[3] d. 1523: Bigland, *Glos.* iii. 901; P.R.O. PROB 11/21, f. 48, copied in Hockaday Abs. ccxcii, 1523. Nephew of Prior Hayward and brother of William Porter the warden of New College, Oxford: above, p. xv; *Visit. Glos. 1623*, 127. J.P. for Glos. 1508–23, reappointed posthumously in error, and justice of gaol delivery at Gloucester 1511, 1520: *Cal. Pat.* 1494–1509, 641; *L. & P. Hen. VIII*, i, pp. 476, 1537; ii, pp. 190, 318; iii, p. 396; iv, pp. 168, 721. Steward of the earl of Northumberland in Oxenhall, steward of Lord Latimer in the hundred of Bledisloe, lessee of Huntley and Bulley and lord of Boulsdon in Newent, resident at Porter's Place at the SE. corner of Newent marketplace: *Glos Military Survey 1522*, 53, 62, 64, 199, 200; Rudder, *Glos.* 564; Glos. R.O. D412/Z3, D1810/1, D5767. Father of Arthur Porter the understeward of Llanthony and the purchaser of the priory at the dissolution: above, p. xxxii.

*Aldermede sub redditu sex denariorum per annum et duas acras terre iacentes in
Acrey nuper in tenura Henrici Garon sub redditu viginti denariorum per annum,
necnon et unam parcellam prati vocatam Smalemede iacentem inter Harsebroke et
Catteland sub redditu octo solidorum per annum.*

*Habendo et tenendo omnia et singula predicta messuagium, terras et prata cum
omnibus suis pertinenciis predicto Ricardo et Elizabethe ac Iohanni filio eorum ad
terminum vite eorum et cuiuslibet eorum diucius viverint. Reddendo inde nobis
prefato priori et conventui et successoribus nostris annuatim durante vita ipsius
Ricardi unam rubiam rosam ad festum Sancti Iohannis Baptiste si petatur pro nobis,
servicium inde debitum et herietta quando acciderint post decessus dictorum
Elizabethe et Iohannis tenencium. Et post mortem ipsius Ricardi predicta Elizabetha
uxor eius ac Iohannes filius eorum inde nobis prefato priori et conventui et
successoribus nostris reddent totum inde integrum redditum prius debitum et
consuetum prout superius percellatum exprimitur, videlicet in toto triginta tres
solidos et octo denarios ad duos anni terminos ibidem equaliter solvendos, sectam
curie et omnia alia servicia inde prius debita et consueta prout consuetum manerii
de Quedesley in se exigit et requirit.*

*Noveritis similiter nos prefatum priorem et conventum attornasse et in loco nostro
posuisse dilectos [f. 3] nobis in Christo Rogerum Porter et Iohannem Chadwell
nostros veros et legittimos attornatos coniunctim et divisim ad intrandum vice et
nomine nostris in omnia et singula supradicta mesuagium, terras et pratum cum
pertinenciis et possessionem ac seisinam inde capiendum, et post huiusmodi
possessionem et seisinam inde captas et habitas, ad deliberandum Rycardo et
Elizabethe ac Iohanni filio eorum plenam et pacificam possessionem et seisinam de
et in omnibus et singulis supradictis mesuagio, terris et prato cum pertinenciis
secundum vim, formam et effectum huius presentis scripti indentati, ratum et gratum
habentes et habituros quicquid dicti attornati nostri vice et nomine nostris fecerint
aut unus eorum fecerit [aut] procuraverit in premissis seu in aliquo premissorum.*

*In cuius rei testimonium uni parti huius scripti nostri indentati penes predictos
Ricardum et Elizabetham ac Iohannem filium eorum remanenti nos prefatus prior et
conventus sigillum nostrum comune ap[p]osuimus, alteri vero parti eiusdem
scripti indentati penes nos prefatum priorem et conventum et successores
nostros remanenti predictus Ricardus et Elizabetha ac Iohannes filius eorum sigilla
sua apposuerunt. Data in domo nostra capitulari Lanthonye predicte primo
die mensis Marcii anno regni Regis Henrici Septimi post conquestum decimo
septimo.*

121. Proxy to fellow canon Walter Keyneloke, fellow canon Thomas Systetur, Mr.
John Aleyn[1] and Nicholas Hillington, B.[Cn. or C.]L., to act for the prior in Ireland.
[f. 3v.] 10 Nov. 1501.

---

[1] B.Cn.L., d. 1506; prebendary of St. Patrick's, Dublin, by 1464, dean there 1465–1506,
chaplain to the king and master of the chancery of Ireland from 1494: Emden, *Biog. Reg.
Oxon. to 1500.*

122. Grant of a corrody to Thomas Hawkyns of Littledean and his wife Joan, sister of Archbishop Henry Dene, as follows:[1]

(a) during Joan's lifetime, every week seven manchet loaves (*myches*), four cheaper *browne lofes* such as are served daily to servants and seven gallons of better ale, and every day a dish of meat or fish such as is served to three brothers of the convent;

(b) [f. 4] for Thomas after Joan's death, an annual render of 40s., victuals and a chamber in the priory like a gentleman servant;

in default of which they may claim 40s. by distraint upon the prior's properties in Glos. 20 Mar. 17 Hen. VII [1502].

123. Lease to John Ballard and to Roger Blake, chaplain and merchant of Drogheda [Louth] (*capell' de Drogheda mercatorem*) of the tithes of corn, hay and thorns (*rampnorum*) [f. 4v.] of Stameen (*Stamenes*),[2] of Newtown,[3] of St. James's and of the land of Furness Abbey[4] held by Richard Canton, which tithes all belong to the rectory of Colp [Meath], for ten years at £5 a year. 20 Oct. 18 Hen. VII [1502].

124. Lease to Richard Hulle of Little Brinsop (*Parva Brynshope*) of a ploughland in Brinsop [Herefs.] with the land, meadow and pasture belonging to it (now held for life by Richard's father Thomas and formerly held by William Crickot) for 40 years at 14s. a year. 1 Oct. 18 Hen. VII [1502].[5]

125. [f. 5] Appointment of Thomas Brownyng, literate (*litteratum*),[6] to hold and supply a grammar school within the priory for canons[7] and boys[8] of the house for life by self or deputy, receiving (a) a tenement built by the prior in Severn Street, with a garden, (b) food and drink, including a loaf and ale every night, (c) a priory gentleman's gown annually and (d) 4 marks a year paid quarterly. He may teach

[1] Amended from **116** above to the corrodians' advantage and backdated.
[2] Containing 180 a. of arable of which 100 a. were sown annually: *Irish Cart. Llanth.* p. 181.
[3] Containing half a ploughland of which 30 a. were sown annually: ibid.
[4] At Beymore and Beybeg, containing 4 ploughlands of which 180 a. were sown annually: ibid. p. 52 n., p. 181.
[5] At the final words *anno suprascripto* the stroke of the last *p* descends into the lower margin and is bound with a scroll bearing the incomplete motto *Timentibus Deum nichil deest nec his*: cf. below, **223** n.
[6] Resident in the parish of St. Mary de Crypt in 1513: Glos. R.O. GBR/B2/1, f. 226.
[7] As required by Pope Benedict in 1339 and by an act of the Augustinian general chapter of 1434: Salter, *Chapt. Augustin.* 83, 229.
[8] e.g. singing boys and servants at mass: cf. below, **289**, **491**; Nicholas Orme, *Education in the West of England 1066–1548* (Exeter, 1976), 8.

other scholars within the priory and receive their fees[1] provided that they do no harm
while staying there. 12 Sept. 1502.

*Hec indentura facta duodecimo die mensis Septembris anno regni Regis Henrici
Septimi post conquestum decimo octavo inter Dominum Edmundum priorem domus
et ecclesie Beate Marie de Lanthonia iuxta Gloucestriam et eiusdem loci conventum
ex parte una et Thomam Brownyng litteratum ex parte altera testatur quod inter
partes predictas talis conveniencia facta est prout sequitur, videlicet quod dictus
Thomas in propria persona sua infra prioratum Lanthonie predictum in quodam
loco conveniente sibi per dictos priorem et conventum assignato a die Sancti
Michaelis Archangeli proxime futura post datam presencium durante vita sua
naturali dum potens sit in corpore, et si ad impotenciam corporis sui devenerit tunc
per suum deputatum in sciencia grammaticali sufficienter imbutum, scolam
grammaticalem tenebit et stupabit et omnes et singulos canonicos et pueros in
eodem existentes prioratus illius ad scolam illam venientes libenter et diligenter in
predicta sciencia grammaticali meliori modo quo poterit secundum scire suum
fideliter instruet, informabit et congruis temporibus in dies docebit.*

*Capiendo et habendo pro sua doctrina et diligenti labore suo in dicta sciencia sic
exercendis[2] a dictis priore et conventu annuatim durante termino predicto unum
tenementum cum gardino adiacente pro manso suo in quodam vico Gloucestrie
vocato 'Severnstrete' modo sibi limitatum et assignatum, de costis et expensis
ipsorum prioris et conventus edificatum et reparatum ac insuper reparandum.*

*Et ulterius idem Thomas in dies habebit infra prioratum predictum esculenta et
poculenta sibi congrua, honesta et sufficiencia, et erga noctem singulis diebus pro
sua liberata unum panem cum conveniente porcione cervisie,[3] et annuatim unam
togam de secta generosorum prioris Lanthonie qui pro tempore fuerit sicut ipsum
priorem aliis generosis pro liberatura sua dare et distribuere contigerit, et quatuor
marcas legalis monete Anglie ad quatuor anni terminos usuales, videlicet ad festa[4]
Nativitatis Domini, Annunciacionis Beate Marie, Nativitatis Sancti Iohannis
Baptiste et Sancti Michelis Archangeli per equales porciones sibi fideliter solvendas
durante predicto termino.*

*Et bene licebit prefato Thome recipere et docere infra prioratum predictum in loco
sibi assignato alios scolares tot quot ad se venire contigerit, ad usum et ad opus
suum proprium ab ipsis recipiendo scolagium prout inter ipsos concordatum fuerit,*

---

[1] This clause allowed the priory's monastic grammar school to break the monopoly of
public education enjoyed by its secular grammar school in Gloucester, a monopoly which the
priors defended at law in 1286–9, 1380–1410 and 1513: ibid. 57–64. From 1373 until some
time before 1535 the latter school occupied a house at no. 6a Longsmith Street which the
priors enlarged in 1396 and let with the mastership: P.R.O. C 115/73, f. 32 (30); Reg.
Brockworth, f. 78; Reg. Chirton, ff. 62, 108v., 187; *Glouc. Rental 1455*, 22. The priory also
gave a site in 1529 for the Crypt Grammar School, which opened in 1539: Austin, *Crypt
School*, 27–8.
[2] MS. *exercendum.*
[3] MS. *cervicie.*
[4] MS. *festum.*

sine aliqua contradiccione dictorum prioris et conventus et successorum suorum durante termino predicto, sic quod ipsi scolares seculares nullum dampnum, preiudicium nec detrimentum prioratui predicto facient nec fieri procurabunt quoquo modo dum fuerint ibidem residentes et sobrie et honeste viventes.

Et ad omnes et singulas istas convenciones ex parte ipsius Thome bene et fideliter observandum idem Thomas coram priore et conventu suprascriptis[1] corporale prestitit sacrum.[2] In cuius rei testimonium uni parti huius indenture penes prefatum Thomam remanenti nos prefatus prior et conventus sigillum nostrum[3] commune apposuimus, alteri vero parti eiusdem indenture penes prefatum priorem et conventum et successores suos remanenti ego predictus Thomas sigillum meum apposui. Data in domo nostra capitulari Lanthonie predicte die et anno suprascriptis.

126. Lease to John Rollys of Haresfield (*Harsfeld*) and his sons Thomas and William [f. 5v.] of property there for 60 years at £13 9s. 8½d. a year as follows.[4]

(a) Tithes of corn, flax, hemp, pasturage and fruit belonging to the rectory (except in Haresfield park[5]) at £9 6s. 8d.

(b) Tithes of hay similarly (except in Haresfield park) at 12s.

(c) Haresfield manor[6] with its demesne land, meadow and pasture (including 3 a. of meadow at *Rixbrugge* and 3 a. of meadow in *Moretonnes Mede*[7]) at £3.

(d) A messuage and 14 a. 3 r. of land (formerly held by John Scotte[8] and lately by Richard Holder) at 11s. for rent and 0½d. for herring-silver.[9]

The lessees will pay a heriot of 3s. 4d. and other customary services on a death, and at least one of them will live on the estate. The prior will maintain the manorial buildings. The lessees will collect rent from the prior's tenants,[10] [f. 6] rendering annual accounts and receiving annually a gown or an allowance of 6s. 8d. They will also have five wagon-loads a year of bundled fuel from *Lez Scarre* in the prior's

---

[1] MS. *suprascripta.*

[2] MS. *sacrarium.*

[3] MS. *nostre.*

[4] John, Thomas and William Rowlys still lived in Haresfield in 1522 possessing goods valued at respectively £14, £8 and nil: *Military Survey of Glos. 1522*, 186. Thomas (d. 1549) renewed the lease in 1536 and purchased (c) and (d) from the Crown in 1543, his family holding them with the tithes of the rectory until 1606: *Glevensis*, xxxiii. 55; *V.C.H. Glos.* x. 192, 194; Hockaday Abs. ccxxxiii, 1543.

[5] Tithes of pasturage in the park were held in 1539 by John Partridge and John Sanford for 6s. 8d. a year; *Glevensis*, xxxiii. 55. The park was hunted from Parkend Lodge at SO 780105: *V.C.H. Glos.* x. 189–90.

[6] Comprising a house and 120 a.: *V.C.H. Glos.* x. 192.

[7] Strips of common meadow at Epney near Moreton Valence including 1½ a. in Tween Dyke around SO 770107: P.R.O. C 115/77, s. ii no. 82.

[8] Probably including Scott's Acre, so called in 1816, at SO 818098 W. of The College: *Glevensis*, xxxiii. 48, 54.

[9] In lieu of herrings for the priory: *O.E.D.*

[10] Seven tenants rendering a total of £4 12s. 10¼d. in 1539: *Glevensis*, xxxiii. 54.

wood.[1] The Nativity of St. John the Baptist 18 Hen. VII [24 June 1503].

127. Presentation of John Hoore, chaplain, to the vicarage of Canon Frome [Herefs.] vacant by the resignation of Roger Home. 9 Mar. 1502[/3].

128. Letter of fraternity to Richard and Elizabeth Chapman. 22 Mar. 1502[/3].

Edmundus permissione divina prior monasterii sive prioratus Lanthonie iuxta Gloucestriam et eiusdem loci conventus Ricardo Chapman et Elizabethe consorti sue salutem in omnium Salvatore et per oracionum suffragia celestium consequi premia gaudiorum.[2] Quamvis ex caritate debita teneamur devote supplicacionis instancia divine pietatis aures pulsare iugiter pro universali salute, specialius tamen illis communicare [f. 6v.] *tenemur et intendimus quecumque spiritualia bona de quorum devocione erga nos et prioratum nostrum predictum[3] certa fide et experiencia didicimus. Nos igitur unanimi voluntate et concensu libentissime vobis concedimus in vita vestra pariter et in morte plenam participacionem omnium meritorum et suffragiorum nostrorum que per nos operari dignabitur clemencia Salvatoris tam in missis, horis, oracionibus, vigiliis, abstinenciis, disciplinis, elemosinis et ieiuniis quam hospitalitatibus ac quibuscumque aliis beneficiis in ecclesia nostra que fient imperpetuum, ut multiplici fructu suffragiorum suffulti celerius ac felicius Christo annuente eternam beatitudinem mereamini adipisci. Data in domo nostra capitulari Lanthonie predicte sub sigillo nostro communi vicesimo secundo die mensis Marcii anno Domini millesimo quingentesimo secundo.*

129. Presentation of John Drury, chaplain, to the vicarage of Windrush (*Wynryche*) vacant by the resignation of William Smythe. 1 Apr. 1504.

130. Proxy to William Yate vicar of Marden [Wilts.] and Roger Bacheler to act for the church of Chirton [Wilts.]. 20 Apr. 1504.

Pateat universis per presentes quod nos Dominus Edmundus, prior monasterii sive prioratus Lanthonie iuxta Gloucestriam ordinis Sancti Augustini Wigorniensis diocesis, et eiusdem loci conventus, ecclesiam parochialem de Chirinton Saru' diocesis in proprios usus nostros canonice optinentes, in omnibus causis et negociis coram quibuscumque iudicibus, ordinariis, delegatis, subdelegatis et eorum commissariis quibuscumque motis vel movendis nos aut dictum prioratum nostrum et ecclesiam nostram predictam qualitercumque tangentibus, quociens nos abesse vel adesse contigerit, dilectos nobis in Christo Willelmum Yate, vicarium de Mareden, et Rogerum Bacheler coniunctim et divisim et quemlibet ipsorum in solidum et per se, ita quod non sit melior condicio occupantis sed quod unus eorum

---

[1] Now Halliday's wood around SO 833089, formerly Harescombe Scar: C. & J. Greenwood, *Map of Glos.* (1824); P.R.O. C 115/77, s. ii no. 50.

[2] MS. *gaudeorum.*

[3] The MS. has here the redundant words *vos habere.*

inceperit alius prosequi valeat mediare pariter et finire, nostros et predicti prioratus nostri facimus et constituimus procuratores, negociorum gestores et nuncios speciales per presentes, dantes et concedentes eisdem et cuilibet[1] eorum, per se et in solidum, potestatem generalem et mandatum speciale nomine nostro et dicti prioratus nostri agendi et defendendi, [tam] de calumpnia quam de veritate dicendi ac quolibet alio modo licito in animas nostras iurandi, status nostri et dicti prioratus nostri reformacionem, in integrum restitucionem, dampna, expensas et interesse ac sequestrorum relaxacionem petendi [et] recipiendi, crimina et defectus obiciendi et obiectis respondendi, necnon in visitacionibus quorumcumque episcoporum seu aliorum prelatorum ac in [f. 7] congregacionibus et convocacionibus cleri et sinodis comperendi et interessendi, provocandi et appellandi, provocacionum et appellacionum causas prosequendi, alium procuratorem vel procuratores loco suo substituendi, substitutum[2] vel substitutos per eosdem vel eorum aliquem revocandi procuratorisque officium in se reassumendi quociens ipsis vel eorum alicui videbitur expedire, ac omnia alia et singula faciendi que in premissis vel circa ea necessaria fuerint vel oportuna et que per veros et legittimos procuratores poterunt exerceri, eciam si mandatum exigant speciale.

Pro eisdem vero procuratoribus nostris et ipsorum aliquo ac quocumque substituendo per ipsos vel eorum aliquem rem ratam haberi et iudicatum solvi omnibus quorum interest vel poterit interesse promittimus et cauciones exponimus sub dicti prioratus nostri rerum omnium ypotheca. In cuius rei testimonium sigillum nostrum commune ad causas fecimus hiis apponi. Date in domo nostra capitulari Lanthonie predicte vicesimo die mensis Aprilis anno Domini millesimo quingentesimo quarto.

131. Proxy to John William and Thomas Philipp, chaplains, to act for the church of Caldicot (*Caldecote*) [Mon.]. 20 Apr. 1504. [Abstract in MS.; cf. **130**]

132. Title of Dudstone hospital[3] granted to Robert James, clerk, in the form of a letter to the bishop of Hereford presenting James for ordination. 12 May 1504.

Copia tituli concessi Roberto James clerico.

Reverendo in Christo patri ac domino Adriano [de Castello] dei gracia Herfordensi episcopo seu cuicumque alteri antistiti graciam sedis apostolice ac execucionem sui officii obtinenti ipsorumve seu alicuius eorundem vicario in spiritualibus generali vestri si placet humiles et devoti prior monasterii sive prioratus Lanthonie iuxta Gloucestriam ordinis Sancti Augustini Wigorniensis diocesis et eiusdem loci conventus obedienciam et reverenciam tanto patri debitas cum honore. Paternitati[4] vestre Reverendum Robertum James, clericum, latorem presencium per has litteras patentes ad titulum domus nostre de Duddeston

---

[1] MS. *cuiuslibet.*
[2] MS. *substitutos.*
[3] Otherwise called St. Mary Magdalen's hospital, in London Road, Gloucester: *V.C.H. Glos.* ii. 122; iv. 353–4.
[4] MS. *Paternitate.*

presentamus, rogantes attencius quatinus prefatum Robertum ad omnes sacros ordines ad eundem titulum dignemini misericorditer promovere. In cuius rei testimonium sigillum nostrum commune presentibus est appositum. Date in domo nostra capitulari Lanthonie predicte duodecimo die mensis Maii anno Domini millesimo quingentesimo quarto.

133. [f. 7v.] Presentation[1] of William Hareberd, literate (*litteratum*),[2] to the rectory of Cusop (*Cuyshope*) [Herefs.] vacant by the death of William Thomas. The presentation is made by the prior and convent of Llanthony-by-Gloucester as proprietors, by consent of interested parties, of the priory of [Llanthony] St. John in Wales and thereby as patrons[3] of the church or free chapel of Cusop. 28 Oct. 1504.

134. Presentation of Thomas Gronow[4] to the rectory of Colesbourne (*Collesburne*) vacant by the death of Roger Wever. 29 Jan. 1504[/5].

135. Lease to William Lewson, *milner* of Mordiford [Herefs.], and his wife Alice of a watermill[5] there lately held by Thomas Garson, with the buildings, land and watercourse belonging to it, for 30 years at 8s. a year. The lessees will make suit to the prior's court [f. 8] at Fawley (*Falley*) [then in Fownhope, now in Brockhampton, Herefs.] and will scour the watercourse and otherwise maintain the property, especially the common way called *Lez Botte*[6] over which water runs to the mill (*super quam aqua currit ad dictum molendinum*). 4 Aug. 18 Hen. VII [1503].

136. Bond of John Bromyche of Tewkesbury and William Leuson in £5 to perform the covenants of the above lease. 4 Aug. 18 Hen. VII [1503].

137. Letter of fraternity to Richard Alexander and his wife Isabel.[7] 8 Sept. 1505. [Abstract in MS.; cf. **128**]

---

[1] The initial letter of the initial word *Reverendo* (addressing the bishop of Hereford) has a loop extending into the left margin and containing a human face.

[2] Instituted 26 Mar. 1505 through his proctor Richard Hyeward, chaplain: *Reg. Mayew*, 273.

[3] Cusop church was given to the priory by Ranulph de Baskerville before 1141 and allocated to Llanthony in Wales in 1205: P.R.O. C 115/75, f. 214 no. 22; f. 247v. no. 11. The claim to patronage reflects the legal challenge described in **215** below.

[4] d. by 1530; B.A., B.C.L., rector of Colesbourne 1505–8, rector of Stratton from 1508, subdean of Chichester from 1513 and registrar of the abbot of Gloucester in 1527: Emden, *Biog. Reg. Oxon. to 1500*; below, **181**.

[5] The priory acquired two mills here before 1199: Dugdale, *Mon.* vi. 137. The mill site, on the south side of the village in Fownhope parish (below, **337**), is evidently that still extant at SO 571372, fed by a leat from a weir on the Pentaloe Brook at SO 577373.

[6] Either the road to Woolhope, which crosses the leat at SO 575372, or a lower track at SO 573372.

[7] A Richard Alexaunder, worth £50 in goods, was the richest householder in Charlton Kings in 1522: *Military Survey of Glos. 1522*, 46.

138. [f. 8v.] Presentation of Edward Finche, M.A., chaplain,[1] to the vicarage of Great Barrington (*Bernynton Magna*) vacant by the death of Richard Alen. 10 Feb. 1505[/6].

139. Title (for the purpose of ordination) granted to John Smythe. 10 May 1505. [Abstract in MS.; cf. **132**]

140. Presentation of Richard Gowre, chaplain, to the vicarage of Caldicot [Mon.] vacant by the death of William Lewys. 1 Sept. 1505.

141. Title (for the purpose of ordination) granted to Henry Locoke, clerk. 5 Sept. 1505. [Abstract in MS.; cf. **132**]

142. [f. 9] Proxy to Walter Myll, vicar of Kington [Herefs.],[2] and John Chadwell, clerk, to exercise testamentary jurisdiction over the estates of those deceased in the parish of Kington[3] after 14 Aug. 1490. 18 July 1505.

Frater Edmundus, permissione divina prior monasterii sive prioratus Lanthonie iuxta Gloucestriam ordinis Sancti Augustini Wigorniensis diocesis et eiusdem loci conventus, iurisdiccionem specialem ordinariam[4] et immediatam in ecclesia parochiali de Kyngton Herefordiensis diocesis et tota eiusdem parochia nobis et prioratui nostro canonice appropriatis optinentes et exercentes [ab] antiquo, dilectis nobis in Christo Domino Waltero Myll, perpetuo vicario ecclesie parochialis de Kyngton predicte, et Iohanni Chadwell clerico salutem in sinceris amplex[ion]ibus Salvatoris. Ad audiendum compotus et ratiocinia omnium testamentorum quorumcumque decedencium ac administratorum bonorum ab intestato defunctorum in parochia predicta decedencium a quartodecimo die mensis Augusti anno Domini millesimo quadringentesimo nonagesimo, ac eosdem executores et administratores ab officiis, oneribus et administracionibus suis huiusmodi acquietandum et liberandum, ipsisque litteras testomoniales super hoc faciendum, ac in casu quo male seu indebite administraverint canonice puniendum, omniaque alia et singula faciendum et expediendum que in premissis aut alias dictam nostram iurisdiccionem concernencia pertinent et incumbent, vobis committimus vices nostras cum

---

[1] d. 1539; D.M. in 1518, vicar of Great Barrington 1506–9, prebendary of Salisbury 1514–39, prebendary of Chichester 1518–36, rector of Ross-on-Wye (Herefs.) 1521–39, archdeacon of Wilts. 1522–39, prebendary of St. Stephen's chapel, Westminster, 1522–30 and physician to Cardinal Wolsey 1528: Emden, *Biog. Reg. Oxon. to 1500*; below, **187**.

[2] d. 1506; vicar of Kington 1484–1506 and vicar of Mordiford (Herefs.) at his death: *Reg. Myllyng*, 200; *Reg. Mayew*, 274; below, **144**.

[3] Kington church with its chapels of Huntington and Brilley (Herefs.) and Michaelchurch-on-Arrow (Radnors.) was given to the priory by John Bohun as lord of Huntington in 1327–8 and appropriated in 1349: P.R.O. C 115/75, s. xix nos. 1–6, 14; *Charters and Records of Hereford Cathedral*, ed. W. W. Capes (Hereford, 1908), 217–19. The privilege of proving wills, which reflects the status of Huntington as a marcher lordship (cf. 27 Hen. VIII c. 26, s. 12) reverted to the bishop in 1539 under the Dissolution Act: 31 Hen. VIII c. 13, s. 23.

[4] MS. *ordinare.*

cuiuslibet cohercionis canonice potestate; ratum et gratum habituri quicquid iidem Dominus Walterus Myll et Iohannes Chadwell nomine nostro fecerint aut unus eorum fecerit in premissis. Data in domo nostra capitulari sub sigillo nostro communi decimo octavo die mensis Iulii anno Domini millesimo quingentesimo quinto.

143. Release by Joan Hawkyns of Littledean, widow, to Robert Coofe chaplain, John Chadwell, Richard Pere and their heirs of title to a tenement and curtilage between the bridges of Gloucester which was lately granted to her for life by John Carwent.[1] St. Hilary [13 Jan., year omitted].

144. [f. 9v.] Presentation of John Batty, chaplain,[2] to the vicarage of Kington [Herefs.] vacant by the death of Walter Myll.[3] 12 Oct. 1506.

145. Lease to John Stephens alias Yeong of Turkdean, his wife Isabel and their son John Yeong[4] of the manor of Turkdean[5] with a dovecot, houses, land, meadow and pasture belonging to it for 30 years at 30s. a year. The lessees will

    (a) maintain the property and its walls, ditches and hedges, except that the prior will find shingles and pegs (*assulas et clavos assulinos*) for the dovecot and other buildings, and

    (b) feed the priory's steward or understeward, their two servants and their three horses twice a year when they come to hold court. 20 Oct. 19 Hen. VII [1503].

146. [f. 10] Title (for the purpose of ordination) granted to Robert Hale, clerk.[6] 22 Oct. 1506. [Abstract in MS.; cf. **132**]

147. Lease to James Smyth, chaplain, of

    (a) the chapel of Tillington (*Tyllynton*) [in Burghill, Herefs.] and the land, tenements, meadow and pasture belonging to it and

    (b) the pasturage of the churchyard of Burghill (*Borowghyll*)

for life at 20s. a year. He or his deputy will celebrate mass in the chapel daily. 15 Dec. 1506.

---

[1] Above, **117**.

[2] Of Nevern (Pemb.), vicar of Kington 1506–13 and of Llanafanfawr (Brec.) from 1513: below, **281**. He or a namesake was vicar of Weobley (Herefs.) in 1511: below, **228**, **242**.

[3] Vicar since 1484: *Reg. Myllyng*, 200.

[4] A John Yong, worth £16 in goods, still lived in Turkdean in 1522: *Military Survey of Glos. 1522*, 119.

[5] Nether Turkdean or Lower Dean manor, which was relet to William Walter in 1534. The manor house retains a former chamber block, extending west from the centre of the east front, which has Tudor windows and a heavily beamed ceiling of about this time: *V.C.H. Glos.* ix. 223–4.

[6] Vicar of Wotton-under-Edge in 1532: Hockaday Abs. xxv, 1532 subsidy.

148. [f. 10v.] Proxy to Masters Henry Martyn commissary,[1] John Walker clerk, Roger Boghan and Richard Welynton to act for the priory's churches in the diocese of Hereford. 10 Mar. 1506[/7].

[ff. 11–16 were in the middle of a quire and are lost. Entries **149–60** and part of **161** are supplied from the index in the MS.]

149. [f. 11] Grant of a yearly pension to Joan Hawkyns of Littledean.

150. Lease to William Malet of property at Alvington. (*Alvynton*: *copia indenture Willelmi Malet pro firma ibidem.*)

151. [f. 12] Stock at Alvington delivered by indenture to the above lessee.

152. Indenture with Thomas Hays of Hereford.

153. [f. 13] Lease to John Aleyn[2] of the tithes of Longford and Wotton by Gloucester.[3] (*Langford et Wotton iuxta Gloucestriam*: *copia indenture Iohannis Aleyn pro decimis ibidem.*)

154. Indenture with Humphrey Bleke of Stanton Lacy, Salop.

155. [f. 14] Indenture with Hugh Hyggones, priest of Orcop, Herefs.[4]

156. Indenture with John Bakar of Weobley, Herefs.

157. [f. 15] Indenture with (*Domini*) Hugh Merycke of Ballingham (*Balyniam*), Herefs.[5]

---

[1] d. 1524; B.Cn. & C.L., prebendary of Hereford 1504–24, commissary of the diocese *c.* 1507–11 and vicar general 1516, residentiary canon 1511–24, archdeacon of Shropshire 1516–24 and incumbent of many parochial benefices including a rectory in the prior's gift at Llanwarne 1520–4: Emden, *Biog. Reg. Oxon. to 1500*; *Reg. Mayew*, 82, 102, 279; below, **374**.

[2] d. 1524; tanner, sheriff of Gloucester 1503 and alderman from 1517, resident in St. John's parish: *V.C.H. Glos.* iv. 53, 375; Fosbrooke, *Glouc.* 208: P.R.O. PROB 11/21, f. 129v. copied in Hockaday Abs. ccxv, 1524.

[3] For 56s. 8d. a year, as Edward Alen still held them in 1535: *Valor Eccl.* (Rec. Com.), ii. 424.

[4] Probably a lease of a portion of tithes for 14s. 4d. a year, in the same form as **113** above and signifying Hyggones's appointment to the cure of a dependent chapel or church given to the priory by Ranulph de Baskerville before 1141: *Valor Eccl.* (Rec. Com.), ii. 426; P.R.O. C 115/75, f. 214 no. 22.

[5] A lease of the greater and lesser tithes, oblations and revenues of Ballingham rectory for life at 27s. 8d. a year, dated Michaelmas 22 Hen. VII (1507). Merycke, a clerk, still held the lease in 1535 and 1546: *Valor Eccl.* (Rec. Com.), ii. 426; *L. & P. Hen. VIII*, xxi (1), p. 357.

158–9. Two quittances to the abbot of Kingswood.

160. Indenture with Richard Lynet of Prestbury (*Presbury*).

161. [f. 16] Citation to a visitation of the priory by Thomas Alcock, D.Cn. [& C.]L.,[1] vicar general of Silvestro [de' Gigli] bishop of Worcester, [f. 17] on Wednesday [28 June] the eve of St. Peter. Given under the prior of Worcester's seal at Worcester, 13 May 1503.

162. [f. 17v.] Certificate acknowledging that the above was received on 7 June. 18 June 1503.

163. Lease to William Haukyns[2] of Sher[r]in[g]ton[3] in Pembridge (Herefs.) and to Thomas Fletcher of Weobley of property at Weobley (Herefs.), namely
   (a) the manor with demesne meadow and pasture, rents and services of free and customary tenants, view of frankpledge, courts and court fines and the profits of the manor and glebe and
   (b) the rectory with tithes of corn and hay
for 21 years, rendering annually £18, four seams [i. e. packhorse loads] of wheat, two seams of oats [f. 18] and straw for strewing the church. The lessees will maintain the *Canon Barne* and the messuage north of it. 10 Apr. [year omitted].

164. Manumission of Robert Bysshoppe, neif of Hempsted, and his issue. 21 Sept. 1506.

Universis pateat per presentes quod nos Edmundus, prior ecclesie Beate Marie Lanthonie iuxta Gloucestriam, et eiusdem loci conventus manumisimus et ab omni iugo servitudinis et nativitatis quantum ad nos et successores nostros attinet absolvimus atque liberum dimisimus Robertum Bysshoppe, nativum nostrum pertinentem manerio nostro de Heyhamstyd, cum tota sequela sua, ita quod nec nos [nec] successores nostri erga predictum Robertum et eius sequelam, ut prefertur, aliquam calumpniam et demandam racione nativitatis predicte exigere seu vendicare poterunt, [f. 18v.] sed abinde sumus exclusi per presentes imperpetuum. In cuius rei testimonium sigillum nostrum commune presentibus est appositum. Data in domo nostra capitulari Lanthonie predicte 21 die mensis Septembris anno regni regis Henrici Septimi vicesimo secundo.

165. Citation to a visitation of the priory by Silvestro [de' Gigli] bishop of

---

[1] d. 1527; graduate of Bologna, archdeacon of Worcester 1483–after 1518, archdeacon of Ely 1496–1527, chancellor of Worcester 1503–8, prebendary of Hereford until 1523, master of Jesus College, Cambridge 1515–16: J. & J. A. Venn, *Alumni Cantabrigienses to 1751*, i (Cambridge, 1922), 12, corrected by Le Neve, *Fasti 1300–1541, Monastic Cathedrals*; op. cit., *Hereford.*
[2] Esq., d. 1530: *Visit. Herefs. 1569*, 40; *Hereford Probates 1407–1581*, 244.
[3] Sherrington Manor at SO 375546.

Worcester or his commissary on Thursday 22 Apr. 1507. Worcester palace, 27 Feb. 1506[/7].

Silvester, permissione divina Wigorniensis episcopus, dilectis nobis in Christo priori et conventui domus sive prioratus Lanthonie iuxta Gloucestriam nostre diocesis salutem, graciam et benediccionem. Cura regiminis suscepti nos sollicitat pariter et compellit ut circa utilitatem subditorum nostrorum in hiis precipue per que animarum saluti et locorum indempnitati consulitur solicite intendamus. Quapropter vos et monasterium sive prioratum vestrum tam in capite quam in membris ad viciorum extirpacionem, morum reformacionem et divini cultus augmentum, annuente Domino, actualiter visitare intendimus.

Vos igitur, domine prior predicte, tenore presencium premunimus ac peremptorie citamus, et per vos omnes et singulos confratres et concanonicos dicte domus sive prioratus vestri presentes, et alios si qui fuerint absentes qui nostre visitacioni huiusmodi tenentur interesse de iure seu consuetudine citari volumus et mandamus quod compareatis et compareant coram nobis aut nostro in hac parte commissario in domo capitulari prioratus vestri predicti die Iovis videlicet 22 die mensis Aprilis proxime iam futuri cum continuacione et prorogacione dierum tunc sequencium si oporteat, visitacionem nostram predictam iuxta iuris exigenciam et preteriti temporis morem debite et legittime subituri, vosque, domine prior predicte, titulum officii vestri necnon litteras et munimenta quecumque dictam domum sive prioratum vestrum ac ecclesias et beneficia eidem pertinencia et concernencia ibidem exhibituri et ostensuri, vos insuper, domine prior antedicte, ac officiarii et ministri dicti prioratus vestri compotum administracionis vestre et suorum officiorum ac statum dicti domus exhibituri, veritatemque quam noveritis et quilibet eorum noverit adtunc a vobis et eis inquirendo visitacionem nostram concernentem dicturi et deposituri, ulteriusque facturi et recepturi coniunctim et divisim quod huiusmodi visitacionis nostre qualitas et natura in se exigunt et requirunt. Vobis eciam, prefate domine prior, inhibemus et per vos ceteris officiariis et ministris dicti prioratus vestri inhiberi volumus et mandamus ne quicquam in preiudicium visitacionis nostre predicte attemptetis seu attemptent, faciatisve aut faciant aliqualiter attemptari.

De diebus vero recepcionis presencium ac de omni eo quod feceritis in premissis nos aut nostrum in hac parte commissarium dicta die et loco una cum omnibus nominibus et cognominibus omnium et singulorum confratrum et concanonicorum vestrorum citatorum distincte et aperte certificetis litteris patentibus autentice sigillatis hunc tenorem habencium. Data sub [f. 19] sigillo nostro in palacio nostro Wigornie penultimo die mensis Februarii anno Domini millesimo quingentesimo sexto et nostre consecracionis anno octavo.

166. Certificate acknowledging that the above was received on 4 Mar. 21 Apr. 1507.

Reverendo in Christo patri ac domino Domino Silvestro dei gracia Wigorniensi episcopo vestrove in hac parte commissario seu commissariis quibuscumque suus humilis et devotus frater Edmundus prior monasterii sive prioratus Lanthonie iuxta Gloucestriam ordinis Sancti Augustini dicte vestre diocesis obedienciam et reverenciam tanto patri debitas cum honore. Mandatum vestrum reverendum infrascriptum quarto die mensis Marcii proximi iam elapsi cum ea quam decuit

*reverencia recepi cuius tenor sequitur et est talis: Silvester permissione divina etc.,
ut supra. Cui quidem mandato vestro reverendo secundum vim, formam et effectum
eiusdem parui et parebo in omnibus contentaque in eodem perfeci iuxta vires.
Nomina vero et cognomina concanonicorum et confratrum meorum citatorum una
cum plenaria designacione officiorum suorum presens scedula continet hiis annexa.[1]
Data sub sigillo meo vicesimo primo die instantis mensis Aprilis anno Domini
millesimo quingentesimo septimo.*

167. Lease to William Stevyns, cordwainer, and his wife Edith of a shop[2] by All
Saints' church and two gardens[3] in Bell (*Travey*) Lane, Gloucester. 23 Mar. 1507.

*This indenture made the 23 day of Marche in the yere of the regne of King Henry the
VII the 22 betwene Edmund Forest prior of the howse & monastery of Lanthony
besyde Gloucester and the covent of the same on the oone partie and William
Stevyns, corveser, and Edyth hys wyffe of the seyd towne of Gloucester on the othir
partie witnesseth that the sayd prior and covent of the same hows have putt & to
ferme lett to the sayd William & to Edyth his wyffe, and to eyther of them lengyst
lyvyng, on shoppe joynyng to the church wall of Alhallous late in the holdyng of
John[4] Williams, with 2 gardens lying in Travey Lane late in the holding of Garett
Vannez[5] lying next to a tenement of the sayd William's[6] in the seyd lane, for the terme
of 40 yere then next after the date of this indenture. To have & to hold the seyd
shoppe with the sayd gardens to the seyd William & Edyth his wyffe during the terme
of 40 yere aforeseyd and to eyther of them lengist levyng, paying yerely to the*

[1] Not annexed to the registered copy.
[2] The shop, which Stevyns still held in 1535, stood 50 ft. S. of the high cross in front of the
present no. 2 Southgate Street and flanked the S. chancel wall of All Saints' church,
projecting into the street at the SE. corner: Glos. R.O. GBR/J5/4; P.R.O. C 115/73, f. 26 (24)
no. 50; *Glouc. Rental 1455*, 4; plan of the demolished church, *Trans. B.G.A.S.* xix. 144 pl. iv.
In 1228 × 40 it measured 15 ft. 3in. from E. to W. and 7 ft. 7 in. from N. to S.: P.R.O. C
115/75, f. 45v. no. 76, f. 96v. = C115/81, ff. 6, 24 = C115/84, ff. 36–7 nos. 111, 114. By 1509
it also included an encroachment into the street for which the prior paid the borough 12d. a
year: Glos. R.O. GBR/J5/3. It was demolished in 1750–1 to widen the highway and enlarge
the tolsey: Gloucester Improvement Act, 23 Geo. II, c. 15; *V.C.H. Glos.* iv. 249.
[3] The two gardens, which Stevyns still held in 1535, comprised the fifth plot from the W. on
the S. side of Bell Lane and a plot adjacent on the S. extending to Mary Lane. A tenement
built in the N. plot by Thomas Gildeford before 1442, when both were in dispute, was
evidently removed in the mean time when the priory repossessed them: Glos. R.O. GBR/J5/4;
P.R.O. C 115/73, ff. 27–30 (25–8) nos. 54, 60; *Glouc. Rental 1455*, 18b.
[4] Marginal gloss: *Philippe & Mathewe.*
[5] Gerard van Eck (d. 1506), clothier, sheriff 1497 and mayor 1499 and 1505, who lived
nearby: *L. & P. Hen. VIII*, i (1), p. 239; P.R.O. PROB 11/15, f. 89, copied in Hockaday Abs.
ccxvi, 1506; Glos. R.O. GBR/J5/3.
[6] Probably Stevyns' dwelling, since he lived in the parish of St. Mary de Crypt: Glos. R.O.
GBR/B2/1, f. 226. He there succeeded Thomas Stephens, M.P. for Gloucester 1420, 1422–3,
1427–32 and 1442, who in 1442 held tenements in the fourth and sixth plots on the S. side of
Bell Lane with much other property in the town: *Hist. of Parl., Biographies 1439–1509*;
Glouc. Rental 1455, passim.

seyd prior & his successors during the sayd terme 11s. 8d. of lawfull money of
Englond to be paid quarterly at 4 fests of the yere, that is to say at the fest of the
Annunciation of Our Lady next aftur the date of these indentures 2s. 11d. [f. 19v.]
and at the feste of Seint John the Baptist next aftur 2s. 11d.,[1] *at the feste of Seint*
Michaell tharchangell 2s. 11d. and at the fest of Crystmas 2s. 11d. And yff it so
happe the sayd rent of 11s. 8d. or eny parte thereof be unpaid a month aftur eny of
thes sayd fests in parte or in the hoole then it shall be lawful to the sayd prior and
his successors to reentre into the sayd shoppe and gardens and to make new graunts
where plesyth them best. Furthermore the sayd William & Edyth byndyth them by
these present indentures to keep al manner off reparacions of & uppon the sayd
shoppe and gardens uppon there own propur cost and charge during the sayd terme,
excepte grosse timbur as sills and bemys the wiche the seyd prioure and his
successors shall deliver or cause to be delyveryd as ofte and as requirith. In
witnesse wherof the parties aforesayd enterchangeabully have sett to ther sealis the
day and yere aforesayd. And furthermore the sayd William and Edyth shall leve the
seyd shoppe and gardens at the end of the sayd terme in as good state as they
fownde it.

168. Lease to John Scherman and Thomas Hanscombe of Lyndeford watermill[2] in
Henlow [Beds.] for 30 years at 53s. 4d. a year. The lessees will maintain:

  (a) the walling and roofing of the millhouse with battens, pegs, stone tiles
(*findulis, clavis assulinis, petris tegul'*) and *lez crestis*,

  (b) the millstones and

  (c) the *coggewhelis & waturwhiles* with brass and ironwork and everything
necessary for the machinery (*goyngwarke*) and *waterwarke*.

  [f. 20] The prior will find and carry trees for the great timbers and small tree
stocks for the *waterbordis* and will pay for *stobullingwarke*[3] carpentry but not for
sawingwarke. In case of default he may distrain upon the lessees' cattle. 26 Apr.
1507.

169. Appointment of William Grene alias Chymemaker[4] to maintain a clock and
bells in the priory. 8 July 1507.[5]

This indenture made the 8 day of Julii in the yere of the regne of Kyng Henry the VII
the 22 betwene Edmund Forest prior of the howse and [church] of Lanthony besyde
Gloucester on the oon partie and William Grene otherwise callid William
Chymemaker of the seyd towne of Gloucester on the other partie witnessith by these

---

[1] MS. *2s. 6d.*

[2] One of three mills on the Ivel in Henlow and one of two there which belonged to the
priory: *V.C.H. Beds.* ii. 283.

[3] *O.E.D.* gives *stobulling* or *stubbling* in the sense 'clearing land of stubble'. Here it is
probably used for *scappling*, 'squaring with the axe'.

[4] Resident in St. John's parish: Glos. R.O. GBR/B2/1, f. 226.

[5] Compare the abbot of Gloucester's appointment of a blacksmith to maintain a chime on
eight bells in 1525, printed in *Hist. & Cart. Mon. Glouc.* (Rolls Ser.), iii, pp. cx–cxi.

present indenturis that the seyd William have promised and graunted unto the sayd prior & covent of the same to keep all manner of reparacions of and uppon the chyme and clocke on myn owne propur cost and charge to the seyd prior and monasteri pertaining with all maner ropis and wyris[1] to the seyd chyme and clocke. And also the seid William promisith by these present indenturis to kepe all maner of yre[n]warke[2] of the bellis perteyning to the seid monasteri uppon his owne propur cost and charge as long as the seid William do & kepe the seid charge.

For the wiche service the seid prior graunteth by these present indenturis to the seid William 20s. of lawfull money of Englond to be payid quarterly as other of his servants be paied, and also at every generall del[iver]yng of lyverey a lyverey gowne of 3 brode yards and an half of clothe of yeman's clothing. To the wiche promises well and truly to be performed & kepte on bothe parties the parties aforseid enterchaungabully have sette to ther sealis the day & yere aforeseyd.

170. [f. 20v.] Grant to David and Joan Jonys of Llanwarne (*Lanwaren*) [Herefs.], their son William and David's and William's issue of property there[3] for 60 years at 29s. 11d.[4] a year as follows.

A parcel formerly held by David Purdy extending lengthways into *Nethermore*, rent 20d.

Land and a tenement formerly of Philip Longe extending lengthways to the *Amor* brook and widthways between land of Thomas Lanwaren and *Morecroft* formerly held by Rees Carpentar, rent 20d.

A parcel formerly held by Richard Pers, rent 20d.

A parcel formerly of Philip Longe extending lengthways by *Overmoresside* formerly held by John Morys, rent 2s. 0d.

Burimere Forlong formerly held by William Daniell, rent 2s. 9d.

A parcel in *Morefield*[5] formerly held by Reginald Jones, rent 18d.

Parcels in *Schep Strete* and at Llanwarne Cross formerly held by John William, rent 3s. 6d.

Pole Meadowe in the demesne of Monkton, rent 3s.8d.

Land called *Overmore*, rent 18d.

Marle Forlong, rent 4s. 0d.

The lessees will render suit of court and heriot. [f. 21] 25 June 22 Hen. VII [1507].

171–2. Titles (for the purpose of ordination) granted to Roger Pecke, clerk,[6] and

---

[1] Probably ropes for the weights and wires to the clapper(s).

[2] i.e. clappers and staples, straps and gudgeons.

[3] The priory's estate at Llanwarne, including Monkton, was given by Hugh de Lacy (d. *c.* 1115): P.R.O. C 115/75, f. 213 no. 19.

[4] The total of the separate rents is only 23s. 11d.

[5] Around SO 502271 E. of Hill Gate, within the boundary of Monkton township nearest to Llanwarne village: *Herefs. Field-Name Survey, Llanwarne*, 7.

[6] Ordained subdeacon 8 Apr. 1508 and priest 23 Sept. 1508 by the bishop of Hereford: *Reg. Mayew*, 248, 250.

Richard Caple, clerk.[1] 11 Sept. 1507. [Abstracts in MS.; cf. **132**]

173. Lease to Philip and Isabel Yorke and their son Thomas[2] of a messuage and adjacent land and pasture at Llanwarne [Herefs.] (formerly held by David Gernes and later by Philip's father Thomas, [f. 21v.] who remains in possession for life) for 60 years from Michaelmas last past at 7s. 2d. a year and heriot. 10 Dec. 23 Hen. VII [1507].

174. Presentation of Henry Osburne to the vicarage of Barton Stacey [Hants.] vacant by the death of William Bucknell. 14 Sept. 1507.

175. [f. 22] Title of Dudstone hospital (for the purpose of ordination) granted to John Perman. 20 Sept. 1507. [Abstract in MS.; cf. **132**]

176. Quittance to the abbot of Kingswood. 30 Sept. 1506 or 1508 (*anno Domini 1508 et anno regni Regis Henrici VII 22*). [Abstract in MS.; cf. **44**]

177. Presentation of Richard Shoyer B.A., clerk,[3] to the vicarage of Painswick vacant by the death of Richard Kay. 20 July 1507. [Abstract in MS.; cf. **39**]

178. Lease [in English] to David ap Ric of Llanwarne [Herefs.] and his children Joan and John of a messuage and appurtenances there lying between land formerly of Thomas Smyth on the north and the prior's land formerly held by John Hendry on the south-west and abutting the prior's land formerly held by John ap Gwillim David, for 60 years at 4d. a year [f. 22v.] and heriot of 2s. 0d. 10 Dec. 23 Hen. VII [1507].

179. Licence to Roger Taylor alias Edwards to sublet a house at Canon Frome [Herefs.].[4] 8 Jan. 1508.

Memorandum that I Edmund Forest, prior of Lanthony besydes Gloucester, have geve lycens to Roger Taylor otherweys called Roger Edwards to putt suche persons in his howse in Canon Frome as plesith hym for the space of sevyn yere foloing only after the date of this present wryting, to occupy the said howse & the landis thereto

---

[1] Supplicant for B.A. at Oxford 5 May 1507: Emden, *Biog. Reg. Oxon. 1501–40.*

[2] Philip Yorke d. 1525–6, Thomas (of Llandinabo) d. 1534–6: *Hereford Probates 1407–1581*, 228, 258.

[3] The prior's kinsman: above, pp. xx–xxi. The title is premature as Shoyer used this benefice to finance his studies and was not admitted B.A. nor ordained acolyte until 1510: Emden, *Biog. Reg. Oxon. 1501–40.* He resigned on a pension out of the benefice by 1532: Hockaday Abs. xxv, 1532 subsidy. He held rectories in the prior's gift at All Saints, Gloucester, 1509–11 and at St. Mary de Crypt, Gloucester, *c.* 1509–17: below, **191**, **351**.

[4] Canon Frome was given to the priory by Hugh de Lacy (d. *c.* 1115): P.R.O. C 115/75, f. 213 no. 19.

belonging unto the tyme that the seid seven yere be fully endyd, wych 7 yerys shal be parte of the yeris in his indenture. For the wych lycence the said Roger hath geve to the seid prior the day of the making of this presentis, that ys to sey the Saturday next after the fest of Seynt Edward king and confessor the 23 yere of the regn of Kyng Henry the VII, 13s. 4d. in the name of an hariett according to the lease or graunt of his indenture. Per me Edmund priorem Lanthonie predicte.

180. Lease to William and Matilda Smyth and their son Thomas of customary land at Monkton [in Llanwarne, Herefs.], namely

(a) [f. 23] a messuage lately held by Richard Pers,

(b) three crofts of customary land lately held by John Turnor between *le Holewey* and *Sondays* Well (*Walle*) and

(c) an acre lately held by David Perdy and William Willmot

for 60 years for 18s. a year, suit of court at Llanwarne and heriot. The lease is void unless William [re]pays to Mabel Perse of Llanwarne 55s. and other sums which she is paying as a fine to the prior and other officials of Llanthony. The Purification 23 Hen. VII [2 Feb. 1508].

181. Presentation of Roger Dale to the rectory of Colesbourne (*Collisburn*) vacant by the resignation of T. Gronowe. 2 Nov. 1508. [Abstract in MS.; cf. **39**]

182–3. Titles of Dudstone hospital (for the purpose of ordination) granted to Henry Gwillim[1] and William Bowghan,[2] clerks. 8 Nov. and 14 Dec. 1508. [Abstracts in MS.; cf. **132**]

184. [f. 23v.] Lease to William Grevell, serjeant at law,[3] and his wife Margery of

---

[1] Chaplain at Tirley in 1522: *Military Survey of Glos. 1522*, 175.

[2] Alias Voughan, ordained acolyte 1508, deacon 24 Mar. 1509 and priest 22 Sept. 1509 by the bishop of Hereford: *Reg. Mayew*, 248, 251, 253.

[3] Of Arle in Cheltenham and Upper Lemington in Todenham, d. 1513: *Visit. Glos. 1623*, 70; C. T. Davis, *Monumental Brasses of Glos.* (1899), 113–5. J.P. for Glos. 1486–1513 and for ten other counties between 1496 and 1513, commissioner of gaol delivery at Gloucester 1488–1513, Worcester 1497–1501, Hereford 1502 and Oxford and Newgate 1509–13, commissioner of oyer and terminer in Wales and the Marches 1502–3, serjeant at law 1504–13, justice of assize in the SW. 1505–6, justice in eyre at Usk 1507, justice of assize for Oxford circuit and justice of Common Pleas 1509–13: *Cal. Pat.* 1485–94, passim; 1494–1509, p. 353 & passim; *L. & P. Hen. VIII*, i. 31 & *passim*. Ultimately lord of Arle and Upper Lemington, Elmstone in Elmstone Hardwicke, Dorn in Batsford and Aston Magna in Blockley, with more than 1,000 sheep at Lemington and other flocks on leased land at Puckham in Sevenhampton, Ditchford in Blockley, Broad Campden in Chipping Campden and 'Calcote'; donor of bequests towards rebuilding the south aisle of Todenham church, the cloister of Winchcombe Abbey and the church of Llanthony Priory, his executors including Robert Wye husband of his daughter Alice: P.R.O. PROB 11/17, f. 96, copied in Hockaday Abs. cxlvii, 1513; P.R.O. C 142/28/73; *V.C.H. Glos.* vi. 252, 255, 258; viii. 53; *V.C.H. Worcs.* iii. 269; for Arle, *Trans. B.G.A.S.* xxxvi. 288–303.

land, tenements, meadow and pasture at Redgrove[1] in the parish of Cheltenham (except the grove and great trees growing inside and outside it) for life at 6s. 8d. a year. Rents, homage, escheats, suit of court and profits of justice from the prior's tenants are reserved to the prior. The prior's attorneys John Seborne and Richard Dobyns will deliver seisin. 6 Mar. 23 Hen. VII [1508].

185. [f. 24] Lease to Thomas and Isabel Salmon of Barton S[t]ac[e]y, Hants., and their son [   ] of the rectory there with greater and lesser tithes and emoluments of the rectory or glebe, except the advowson, for 40 years at £17 a year. The lessees will

(a) feed the cellarer and the steward, their servants and their horses when they come to superintend the rectory and collect dues,

(b) pay a pension due to the abbot of Hyde by Winchester and fees due to the archdeacon of Winchester and

(c) repair houses, walls and fences in the rectory.

[f. 24v.] In case of default the prior may distrain upon the lessees' oxen and cattle. 10 Mar. 23 Hen. VII [1508].

186. Presentation of William Halpeny to the vicarage of Prestbury vacant by the death of Richard Asplene. 6 Dec. 1508. [Abstract in MS.; cf. **39**]

187. Presentation of Hugh Elynden to the vicarage of Great Barrington (*Bernynton Magna*) vacant by the resignation of Edward Finche. 10 Apr. 1509. [Abstract in MS.]

188. Presentation of Christopher Winshipp[2] to the vicarage of Awre vacant by the death of Thomas Wyck.[3] 10 Apr. 1509. [Abstract in MS.]

189. [f. 25] Title of Dudstone hospital (for the purpose of ordination) granted to James Godwyn, clerk.[4] 10 Sept. 1509. [Abstract in MS.; cf. **132**]

190. Quittance to the abbot of Kingswood for 20s. as **44** above. 30 Sept. 1 Hen. VIII [1509].

---

[1] In 1535 the priory's Redgrove estate yielded 13s. 3d. from free tenants and 46s. 8d. from customary tenants: *Valor Eccl.* (Rec. Com.), ii. 427. Known in 1360 as Hatherley manor, it was acquired piecemeal in the 12th and 13th centuries and comprised scattered properties at Alstone, Arle, Up Hatherley and Harthurst in Cheltenham, at Hayden in Boddington, at Brickhampton in Churchdown, at Staverton and Down Hatherley and at Brawn in Sandhurst: *Camd. Misc.* xxii. 18, 46; P.R.O. C 115/77, sect. v. Redgrove itself, acquired as a grove at Harthurst, survived into the 19th century as the grounds of New Arle Court around SO 913216: P.R.O. C 115/77, sect. v nos. 71, 74; *Cheltenham Local Hist. Soc. Journal*, vi. 19–22.
[2] Instituted 21 Apr.: *Reg. Mayew*, 277. Chaplain of Randwick in 1498: *Reg. Morton*, ii. 137.
[3] Vicar since 1483: *Reg. Myllyng*, 193.
[4] Supplicant for B.A. at Oxford 25 Nov. 1508; possibly rector of Road (Som.) from 1515: Emden, *Biog. Reg. Oxon. 1501–40.*

191. Presentation of Richard Sheyer, B.A., clerk,[1] to the rectory of All Saints, Gloucester, vacant by the death of T[homas] Numon alias Dyar. 14 Sept. 1509. [Abstract in MS.; cf. **39**]

192. Presentation of Thomas Fleuing to the vicarage of Windrush (*Winrich*) vacant by the death of John Drury. 19 Jan. 1509[/10]. [Abstract in MS.]

193. Presentation of Richard Morys to the rectory of Colesbourne (*Collesburne*) vacant by the death of Roger Dale. 20 Jan. 1509[/10]. [Abstract in MS.]

194. Presentation of John Winston to the vicarage of Awre vacant by the death of Christopher Winshipe. 11 Mar. 1509[/10]. [Abstract in MS.]

195. [f. 25v.] Presentation of John Tycull to the vicarage of Prestbury vacant by the resignation of William Halpeny. 8 Mar. 1509[/10]. [Abstract in MS.]

196. Lease to Ralph Krymshawe vicar of Stanton Lacy (Salop.), William Cheyne mercer of Ludlow (Salop.) and Richard Bragott weaver of Ludlow,[2] of the parsonage, glebe, tithes, rents and profits of justice of Stanton Lacy. 26 June 1508.

This indenture made the 26 day of June the 23 yere of the regne of King Harry the VII betwene Edmund prior of the howse and churche of owre lady Seint Mary the Virgyn off Lanthony besides Gloucetur and the covent of the same place of the on partie and Syr Rauffe Krymshawe vicary of Stanton Lacy in the counte of Salop, William Cheyne of Ludlowe in the seid count[e] mercer and Richard Bragott of Ludlowe forseid wever and every of them on the other partie witnesseth that the seid prior and covent by ther hoole assent and concent have dimised and lett to ferme to the forseid Syr Rauff, William & Richard ther parsonage of Staunton Lacy in the seid counte with all tythes, offryngs, presents and emoluments to the seid parsonage or glebe belonging, groing or pertenyng and all rentis of the seid prior and covent with the amerciaments, profitts & vantagees of the lawe daies & cowrtt of the same prior, covent & ther successours in Staunton Lacy beforeseid, the advoson of the churche ther only excepte.

To have, perceive & occupie the seid parsonage and glebe and all other the premisses withe ther appurtenants, excepte before excepte, to the same Sir Rauff, William and Richard from the fest of the Nativite of Seint John the Baptist last past before the date of these presents unto the ende & terme of 12 yerys then nexte immediatly folowyng and to be comple[te]d, yelding therefore yerely during the seid

---

[1] The prior's kinsman, not admitted B.A. until 1510: above, pp. xx–xxi; **177** n. Since Numon alias Dyar was also rector of St. Mary de Crypt 1496–1509 and since Robert Stynchecombe succeeded Sheyer as rector of All Saints in 1511 and of St. Mary de Crypt in 1517 it follows that Sheyer was rector of All Saints 1509–11 and of St. Mary de Crypt *c.* 1509–17: Fosbrooke, *Glouc.* 163 corrected by *Glouc. Corp. Rec.* p. 418; below, **300** n, **351**.

[2] d. 1520: *Hereford Probates 1407–1581*, 207.

*terme at the feaste of the Annunciacion of owr lady Seint Marie the Virgin and the
Nativite of Seint John the Baptist to the seid prior, covent and ther successours £18
6s. 8d. by even porcions.*

*And the foreseid Sir Rauff, William & Richard graunte and conventen by these
presents that they or on of them shall as well provide and fynde a steward for the
seid lawedays and courts too tymys in the yere to be holdin att ther owne costs &
charges, as to provide and fynde for the cellerer and the steward of Lanthony
beforeseid, for them and ther servaunts convenient mete, drinke and loggyng and for
there horses sufficient hey, lytter and provaunder at Ludlowe beforeseid at ther owne
costis and charges as often as they or eny of them shall happen to come to Staunton
Lacy beforeseid for eny cause or besenes of the seid prior, covent and ther
successours during the seid terme.*

*And if it happen the seid rent of £18 6s. [f. 26] 8d. to be byhynd onpayed at
Lanthony beforeseid to the seid prior, covent and ther successours by the space of a
monthe after eny of the seid feasts when it oweth to be paide, that then the forseide
Sir Rauff, William and Richard and every of them covenanten and graunten to the
seid prior, covent and successors to forfaite 20s. in name of a peyne as oft as it shall
happen the seid rent to be so behynde and unpayd. And if it happen the seid rent to
be byhynd in parte or in all by the space of too monethis after eny of the seid feasts
when it owith to be paide during the seide terme, then the same Sir Rauff, William
and Richard and ether of them to forfaite by these presents to the said prior, covent
and successors 20s. in name of a peyne, and that then it shal be lawfull to the seid
prior, covent and ther successors into the seid parsonage, glebe & other the
premisses with ther appurtenaunce to reentre and that to have and enjoy in there
first astate, this lese notwithstanding.*

*In witnesse whereof the seid prior and covent to the on partie of these indentures
remaynyng with the forseid Sir Rauff, William and Richard have putt ther comen
seale, and to the other parte remaynyng with the seid prior and covent the forseid
Sir Rauff, William and Richard severally have put there seales the v[er]y day and
yere above writen.*

197. Bond of William Cheyny and Richard Braggot in £20 to perform the covenants
of the above lease. 23 June 1508.

*Noverint universi per presentes nos Willelmum Cheyny de Ludlowe in comitatu
Salopie, 'mercer', et Ricardum Braggot de Ludlow in comitatu Salopie, 'wever',
teneri et firmiter obligari Edmundo priori domus et ecclesie Beate Marie de
Lanthonie iuxta Gloucestriam in viginti libras sterlingorum solvendas eidem priori
et successoribus suis in festo Sancti Michelis Archangeli proxime futuro post datam
presencium, ad quam quidem solucionem bene et fideliter faciendam obligamus nos
et utrumque nostrum per se pro toto et in solidum, heredes et executores nostros per
presentes sigillis nostris sigillatas. Data in vigilia Nativitatis Sancti Iohannis
Baptiste anno regni Regis Henrici Septimi vicesimo tercio.*

*The condicion of this obligacion is suche. If the within bounden William and
Richard and either of them fullfyll, kepe and performe all and singler covenants and
agrements specified in certen indenturis made betwene Edmunde, prior of the howse*

*and churche of Lanthoni besides Gloucetur, and covent of the [f. 26v.] same place of
the on parte and on Sir Rauff Krymshawe, wicarie of Staunton Lacy in the counte of
Salop, clerke, and the foreseid William & Richard and either of them of the other
partie, of date of 26 day of June the 23 yere of the reigne of King Herry the VIIth,
then this obligacion be woide, or els to stond in his strength and vertue.*

198. Lease to John Nicolas of the tithes of the north part of Conock[1] in Chirton,
Wilts. 15 Aug. 1509.

*This indentur made in the fest of the Assumpcion of Oure Lady in the yere of the
regne of King Henry the VIIIth the first yere betwixt Edmunde Forest, prior of the
howse and monasterii of Lanthon besyde Gloucetur, and the [covent] of the same on
the on partie and John Nicolas of the parishe of Chyrynton in the counte of
Wyltshire[2] on the other partie witnesseth that the seid prior and covent have put and
to ferme let to the seid John Niclas the tethe of[3] the northe parte of Conocke the
whiche the seid prior and covent hath within the seid Conocke. To have and to hold
the seid ferme of the Connok to the seid John Niclas and to his assignes for the
terme of his lyffe, pay[i]nge yerely unto the seid prior and his successors £6 of
lawfull money of Englond to be paide at 2 termes of the yere, that is to sey at Hocke
Tuysday[4] 60s. and at the fest of Seint Jamis the Appostell [27 July] 60s. by evyn
porcions. And yeff hit so happe the seid rent of £6 be behynd in parte or in the hole
[a] fortnyth aftur eny of the seid dais of peyment, that then the seid John Niclas shall
bring to the seid howse of Lanthony within the moneth, in peyne of forfetting, 40s. to
the seid prior and his successors over the sum of £6, and to forfette his indenture at
the plesure of the seid prior and his successors. To the wiche promyse well and truly
to be performed the seid prior and covent on the on partie and the seid John Niclas
on the other partie enturchaungeable have put to ther seales the day and the yere
aboveseid.*

199. [f. 27] Citation to a visitation of the priory by Silvestro [de' Gigli] bishop of
Worcester or his commissary on 23 May. Worcester palace, 28 Mar. 1510.

200. Certificate acknowledging that the above was received on 16 Apr. 21 Apr.
1510.[5]

201. Lease to John ac Mericke,[6] his son Thomas and [Thomas's] wife Alice of
property in the demesne of Monkton [at Llanwarne, Herefs.] previously held by

---

[1] Nicolas still held these tithes for £6 a year in 1535: *Valor Eccl.* (Rec Com.), ii. 428.
[2] MS. *Wylsthire.*
[3] MS. *of of.*
[4] The second Tuesday after Easter day: *O.E.D.*
[5] The MS. has *millesimo quingentesimo septimo*, which is clearly wrong as the citation is
dated *millesimo quingentesimo decimo et nostre consecracionis anno undecimo.*
[6] Of St. Weonards, d. 1515: *Hereford Probates 1407–1581*, 197.

David Halocke, viz. a messuage, *Medilfyld* meadow adjacent extending to *Keudynans Broke*[1] and two closes beyond *le Porte Wey*,[2] [f. 27v.] all for 70 years at 16s. a year and heriot. Michaelmas 2 Hen. VIII [29 Sept. 1510].

202. Lease to John Hoskyns of Monkton [in Llanwarne, Herefs.], his wife [   ] and their son [   ] of property there, viz. a messuage with a croft adjacent,[3] *Wilmaston* meadow, *Litle Feld* and *Nether Litle Feld*,[4] a field called *le Medow* at *le Crosse*,[5] *Litle Feld Medow, Henry Felde* and *Henryfelde* meadow,[6] *Parkys Forlong* croft, *Wentys Close*,[7] *Caudynan* close[8] extending to *Meryvales Crosse, Wethibed Felde, Hunthyll* field, an acre at *Over Hunthill, Gosty Closse* and *Monehill* field, all for 70 years at 26s. a year and heriot. Michaelmas 2 Hen. VIII [29 Sept. 1510].

203. [f. 28] Appointment of Robert Wye[9] as steward of manors, lands and tenements in Glos. and Wilts., to perform the office by self or deputy at the ancient fee of 40s. a year. 8 Dec. 2 Hen. VIII [1510].

204. Subsidy Roll quittance for £6 8s. as the first moiety of a clerical subsidy of

---

[1] Relet to ac Mericke in 1513 with a fuller description locating this part of the property at SO 495258 and identifying Keudynans Brook with Cold Brook: below, **278**.

[2] The Hereford–Monmouth road.

[3] Probably Upper Monkton Farm at SO 491264, now a house of rubble and timber framing dated to the early 17th century: *Inventory of Herefs.* (Royal Commission on Historical Monuments, 1931), i. 178. It lies among, and in 1840 ran with, the fields which are identified below from the tithe map of that date: *Herefs. Field-Name Survey, Llanwarne*, 8.

[4] Alias Upper and Lower Light Field around SO 494266.

[5] At Decon's Cross: below, **458**.

[6] Alias Hendre Field around SO 493261. The MS. repeats *medow* after the first *Henry Felde*, an error which is corrected in **458**.

[7] Alias Woonty Close around SO 495260.

[8] Alias Cae Daniels at SO 492259. The MS. has *Caudyvan* or *Candyvan*, the 6th letter being corrected here on the evidence of the later form.

[9] Of Rodmarton and Lypiatt Park in Stroud, d. 1544, heir of his grandfather Thomas Whittington and son in law of the lawyer William Grevell: *L. & P. Hen. VIII*, i, p. 221; *Visit. Glos. 1623*, 187; above, **184** n. J.P. for Glos. 1508–44, Wilts. 1515–44 and Worcs. 1532–42, commissioner of gaol delivery at Gloucester 1511, 1530, 1537–9 and 1544, nominee for shrievalty of Glos. 1514, 1520 and 1522, commissioner delivering Glos. tax assessments 1523 and 1534 and commissioner of oyer and terminer for various counties 1538–44, fined for refusing knighthood 1536: *Cal. Pat.* 1494–1509, 641; *L. & P. Hen. VIII*, i–xx passim. Escheator of Glos. 1517, 1527 and 1543: *List of Escheators* (List & Index Soc. lxxii, 1971), 54. Lord of Upper Lypiatt in Bisley, of Frampton Mansell in Sapperton, of Rodmarton, of Pitchcombe, of Bentham in Badgeworth, of Corse and of Longdon in Worcs., lessee of land at Icomb and Minchinhampton and at Lowsmoor in Avening and owner of houses and land in Gloucester, Cheltenham and Tewkesbury: P.R.O. PROB 11/30, f. 149, copied in Hockaday Abs. cxxiv, 1544; P.R.O. C 142/73/83; *V.C.H. Glos.* viii. 276; xi. 111, 236; *V.C.H. Worcs.* iv. 115; *Military Survey of Glos. 1522*, 44, 97–8, 115, 160, 179.

£40,000 granted in year 12 [Hen. VII, i.e. 1497][1] as assessed by John [Ingleby] bishop of Llandaff on the prior's spiritualities and temporalities in that diocese and paid in the Treasury on 25 Nov. in year 24 [Hen. VII, i.e. 1508].

205. Undertaking by the warden and college of vicars choral of Hereford, in return for a gift of £100 from the late Henry Dene archbishop of Canterbury, to sing dirges and requiem masses and say prayers for his soul. 28 Oct. 1504.

Thys indenture made the 28 day of Octobyr the 20 yere of the reigne of Kyng Henry the VII betwin Edmunde priour of the monastery of oure Blyssid Lady of Lanthony by Glouceter and covent of the same place of thoon partie and the custos and vicaryes in the qwere of the cathedrall chirche of [f. 28v.] *Hereforde of thothur partie witnessith:*

Where the Most Reverende Fathur in Gode Henry Dene late archebysshop of Canturbury delyvered to the same prioure a hundred poundes sterlingys to be delyvered to the said custos and vycaryes to thentente that they therwyth shuld purchase londys and tenementys to thyerly valour of 5 poundys sterlyngys over all chargys, and the same to make suer aftur thordour of the lawe to them and their successours for evere, and the same custos, vicaryes and their successours to doo for the same certein orations and prayers for the soule of the saide late archebysshop as hereafter shall appere, the whiche sume of £100 the saide custos and vicaryes knolege themsilf the day of the makyng of theys presents of the said prior to have recevid, the said priour and his successours thereof to be acquite and dischargid for evere; and the same custos and vicaryes in consideracions of the premisses according to thentente aforesaid by theis presents covenanten and graunten for them & their successours to the said prior and his successours that they before the feste of Sainte Michaell tharchaungell that shal be in the yere of oure Lord God 1506 shall purchase londis and tenementys of thyerly valour of fyve poundys sterling over all charge to them and their successours.

Also the said custos and vicaryes for them and theyr successours by theys presents grauntyn and covenaunty[n] to the said priour and his successours that they and their successours for ever from hensforth yerly betwin the festys of the Purificacion and thannunciacion of oure saide Blissid Lady shall synge or cause to be songyn a solempne Dirige after Evynsong within the qwere of the said cathedrall chirche, and on the morowe nexte insuing shall syng or cause to be songyn a solempne masse of Requiem at the high aulter within the said chirch for the soule of the said late archbisshop, the same Diriges and massez to be don with like solempnite, ringyng and all othur observances as in the saide chirche is usyd to be don for the soule of John Stanburi sometyme bysshop of Hereford.[2]

Also the same custos and vicaryes and their successours yerely after every of the said masses shall incontinente distribute or cause to be distributyd among themself to every vicary than there being present at the said Dirige and masse 8d., every decone than there present 4d., and to every querester and sexten than there present 2d.

---

[1] At a convocation of Canterbury province assembled on 23 Jan. 1497: Wilkins, *Concilia*, iii. 645.

[2] By deed of endowment of 1491: *Reg. Stanbury*, xii.

Also the same custos and vicaryes for them and their successours by these presents grauntyn that all suche revenuez and profits of the said londys and tenements that yerly shall fortune to growe and remayne above the costys and chargys of the premissez shal be imploied in comyn to thuse and profits of the said custos, vicaryes and successours.

Also the said custos, vicaryes and their successours every day for ever after theire dyner within the said college[1] whan they say 'De profundis', than they shall pray for the soule of the said late archebisshop. And whan they have saide 'De profundis', they shall saye theys wordys: 'God have mercy upon the soule of Henry Dene, late archbisshop of Canterbury and before that priour of Lanthony by Gloucester.'

And after every there commen soper by them in the said college had, they shall pray for the soule of the said archbisshop as they use & doo for the soules of theire founders.

In wittenes whereof to thoon partie of theys presente indenturs remaynyng with the said custos and vicaryes the said prior and covent have sett their commen seall, and to the othur of the same indenturs remaynyng with the said priour and covent the said custos and vicaryes have sette theire commen seall the day and yere abovesaid.

206. Bond of the vicars choral [f. 29] in 200 marks to perform the covenants of the above. 28 Oct. 20 Hen. VII [1504].

207. Purchase from Dean Thomas Wolsey[2] and the chapter of Hereford for £60 of

(a) a quitclaim of 60s. annual rent on the prior's manor, lands and tenements in Widemarsh Moor [in Hereford],[3] a rent previously disputed between the late Dean John Hervy and the late Prior Henry [Deane] and

(b) [f. 29v.] the right of estovers for the repair of Carey Weir [then in Fownhope, now in Brockhampton], Herefs., from Caplar Wood [in Fownhope], to be delivered by the bailiff of Woolhope (*Hopwolweth*) manor or taken in default.[4] 7 Jan. 2 Hen. VIII [1511].

---

[1] Built 1472–5: Philip Barrett in *Hereford Cathedral: a History*, ed. G. Aylmer and J. Tiller (London, 2000), 445.

[2] The future cardinal and Lord Chancellor, prebendary of Hereford 1508–13, dean there from at least 1509 to 1512, king's almoner and dean of Lincoln 1509–14: Le Neve, *Fasti 1300–1541, Hereford*; Emden, *Biog. Reg. Oxon. to 1500*.

[3] A rent charge confirmed to the dean and chapter in 1219: *Charters and Records of Hereford Cathedral*, ed. W. W. Capes (Hereford, 1908), 49. Altogether the prior's property in Hereford in 1535 comprised a mill yielding 20s. a year, a tenement in Widemarsh Street yielding 20s. and Widemarsh manor yielding 30s. for the manor site, £11 13s. 9d. from customary tenants and 7d. from court perquisites: *Valor Eccl.* (Rec. Com.), ii. 428, 431; cf. *Tax. Eccl.* (Rec. Com.), 170. This, however, included a messuage and 44 acres in the moor to which the rent charge did not apply as they were acquired in 1292: *Cal. Pat.*1281–92, 477. Widemarsh manor house may be that known in the 18th century as Prior's Moor at SO 504408 north of Widemarsh Brook, with Widemarsh Mill to the E. and Canon Moor, in which the dean and chapter of Hereford were the prior's tenants, to the S.: H. Price, *Map of Hereford* (Hereford, 1802); cf. below, **209**.

[4] The vendor's copy remains in Hereford Cathedral Library.

208. Quittance from Dean Thomas Wolcy for £20. 10 Jan. 2 Hen. VIII [1511].

209. Quittance to Dean Thomas Wolsey and the chapter of Hereford for 9s. 6d. annual rent on lands and tenements held by them in Canon Moor [in Hereford].[1] 7 Jan. 2 Hen. VIII [1511].

210. [f. 30] Grant to John Breynton, gentleman,[2] for trust in his circumspection, fidelity and industry, of 20s. yearly rent for life from the prior's lands and tenements in Bishop's Frome (Herefs.), with payment of 1d. as livery of seisin. 20 Jan. 2 Hen. VIII [1511].

211. Presentation of Richard Barnard, chaplain, to the rectory of Colesbourne (*Collesburn*) vacant by the death of Richard Morys. 21 May 1510.

212. [f. 30v.] Presentation of Hugh Grene, chaplain,[3] to the vicarage of Canon Frome (Herefs.) vacant by the death of John Hoore. 16 Aug. 1510.

213. Presentation of John Wadynton, chaplain, to the vicarage of Little Barrington (*Parva Bernynton*) vacant by the death of William Belchere. 9 Jan. 1510[/11].

214. Proxy to William Lewis, vicar of Caldicot [Mon.], and William Bays to act for the church of Caldicot [as in **130** above]. [f. 31] 18 Apr. 1504.[4]

215. On the appropriation of Llanthony Prima.
    The royal escheator George Traheren, sitting at Weobley (Herefs.) in 1503–4, escheated the property of Llanthony Prima Priory on the false grounds that it was vacant from the death of Prior John Penbrugh on 8 August 1469.[5] On a traverse the king's council found that Llanthony Prima was lawfully appropriated to Llanthony-

---

[1] A rent charge acquired *c*. 1147: *Trans. B.G.A.S.* lxiii. 14; cf. *Valor Eccl.* (Rec. Com.), iii. 6.
    [2] d. 1527, lawyer of Stretton Sugwas (Herefs.), Hereford and London; commissioner of gaol delivery at Hereford 1490–1512 and at Worcester 1501, M.P. for Herefs. 1491–2, J.P. for Herefs. 1496–1527; lord of Stretton Sugwas and owner of 300 acres there and at Credenhill, of 1,130 acres and ten messuages at Mordiford, Nether Shellwick (in Holmer) and Dilwyn, of Burmarsh in Bodenham and of land at Wellington all in Herefs.: *Hist. of Parl., Biographies 1439–1509*; *Visit. Herefs. 1569*, 13; Duncomb, *Herefs., Hundred of Grimsworth*, 163; P.R.O. C 142/46/94.
    [3] Instituted 21 Aug.: *Reg. Mayew*, 278. Incumbent of Canon Frome 1510–29 and Little Marcle (Herefs.) from 1525: *Reg. Bothe*, 338, 343. To be distinguished from his namesake the prebendary (d. 1524): cf. **281** n.
    [4] The date is incorrect, as two others became proctors of Caldicot on 20 Apr. 1504: above, **131**.
    [5] Disregarding *inter alia* the election of John Adams, last prior before the appropriation: Dugdale, *Mon.* vi. 139.

by-Gloucester,[1] and after a suit to the council lasting five terms the property was restored. For a payment of 100 marks to the king's receiver John Heron at Westminster on 10 Mar. 1504 the king confirmed the appropriation by letters patent.[2]

Memorandum quod ubi monasterium Lanthonie Prime in Wallia cum percinenciis fuit legitime appropriatum, unitum et incorporatum monasterio Lanthonie iuxta Gloucestriam in tempore reverendissimi patris Domini Henrici Dene quondam Cantuariensis archiepiscopi et prioris Lanthonie predicte, et per ingentes labores et maximas expensas eiusdem reverendissimi patris domini prioris extiterit per auctoritatem et licenciam illustrissimi principis Edwardi Quarti nuper regis Anglie, fundatoris Lanthonie Prime supradicte racione et in iure comitatus Marchie, sicut in litteris suis patentibus et sub plumbo summi pontificis[3] necnon sigillo capituli Menevensis ecclesie confirmatur, ut in appropriacione monasterii predicti plenius intuentibus apparet; nichilominus persuasum est per quandam falsam inquisicionem captam apud Webley in comitatu Herefordie coram Georgio Traheren escaetore domini Regis Henrici Septimi anno eiusdem regis decimo nono cuius tenor hic sequitur et est talis, videlicet:

> *Monasterium predictum Lanthonie Prime in Marchia Wallie a tempore cuius contraria memoria hominum non existit fuit de donacione, fundacione et patronatu domini regis et progenitorum suorum, ad quem quidem prioratum tunc vacantem Henricus Rex Anglie Sextus quendam Iohannem Penbrugh presentavit, qui quidem Iohannes Penbrugh virtute eius presentacionis ad illum prioratum dimissus, institutus et installatus exstituit prout iustum fuit. Et predictus Iohannes videlicet octavo die mensis Augusti anno regni Regis Edwardi Quarti post conquestum nono obiit. Per cuius mortem prioratus predictus vacuit et adhuc vacat, per quod donacio, presentacio et concessio eiusdem prioratus ad dominum regem pertinent ac omnia exitus et proficia eiusdem prioratus tempore vacacionis eiusdem eciam ad dominum regem pertinent et de iure pertinere debent. In cuius rei testimonium etc.*

Unde, per cuius false inquisicionis colorem, Dominus Edmundus Forest, prior Lanthonie iuxta Gloucestriam, amotus et expulsus fuit a possessionibus Lanthonie Prime supradicte, donec tandem idem prior accessit ad illustrissimum principem dominum Regem Henricum Septimum et peciit ab eo licenciam faciendi traversiam suam iuxta formam et statuta legis Anglie, per quam veritas appropriacionis Lanthonie Prime et falsitas inquisicionis predicte magis patefierent. [f. 31v.] Unde traversia sua incepta simul et finita, visis et intellectis omnibus munimentis concernentibus appropriacionem Lanthonie Prime predicte, inventum est per consiliarios domini regis predicti quod dictum monasterium Lanthonie Prime

---

[1] The finding led to an indenture of 12 Nov. 1504 whereby the king claimed the patronage of both priories by right of his duchy of Lancaster and the prior and convent undertook not to elect a new prior without his licence. They acknowledged the indenture in their chapter house on 8 Jan. 1505 before William Greville, serjeant at law: *Cal. Close* 1500–9, 173.

[2] Dated 2 May 1505: *Cal. Pat.* 1494–1509, 403 confirming *Cal. Pat.* 1476–85, 284.

[3] In 1481: *Cal. Pat.* 1476–85, 284; *Cal. Papal Letters* 1471–84, 912; cf. above, **107**.

predicte fuit legitime appropriatum monasterio[1] Lanthonie iuxta Gloucestriam, et quod illa inquisicio capta apud Webley per predictum escaetorem fuit falsissima. Unde post maximas expensas et longissimam sectam ad consiliarios domini regis predicti, videlicet per sectam quinque terminorum integrorum, idem Dominus Edmundus prior Lanthonie iuxta Gloucestriam per predictum illustrissimum principem Dominum Regem Henricum Septimum ad omnes possessiones suas concernentes Lanthoniam Primam fuit iterum restitutus, ut patet per materiam recordi in custodia domini prioris remanentem et cum appropriacione predicta quiescentem.

Pro cuius quidem favore et benevolencia in veritate materie predicte habita simul et obtenta, predictus Edmundus prior dedit prefato regi centum marcas auri solutas ad manus Iohannis Heron receptoris domini regis predicti, ut patet per billam inde scriptam et manu eiusdem Iohannis signatam, cuius tenor hic sequitur.

This present bill made at Westminster the 10 day of March the 19 yere of our souveragne lorde Kyng Henry the VII witnessyth that John Heron hath recevid in the name and for the use and behove of oure souveraigne lorde of the prior of Lanthon besydes Gloucetur one hundrith markes sterling for the king's favor to be obteigned in certen peticions put unto his highnes. In wittnesse hereof the foresaid John Heron unto these presentes writings hath subscribed his name and sette his seal the day & yere abovesaid. By John Heron, 100 marc.

Pro qua quidem summa 100 marcarum pre manibus soluta prefatus Dominus Rex Henricus VII predictam appropriacionem Lanthonie Prime confirmavit, ut patet per litteras suas patentes et in custodia domini prioris cum appropriacione predicta similiter remanentes.

216. On the redemption of the priory's possessions in Ireland.

Gerald earl of Kildare, King Henry VII's deputy in Ireland,[2] took two thirds of the priory's possessions there under colour of the 1379 ordinance against absentees and enjoyed them for many years.[3] When he crossed to England in 1503–4 Prior Forest met him, and the parties' counsellors made a final concord in St. Paul's cathedral. Since the ordinance applied to temporalities rather than spiritualities, the earl released the possessions for

(a) £40,

(b) £6 13s. 4d. to his countess and

(c) £5 13s. 4d. to his counsellors for buying ordinary doublets

(a total of £52 7s.[4] paid at Richmond [Surrey] in 1503–4 by the prior in the presence

---

[1] MS. *monasterium.*

[2] d. 1513, lord deputy 1479–92, 1496–1513. His relations with the priory may have been soured in 1494 when Prior Deane, as chancellor, participated in his attainder in the Irish parliament: *D.N.B.*

[3] In 1369–70 the king's lieutenant in Ireland had seized the same property on the same grounds under an ordinance of 1361: Reg. Brockworth, f. 26. The ordinance cited here was made at a parliament of 24 Apr.–27 May 1379: *Rotuli Parliamentorum* (London, 1783), iii. 85–6.

[4] Rounded up to the nearest whole number of shillings.

of fellow canon Walter Kenelocke the priory's proctor for Duleek [Meath]);
  (d) expenses for them as mentioned in the prior's detail book for the year and
  (e) a yearly fee of £10 in Irish money for life.
Entered in 1510–11.

Memorandum quod cum ordinatum fuit tempore Ricardi Secundi regis Anglie per
actum parliamenti apud Westmonasterium, videlicet anno sui regni 3,[1] quod omnes
homines, cuiuscumque status essent, habentes aliquas possessiones in terra Hibernie
continue post ordinacionem predictam se illuc traherent et ibi moram facerent pro
defensione terre predicte, ut patet per materiam recordi in Gallica lingua scriptam
in registro Domini Willelmi Cherinton quondam prioris Lanthonie folio 105,[2] aut si
aliqua causa racionali ibidem personaliter interesse non possint[3] tunc teneantur
invenire ibidem homines defensabiles in loco suo ad defensionem terre predicte,
habito respectu ad quantitatem et valorem terrarum et possessionum eorundem, et
hoc sub certa pena ut patet in eadem ordinacione facta; cum igitur prior et
conventus Lanthonie iuxta Gloucestriam habent ibidem diversas possessiones tam
spirituales quam temporales in auxilium domus sue predicte sibi datas, et quia in
Anglia ex causa fundacionis ecclesie sue predicte pro divinis et aliis ibidem
faciendis residere[4] et commorare teneantur, premissis igitur pie consideratis
concessum est per Henricum Sextum, Edwardum Quartum et alios nobilissimos
reges Anglie prefatis priori et conventui Lanthonie ac eorum successoribus
imperpetuum quod seipsos non solum absentant a terra predicta sed eciam quod
licite valeant omnibus possessionibus suis ibidem gaudere et eas disponere atque in
Angliam abducere et cariare prout sibi commodius et utilius videatur expedire,
absque aliquo quocumque impedimento regum Anglie aut ministrorum suorum, ut
patet per diversas litteras patentes[5] diversorum regum Anglie in custodia domini
[prioris] remanentes; sic tamen quod idem prior et conventus et successores sui
semper onerentur fore [f. 32] *contributores ad defensionem terre predicte sicut et*
alii religiosi sint, et hoc iuxta quantitatem et valorem possessionum suarum ibidem,
et quod idem prior et conventus Lanthonie predicte per procuratores suos in terra
predicta inveniant[6] homines ibidem defensabiles cum necessitas cogit et sicut
contributores ad defensionem terre predicte more aliorum religiosorum secundum
quantitatem possessionum suarum, ut predictum est.
  Nichilominus quidam dominus Geraldus, comes de Kyldare et deputatus domini
Regis Henrici Septimi ibidem, sub colore ordinacionis supradicte contra absentes,
duas partes possessionum nostrarum ibi possidebat et multis annis eis gaudebat.
Donec tandem ex inspiracione Spiritus Sancti idem comes, transfretando ad

---

[1] *Recte* anno 2.
[2] Reg. Chirton, f. 105.
[3] MS. *poterant.*
[4] MS. *resedere.*
[5] Original grants by Henry VI in 1425 and by Edward IV in 1481 were confirmed by Henry
VII in 1496 and 1497 but the priory had lost the patents of confirmation: *Cal. Pat.* 1476–85,
246; 1494–1509, 73, 106; below, **326**.
[6] MS. *inveniunt.*

dominum Regem Henricum Septimum prenominatum, circa 19 sui regni annum in Angliam venit. Ad quem quidem comitem salutandum et conveniendum dominus Edmundus Forest prior Lanthonie supradicte una cum suis eruditis consiliariis accesserunt, et habita matura communicacione in ecclesia Sancti Pauli aput Londinium inter utriusque partis consiliarios de duabus partibus predictis, tandem omnis lis et controversia inter partes predictas in hunc modum sopita est.

Quia videlicet statutum predictum magis se extendit ad temporales quam ad spirituales possessiones, et quia nostre possessiones ibidem magis consistunt in spiritualibus quam in temporalibus, igitur premissis consideratis idem comes ex sua bona consciencia a duabus partibus predictis seipsum exonerabat et manus suas imperpetuum ab illis amovit, ac illas nobis predicto priori et conventui ac successoribus nostris pro se penitus relaxabat.

Pro qua quidem relaxacione facta ordinatum erat per utriusque partis consiliarios quod predictus prior daret predicto comiti summam quadraginta librarum sterlingorum, et uxori eiusdem comitis summam sex librarum et tredecim solidorum ac 4 denariorum, et consiliariis eiusdem comitis quinque libras et 13s. 4d. ad emendas illis diploides feriales: summa totalis, quinquaginta due libre auri et septem solidi, ultra expensas super eos factas ut patet per unum librum de percellis eiusdem prioris de anno supradicto. Quam quidem summam quinquaginta duarum librarum et septem solidorum idem prior solvit ad manus predictorum apud Richemond in presencia fratris Walteri Kenelocke, procuratoris nostri apud Dewlicke, anno quo supra.

Preterea partes predicti ordinaverunt quod idem comes haberet quoddam annuale feodum de decem libris pecuniarum Hibernicarum solvendum annuatim per procuratorem nostrum apud Dewlicke, quod quidem feodum idem comes habet sub sigillo nostro conventuali durante vita sua tantum.

Et ulterius notandum quod ubi ante conclusionem huius rei a predicto comite et ministris suis circa res nostras in Angliam vehendas non modicum gravamen passi sumus, tunc ex eo tempore ex quo[1] *omnia hec facta sunt idem prior et conventus ac procuratores sui apud Dewlicke in Hibernia predicta de 2 partibus predictis pacificam habuerunt posessionem. Et ne hec amica[bi]lis et finalis concordia inter partes predictas aliquando in oblivionem verteretur, predictus Edmundus prior hoc scriptum hic in registro suo registrari et annotari fecit anno secundo Henrici Octavi.*[2]

217. On the redemption of Okle Clifford [then in Oxenhall,[3] now in Newent].

Prior Henry Dene purchased the demesne and appurtenances of Okle[4] by Newent

---

[1] MS. *qua.*

[2] MS. *Henrico Octavo.*

[3] *Military Survey of Glos. 1522,* 62.

[4] Okle Clifford: Dugdale, *Mon.* vi. 140. In 1535 it yielded rents of £4 from the manor site and demesne, 21s. 8d. from free tenants, £4 6s. from customary tenants, 20s. fron Waterdine pasture and 10s. from three groves, with 11d. in court perquisites: *Valor Eccl.* (Rec. Com.), ii. 425.

from Robert Hyett of Newland[1] and N. Pansfoote of Twyning. After Dene's death John Roberts of Newland[2] claimed the property by right of his wife Matilda daughter of William Dwlle,[3] showing a pedigree and a sealed deed. Mr. John Kyngismyll, justice,[4] for the Robertses, and Mr. William Grevell, serjeant at law, for Prior Forest, inspected the documents and concluded that the Robertses should release their deed and their claim to the prior by a final concord for £60,[5] a sum which the prior paid to the Robertses in the presence of both parties' lawyers at the Newark[6] near Hempsted on 7 Aug. 1507. Entered in 1510–11.

Memorandum eciam quod ubi venerandus pater Dominus Henricus Dene, quondam Cantuariensis archiepiscopus et prior Lanthonie, perquisivit de quodam Roberto Hyett de Newland et N. Pansfoote de Twynnyng dominium de Ocle iuxta Newent cum pertinenciis suis, ut per statum et evidencias [f. 32v.] predicto[7] honorando patri factas plenius apparet, nichilominus post decessum predicti reverendi patris Henrici Dene supervenit quidam Iohannes Roberts de parochia de Newland predicta et peciit a Domino Edmundo Forest tunc priore Lanthonie et successore eiusdem reverendi patris H. D. predicti totum dominium de Ocle predictum cum suis pertinenciis, et hoc de iure Matildis uxoris sue filie cuiusdam Willelmi Dwlle et recte heredis ad manerium predictum, ut patet per quandam scedulam[8] de 'la petygre' et quandam cartam talliatam in custodia domini remanentes.

Unde conclusum est inter predictum priorem, predictum Iohannem et predictam Matildam quod utraque pars eligeret sibi iurisconsultum ad audiendum, determinandum et finiendum lites sic inter partes predictas dependentes. Unde visis

[1] d. before 1485, when resident at Littledean: *Cal. Pat.* 1476–85, 469. Porter of St. Briavels castle 1460–80, rider of Dean Forest 1460, receiver there 1461–80 and gaveller 1464–81: *Cal. Pat.* 1452–61, 638; 1461–7, 18, 24, 361; 1476–85, 204, 287. Owner of land and tenements in Newland at Poolway, Coleford, Millend, Clearwell and Redbrook, in Staunton and in St. Briavels: Glos. R.O. D1677/GG/252, D2244/165, 174, 178, 180, 187, D2957/86/8.

[2] Of Clearwell in Newland: Glos. R.O. D2957/214/53, 70.

[3] Of Newland; d. 1481, or a namesake who d. 1525 and was lord of a Dean Forest mesne until 1513: *Hereford Probates 1407–1581*, 94, 229; Glos. R.O. D2957/214/57.

[4] Of Freefolk in Laverstoke (Hants.), d. 1509: P.R.O. PROB 11/16, f. 128v. M.P. for Heytesbury (Wilts.) 1491–2, commissioner of oyer and terminer in the midlands 1493, J.P. for Hants. 1493–1509, Glos. 1504–9 and temporarily for 23 other counties, serjeant at law from 1494, king's serjeant at law from 1497 and justice of Common Pleas from 1504: *Hist. of Parl., Biographies 1439–1509*; *Cal. Pat.* 1494–1509, 354. Justice of assize 1502–9 and commissioner of gaol delivery at various places between 1495 and 1509, in which capacity he sat with William Greville at Gloucester in 1506: ibid. 488 & *passim*.

[5] For £200 according to a final concord dated 27 Oct. 1507 whereby John and Matilda Roberts conveyed to Richard Spencer and Richard Peere (presumably on the prior's behalf) the manor of *Ocleys Court* and 3 messuages, 200 a. of land, 100 a. of pasture, 20 a. of wood and 100s. rent in Okle and Newent: P.R.O. CP 25/1/79/97, no. 74.

[6] 'A pretty house of stone': John Leland in *Trans. B.G.A.S.* xiv. 244. It was rebuilt on another site, as the present Newark House, for John Viscount Scudamore in 1690–6: B.L. Add. MS. 11046/vi, f. 31. Dr. Bridgett Jones supplied this reference.

[7] MS. *predictas*.

[8] MS. *scelulam*.

et intellectis munimentis et evidenciis utriusque partis per probos et discretos viros Mr. Iohannes Kyngismyll iudicem ex parte dictorum Iohannis et Matilde et Mr. Willelmum Grevell servientem ad legem ex parte dicti prioris itinerantes aput Gloucestriam, ordinatum, diffinitum et conclusum est quod dicti Iohannes et Matilda pro se et heredibus suis imperpetuum relaxarent predicto Domino Edmundo priori Lanthonie et successoribus suis predictam cartam talliatam et totum titulum suum quem ad predictum manerium de Ocle cum pertinenciis pretendebant habere, quod et fecerunt. Et quia predicta Matilda fuit tunc sub potestate viri sui, igitur adducta coram predicto Mr. Iohanne Kyngismyll iudice spontanea voluntate et non coacta totum titulum suum quod iure hereditario in predicto manerio de Ocle habere deberet publice prefato Domino Edmundo priori Lanthonie et successoribus suis imperpetuum relaxavit.

Pro quorum quidem relaxacione et predicte Matilde publica coram predicto iudice confessione, statutum et ordinatum fuit per predictum Mr. Iohannem Kyngismyll et Willelmum Grevell quod predictus Dominus Edmundus prior pro hac finali concordia et perpetua pace inde habenda daret predictis Iohanni Roberts et Matilde uxori eius summam sexaginta librarum, quam quidem summam £60 predictus prior solvit Iohanni et Matilde simul in una summa apud 'le Newarke' prope Hempstid in presencia predictorum Mr. Iohannis Kyngismyll et Mr. Willelmi Grevell, ut manifestius patet per librum eiusdem prioris de percellis, viz. Sabbato ante festum Sancti Laurencii martyris anno regni Regis Henrici VII 22.

Et ne talis finis et amicabilis concordia in processu temporum oblivioni[1] fortassis daretur, predictus prior hanc notam hic in registro suo intitulari fecit, anno videlicet secundo Henrici Octavi.[2]

218. On the redemption from William Burggis[3] of Longdon [Worcs.] of title to lands and tenements in Quedgeley (*Quedesley*), Whaddon, Elmore and Arlingham (*Erlingham*) which Thomas Morgan and J[ohn] Hilley of Gloucester previously sold by deed (*cartam*) and release to Prior Henry Dene, having had them of the feoffment of Thomas Tethegy and William Knyght. After Dene's death Burggis claimed the properties, exhibiting a sealed deed, a levied fine[4] and other muniments (*cartam talliatam, finem levatum et alia munimenta*). When both parties' lawyers had inspected the documents [f. 33] Burggis released his claim by a final concord and

---

[1] MS. *oblivione.*

[2] MS. *Henrico Octavo*

[3] Alias Bridges (d. 1523), lord of Eastington in Longdon by right of his wife Alice, lord of Ketford in Dymock by inheritance and brother of Sir John the lord mayor of London: *Visit. Glos. 1623,* 234; *Visitation of Worcs. 1569* (Harleian Soc. xxvi), 25; *V.C.H. Worcs.* iv. 115; J. E. Gethyn-Jones, *Dymock down the ages* (privately printed, 1966), 33.

[4] Probably a final concord of 20 Jan. 1463 whereby John and Elizabeth Garun conveyed land in Quedgeley and other places to Thomas, Matilda and John Brugge: P.R.O. CP 25/1/294/74, no. 9.

handed them over to Prior Forest for 20 marks[1] paid by the prior's deputies Henry Sheyar and John Chadwell. Entered in 2 Hen. [VIII, 1510–11].

219. On the redemption from Thomas Waren of Stonehouse (*Stonhowse*) of title to lands and tenements in the demesne of Haresfield (*Harsfeelde*) called *le Pynchons* which Prior Dene previously purchased from Richard Frenshe, property worth 12s. gross, 7s. 10d. net and owing service and pleas to the chief lord of the fee. Waren had paid 5 marks to the rightful heirs of the property for a title (*statum*) to it and certain muniments concerning it. When Prior Forest succeeded he met Waren who released his claim and handed over the documents on being repaid the 5 marks. Entered in 2 Hen. VIII [1510–11].

220. [f. 33v.] On lands and tenements purchased by Prior Henry Dene from John Harsfeld.
(a) Rodmoor[2] in the demesne of Haresfield, let to men surnamed Serynen and Berd[3] at an initial rent of 8s. which was increased to 10s. by a court of Llanthony and Haresfield in March 1511.
(b) Waren's Lease in the demesne of Standish, let to John Bonde[4] for 9s. a year by a court held at Llanthony in March 1511.

Preterea sciendum est quod prefatus honorandus pater Dominus Henricus Dene quondam Cantuarensis archiepiscopus sepedictus perquesivit certas alias terras et pasturas de quodam Iohanne Harsfeld vulgariter vocatas 'Roddore', quas quidem terras duo homines cognominati Serynen et Berd modo tenent. Et solebant reddere prefato priori Domino Henrico Dene pro predictis terris et pasturis 8s. per annum, et iam reddent Domino Edmundo nunc priori 2s. amplius de meremento redditus. Summa igitur totalis nunc 10s. est, ut patet per rotulam curie de Lanthonie et Hersfeld ad terminum Annunciacionis Beate Marie ibidem tente anno regni Regis Henrici Octavi 2.

Item prefatus honorandus prior Dominus Henricus Dene Cantuariensis episcopus et prior Lanthonie predicte perquesivit a predicto Iohanne Harsfelde alias terras et pasturas infra dominium de Standish vulgariter vocatas 'Warynnis Leese' ut patet per cartas inde factas et in custodia prioris Lanthonie remanentes, quas quidem Iohannes Bonde modo tenet et reddet per annum 9s. ut patet per rotulam curie tente apud Lanthoniam predictam termino Annunciacionis Beate Marie supradicto, anno eiusdem Regis Henrici VIII similiter secundo.

[1] For 40 marks according to a final concord dated 27 Oct. 1505 whereby William and Alice Brugge conveyed to Henry Shoyer and John Chadwell (evidently on the prior's behalf) 36 a. of land, 6 a. of meadow and 6d. rent in Quedgeley: P.R.O. CP 25/1/79/97, no.64.
[2] At SO 774116 NW. of Oakey Farm: map, Glos. R.O. Q/RI/74.
[3] Names represented in 1522 by Thomas Serney and John Berde both of Standish: *Military Survey of Glos. 1522*, 183.
[4] d. by 1539, when Alice Bond held it: *Glevensis* xxxiii. 54. He owned goods worth £19: *Military Survey of Glos. 1522*, 186.

221. Note that, lest any of the property purchased by Prior Dene should be escheated under the Statute of Mortmain, Prior Forest purchased the following pardon.

222. The king's[1] general pardon to Edmund Forest alias Shyar, prior of Llanthony-by-Gloucester [ff. 34–8] and of Llanthony in Wales, and to his convent, for all offences committed before 23 Apr. 1 Hen. VIII [1509]. [f. 38v.] Westminster, 9 July 1 Hen. VIII [1509].[2]

223. Letter under the royal signet announcing the birth of a prince.[3] Richmond [Surrey], 1 Jan. [1511].

Trusty and welbeloved in God, we grete you welle. And where it hath pleased almighty God oure maker of his infynite grace and goodnesse to send unto us at this tyme good spede in the deliveraunce and bringing furthe of a prince, to the greate reioysing and comfort of my lorde, us and al his loving subgietts of this his kingdome, for whiche singular grace we have especial cause to geve thanks and praising to our said maker, as so we right hertely doe; and forsomoche as we trust that this oure good spede is to youre comfort, advertise you thereof by these our letters; desiring and praying you to geve with us for the same unto oure said maker honour, lawde and praise, and to pray for the good helthe, prousperite and preservacion of the said prince. Yeven under oure signet at my lord's manor of Richemont the furst day of January.

224. Manumission of John Shepard alias Teste and his sons Thomas and Gerard, neifs of Hempsted (*Heyhamsted*), and their issue [as **164** above]. 17 Jan. 18 Hen. VII [1503].

225. [f. 39] Appointment of John Hogge lately of Gloucester, carpenter, alias John Dekyns, carver,[4] to work on buildings and other necessary works in and outside the convent, receiving
   (a) for life, a chamber in the priory lately occupied by John Carewent, with waste timber from Gloucester and elsewhere for winter fuel there,
   (b) as long as he can work, a pension of 1d. a day (including holidays) with victuals and an artificer's gown, and
   (c) when he can work no longer, alms of 20s. a year. [No date.]

---

[1] The initial letters of *Henricus* here and of *Trusty* in **223** below are ornamented with foliage and interlaced flourishes and are executed in double strokes bound with scrolls inscribed *Timentibus Deum nichil deest nec [h]is qui eum diligunt in veritate* (illus. above, p. xxxviii). The opening words from Psalm xxxiv. 9 'They that fear God lack nothing' occur elsewhere as Prior Forest's motto: above, p. xxii. They are here extended with a paradoxical allusion to Psalm cxxii. 6, 'nor do they that truly love him'. For [h]*is* cf. **124** n.
  [2] Calendared in *L. & P. Hen. VIII*, i, p. 226.
  [3] Henry duke of Cornwall, b. at Richmond 1 Jan., d. there 22 Feb. 1511: *Complete Peerage.*
  [4] Resident in Trinity parish and tenant of land beside the town ditch N. of the E. gate: Glos. R.O. GBR/B2/1, f. 226; GBR/J5/3.

Omnibus Christo fidelibus ad quos presens scriptum pervenerit Edmundus, permissione divina prior domus et ecclesie Beate Marie de Lanthonia iuxta Gloucestriam, et eiusdem loci conventus salutem in Deo sempiternam. Noveritis nos prefatum priorem et conventum dedisse, concessisse et per hoc presens scriptum nostrum confirmasse Iohanni Hogge nuper de Gloucestria, carpenter, alias dicto Iohanni Dekyns nuper de Gloucestria, carver, quandam diurnam pensionem videlicet 1 denarium per diem tam diebus festivis quam aliis diebus tam diu [quam] dictus Iohannes potest laborare in operacione dicti domini prioris et eiusdem loci conventus, tam in edificiis domorum quam in aliis operacionibus necessariis eiusdem et extra locum ad placitum dicti domini prioris vel eius deputati, si predictus Iohannes possit laborare, cum victu ac una toga sicut ut decet talem artificem habere.

Et eciam dictus prior concessit prefato[1] Iohanni Hogge alias Dekyns unam cameram quam Iohannes Carewent nuper occupaverat in dicto prioratu ad terminum vite sue. Ac eciam dictus prior concessit prefato Iohanni Hoggs alias Dekyns omnia focalia de exitu meremii que dicuntur fewell in willa Gloucestrie et extra ad cameram dicti Iohannis in tempore yemali. Ac eciam noveritis nos prefatum priorem et conventum dedisse et concessisse dicto Iohanni Hoggs alias Dekyns in elemosinam annuatim ad terminum vite sue 20s. cum omnibus predictis concessis quando dictus Iohannes amplius laborare non potest in arte sua.

Habendo et percipiendo omnia predicta ut predicuntur ad terminum vite sue etc. In cuius rei testimonium sigillum nostrum commune est appensum.

226. On an arbitrators' award appropriating a chantry at Tillington chapel in Burghill [Herefs.] to the priory of Llanthony in Wales. [1453 × 8].[2]

Memorandum that thereas there was a replegiare [i.e. writ of replevin] *ysuyde by the priour and the covent of Lanthoney in Walis apon a distresse ytake by Harry Oldcastell,[3] lorde of the manor of Tyllynton with all the appertenances as in the wright of Elsabet his wiffe by a joynt asstate that she hadde with John of Milborne[4]*

---

[1] MS. *prefati.*

[2] Dated soon after Simon Milburne's majority: see below.

[3] Son and heir of the Lollard rebel Sir John Oldcastle, Lord Cobham (d. 1417), of whose property he recovered Almeley manor (Herefs.) in 1431 and tenements at Baysham in Sellack, King's Caple and Brockhampton (Herefs.) in 1444; M.P. for Herefs. 1427, 1442 and 1453 and J.P. there 1456–8: *Complete Peerage*, x, appendix 'Sketch pedigree to illustrate Oldcastle' & n.; *Hist. of Parl., Biographies 1439–1509.*

[4] From Sir William of Eynesford, who is mentioned below, Tillington descended as follows (cf. *Visit. Herefs. 1569*, 36, 90):

(a) Sir William's nephew John of Eynesford alias Eylesford, Kt. (d. 1396) and his wife Isabel (d. 1421), who later married Richard de la Mare: *Calendarium Inquisitionum post mortem* (Rec. Com.), iii. 189; iv. 59; *Reg. Trefnant*, 35.

(b) Sir John's daughter Elizabeth and her husband Peter Milborne: C. J. Robinson, *Mansions and Manors of Herefs.* (London, 1872), 54.

(c) Their son John Milborne (d. 1436) and his wife Elizabeth (daughter of Walter Devereux) who also held jointly the manors of Munsley (Herefs.), Westbury Burghill and Bulley (Glos.) and Holme (Lincs.): *Calendarium Inquisitionum post mortem* (Rec. Com.), iv. 175; *Cal. Close 1435–41*, 75; *V.C.H. Glos.* x. 87.

not yore ago her husbonde heveryter [i.e. inheritor] *to the saide manor (the wyche dystresse was takon by the seyde Harey apon the seyde priour as person of the churche of Burghull for the wytdraugto* [i.e. withdrawal] *of a prestes servyce for 3 days in the weke within the chapell of Tyllynton[1] bryngyng with him bred, wyne and wax, that ys to say Sonday, Wenysday and Fryday, and also the lenton and midwyntour every day and every holy day throght the yere, the wyche servyce and charge as hit is surmyttyd by the sayde Harry hath byn boron by the sayde priour and covent and her predecessors without eny interupcion soth the tyme that no mynde ys into now); that the seyde prior sayth that by eny evidens that he kan fynde within her hows ne in no othir place he owght nott to bere no such charge, for they sayn all the lyvelode that they hav within that lordeshippe othir ony othir that was yevyn by eny lorde of the sayde Tyllynton was yevyn frely in puram et perpetuam elemosinam* [i.e. in frankalmoin] *without eny charge, and so thinkyt him and his concell hy owght not to bere that charge inlasse then there were a cause.*

And hongynge this seyde ple att the comyn lawe, att the instance of certeyn frendes of both sides this matr & all other maters and debates weren putt in ordinaunce and rewarde and jugement (by sufficyant surete foundon) of Watkyn Devereux[2] and John Monynton,[3] the wiche arbitrors by the avice and councell of owr soverayne father in God the bysshope of Herforde, after the mater yherde on both sydes, for the awrireste [i.e. most awry claims] *that they seon on both sydez they findon a mene way by the wysdom and goodwyll of owr seyde* [f. 39v.] *father in God the busshupp and with the grace of God to Goddis pleasaunce, the wiche by reson with that that it may stonde be comon ryght and not ayenst the lawe spirytuall ne temporall, but stondon firme and stabull by the avice of goode concell of bothe lawes, most nedis torn to ese of bothe hem, as it is though[t] by the seyde arbitours, the wiche mene way is this.*

They findon by the olde evedens and recordes that there was a chaunterye yfunded

---

[1] St. Michael's: *Cal. Pat.* 1340–3, 63. The chapel site, at Tillington Court, is mentioned in 18th-century deeds and was occupied by a dovecot from *c.* 1700: *Trans. Woolhope N.F.C.* 1930–2, 62.

[2] Probably not Sir Walter Devereux of Weobley and Bodenham, Herefs. (d. 1459), five times M.P. for the county, but his namesake son and heir (1432–85) who was knighted at Towton 1461 and created Baron Ferrers of Chartley (Staffs.) 1461. The latter, as an esquire, was M.P. for Herefs. 1460 and by marriage to Anne Ferrers in 1453 was lord of 10 manors in Berks., Hunts., Northants., Oxon., Staffs. and Warws. As Baron Ferrers he was at various times J.P. for six counties, commissioner of oyer and terminer for Wales and 12 counties, constable of Aberystwyth, Brecon and Hay, tutor to the prince of Wales and K.G.: *Hist. of Parl., Biographies 1439–1509; Complete Peerage; Cal. Pat.* 1467–77, *passim*; 1476–85, 50, 145, 560–1, 570.

[3] Trustee from 1417 of the jointure of John and Agnes Merbury, which he conveyed in 1438 to Walter (later Sir Walter) Devereux as Agnes's son. It comprised the castle and manor of Weobley (Herefs.) and other estates in seven counties: *Cal. Fine R.* 1437–45, 31–3.

by Sir Will of Eynesforde,[1] *sumtyme lorde of the said manor, of a prestes servyce to be don within the seid chapell of Tyllynton in perpetuete, and thereto yaf and mortest* [i.e. amortised] *to susteyn that divine service within the seyd chapell, to pray for him and his auncetors ant to do sertayne observaunce, that is to sey in every fest of 9 lessons to sey Placebo and Dirige for hym and all Crision* [souls], *and to susteyn this divine servyce yaf 3 mes[suag]es, 6 score and 3 acres of londe erabull* [i.e. arable] *and 3 acres of medowe lyynge be metes and boundes within the said lordeshipp of Tyllynton and Burghull;*[2] *and ordeyned that whosoever were lorde of Tyllynton shulde be patrone, and yf the servyce were woyde by a month and no man presented, that the busshupp shulde presente, so that he were an able prest to observe and kepe his charge aftur the forme of the composicion that was made betwene the patron and the first presente[e].*

And forsomuche as the londe is nott so much werth nowe[3] *as it was sumtyme, ne prestes so grete chepe as they weren of olde tyme, as nowe there will no prest seche after that servyce ne in no wise bere that charge, for the lyvelode is to[o] pore for eny preste to leve apon, as every man seyth, and so the sayd servyce stont and hath yore voyde; whereapon the arbytros abovesayde by the wysedome and good concell of owr seyd fathir in God the busshupp hav ordeyned and rewarded, with that that it may lawfully stonde by the avice of good concell on both sydes bothe spirituall and temporall, that the sayde Harry Oldecastell and Elsabeth his wife, the wiche hathe a joynt asstate in the tayle, here son and heyre beying within age, that is to say the son of John of Mylborne,*[4] *shullon suffre, devise and ordeyne by wey of presentacon or eny othir graunt that lawe woll in eny wyse suffre, by the avice of concell as it is above said, that the sayde prior and covent shall have the seyd lyvelode and lande to them & there successors for evermore, and they to fynden an able preste*[5] *to syng*

---

[1] Also called 'of Eyllesford' and 'of Kent', owner of land in Herefs. by 1328 and in Surrey by 1338: *Cal. Close* 1327–30, 379; 1333–7, 347; 1337–9, 407. He also acquired the manor of Westbury Burghill (Glos.) in 1334 and Scottish lands in 1335, and in 1340 was granted an annuity of £20 at the Exchequer: *Cal. Pat.* 1334–8, 61; 1338–40, 441; 1345–8, 279; cf. *V.C.H. Glos.* x. 87.

[2] Sir William of Eynesford and Roger of Burghill originally gave 100 a. of land, 6 a. of meadow and 3 a. of wood for two priests to celebrate divine service daily under a mortmain licence of 1340: *Cal. Pat.* 1340–3, 63. Sir John of Eynesford redefined the gift under an episcopal licence of 1395 to comprise scattered properties of the extent described here: *Reg. Trefnant*, 30–6.

[3] 33s. 4d. in 1535: *Valor Eccl.* (Rec. Com.), iii. 34.

[4] Simon Milborne (1432–1522), lord of Tillington and Westbury Burghill (Glos.) by inheritance and of Icomb (Glos.) by marriage: *Visit. Herefs. 1569*, 36, 90; Duncumb, *Herefs., Hundred of Grimsworth*, 52; P.R.O. C 142/81/243; *V.C.H. Glos.* x. 87; *V.C.H. Worcs.* iii. 415. J.P. for Glos. 1473 and Herefs. 1473–5, 1483–96, sheriff of Herefs. 1463, 1479 and commissioner of gaol delivery at Hereford 1487–90: *Cal Pat.* 1467–77 and later vols., Commissions of the Peace; *Cal. Pat.* 1485–94, 213, 319; *Cal. Fine R.* 1471–85, 178; Duncumb, *Herefs.* i. 144–5.

[5] Cf. above, **147**; below, **466**. Prior Hart evidently sold a turn of the advowson, since three trustees (Thomas Monyngton, Griffin Barton Esq. and Sibyl Breyntone) presented to the living in 1529, and in 1535 the chaplain received the gross income: *Reg. Bothe*, 343; *Valor Eccl.* (Rec. Com.), iii. 34.

*within the said chapell every day throught the yere, bryngyng with hym brede, wyne
and wax, and in especiall to pray for the fownder of that servyce and for his
auncetors, and also bere and do all othir charges the wiche ben comprehendyd
within the old composycon. And this ydon and this charche observed & kept in all
maner degre, that then the sayd prior & covent to ben discharged of the fyrst
servyce, that is to say for to fyndon a prest for 3 days in the weke.*

227. Title of Dudstone hospital (for the purpose of ordination) granted to Patrick
Keryn, clerk [as **132** above]. [f. 40] 15 Mar. 1510[/11].

228. Letters patent from Richard [Mayew], bishop of Hereford, on the vicar's
portion at Weobley (Herefs).
   When this matter was disputed between Edmund prior of Llanthony as rector of
Weobley[1] and John Batty, vicar there, they chose as arbitrators John Wardroper,
B.Cn. & C.L., archdeacon of Stafford and residentiary canon of Hereford,[2] and
Henry Martyn, B.Cn. & C.L., canon of Hereford. The arbitrators awarded to the
vicar and his successors:
   (a) a messuage by the canons' yardland,
   (b) altarage, viz. oblations,
   (c) tithes of wool, lambs, piglets, calves, chickens, geese, eggs, flax, hemp, leeks
and pasturage, except the pasturage of Weobley Little Park and the first *tacke* of the
Great Park Meadow which belong to the rector,
   (d) the second *tacke* of that meadow,
   (e) other small tithes and
   (f) two pack-horse loads (*summas*) of wheat and one of oats yearly from the
prior's *Canon Barne* at Weobley.
[f. 40v.] [Stretton] Sugwas manor [Herefs.], 28 Mar. 1511.

229. Proxy to [   ] to act for the prior in Ireland [as in **65** above, except that the
proctors are not to demise tithes or revenues of churches for terms of more than
three years]. [f. 41] 20 May 1511.

230. Letter [from the authors of the commission **231** below] to the priors of
Llanthony and Haverfordwest [Pemb.] on collecting money for St. Mary's College,
Oxford.[3] [7 May 1511.]

*To the ryght worshipfull brethern in God priors of Lanthony and Herford, visitors of
Saint Augsten's religion, and to either of them, be this delyveryd in goodly hast.*

---

[1] Weobley church was given to the priory by Gilbert de Lacy before 1158: P.R.O. C 115/75,
f. 216 no. 25.
[2] d. 1515; papal notary public 1488, prebendary of Lichfield and archdeacon of Stafford
1501–15, rector of Stow-on-the-Wold 1502–15, vicar general of Hereford diocese from 1504,
prebendary there 1506–15, residentiary canon 1508–13 and official 1511–15: Emden, *Biog.
Reg. Oxon. to 1500.*
[3] Cf. above, p. xxiii.

Ryght worshipfull brethren in Christ, due recommendacions had, we have send unto yeu a commyssion for the colleccion of certayn multiz and peynes [i.e. fines and penalties] *of oure brethren being absent at oure last chaptor held at Leicester,*[1] *and certen contribucions graunted at the same chaptor unto the edifying of Oure Lady College in Oxford, whos names and sommes do folowe in the said commission. We have also received lettres of late from the worshipfull of the same universite exorting us goodlie to provide remedy among us for the reparacion of the same college, wiche as we all knowe is ruinose and desolate. And as we have be enformed, the scolars studentiz of oure religion be compelled to enhabett themselffs in other colleg[es] & places of the same universite,*[2] *wich may be well taken for a slaunder and rebuke of oure hole religion.*

In avoiding of wich inconvenience & of all other that may herupon ensue we require you to gyve your diligence in all goodly hast in excecuting of this commission to the performaunce of the said charge, and all such persones of oure religion that be not expressed in the same commission, that ye goodly do exorte them and move them for their charitable contribucions unto the same. And thus doing we shall avoide the displeasor of the hoole [f. 41v.] *universite and deserve thanks of Almyghty God. Good brethern, we send to you the names of the multacions* [i.e. fines to be collected] *within yer progresse, to redy yeu suerly therein of wich ye*[3] *be oncerten, praying yeu forther effectually to exorte all such as shold have scolers at the universite and as yet have noon, for defaulte whereof straite commissions shal be directed to them except they shortly doo their dutiez in executing the premisses.*

We forther, regarding as well your paynes, labors and trobly jorneis as the costs and expenses of religious places (not willing them to be double charged), considering the generall chaptor is but a yere hens to com, we therfore woll that ye determyn yourselfs fully to execute this commission and the contents of the same toguyders in this your visitacion all in oon. And thus we commyt yeu to Allmyghti Jhu who preserve yeu. Amen.

231. Commission from Richard [Pescall] abbot of Leicester, Henry [Cocks] abbot of Northampton and Ralph [Maxfeld] abbot of Kenilworth [Warws.],[4] presidents of the last general chapter of the Augustinian order held at Leicester, to the priors of Llanthony and Haverfordwest (*Herford*) [Pemb.] to collect, within the limits of their visitation,[5] contributions to the building and repair of St. Mary's College at Oxford and the undermentioned fines as agreed at that chapter, and to pay them to the abbot of Osney [Oxon.] and William Wall, prior of regular students at Oxford,[6]

---

[1] At Trinity 1509: Salter, *Chapt. Augustin.* 126.

[2] Contrary to an order from the chapter of Barnwell (Cambs.) of 1506: Salter, *Chapt. Augustin.* 125.

[3] MS. *we.*

[4] Surnames supplied from *V.C.H. Leics.* ii. 19; *V.C.H. Northants.* ii. 130; *V.C.H. Warws.* ii. 89.

[5] i.e. the dioceses of Worcester, Hereford and St. David's: Salter, *Chapt. Augustin.* 130.

[6] d. 1536–7; B.Th. 1512, canon of Kenilworth, prior there in 1516 and abbot 1516–36: Emden, *Biog. Reg. Oxon. 1501–40.*

by 25 July. 7 May 1511.[1]

Fines for not attending [at Leicester in 1509]:[2]

Butley Priory [Suff.] 40s.

Chirbury Priory [Salop.] 6s. 8d.

[Canons] Ashby Priory [Northants.] 20s.

Cirencester Abbey £10

Dunstable Priory [Beds.] £5

Dodford Priory [Worcs.] 10s.

Caldwell Priory [Beds.] 6s. 8d.

Haverfordwest (*Haferfordia*) Priory [Pemb.] 10s.

Ravenstone Priory [Bucks.] 6s. 8d.

Bardsey (*Bradsey*) Abbey [Caern.] 40s.

Huntingdon Priory 20s.

Penmon Priory [Anglesey] 10s.

Bushmead Priory [Beds.] 10s.

Beddgelert (*Beytokeleyte*) Priory [Caern.] 10s.

Stonely Priory [Hunts.] 6s. 8d.

St. Tudwal's (*Medestedewale*) Priory [Caern.] 10s.

[f. 42] Burscough (*Bureshogh*) Priory [Lancs.] 40s.

Pynham Priory (*de Colceto iuxta Arundell*) [Suss.] 6s. 8d.

[Church] Gresley Priory [Derb.] 6s. 8d.

Southwark Priory [Surr.] 13s. 4d.

Breadsall Priory (*de parco de Bradesale*) [Derb.] 3s. 4d.

Reigate Priory [Surr.] 13s. 4d.

Cholesburne Priory [unident.] 10s.

Tandridge Priory [Surr.] 13s.4d.

Pinkeney Priory [unident.] 6s. 8d.[3]

Bradenstoke Priory [Wilts.] £5

Sandleford Priory [Berks.] 13s. 4d.

Anglesey Priory [Cambs.] 40s.

Fines for not having scholars at Oxford:[4]

Colchester (*Cecestria*) Priory [Essex] £5

Nostell Priory [Yorks.] £5

Leicester Abbey £5

Kirkham Priory [Yorks.] 40s.

Dunstable Priory [Beds.] £5

Newburgh Priory [Yorks.] £5

St. Frideswide's Priory [Oxford] 20s.

Bolton Priory [Yorks.] £3

Haughmond Abbey [Salop.] 20s.

Thurgarton Priory [Notts.] £3

Cirencester Abbey £5

Carlisle Priory [Cumb.] £5

Southwark Priory [Surr.] £3[5]

Newark Priory [Surr.] (*de Newloco iuxta Gilford*) 40s.

---

[1] Similar clauses and schedules were included in a commission from the same authorities, dated 30 Aug. 1511, to the priors of Newnham (Beds.) and Launde (Leics.) to visit the archdeaconries of Oxon., Bucks. and Beds., and are printed in the original language and spelling in Salter, *Chapt. Augustin.* 185–7.

[2] This list is as agreed in 1509, although Dodford was a Premonstratensian house. The list supplied to the priors of Newnham and Launde added the names of Stone Priory [Staffs.], Trentham Priory [Staffs.] and Walsingham Priory [Norf.]: ibid. 128–9, 187.

[3] Cholesburne alias Heelburg and Pinkeney alias Pionia were in or near the diocese of Hereford, Pinkeney being possibly the Arrouaisian priory of Wormsley by King's Pyon (Herefs.): Salter, *Chapt. Augustin.* 269, 272, 276–8.

[4] 44 houses were required to do this: ibid. 99–100, 129–30.

[5] By an error which is found also in the prior of Newnham's copy, two entries 'Southwick Priory [Hants.] £3' and 'Southwark Priory £5' are here confused: ibid. 130, 187.

232. Prior Forest's citation of John [Hagbourne], abbot,[1] to a visitation of Cirencester Abbey on 17 Aug.[2] 20 July 1511.[3]

233. The abbot's reply seeking deferral from 3 to 17 Aug. Bradenstoke [Priory, Wilts.], 20 July 1511.

Ryght honorabull fadyr yn Gode and my syngular frynd, y hertyly recummend me unto yew. Soe hit ys a servant of yewrs hathe dylyverd me a cytacion for me & my brethern to [f. 42v.] *apere afore yew yn my chapter howse the 3 day of August next enseewyng. Y and my brethren schal be glad to apere afore yew, but methinkkyth the day very schort & to me specyally grevys for mony consyderacions, as my servant can enforme yew. Wherefore yff hit shall plese yew to change the day & defer hit to the 16 or 17 day of the sayde monthe of August ye may doo me grete plesure, and not oonly to me but to such as y am nowe enbesyd* [i.e. embusied] *fore, and then ye shal be hertyly welcum. And glad y wold to doo the best chere to you as my howzss woll yeve. Be Godd's grace, who ever preserve yew. Amen. Fro Bradstocke in hast, celebritate Sancte Margarete;* [signed] *with the hond of yewrs to his power, John abbott of Cysstetur.*

234. Prior Forest's reply agreeing. 20 July 1511.

To the right reverend father in God and my especiall goode lover thabbot of Cyrcetor this letter be delyverid spedily.

Reverend father in God, I recummend me to you in my most lovyng maner. So ys hit that y have recevyd your discrete and gentill lettur, by the wiche y perceve that ye thinke your day of apparans very shorte and wold gladly have lenger respite for urgent causis and diverse consideracions you moving in that behalfe. Father, y am right well content and plesid, consedering your besynes, to differre my day of visitacion limited in the mandate or citacion directed to your fatherhode and my good bretheryn and yours, and to be withe you the dayis prefixed in your lettur, that ys to say the 16 day of August at Circetur at bedde in the town and the 17 day of the same monyth, that ys the morow folowyng, to be with you at 10 of the bell in your chaptur house.

Howbehit, y fere me that y shall have but lytyll thanks of our presidents for the prolongyng of tyme, considering that they all in on assent have appoyntyd my tyme by their writing autenticall, as I shall ferther declare unto you at owr next meting. Notwithstandyng, yf anything be objecte or cast unto my charge at the next generall chaptur, as in disobeing there writing by reson of brokyng of the day appointid, y shall for your sake & resonable desyre answer thereto as God shall put in my mynd. And thus our Lorde preserve you and send you as well to fare as your own kynde

---

[1] d. 1522; B.Th. 1500, prior of St. Mary's College, Oxford, in 1501, S.T.P. by 1504 and abbot of Cirencester 1504–22: Emden, *Biog. Reg. Oxon. to 1500*; *Trans. B.G.A.S.* cxi. 138. J.P. for Glos. 1510–14: *L. & P. Hen. VIII*, i, p. 1537.
[2] The original version of the citation had 3 Aug., as shown by **233** below.
[3] On the dating and that of the two letters that follow, see above, p. xl.

harte kan thinke. Wrote at Lanthony besyde Gloucetur on the feest of Saint Margarete with the hand of your brother and fast lover, Edmunde, prior.

235. Proxy to [f. 43] [fellow canons] Thomas Systetur and Robert Occle to act for the prior in Ireland [as in **229** above]. [f. 43v.] 16 Sept. 1511.

236. Certificate of John [Hagbourne] abbot of Cirencester acknowledging that on 1 Aug. he received Prior Forest's citation dated 15 July[1] to a visitation on 17 Aug. [f. 44] and that on 2 Aug. he cited his fellow canons, listed below, to appear.[2] Cirencester chapter house, 9 Aug. 1511.

The lord abbot; the lord prior; Dom John Bristowe; Dom John Durrisley, chamberlain, pittancer and kitchener; Dom John Dorney; Dom John Payneswyke, hosteler; Dom John Aston, chaplain and warden of the Lady Chapel; Dom John Blake, cellarer, almoner and warden of Cheltenham parish church;[3] Dom Richard Syssetur, warden of the parish church of St. John the Baptist of Cirencester, sacrist and warden of the infirmary; Dom William Burforde, warden of the refectory; Dom William Cernay, precentor; Dom Richard Brodwel; Dom Thomas Bray, subsacrist; Dom William Hakeborne; Dom Thomas Compton; Brothers Thomas Brynkeworth, John Pulham, John Rowell, William Frome, Robert Cheltinham, William Burton and Richard Hereforde; absent: Dom William Minsterworth; absent in apostasy: Dom John Saperton and Dom Thomas Frome.

237. Prior Forest's citation of Thomas [Atwood], prior, to a visitation of Studley Priory [Warws.] on 4 Aug. [f. 44v.] 20 July 1511.

238. Certificate of Thomas Atwodde, prior of Studley, acknowledging that on 22 July he received Prior Forest's citation and cited his brethren to appear, viz. William Tutbery subprior, William Alcestur, John Eton, William Cowgton, John Yardesley and Richard Ippysley priests and William Warwike and William Bromysgrove acolytes.[4] 28 July [1511].

239. Concerning William Welshe's homage for the fee of Netheridge[5] in Quedgeley, rendered 4 Dec. 1511.

---

[1] The true date of the citation was either 20 July as in **232** or a few days later if time is allowed for the transmission of the letter **233** above.

[2] The abbey had gained 14 canons and lost 13 since 1498, John Dur(ri)sley remaining chamberlain and kitchener throughout: *Reg. Morton*, ii. 131.

[3] Canon John Dursley was warden of Cheltenham parish church in 1498, as Canon Nicholas Fairford had been in 1378: *Reg. Wakefield* (Worcs. Hist. Soc. 1972), p. 156; *Reg. Morton*, ii. 131. Michael Greet supplied these references.

[4] The priory had gained 5 canons and lost 2 since 1498, Atwood and Tutbury remaining in office throughout: *Reg. Morton*, ii. 133.

[5] An estate of 80 a. which the Welshes held in fee from the priory from the late 13th century: *V.C.H. Glos.* x. 218–19.

In settlement of a dispute, [f. 45] as recorded in f. 138 of his register,[1] Prior Wyche at Llanthony on 8 June 8 Hen. V [1420] sealed an indenture confirming to James son of the late Giles le Welshe of Woolstrop (*Wolstrope*) [in Quedgeley] and his heirs the subinfeudation of *Netherruge in Quedesley* for:

(a) service of one knight's fee,

(b) yearly rent of 1 lb. of pepper,

(c) suit of court at Llanthony every Michaelmas and Easter,

(d) relief of 100s., homage and fealty

in the presence of William Beaucham[p] of Powicke [Worcs.] Kt.,[2] John Pauncefot Kt.,[3] Thomas Mulle of Harescombe,[4] Robert Whitinton[5] and others.

Accordingly William, son and heir of another James le Welshe, did homage for the same and paid 100s. to Prior Forest and 3s. 4d. to his chamberlain in Llanthony chapter house on the eve [20 Sept.] of St. Matthew 1511,[6] [f. 45v.] kissing the prior while kneeling and clasping his hands between the prior's knees, as follows. [Here the language changes.]

I knowlege myselfe to do you both feate and homage for suche certen lande as myne antecessors in tymes passede hathe holden of youe and youre predecessors by knyght service in the ritht of your churche and monastery of owr Blessyd Lady of Lanthony named Netheruge lying within the lordshipp of Queddysley in the counte of the towne of Glouceter, and to bere you feythe above all men saf the faythe of myne allercaunce [i.e. allegiance].

[1] Reg. Wyche, P.R.O. C 115/76.

[2] d. by 1422; constable of Gloucester castle from 1392–3, sheriff of Worcs. 1401 and of Glos. 1413: *V.C.H. Worcs.* iv. 186. Warden of the priory 1401: *Trans. B.G.A.S.* lxiii. 108. In addition to Powicke (Worcs.) he was lord of Boddington (Glos.): *V.C.H. Glos.* viii. 190.

[3] 1368–*c.* 1445; knighted 1394, M.P. for Glos. 1413 and 1421, J.P. there 1422–3 and 1432–8, sheriff of Glos. 1422, 1426 and 1434 and of Herefs. 1437, lord of Hasfield (Glos.), Crickhowell (Mon.), Cowarne (Herefs.) and Bentley Pauncefoot (Worcs.): *Hist. of Parl., Commons 1386–1421* correcting *Trans. B.G.A.S.* lxxi. 132–5; *V.C.H. Worcs.* iii. 226.

[4] Either the younger Thomas (d. 1460), for whom see above, **40** n., or his namesake father (d. 1422). The father was J.P. for Herefs. 1399–1419 and Glos. 1404–22, commissioner of gaol delivery at Hereford 1399, commissioner of oyer and terminer for Glos. 1402 and Worcs. 1405, M.P. for Glos. 1407 and 1411, escheator of Herefs. 1412, steward to the duchy of Lancaster in Herefs. and Glos. 1416–17, lord by inheritance of Traymill in Thorverton (Devon) and lord by marriage of Harescombe and Duntisbourne Rous (Glos.) and Avenbury, Allensmore and Tregate in Llanrothal (Herefs.): *Hist. of Parl., Commons 1386–1421*; *Trans. B.G.A.S.* x. 124, 128.

[5] d. 1423, elder brother of Richard Whittington (d. 1423) the mercer and mayor of London. M.P. for Glos. six times between 1384 and 1414, tax collector there 1384, J.P. 1390–7 and 1399–1423, escheator 1392–4, 1401 and 1409, justice of assize in Glos. and Som. 1395–6, constable of Dean Forest 1398, forester of Corse 1400–23, commissioner of oyer and terminer for Glos. and Worcs. 1401, sheriff of Glos. 1402, 1407 and 1412 and lord of Pauntley (Glos.), Staunton (then Worcs., now Glos.), Sollers Hope and Hopton in Stoke Lacy (Herefs.): *Hist. of Parl., Commons 1386–1421*; *V.C.H. Worcs.* iv. 199–200; P.R.O. PROB. 11/3, f. 8v. copied in Hockaday Abs. cccx, 1424.

[6] The date and the sum paid to the chamberlain, as given here, are contradicted below.

And in wittenes of this homage to my lorde abovesaid to be made and don, I the said William Welshe personally in the chaptur howse of the churche and monastery of owr Blessyd Lady of Lanthony aforesaid, in the presens of all the covent there and on[e] Robert Wye then beyng chyff stewarde of the said churche and monastery and oon John Arnold,[1] lerned, reteyned of councell with the said William Welshe then beyng, Richard Monyngton, William Phelipps, Richard Chi. clerke, John Coke,[2] John Crosse and John Berde wyth mony other, and for a recongnicion of the premisses, I the said William Welshe have paid for a relef in golde and silver for the said lande named Nethurruge unto the hande of oon William Heywode, notary papall and imperiall, to the use of the said lorde, 100s. of good and lawfull money of Englond in the chaptur howse of Lanthony aforesaid the 4 day of December the yere of the reigne of King Henry the VIII the 3 [1511].

And so the said William Welshe for the said lande is admitted a franke servaunt. And the said William hathe paid to the chamberleyne of the said lorde, of an old laudable custom, 6s. 8d.

---

[1] d. 1545; resident in 1509 at Cardiff (Glam.), Mathern (Mon.), Sudeley (Glos.) and London: *L. & P. Hen. VIII*, i, p. 223. J.P. for Usk, Caerleon and Trelleck (Mon.) 1515, J.P. for Glos. 1515–45, nominated as sheriff there 1530, 1532, commissioner for compounding in N. Wales 1534, commissioner for the survey now known as *Valor Ecclesiasticus* in Glos. and Bangor diocese 1535, protonotary of the Council of Wales 1535–*c.* 1540: *L. & P. Hen. VIII*, ii–xx *passim.* Steward of Dursley by 1522 and of Westbury-on-Severn from 1526: *Military Survey of Glos. 1522*,153; *Trans. B.G.A.S.* vi. 133. Steward of Thomas Lord Berkeley (d. 1532): John Smyth, *Lives of the Berkeleys* (Gloucester, 1883 ed.), ii. 241. Steward of Flaxley Abbey and of courts and hundreds for Gloucester Abbey: *Valor Eccl.* (Rec. Com.), ii. 418, 486. Commissioner for suppression of monasteries in Glos. 1539–40: *L. &. P. Hen. VIII*, xiv (2), 241, 260, 267; xv. 8, 11. Resident from 1523 at Highnam, where he acquired the manor by lease 1516 and by purchase 1542 and rebuilt the house; lord of Boseley in Westbury-on-Severn, lessee of the manors of Lassington, Rudford, Highleadon and Upleadon and owner of 120 a. at Longford and 420 sheep at Eastington near Northleach: *L. & P. Hen. VIII*, iv, p. 2376; xvii, p. 157; *V.C.H. Glos.* ix. 122; x. 18–19, 92; Smyth, *Lives of the Berkeleys*, ii. 222; P.R.O. PROB 11/31, f. 16, copied in Hockaday Abs. clii, 1546. Bencher of Lincoln's Inn by 1524: *Records of Lincoln's Inn, the Black Books* (London, 1897), i. 208. For his son (Sir) Nicholas cf. above, p. xxxi.

[2] Mercer, d. 1528; b. at Minsterworth, sheriff of Gloucester 1494, 1498 and mayor 1501, 1507, 1512, 1518, resident there in 1513 in St. Nicholas's parish but buried in St. Mary de Crypt: Austin, *Crypt School*, 14–27, 136–44; Glos. R.O. GBR/B2/1, f. 225v. Wealthiest man in Gloucester in 1524, assessed at £300: *V.C.H. Glos.* iv. 54. Owner of land at Minsterworth and purchaser in 1512 of Buckland Place in Badgeworth with six messuages and 64 a., in 1524 of a mill at Ebley in Stonehouse with 37 a. and in 1526 of Curteys at Oxlinch in Randwick: Glos. R.O. D3270/C1 (133), C6 (16), C8 (134); GBR/J1/1181, 1194, 1202–5. He bequeathed vestments worth 33s. 4d. to our Lady's altar in the priory: Austin, *Crypt School*, 138.

240. [f. 46] Letter of fraternity to Robert Poyntz, Kt.[1] [as **128** above].1 Oct. 1511.

[f. 46v. is blank. The last four lines of the above entry are repeated at the top of f. 47 in another hand.]

241. [f. 47] Letter of fraternity to Mr. Thomas Poyntz[2] and his wife Joan.[3] 1 Oct. 1511.

242. Proxy to John Batty, vicar of Weobley [Herefs.]. 16 Sept. 1511. [Abstract in MS.; cf. **130**]

243. Title of Dudstone hospital (for the purpose of ordination) granted to John Peggyn.[4] 16 Sept. 1511. [Abstract in MS.; cf. **132**]

244. Quittance to the abbot of Kingswood. [f. 47v.] 30 Sept. 1511. [Abstract in MS.; cf. **44**]

245. Lease to James and Catherine Hooper[5] and their son Richard of property at Bishop's Frome (Herefs.), viz.
   (a) rectorial tithes of grain and hay,

[1] Of Iron Acton, d. 1520. Sheriff of Glos. seven times between 1468 and 1501, sheriff of Hants. 1482: *Cal. Fine R.* 1461–71, 1471–85, 1485–1509 *passim*. J.P. for Glos. 1485–1515: *Cal. Pat.* 1485–94 and later vols., Commissions of the peace; *L. & P. Hen. VIII*, i, p. 1537; ii, pp. 190, 318. Esquire of the body to Edw. IV 1483, knighted at Rodmore 1485, constable of St. Briavels 1485–90, steward of the bishop of Worcester in Glos. 1488–1519, royal steward of Berkeley 1492–1520, steward of Bristol and Kingswood Abbeys, vice-chamberlain to the queen from 1509 and inclosure commissioner 1517; lord of Iron Acton, Alderley, Elkstone, Hill, (Little) Marshfield, Brokenborough in Almondsbury, Gaselyn's in Frampton Cotterell, Sturden in Winterbourne and Stanshawe's in Yate and owner of nos. 11–14 and 23 Wine Street, Bristol, resident at Greyfriars in London; buried at Gaunt's hospital, Bristol, in the Jesus chapel which he built and endowed: Sir John Maclean, *Memoir of the Family of Poyntz* (Exeter, 1886), 62–7, 95, 98–9; Christopher Dyer, *Lords and Peasants in a Changing Society* (Cambridge, 1980), 380; *Historic Churches & Church Life in Bristol* (B.G.A.S. 2001), 101; *Trans. B.G.A.S.* lxxiii. 123; *V.C.H. Glos.* v. 415; vii. 212; Leech, *Topog. Bristol*, i. 177, 180.
[2] Sir Robert's younger brother, d. after 1520; esquire of the body to Hen. VII 1488, granted a royal annuity 1489, royal steward of Bisley hundred from 1495: Maclean, *Family of Poyntz*, 61–3, 99. Commissioner of gaol delivery at Hereford 1494, Gloucester 1497 and Shrewsbury 1498, J.P. for Glos. and Herefs. 1496–1515, Salop. 1496–1510 and Worcs. 1502–7, sheriff of Glos. 1510, esquire for the body to Hen. VIII 1516, inclosure commissioner 1517: *Cal. Pat.* 1485–94, 476; 1494–1509 *passim*; *L. & P. Hen. VIII*, i, ii *passim*.
[3] d. after 1512; formerly wife of Sir Walter Devereux, Lord Ferrers (1432–85), after whose death she remained lady of the castle and manor of Weobley with King's Pyon and other places in Herefs.: *Complete Peerage*, s.v. Ferrers; cf. **226** n.
[4] Ordained acolyte 20 Sept., subdeacon 20 Dec. 1511 and priest 5 June 1512 by the bishop of Hereford: *Reg. Mayew*, 255–7.
[5] James still held the lease in 1535: *Valor Eccl.* (Rec. Com.), ii. 425.

(b) the rectory buildings and glebe as they were in the time of Richard Welyngton and

(c) the barn newly built by the late vicar Thomas Brugge

for 40 years at 10 marks a year for the tithes and 40s. a year for the buildings. The prior will find any timbers for repairing the rectory buildings [f. 48] and any timbers and stone tiles for repairing the barn. The lessees will maintain banks and breaches (*ripas et rupt'*) on the stream belonging to the glebe and will build on the glebe, within four years, a dwelling house for which the prior will give four oaks. The lessees will pay a procuration of 4 marks at the bishop's triennial visitation but may deduct it from their rent. The Purification 2 Hen. VIII [2 Feb. 1511].

246. Bond of Roger Homme, chaplain,[1] and John Gyney and James Hooper both of Bishop's Frome in £40 to perform the covenants of the above lease. [f. 48v.] The Nativity of St. John the Baptist 3 Hen. VIII [24 June 1511].

247. Lease to Richard Malcote, vicar of Henlow [Beds.], to William Watefild and Thomas Bathe, proctors of Henlow church, and to their successors of a plot measuring 100 ft. by 40 ft. by the churchyard there on the west (*iuxta cimiterium ibidem ex parte occidentali*) for building a *churche howse*, for ever at 2d. a year. 24 Sept. 2 Hen. VIII [1510].

248. [f. 49] Lease to Richard Philpott chaplain, Margaret widow of Richard Herbert[2] and her sons George and Matthew of the rectory buildings and tithes of corn at Caldicot [Mon.] for 30 years at £16 a year. 26 Apr. 3 Hen. VIII [1511].

249. [f. 49v.] Lease to Margaret, widow of Richard Herbert Esq., and her sons George and Matthew of property at Llantrisant [Mon.] lately held by Walter Herbert Kt.,[3] viz. a ruinous messuage,[4] 5 a. of demesne land and two pastures, formerly two islands, called *lez Stones* alias *Gregoise*,[5] for 30 years, rendering 46s. 8d. a year, suit to the prior's court there and heriot. 26 Apr. 3 Hen. VIII [1511].

---

[1] Alias Home, d. 1527, vicar of Canon Frome to 1503 and of Stretton Grandison to 1527: *Hereford Probates 1407–1581*, 234; above, **127**; cf. *Reg. Bothe*, 340.

[2] Of Ewyas (Herefs.), d. 1510, illegitimate son of William earl of Pembroke (d. 1469) and father of another William earl of Pembroke (1506–52): *Complete Peerage*. Gentleman usher to Hen. VII, receiver and farmer of the town and lordship of Abergavenny and from 1509 constable and porter of Abergavenny castle: *Cal. Pat.* 1485–94, 424; *L. & P. Hen. VIII*, i, pp. 70, 276, 337. Buried under an effigy in Abergavenny Priory: Bradney, *Mon.* i. 165; ii. 13.

[3] d. 1507, brother of William Herbert earl of Huntingdon (d. 1491); royal steward from 1486 of Talgarth and Cantref Selif (Brec.); lord from 1505 of the castles and manors of Raglan and Chepstow with Dingestow, Penrose and Redwick in Magor (Mon.) and the manor of Tidenham (Glos.): *Cal. Pat.* 1485–94, 88; *Cal. Close* 1500–9, pp. 196, 200; *Cal. Inq. p.m. Hen. VII*, iii, p. 447.

[4] In 1535 a capital messuage called Gregos: *Valor Eccl.* (Rec Com.), ii. 429.

[5] Let separately in 1543 for 2s. 4d. as 2 a. of land and 2 a. of pasture, and belonging in the 20th century to a house called Ty Mawr 100 yd. N of the church: Bradney, *Mon.* iii. 152.

250. [f. 50] Lease to Thomas Sebrygte, fishmonger of Gloucester, his wife Eleanor and their children John, Isabel and Catherine of

(a) [f. 50v.] a tenement[1] [in Gloucester] at the end of St John's (*Grase*) Lane opposite the door of St. Mary de Grace, lately held by William Goldsmyth and belonging to the sacrist of Llanthony, and

(b) a stable[2] in St. John's (*Grase*) lane belonging to the collector of Gloucester rents, between William Rede's garden[3] and a stable of the prior

for 40 years, rendering 33s. 4d. a year and suit to the prior's court in the church of St. Owen. The lessees will live in the tenement; they will maintain the tiling of the roofs with nails and battens (*tecta in tegulacione cum clavis et findulis*) and the walls called *mudde walle*, but if a new building is to be erected the prior will find timber. The Nativity of St. John the Baptist 3 Hen. VIII [24 June 1511].

251. [f. 51] Appointment of William Phelipps as porter (*ianitor*) of Llanthony Priory in Wales,[4] receiving

(a) 6s. 8d. a year,

(b) a gown a year, with 5s. at the discretion of the proctor and

(c) seven quarts a week of conventual ale from the cellarer of Llanthony in Wales. 9 Dec. 3 Hen. VIII [1511].

252. Lease to John and Christine Nicholas at Chirton, Wilts., and their son [   ] of property there formerly held by Richard Nasshe, viz. the manor house and buildings with demesne land, meadow and pasture, amercements, strays, customary fines, view of frankpledge and courts and   tithes of Chirton township, for 50 years, rendering yearly £10 6s. 8d. to the prior and 1 lb. of pepper to the abbess of St. Mary in Winchester. The lessees will fulfil the obligations listed [as in **50** above, except that they are required additionally to feed the subcellarer and are not required to leave the land sown]. [f. 51v.] Michaelmas 3 Hen. VIII [29 Sept. 1511].

[1] The front part of no. 14 Westgate Street, measuring 18 ft. 5in. by 33 ft. 10 in. in the 13th century when the prior of Llanthony-by-Gloucester held it from St. Margaret's hospital of the fee of Llanthony in Wales. By 1442 it was held by the prior of St. Oswald's, from whom Prior Deane evidently redeemed it: P.R.O. C 115/73, f. 61 (59)v. no. 121; C 115/75, f. 50v. no. 280 = C 115/81, f. 85v. = C 115/84, f. 85v. no. 218. Sebrygte probably rented the back of the same burgage from the abbot of Gloucester, as did his predecessor in title Thomas Berston: *Glouc. Rental 1455*, 59b.; cf. P.R.O. C 115/73 as above.

[2] About 70 ft. distant on the E. side of the lane behind no. 11 Northgate Street, where two stables were built after 1442 on the site of former cottages. Sebrygte held the N. stable under this lease and both by 1535: P.R.O. C 115/73, f. 60 (58)v. no. 119; Glos. R.O. GBR/J5/4.

[3] On the NE.; annexed to the Swan at nos. 13–15 Northgate Street, which John, Jane and William Reed held successively from the abbot of Gloucester, but also encroaching on the prior of Llanthony's land behind other stables in the lane: P.R.O. C 115/73, f. 60 (58) nos. 118–9; C 115/84, gloss to f. 115; *Glouc. Rental 1455*, 73b, 127.

[4] The porter's lodge comprised a large and handsome room over the outer gatehouse and wings to the W. and SW.: *Archaeologia Cambrensis*, 6th Ser. xvi. 58–9; plan, *Monmouthshire Antiquary*, v. 50.

253. Lease to Robert and Alice Mynott of Hempsted and their sons Thomas and Walter of

(a) Horsepool fish weir at the Rea [in Hempsted][1] with an osier bed (*persh*),[2] tree prunings in the Neyt and prunings of willows opposite Arland[3] and

(b) a long osier bed between Orlbern Ford and Oxleaze with tree prunings and willow prunings in the Hay and between Oxleaze and the Severn,[4] prunings of willows in Hayward's Way[5] between Moor Stile and Cowleaze, prunings of willows bordering Bagges Persh and around Canmore Mead and thorn bushes and dead willows in all the places mentioned, except brushwood required by the prior for fencing the Hay

for 60 years at £4 a year. The lessees will maintain the weir, unless it is destroyed by the king's officers,[6] but the prior will find half of the great timbers of the weir called reeds, reasons [i.e. lintels], weel-trees and aisletrees[7] and the lessees will carry them to site. They will renew dead willows; they may keep flotsam except boats. They will occupy the buildings in the Neyte except when the prior is there, and the prior will repair such buildings. 1 Feb. 1502.

Hec indentura facta primo die mensis Februarii anno regni Regis Henrici Septimi decimo septimo inter Edmundum Forest priorem domus et ecclesie Beate Marie Lanthonie iuxta Gloucestriam et eiusdem loci conventum[8] ex parte una et Robertum Mynott de Hempsted, Aliciam uxorem eius, Thomam et Walterum filios dictorum Roberti et Alicie ex altera, testatur quod predicti prior et conventus tradiderunt,

[1] The Rea or Horsepool Neyte, at SO 809163, was a detached part of the Llanthony estate from 1540 and was plotted on an estate map of *c.* 1790 as an inhabited eyot at the confluence of Daniel's Brook and the Severn: P.R.O. C 66/700, m. 41 (cf. *L. & P. Hen. VIII*, xvi, pp. 383–4); Glos. R.O. D134/P8. A moiety of Horsepool weir was given to the priory in 1141 and the other moiety *c.*1173: *V.C.H. Glos.* iv. 426. In 1276 the canons were using the fish house there as a place of retreat: *Trans. B.G.A.S.* lxiii. 56–7.

[2] For the meaning see A. H. Smith, *Place-Names of Glos.* (Eng. Place-Name Soc.), ii. 167; iv. 160.

[3] Beside the Severn at SO 807168: Glos. R.O. GDR/T1/99.

[4] Oxleaze at SO 807173 (to be distinguished from the Oxleaze mentioned in **31** above) and the Hay at SO 807170 both lay beside the Severn, which was evidently lined with osiers upstream to Orlbern Ford: Glos. R.O. D134/P8.

[5] Connecting Moor Stile at SO 815175 with Cowleaze at SO 810177: ibid. Now part of an approach road to a W. extension of Sudmeadow refuse tip, which has covered most of the places mentioned.

[6] Weirs on the Severn were destroyed by royal command in 1535, after which the Rea fishery yielded only 3s. 9d. rent: *L. & P. Hen. VIII*, ix, pp. 50, 166; xiv (1), p. 60; *Valor Eccl.* (Rec. Com.), ii. 430.

[7] The mouth of the weir was lined with wattle fences or barriers directing the fish into a narrow throat containing funnel-shaped basketwork traps called weels or putts. The great timbers listed here made up portal frames and intermediate members standing astride the traps: cf. J. M. Steane, M. Foreman and D. J. Pannett in Michael Aston (ed.), *Medieval Fish, Fisheries and Fishponds in England* (British Archaeological Reports, clxxxii, 1988), 171–4, 371–3.

[8] MS. *conventus.*

concesserunt et ad firmam dimiserunt prefatis Roberto, Alicie, Thome et Waltero gortum cum gurgite Sabrine ipsorum prioris et conventus apud 'le Ree' vocatum 'Harspole Were' cum toto 'le persshe, loppyng & shruding' omnium arborum crescentium in 'le Neyte', et omnium salicum ex opposito 'le Ardelond', ac 'le longe persshe' crescentem inter Orlbernford et Oxeleso cum 'le loppyng [et] shrudyng' omnium arborum et salicum crescentium in 'le Heye' et inter Oxeleso et Sabrinam et omnium salicum crescentium inter Morestile et Cowlesowe in 'le Heywardeswey' cum omnibus salicum 'loppe & shreude' sepiencium[1] ad 'le Baggespersshe' et omnium salicum circumquaque Canmore Mede ac cum omnibus spinis et putridis salicibus in et super singulis locis predictis; excepta et omnino reservata prefato priori et conventui ac successoribus suis sufficienti et convenienti tineta in 'le Haye' pro clausura eiusdem (quociens necesse fuerit) facienda, claudenda et ad custos et expenca dictorum prioris et successorum suorum reparanda et reficienda.

Habendo et tenendo predictum gortum cum gurgite, piscaria et proficuis eiusdem ac cum omnibus et singulis prescriptis cum suis pertinenciis, excepta tineta preexepta, prefato Roberto, Alicie, Thome et Waltero successive a die Nativitatis Sancti Iohannis Baptiste proxime futuro post datam presentium usque ad finem termini sexaginta annorum proxime extunc sequencium [f. 52] et plenarie complendorum, si ipsi Robertus, Alicia, Thomas et Walterus tam diu vixerint aut aliquis eorum tam diu vixerit. Reddendo inde annuatim prefatis priori et conventui et successoribus suis quatuor libras legalis monete Anglie solvendas ad festum Natale Domini et Nativitatem Sancti Iohannis Baptiste per equales porciones durante termino supradicto, primo termino solucionis inde incipiente in festo Natali Domini proxime post datam presentium.

Et predicti Robertus, Alicia, Thomas et Walterus predictum gortum reparabunt, sustentabunt et manutenebunt sumptibus suis propriis et expencis, tam in grosso meremio quam in aliis necessariis dicto gorto sepito quociens necesse fuerit durante termino predicto, et illum dimittent in tam bono statu in fine termini sui predicti sicut illum in principio eiusdem termini receperunt, si integer steterit et non lesus[2] seu destructus fuerit per dominum regem aut per ministros sive officiarios suos. Proviso semper quod predicti prior et conventus et successores sui invenient dimidiam partem grossi meremii dicti gorti vocati 'reodis', 'resons', 'weletren' et 'iletren' ad reparacionem predicti gorti quociens necesse fuerit durante termino predicto, quod quidem meremium per predictos priorem et conventum et successores suos prefatis Roberto, Alicie, Thome et Waltero aut alicui eorum infra comitatum Gloucestrie assignatum iidem Robertus, Alicia, Thomas et Walterus cariabunt a loco sic assignato usque dictum gortum sumptibus suis propriis et expensis durante termino predicto. Et iidem Robertus, Alicia, Thomas et Walterus durante termino predicto in loco cuiuslibet salicis modo crescentis in locis predictis devenientis putride et corrupte aliam iuvenem plantabunt.

Et predicti Robertus, Alicia, Thomas et Walterus omnia proficua et extrahuras

---

[1] MS. *septancium.*
[2] MS. *lesum.*

super dictum gurgitem[1] Sabrine nantes atque ad dictum gortum pervenientes habebunt, cymbis et naviculis dicto priori et successoribus suis omnino exceptis et reservatis. Et dicti Robertus, Alicia, Thomas et Walterus habebunt occupationem et suum aysiamentum in omnibus domibus ipsorum prioris et conventus in 'le Neto' modo edificatis, aliquo priore Lanthonie predicte personaliter ibidem non existente, et predictis domibus ad custos et expensas predictorum prioris et conventus omnino reparandis.

Et si contingat dictum redditum quatuor librarum in parte vel in toto a retro fore non solutum per quindecim dies post aliquem[2] finem suprascriptum inquo solvi debeat, aut statum sive terminum finium predictorum alicui persone[3] sive aliquibus personis concedi, dimitti sive assignari[4] sine licencia predictorum prioris et successorum suorum, aut omnes et singulas conventiones predictas minime observari, tunc bene licebit prefatis priori et conventui ac successoribus suis in omnia predicta domos, gortum, gurgitem,[5] piscariam etc. cum omnibus proficuis predictis reintrare et illa omnia cum ceteris premissis in manus suas reassumere et possidere, dictosque Robertum, Aliciam, Thomam[6] et Walterum et assignatos suos inde totaliter expellere, presentibus indenturis in aliquo non obstantibus. In cuius rei testimonium partes predicte presentibus indenturis sigilla sua alternatim apposuerunt, datis die et anno supradictis.

254. Letter of fraternity to Richard [Kidderminster] S.T.P., abbot of Winchcombe.[7] 24 Dec. 1511.

Edmundus permissione divina prior monasterii sive prioratus Lanthonie iuxta Gloucestriam et eiusdem loci conventus reverendo in Christo patri ac domino Ricardo Dei gracia Winchilcumbe abbati ac Sacre[8] Theologie Professori egregio. Quoniam de prime prevaricacionis traduce propagati tantam a prothoparentibus nostris infirmitatem contraximus ut nemo nostrum propriis viribus in huius labilis vite via pedes suos valeat de lapsu eripere, necessarium igitur nobis est hanc infirmitatem mutuis sustentare suffragiis orando pro in vicem ut salvemur. Quocirca nos sincere pietatis vestre benignitatem quam erga nos et monasterium nostrum predictum gessistis et in presenti geritis humiliter et devote attendentes vos, reverendissimum patrem antedictum, unanimi assensu et voluntate nostris libentissime recipimus, admittimus et acceptamus in nostrum confratrem et

---

[1] MS. *gurgitum.*
[2] MS. *aliquod.*
[3] MS. *persona.*
[4] MS. *concedere, dimittere sive assignare.*
[5] MS. *gurgitum.*
[6] MS. *Thomas.*
[7] d. after 1531; abbot of Winchcombe 1488–1525, S.T.P. 1497, English delegate to the Lateran council 1512, defender of clerical immunity at St. Paul's Cross, London, 1515: *D.N.B.*; Emden, *Biog. Reg. Oxon. to 1500.* J.P. for Glos. 1494–1508: *Cal. Pat.* 1494–1509, 640.
[8] MS. *sacro.*

dominum specialem et ad omnia et singula bona, beneficia [et] suffragia que per nos et successores nostros operari dignabitur clemencia Salvatoris plenam vobis participacionem omnium meritorum nostrorum, tam in missis, [f. 52v.] horis, oracionibus, vigiliis, abstinenciis, disciplinis, elemosinis ac ieiuniis quam hospitalitatibus ac quibuscumque aliis beneficiis que fient imperpetuum in ecclesia nostra concedenda, ut fructu suffragiorum multiplicato suffulti celerius et felicius Christo annuente eternam in Domino beatitudinem mereamini adipisci; adicientes insuper de caritate nostra speciali[1] ut cum obitus vester nobis fiet nunciatus, pro vobis fiet quod pro caris confratribus nostris defunctis fieri consuevit. Data in domo nostra capitulari Lanthonie predicte vicesimo quarto die mensis Decembris anno Domini millesimo quingentesimo decimo.

255. Letter of fraternity to Thomas Cheltenham, cellarer of Winchcombe Abbey [as **254** above]. 24 Dec. 1511.

256. Nomination by Edward Myll, lord of Harescombe (*Hascombe*),[2] of William Blawiner alias Nicolson, clerk, to the chapel or chantry of Harescombe vacant by the death of James Ladde. [f. 53] Harescombe, 12 May 1512.

257. Presentation of William Nicholson [as above] to Harescombe chapel with the annexed chapel of Pitchcombe (*Pychencombe*), reserving the portion due to the priory. 14 May 1512.

258. Letter of fraternity to Mr. Thomas Wolsey, S.T.P., the king's almoner[3] [as **254** above]. [f. 53v.] 16 May 1512.

259–60. Titles of Dudstone hospital (for the purpose of ordination) granted to Christopher Astun and William Smyth,[4] clerks. 24 May 1512. [Abstracts in MS.; cf. **132**]

261. Presentation of Henry Wyrgge, chaplain, to the vicarage of Little Barrington (*Parva Bernynton*) vacant by the death of John Wadynton. 4 Sept. 1512.

262. Bond of Henry Wyrgge and of Thomas Flymyng, vicar of Windrush (*Wynryshe*), in £20 [f. 54] that Wyrgge will not seek augmentation of the benefice of Little Barrington. 2 Sept. 4 Hen. VIII [1512].

---

[1] MS. *speciale.*

[2] b. 1487, d. after 1552, distant heir of Roger fitzAlan to whom the priory originally conceded the right of nomination in 1181: *Trans. B.G.A.S.* x. 87–9, 95, 126–7 quoting P.R.O. C 115/77, s. ii no. 71 = C 115/83, f. 33. Son and heir of Thomas Myll (d. 1509), cattle farmer: P.R.O. PROB 11/16, f. 158v. copied in Hockaday Abs. ccxxxii, 1509.

[3] Later cardinal and Lord Chancellor: cf. above, **207** n.

[4] A William Smith was chantry priest at Almondsbury in 1532: Hockaday Abs. xxv, 1532 subsidy.

263. Quittance to the abbot of Kingswood as **44** above. 30 Sept. 4 Hen. VIII [1512].

264. [f. 54v.] The king's confirmation[1] of Henry III's letters patent[2] exempting the priory's goods from toll, ferry-toll, pontage and custom (*de theloneo, passagio et pontagio et omni consuetudine*). Westminster, 1 May 4 Hen. VIII [1512], [signed] Studde.

265. The king's mandate to the customers in the port of Bristol [f. 55] to observe the above. Westminster, 13 July 4 Hen. VIII [1512], [signed] Studde.

266. Lease to Richard ap Thomas chaplain, Henry ap Thomas of Caldicot gentleman and Henry's sons Adam, Richard, Thomas, William and Walter ap Thomas of the rectory buildings and tithes of corn at Caldicot [Mon.] for 30 years at £16 a year. Christmas 4 Hen. VIII [25 Dec. 1512].

267. [f. 55v.] The lessees' bond in £20 to perform the covenants of the above lease. St. Stephen 4 Hen. VIII [26 Dec. 1512].

268. Title of Dudstone hospital (for the purpose of ordination) granted to William Gurney, clerk. 20 Jan. 1512[/13]. [Abstract in MS.; cf. **132**]

269. Grant to Charles Somerset Lord Herbert, the king's chamberlain,[3] and to his son Henry[4] of the reversion of the office of steward of Cwmyoy (*Comyowe*), Oldcastle and other manors in Honddu (*Hothnye*) Slade [Mon.] [f. 56] when vacated by the steward David [G]welim Morgan,[5] receiving 40s. a year from the bailiff of

---

[1] Calendared in *L. & P. Hen. VIII*, i, p. 563.

[2] *Recte* Henry II's: P.R.O. C 115/77, s. xxvi (1) no. 12. Confirmed previously in 1309 and 1510: *Cal. Pat. 1307–13*, 162; *L. & P. Hen. VIII*, i, p.170.

[3] d. 1526; knighted at Milford Haven 1485, K.G. and Privy Councillor 1498, ambassador or commissioner to France six times between 1498 and 1525, created Lord Herbert 1503 and earl of Worcester 1514, sheriff of Glam. from 1509 and chancellor there from 1515, royal steward of Ewyas Lacy (Herefs.) and Monmouth from 1503 and Woking (Surr.) from 1511, constable of the castles of Helmsley (Yorks.) from 1487, Painscastle (Radnor) and Montgomery from 1504, Cardiff (Glam.), Monmouth and Three Castles and Ruthin (Denbigh) from 1509, lord of Badminton (Glos.) from c.1485, Gower (Glam.) and Chepstow (Mon.) from 1507 and Raglan (Mon.) from 1509: *D.N.B.*; *Complete Peerage*; Rudder, *Glos.* 254.

[4] d. 1549; appointed jointly with his father as sheriff of Glam., steward of Ewyas Lacy and constable of eight Welsh castles 1510, granted the reversion of his father's Welsh offices 1518, earl of Worcester from 1526 and purchaser of Tintern Abbey 1537: *Complete Peerage*.

[5] Of Llanddewi Skirrid (Mon.) and Arkstone in Kingstone (Herefs.), d. 1524; lord of Llanddewi Skirrid by inheritance, lord of Arkstone (with land at Lulham in Madley, Eaton Bishop and Wormbridge, Herefs.) by marriage to Lucy de la Hay and purchaser of land at Llanwenarth (Mon.): P.R.O. PROB 11/21, f. 145v.; Bradney, *Mon.* i. 277; cf. Herefs. R.O. BF 60/4. Lord of Stoke Lacy, Lawton in Kingsland and Winsley in Hope-under-Dinmore (all in Herefs.) 1488–c. 1502 by marriage to Margaret Wynnesley: *Cal. Close 1500–9*, p. 100. J.P. for Herefs. 1501–15, nominated as sheriff there 1511: *Cal. Pat. 1494–1509*, 642; *L. & P. Hen. VIII*, i, pp. 487, 1538; ii, pp. 70, 313.

Cwmyoy. They may not assign title (*finem facere aut assignare*) to land or tenements nor impose fines (*finem imponere aut taxare*) for felonies or transgressions there without the prior's consent.[1] This grant is void if anyone else proves to have the reversion by grant of the priory of Llanthony Prima. 7 Feb. 4 Hen. VIII [1513].

270. Lease to William Wodde and Thomas Bullocke the younger of certain tithes belonging to the rectory of Kington [Herefs.], viz. tithes of small withies, willows, hay, hemp, pearmains, pears, apples and saplings (*parvis virgulis, salicibus, feno, canabo, volemis, piris, pomis, arbustis*), for nine years at 26s. 8d. a year. The following are reserved to the prior:
    (a) 1 bu. a year of pearmains,
    (b) 1 bu. a year of best *Reddesterys* apples and
    (c) tithes of fruit of the manor now [let] to William Kyngeston.
21 Feb. 4 Hen. VIII [1513].

271–2. [f. 56v.] Titles of Dudstone hospital (for the purpose of ordination) granted to Robert Collyns, clerk, and Thomas Dunne, clerk [as **132** above]. 22 Mar. 1512[/13] and 29 Mar. 1513.[2]

273. Lease to Richard and Catherine Hawkes, gentlefolk of London, and their sons John and William of the tithes of corn and hay of Egleton (*Egilton*), Herefs., which are due to the priory every third year, for 70 years at 40s. triennially. [f. 57] 30 Mar. 4 Hen. VIII [1513].

274. Grant to Arnulf Devyas, chaplain, of the tithes, oblations and other revenues customarily received by the chaplain of Hempsted (*Heihamsted*), provided that he sees to divine service and the cure of souls there.[3] 24 Apr. 1513.

275. Presentation of Thomas Walker, chaplain, to the vicarage of St. Owen, Gloucester, vacant through the profession of the last vicar Nicholas Tele alias Elys as a regular canon of St. Oswald's Priory, Gloucester. 17 Apr. 1513.

---

[1] By grant of Walter de Lacy II (d. 1241) the prior had jurisdiction in Honddu Slade over hunting rights and over assault, murder, bloodshed and breaches of the peace including theft, homicide, rape and arson. No steward, constable, bailiff or forester from elsewhere might enter his jurisdiction, he had gallows and he kept the profits of justice: Dugdale, *Mon.* vi. 138 discussed in W. E. Wightman, *The Lacy Family in England and Normandy* (Oxford, 1966), 140. In 1535 the prior employed a constable of his castle and gaol there: *Valor Eccl.* (Rec. Com.), ii. 431.
[2] MS. *millesimo quingentesimo duodecimo*, evidently in error.
[3] Although a vicarage was ordained at Hempsted before 1428 the cure remained a chaplaincy under the rectory of St. Owen, Gloucester, until 1662: *V.C.H. Glos.* iv. 427.

276. [f. 57v.] Citation to a visitation of the priory by Thomas Hannibal D.Cn. & C.L., vicar general[1] of Bishop Silvestro de' Gigli, on 19 May. Worcester, 22 Feb. 1512[/13].

277. Certificate acknowledging the above. [f. 58] 19 May 1513.

278. Lease to John ap Meurick, John ap Thomas ap Meurick and one son of the latter, and in default of such an heir to John son of Hugh Taylor, of property in the demesne of Monkton [at Llanwarne, Herefs.], viz.

(a) a messuage, land, meadow, pasture, water, woodland and underwood bounded by the Cold Brook (*Col Brocke*), the Hereford–Monmouth road and the branch road to Pendiggott [in St. Weonards] (*viam ducentem a loco vocato Pendevgoyd versus regiam viam predictam*)[2] and

(b) two closes of arable land bounded on all sides by the main road and land formerly of David Wathan

for 60 years at 16s. a year, suit of court and heriot of a best animal. [f. 58v.] Because John ap Meurick has improved the land, and in consideration of 40s., if all the lessees die within the term the next blood relation may have the property if he then offers as large an entry fine as anyone else (*tantum pecunie velit dare domino pro fine suo ad ingressum suum sicut alius*[3] *dare voluerit*). 28 May 5 Hen. VIII [1513].

279. Resignation of Henry Pygge as rector of Stretton Sugwas [Herefs.], with his petition for a pension from the church revenues,[4] delivered at Stretton Sugwas church [f. 59] in the presence of Mr. John Breynton gentleman, Richard Warran, William Vowler, Roger Sutton and John Norman and recorded by John Walker, clerk of Hereford diocese and papal notary public. 26 June 1513.

280. Presentation of Thomas Taylor, chaplain,[5] to the rectory of Stretton Sugwas [Herefs.][6] vacant by the resignation of Henry Pygge alias ap Thomas. 10 July 1513.

---

[1] Appointed to this office 1511, d. 1531; prebendary of York 1504–25 and of Westbury-on-Trym from 1514, rector of Alvechurch (Worcs.) and vicar of St. Nicholas, Bristol, from 1515, royal envoy to the Roman Curia 1523–4, Master of the Rolls 1523–7: *D.N.B.*; Emden, *Biog. Reg. Oxon. 1501–40.*

[2] Straddling the Llanwarne boundary, this property evidently included Prior's Wood at SO 487252 and other parts of the Pendiggott estate in St. Weonards given to the priory before 1146: P.R.O. C 115/75, f. 214v. no. 23.

[3] MS. *aliis* corrected from **444** below.

[4] The bishop awarded him £4 a year and life tenure of the rectory house, 18 a. of glebe equally divided between three fields and half the crops of apples and pears: *Reg. Mayew*, 281.

[5] Instituted 11 July: *Reg. Mayew*, 281. Vicar of the priory's benefices at Stretton Sugwas 1513–15, at Bishop's Frome in 1528 and at Burghill (all Herefs.) by 1535: *Reg. Bothe*, 342; *Valor Eccl.* (Rec. Com.), ii. 427; below, **340**.

[6] Given to the priory by Ralph de Baskerville before 1141: P.R.O. C 115/75, f. 214 no. 22.

281. Resignation of John Batty of Nevern (*Navern*) [Pemb.] as vicar of St. Mary, Kington [Herefs.], in exchange for St. Afan's church, Llanafanfawr [Brec.], delivered in the cloister of Hereford cathedral [f. 59v.] in the presence of William Gowght chaplain and David Bragth literate (*litterato*) of the dioceses of Hereford and St. Asaph, and recorded by Hugh Grene clerk of Hereford diocese and papal notary public.[1] 17 June 1513.

282. Presentation of Richard ap Thomas[2] to the vicarage of Kington [Herefs.] vacant by the resignation of John Battye. 10 July 1513.

283. [f. 60] Bond of Richard ap Thomas vicar of Kington [Herefs.] and John Davis of Radnor in £40 to pay what the vicar owes as follows:
   (a) 13s. 4d. a year to the parson of Kington for Titley church [Herefs.],
   (b) a third of the costs at every bishop's visitation and
   (c) a third of every tenth and subsidy. 16 July 5 Hen. VIII [1513].

284. Order of Richard [of Carew] bishop of St. David's that the priory of Llanthony Prima should pay yearly 20 lb. of wax worth 10s. to St. David's cathedral to keep lights and that the archdeacon of Brecon should have power to demand it. Given at Llanthony Prima at the Invention of Holy Cross [3 May] 1271.

285. Proxy to Ralph Krymshawe and Richard Braggott [f. 60v.] to act for the church of Stanton Lacy [Salop.] [as in **130** above]. 10 Oct. 1513.

286. Lease to Ralph Krymshawe, vicar, and Richard Braggotte of the parsonage of Stanton Lacy, Salop. [as **196** above but omitting William Cheyne as joint lessee]. 26 June 23 Hen. VII [1508].

287. [f. 61] Lease to Richard and Alice Partriche and their sons John,[3] Dennis and Thomas of Podsmead manor [in Hempsted]. 23 Aug. 1508.

This indenture made the 23 day of August in the yere of the reigne of owre soveraigne lorde King Henry the VII the 23[4] *betwene Edmunde Forest priour of the*

<hr>

[1] d. 1524; B.Cn. & C.L., prebendary of Hereford 1504–24 and residentiary canon 1521–4: Le Neve, *Fasti 1300–1541, Hereford*; *Reg. Bothe*, 334–6; below, **300**. To be distinguished from his namesake the vicar of Canon Frome: above, **212**. In the margin beside Grene's attestation is a copy of his mark in the form of a marigold (illus. above, p. xxxix). It is inscribed on the flower *H. Grene*, on a scroll around the stem *Libenter ferto amorem* ('Bring love gladly') and on a scroll at the base *Disce mori* ('Learn to die').
[2] Vicar of Llanafanfawr [Brec.], instituted to Kington by exchange 25 July: *Reg. Mayew*, 281.
[3] The lease was renewed to John Partridge in 1539 and remained in his family until *c.* 1815: *V.C.H. Glos.* iv. 423–4.
[4] 23 Aug. 1508, the date indicated at the end of the penultimate paragraph, was the second day of the 24th regnal year.

howse and monastery of owr Blessed Lady of Lanthony besyde Gloucetur and the
covent of the same of the oon partye and Richard Partriche of Hempsted on that othr
partye witnesseth that the said priour & covent have graunted & to ferme lette to the
said Richarde, Alice his wiffe, Jhon, Deense and Thomas issue of the said Richarde
the syte of the manere of Poddesmede with all suche londs, medous, lesouse and
pastures[1] *that late were in the holding of William Gybbys late fermor there, with all*
maner of grains, catalles & store to the same ferme belongyng wiche the said
William Gibbis hadde by indenture of the said prior and covent, and the particular
parcellis whereof be specified and named more plainly at large in anothr pair of
indentures thereof made betwene the said prior and covent of that oon partye and
the said Richard of the other partye.

To have and to hold the site of the said manere with all the said purtenance to the
said Richarde, Alice his wif, John, Deense and Thomas issue of the said Richard and
to eny of them unto the ende and terme of 60 yeris then next folowyng the date
hereof, if they lyve so longe or eny of them live so longe, paing yerely to the said
prior and his successors as yt apperith evidently in the audite rolis of the said prior,
that is to say 30 qr. of whete, 12 qr. of barly, 20 qr. of pulse,[2] *12 porketts or els 2s. in*
money, [f. 61v.] 12 gees & 12 capons.

Also it is agreed betwene the said parties that the said Richarde, Alice, John,
Deense and Thomas or ther assignes shall carie to the priouris shepehows at
Sheperdes Elmes[3] *40 lods of hey and to Queddesley 4 lods of hey yerely duryng the*
said terme. Also the said Richarde, Alice, John, Deense & Thomas or theire
asseignes shall cary yerely 4 lods of wodd to Lanthony or to the Newerke[4]
whensumever he or eny of them shal be called upon. Also the said Richarde byndith
hymself, his heyris and executors by these presents to pay or cause to be paid the
said 30 qrt. of good and laufull whete yerely duryng the said terme within the yere at
any time that it shal be laufully axed with laufull warnyng, and all grayns to be payd
within the yere as afore is saide.

Also it is agreed by the said parties that the said priour and his successors shall
kepe all maner of reparacions upon the said manor and ferme duryng the said terme

---

[1] The moated manor house occupied the site of the present Betjeman Close. Of the estate, which was surveyed in 1539, vested (as to the freehold) in the Crypt School in 1540 and mapped in 1731, 197 a. lay in a compact block around the house and 15 a. at Frognells, Hempsted Moor and Canmore 1 mile NW.: *V.C.H. Glos.* iv. 423–4; Austin, *Crypt School*, 145–6; Glos. R.O. GBR/J4/1, plan 32a.

[2] In 1535 the render of wheat was valued at £8, of barley at 15s. and of pulse at £3 5s.: *Valor Eccl.* (Rec. Com.), ii. 423.

[3] As described in 1636 this sheephouse was a long building with an iron-bound door of great size and a partly boarded hay loft of four rooms. At the east end a square lobby opened into a small dwelling with a cockloft approached by a ladder: Glos. R.O. D3117/4. Three bays of the 16th-century building, of stone with a collar-beam truss, survive at no. 162 Tuffley Avenue: *Glevensis*, xiii. 12; xxiii. 26 correcting *V.C.H. Glos.* iv. 396. For its purpose cf. *Medieval Archaeology*, xxxix. 136–64.

[4] Cf. above, **217** n.

upon his oune costs & charges, savyng onely the said Richard, Alice, John, Deense and Thomas or their assignes shall carie all maner of stuff to the said reparacions necessarye.

Forthrmore it is agrede betwene the said parties that the said prior and his successors shall have the use of the said prioris chambor within the said manere with the studie, the chapell, the undur parlor with all small houses thereto adjoynyng, the hall, the kechyn, the pantrie and the buttre with other loggyns places for his sarvants as offten & as mony times & as longe as it shall please the said priour and his successours to lodge or tary ther, withowt any interrupcion of the saide Richarde, Alice, John, Deense and Thomas or any of them or any other person or persons in there name.

Also it is agreede by the said parties that the said Richard, Alice, John, Deense and Thomas & every of them during the said terme shall kepe all maner of reparacions of thaching, hegyng, dichyng & enclosyng abowte the said maner & all other places to the same ferme perteynyng that late was in the holdyng of the said William Gibbis upon there oune propur costs and charges.

Forthurmore the said Richard, Alice, John, Deense & Thomas byndeth them, ther heyris and executors by these presents well and truely to performe all suche premises as afore be rehersed. And if it happen the said whete, barly and pulce with all other dueties or any parte thereof as the said Richard hathe paid before the makyng of these present indentures to be behynd unpayd by the space of half a yere, and no laufull distresse to be hadde upon the said maner and ferme, that then it shal be laufull to the said prior and his successours to reentir into the said maner and ferme and to make newe leese and fine for the same at ther pleasure. Also the said Richard, Alice, John, Deense & Thomas byndeth them, ther heyris and executors by these presents to deliver or cause to be deliverid to the said priour or to his successors at thende of the foresaid terme all the foresaid graines, catalle & stoore to the said ferme perteynyng or the prices of the same at thelleccion & choise of the said prior and covent, as in the foresaid other indentures thereof made betwene the said prior and covent on that one parte and the said Richard on that other partie the particular parcells thereof more plainly dothe appere at large.

In witnesse whereof as well the said prior and covent to that one partie of these indentures remaynyng with the said Richard in their chaptur howse of Lanthony have putt there covent seale, as the same Richard, Alice, John, Deense and Thomas to the othr parte of the same indenture remaynyng with the said prioure and covent have putte theire seales. Yeven the day and yere of owre said soveraigne lord the kynges reigne afforesaide and the yere of owre Lord God 1508.

Memorandum that over and beside all the covenants within writen it is forthermore agreed betwene the parties within named that the said Richard, Alice, John, Deense and Thomas or one of them shall yerely during the within writen terme cum to the checker of Lanthony and there to make ther audite and a treue accompte of all their duties and charges comprised within these indentures by the fest of Seint Andrew [30 Nov.] in peyn of forfeyting to the lord 6s. 8d. or at the yeturmost by Cristmas Eve in peyne of forfeiting of their lesse or state.

288. [f. 62] Stock delivered to the above lessees. 23 Aug. 1508.

This indenture made the 23 day of August in the yere of the reigne of owr soveraigne lorde King Henry the VII the 23[1] betwene Edmunde Forest priour of the howse & monasterie of our Blessed Lady of Lanthony besidis Gloucetur and the covent of the same on that oone partie and Richard Partrige, Alice his wiff, John, Deens and Thomas issue of the said Richard on that othr partie witnesseth that the said priour and convent hathe delivered to the said Richard, Alice, John, Deense and Thomas all these parcellis of stuff & store foloing, that is to say:

115 qr. whete, 12 qr. pulce, 17 qr. barly, 3 qr. ots, 31 oxen or 31 marks, 4 kyne or 28s., 1 heyffur or 5s., 1 bull or 5s., 4 porks or 6s. 8d., 4 porketts or 4s. 8d., 8 soukyng pyggs or 2s. 8d., 12 gese or 4s., 9 duckys or 18d., 12 capons or 4s., 20 cocks & hennys or 3s. 4d., 276 eggs or 14d., 8 weyn lods of hey, 2 corne waynys bounden with iron and 2 dunge wayns bond with iron.

The whiche stuff and store, all and every parcell thereof, the said Richard, Alice, John, Deens & Thomas byndyth them & every of them, their heyres and executors to deliver ayen the same stuff unto the said prior or to his successors, or the prices thereof as it is above rated & sett at thelleccion & chois of the said priour or his successors, at thende & terme wyche is specified in anotheir pair of indentures made betwene the said parties concernyng the lettyng to ferme of the syte of the manor of Podesmede with the pertinances, or at any season in the mean season that it may happen the said Richarde, Alice his wiff, John, Deens & Thomas to departe from the said ferme. In witnes whereof ayther of thay said parties to other enterchangeable have put ther seales. Yeven the day and yere abovesaid.

289. Appointment of William Peryeman of Westbury[-on-Severn] as servant and pupil for three years. 25 July 1513.

This indenture made in the fest of Seint Jamys thapostill in the yere of the reign of owre soveraigne lord Kyng Henry the VIII the fyveth betwene Edmund Forest priour of Lanthony besyde Glouceter of the oon partie & William Peryeman the son of Margett Peryeman wydow of the parishe of Wesbery of the othr partie witnessethe that the said William hathe put himself to be the servaunt of the said Edmunde and to dwell with him during the terme of 3 yeris immediately foloing the date hereof, and all the precepts and comaundements lawfull of the said Edmunde the said William shall well and truly and diligently observe and performe during the said terme.

And the said Edmunde shall fynde the said William mete and drinke and clothing[2] bothe wollen and lynen with all othr necessary things to suche a servaunt congrue & mete duryng the said terme. And the said Edmunde shall cause the said William to be taught & informed in playing at organs by the space of oone yere of the said 3 yeres & in gramer the othr 2 yeris residue of the terme afforesaid.[3] In witnesse

[1] *Recte* 24: cf. above, **287** n.
[2] MS. *chothing.*
[3] Cf. above, **125**; below, **491**.

whereof eyther of the said parties to othr to these present indentures
entercheangeable have put their seales. Yeven the day and yere abovesaid.

290. Bill to John Cooke, alderman of Gloucester,[1] for 10½ cwt. 25 lb. of lead. 8 Nov.
1513.

This bill indented made the 8 day of November in the yere of the reigne of King
Henry the VIII the 5th betwene Edmunde Forest prior of the howse and churche of
our Blessed Lady of Lanthony of the oon partie and John Cooke of the toune of
[f. 62v.] *Gloucester alderman of the othr partie witnesseth that the said Edmunde*
hath delivered to the said John a M, half an C & 25 li. of leed to be redelivered to
the said Edmunde or to his successors when he shal be by the said Edmund or his
successors thereto reasonably required. And for the performans of the premisses well
and truely to be donn I, the foresaid John Coke, knolage me to have receyvid the
said leed & over that I bynd me, myn heires & executors to make redeliverance of
the same according to the tenure abive writen. In witnes whereof ayther of the said
parties to these bills indented enterchangeably have putt their sealis. Yeven the day
and yere abovesaid.

291. Bond of John Hill the younger, yeoman of Newnham,[2] in 10 marks to pay 53s.
4d. to the priory in four equal instalments between next All Saints [1 Nov. 1512] and
the second Easter following [16 Apr. 1514]. 9 Aug. 4 Hen. VIII [1512].

292. [f. 63] Lease to Richard Trinder of [South] Cerney, his wife Joan and their son
William of the manor of Cerney as follows:
   (a) the manor buildings[3] and demesne land, meadow and pasture now held by
Richard, except the *stewardes chambr* and a stable next to it,
   (b) great and small tithes on the premises and
   (c) estreats and amercements from tenants and others who come to courts and
view of frankpledge, except rents of free and customary tenants, fines of lands and
tenements, penalties, forfeits of chattels and heriots
for 48 years at £8 13s. 4d a year. The lessees will
   (a) provide food, beds, hay, straw and provender for the cellarer, steward and
understeward, their servants and their horses when they come to hold courts and
courts leet,
   (b) entertain the prior, his men and his horses overnight once or twice a year when
he comes to superintend the manor,
   (c) live on site,
   (d) leave 20 acres ploughed fallow at the end of the term and
   (e) render account at the priory exchequer by St. Andrew's day [30 Nov.] each
year on pain of 6s. 8d. St. Andrew 5 Hen. VIII [30 Nov. 1513].

[1] Cf. above, **239** and n.
[2] Probably of Culver House: *V.C.H. Glos.* x. 39; cf. *Military Survey of Glos. 1522*, 206.
[3] On the site of the present manor house: *Trans. B.G.A.S.* cxvi. 207.

293. [f. 63v.] Bond of the above lessees in £10 to pay £4 in three instalments, i.e. 20s. at the next Purification [2 Feb. 1514], 20s. at St. Andrew following [30 Nov. 1514] and 40s. at St. Andrew next following [30 Nov. 1515]. St. Thomas the apostle 5 Hen. VIII [21 Dec. 1513].

294. Lease to Thomas Faucer, miller of Cricklade (*Creklade*), Wilts., and his daughter and son-in-law Richard and Edith Ludlow of a messuage, a watermill and a yardland of land and meadow now held by Thomas at Cerney Wick (*Wyk*) in the demesne of [South] Cerney, for 37 years at 26s. 8d. a year. [f. 64] The lessees will make suit to the court of [South] Cerney; they will maintain the messuage, the mill with its thatched roof, external and internal millwheels, millstones, pond and leat (*tam in muris et coopertura cum stramine quam in rotis exterioribus et interioribus ac [petris] molaribus cum stagno et cursu aque*) and the hedges and ditches. St. Andrew 5 Hen. VIII [30 Nov. 1513].

295. Bond of the above lessees in £4 to pay 40s. in two instalments at St. Andrew next and that day twelvemonth [30 Nov. 1514 and 1515]. St. Thomas the apostle 5 Hen. VIII [21 Dec. 1513].

296. [f. 64v.] Lease to Maurice and Joan Coope of Monkton in the parish of Llanwarne (*Lanwaren*) [Herefs.] and their son [   ] of a messuage there lately held by John Walker for 60 years, rendering 20s. a year, heriot of the best animal and a consideration of 20s. 8 Sept. 4 Hen. VIII [1512].

297. Record of a court (*halimote*) of the manor of Llantrisant [Mon.] held before Edmund ap Glin ap Hopkin, royal approver [i.e. bailiff]. 16 May 3 Hen. VIII [1511].

Excused: Ieuan ap Jankyn ap Ieuan, Phe[lip] Thomas ap Ior[werth].

[f. 65] Jurors: M. ap Glin Sherall, Glin John ap Ieuan, Ross Thomas ap Phe[lip], John Thomas ap Ieuan, Hopkin ap Jankyn, Thomas ap Ieuan, Thomas ap Richarde, John ap John, Thomas ap John ap M., Glin John ap Glin ap Ior[werth], Watkyn ap Jankyn ap Phe[lip], Jankyn ap Glin ap John.

Findings:

(a) Jankyn ap John, Thomas ap John and Thomas ap John ap Ieuan failed to attend court.

(b) M. ap Glin has destroyed roofing and timber.

(c) There is a gate on the king's highway at *Hebll Freyngke.*

(d) On inspection, *Oyske* Brook is [the boundary] between the king's land called Walter's land and the prior of Llanthony's land of *Gregoes.*

[The following entry is inserted here on an extra half leaf.]

298. Record[1] of an inquisition held at Prestbury by John Hard and William Hamondeshum,[2] on behalf of John [Trefnant] bishop of Hereford, into arrears of

---

[1] Copied from P.R.O. C 115/77, s. vi no. 74.

[2] Alias Amundesham or Amersham. Although he owned land and tenements at Bishop's Cleeve and Gotherington in 1404 his family's property, as surveyed in 1321–2, lay mainly in Prestbury: Glos. R.O. D326/T139/3–4; P.R.O. E 142/32/7.

tithes owed by the bishop as lord to the prior of Llanthony as rector. Saturday and Monday before Michaelmas 13 Ric. II [25 & 27 Sept. 1389].

Present: John Durhurste, Richard Nichol, John Jot, Nicholas Pope, John Temple, Robert Mady and other tenants of the bishop. Findings:

(a) Tithes owed for a watermill,[1] underwood in the park[2] and elsewhere, pasturage, agistment of animals and other matters, according to details compiled by the above men, are £9 8s. 3¼d.

(b) The sum of oblations of money and wax in the manor chapel,[3] and of tithes on the farming of underwood, pannage and agistment in the park and at Puckham (*Puckombe*) [in Sevenhampton] for the last two years, is unknown.

299. Extracts from the accounts of [the bishop of Hereford's][4] bailiffs at Prestbury and Sevenhampton for 1505–13.

Allowed to John Grenehill,[5] bailiff, for tithe of agistment in the park in 21–4 Hen. VII: 4s. a year.

Allowed to the same for tithe of wood (*bosci*)[6] sold in the park in 21 Hen. VII: 7s.

Allowed to Richard Bathorne for tithe of wood sold at Puckham (*Puckcombe*): in 21 Hen. VII 13s. 6¾d., in 22 Hen. VII 15s. 1¾d, in 23 Hen. VII 8s. 2½d. and in 24 Hen. VII 7s. 4½d.

Allowed to the same for [tithe of] agistment of calves in Puckham wood in 24 Hen. VII: 12d.

Allowed to William Raynesford[7] for tithe of agistment in the park in 1–4 Hen. VIII: 4s. a year.

Allowed to the same for tithe of wood sold in the park: in 3 Hen. VIII 4[s.] and in 4 Hen. VIII 16s. 4d.

[f. 65v.] The prior owes the bishop yearly rent of 2s. 6d.

[1] Lower Mill in Mill Street, 200 yd. NW. of the church: *V.C.H. Glos.* viii. 77.

[2] Tithes of vegetation cropped in the park were given to the priory in 1136 when the park was described as formerly villeins' land: Barrow, *Hereford Episcopal Acta 1079–1234*, no. 35. It occupied 280 a. within a larger oval enclosure which includes the present Cheltenham racecourse and is bisected by the present Cheltenham–Evesham road: *Cheltenham Local Hist. Soc. Journal*, iii. 1–3 (with plan); ix. 18–19; xvi. 48–50. For its warden cf. below, **299** n.

[3] Rebuilt in 1344 and located by excavation in 1951: *Trans. B.G.A.S.* lxxxv. 10.

[4] Not the prior of Llanthony's bailiffs, since the tithes described were paid by the bishop's representative to the lessee of the rectory and were not accounted for at the priory: above, **77**, **160**; below, **325**, **484–90**.

[5] Of St. Owen's parish in Gloucester and of Cheltenham, d. 1513 leaving land in Cheltenham, two mills and cash bequests of £88: P.R.O. PROB 11/17, f. 130, copied in Hockaday Abs. cxlvii, 1513. Bailiff of Syon Abbey (Mdx.) in Cheltenham and Slaughter 1481–5: P.R.O. SC 6/853/7–11.

[6] Usually underwood (*subbosci*): P.R.O. C 115/77, s. vi no. 73.

[7] Gentleman, appointed warden of the park by Bishop Mayew in 1513: *Reg. Mayew*, 167–8.

300. Commission to fellow canon William Chaddysley,[1] Mr. Robert Stynchecombe,[2] Mr. Hugh Grene B.Cn. & C.L. and Mr. Richard Hall[3] vicar of Leominster (*Lemster*) [Herefs.] to exercise testamentary jurisdiction, as in **142** above, within the parish of Kington [Herefs.] including the chapelries of Brilley and Huntington [Herefs.] and Michaelchurch[-on-Arrow, Radnors.] (*Brimley, Huntyndon et ecclesia Sancti Michaelis*). 15 Apr. 1514.

301. Title of Dudstone hospital (for the purpose of ordination) granted to William Nangull, clerk. 9 June 1514. [Abstract in MS.; cf. **132**]

302. [f. 66] Proxy to [   ] to attend a convocation of Canterbury province in St. Paul's cathedral, London, on [   ][4] [as **114** above]. 12 June 1514.

303. Presentation of Mr. Nicholas Dixon to the vicarage of Chirton (*Cherynton*) [Wilts.] vacant by the resignation of William Godriche S.T.P.[5] 11 July 1514.

304. Title of Dudstone hospital (for the purpose of ordination) granted to Henry Willis M.A.[6] 20 Nov. 1514. [Abstract in MS.; cf. **132**]

305. [f. 66v.] Presentation of John Phelps, chaplain, to the vicarage of Prestbury vacant by the death of John Tycle. 12 Nov. 1514.

306. Letter of fraternity to Mr. Edmund Goldyng Esq.[7] and his wife Joan. 20 Nov. 1514.

307. [Duplicate of **304** above.]

308. Lease to Nicholas Gylbert[8] of Ewyas Lacy [Herefs.] of the manor of Oldcastle

---

[1] Prior's chaplain in 1515 and subcellarer in 1516: below, **336, 355**.
[2] B.Cn.L. (Oxon.) 1508 and incumbent of parochial benefices in the prior's gift at Brockworth to 1511, Gloucester All Saints from 1511, Gloucester St. Mary de Crypt from 1517 and Tytherington 1530–4: Emden, *Biog. Reg. Oxon. 1501–40.*
[3] One of the name was B.Cn.L. (Oxon.) 1510: ibid.
[4] 22 June 1514: Wilkins, *Concilia*, iii. 658.
[5] Vice-principal of Beam Hall, Oxford, in 1513, rector of St. Martin Outwich, London, 1514–*c.* 1537 and of Hinton-on-the-Green (Glos.) from 1515: Emden, *Biog. Reg. Oxon. to 1500.*
[6] Alias Wyllys; M.A. (Oxon.) 3 July 1514, B. Th. 1530, already ordained acolyte by the bishop of Worcester 1510; sacrist of Corpus Christi College (Oxon.) 1517, vicar of Toddington 1521–41 and Sherborne 1525–54, rector of Uley from 1542 and prebendary of Gloucester 1541–54: Emden, *Biog. Reg. Oxon. 1501–40*; Le Neve, *Fasti 1541–1847, Bristol, Gloucester, Oxford & Peterborough.*
[7] The prior's counsellor, of Piercetown (Meath): below, **311**.
[8] Of the Gronowaid family of Llancillo (Herefs.) but resident at Oldcastle when he d. 1524; owner of 3 farms at Llancillo, 9 farms at Clodock (Herefs.), 9 farms at Michaelchurch Escley (Herefs.) and an estate on both sides of the Usk at Llanwenarth (Mon.): Bradney, *Mon.* i. 227–9; P.R.O. PROB 11/21, f. 131v.

[Mon.] with buildings, [f. 67] land, pasture and meadow for 60 years, rendering annually

(a) 6 seams of wheat, with one heaped measure per quarter and 8 bushels to the seam and

(b) 9 seams of oats, with 16 heaped bushels to the seam.

The prior will find timber, stone and tiles for repairs. The lessee will carry these materials and will be quit of tithes and of oppression from tenants (*oppressione tenencium*); he may assart and enclose (*adcertando et claudendo*), surrendering any improvements at the end of the term. 18 Nov. 6 Hen. VIII [1514].

309. Commission from David ap G[wi]lim ap Morgan, the prior's deputy in Honddu (*Hotheny*) Slade [Mon.], to Thomas Herbert of Abergavenny,[1] son of the late Richard Herbert Esq., to administer justice[2] during pleasure as a lieutenant in Honddu Slade. He may not impose fines without consent. 5 Aug. 6 Hen. VIII [1514].

310. [f. 67v.] Resignation of Mr. William Goodrich S.T.P. as perpetual vicar of Chirton (*Cherinton*) [Wilts.] delivered in a high chamber (*in quadam alta camera*) of Beam Hall[3] of Oxford University in the presence of Mr. John Holder M.A.[4] and John Hauthill, literate (*litterato*) of Worcester diocese, and recorded by Thomas Brerwode B.C.L.,[5] clerk of Coventry and Lichfield diocese and papal notary public. 19 June 1514.

311. Lease to Mr. Thomas Rocheforde, dean of Dublin, and Edmund Goldyng Esq. of Piercetown [Meath], in return for Goldyng's help, of tithes of St. Peter's, Drogheda [Louth], and tithes of 'Curhaston' in Duleek [Meath]. 12 Nov. 1514.

This endenture made the 12th day of November in the 6 yere of the regne of Kyng Henry the VIII betwene Edmunde Forest pryor of the howse & church of our Lady of Lanthony next Gloucester & the covente of the [f. 68] *same of the one partie and Maister Sir Thomas Rocheford dean of Dulyn & Edmunde Goldyng of Peerston*

---

[1] d. 1528–9, illegitimate son of Richard Herbert of Ewyas (d. 1510): Bradney, *Mon.* i. 229; cf. above, **248**. Resident at Abergavenny and Llanwenarth (Mon.), owner of land, herds and flocks at Llanwenarth and purchaser of a dairy farm at Blaen Rhymney (then in Llangynidr, Brec., now in Glam.): P.R.O. PROB 11/23, f. 56v.

[2] Cf. above, **269** n.

[3] In Merton Street, now a 15th-century building with chambers of *c.* 1600: *Inventory of the City of Oxford* (Royal Commission on Historical Monuments, 1939), 166. Goodrich was vice-principal there: above, **303** n.

[4] d. 1544; fellow of Merton College 1511–19 and rector of a moiety of Gamlingay (Cambs.) 1519–44: Emden, *Biog. Reg. Oxon. 1501–40*.

[5] d. 1544; D.Cn.L by 1533, fellow of All Souls College 1511–*c.* 1516, prebendary of St. Paul's, London, 1518–24, president of Exeter consistory from 1519, vicar general and chancellor there from 1521, prebendary of Crediton (Devon) 1521–5 and 1536–44, prebendary of Exeter 1524–44, archdeacon of Barnstaple 1528–44 and chaplain to the king by 1538: Emden, *Biog. Reg. Oxon. 1501–40*.

Landey Esquyer of the othyr partie witnessith that the said prior & covent have covenauntyd and grauntyd & to ferme let to the seid Master Thomas & to Edmunde all the teithes of corne, hey, fyrsses [i.e. furze]*, thornes & tymber belongyng or in any maner of wise apperteynyng to the parsonage of Seint Petur's churche of Droghda in Ireland aforeseyd.*

Also the said prior and covent have covenauntyd & grauntyd to the same Master Thomas Rocheford & to Edmunde Goldyng all the teithis of corne & hey with the appurtenants of Curhaston within the parisshe of Dulyk besyde Peerston Landey in Ireland aforeseyd, for terme of the lyf of the seyd Edmunde Goldyng only, for his laudable councell & lovyng disposicyon had & that is to be had.

To have & to holde all the seid teithis to the seid Maister Thomas & to Edmunde & to their assigns for terme of the lyf of the seid Edmunde Goldyng, yeldyng therfore yerely to the seyd prior & covent & to ther successors, proctours & assigns £8 of lawfull & currant money of Ireland to be paid at 2 termes of the yere, that is to say att the fests of the Purificacion of our Lady and Seynt Peter 'ad vincula', by evyn porcyons duryng the terme aforeseyd. And if it happen the seyd ferme of £8 to be byhynd unpaid in parte or in all after eny of the said fests by the space of won hoole yere, that then it shal be lawfull to the pryor & covent & ther successors, proctours & assigns in all the seyd teithes to reenter & to have ageyn & to enyoye as in ther former enterest & tytle, and the seyd Master Thomas & Edmunde & ther assigns thereof hooly to expell & to put oute, thes endentures in enything notwithstondyng. In witnesse whereof to the won parte of thes endentures remaynyng with the sayd prior & covent the said Master Thomas & Edmunde Goldyng have putt to ther seales, and to the other parte of the same endentures remaynyng with the same Mr. Thomas & Edmunde the seyd prior & covent have put to ther commyn seale. Yevyn the day & yere aboveseyd.

312. Lease [in English] to the same parties of tithes of corn and hay at Ardcath [Meath], except the vicar's portion, [f. 68v.] for 40 years at £16 a year in Irish money. 12 Nov. 6 Hen. VIII [1514].

313. Lease to Richard Coope, *husbandeman* of Ballingham (*Balyniam*) [Herefs.], his wife Agnes[1] and their son Philip of the prior's land, meadow and pasture there including Parson's Close, with *housebote & heybote*, for 45 years at 12s. a year. The prior reserves a right of way from Ballingham to his Carey Mill.[2] 25 Mar. 6 Hen. VIII [1515].

314. [f. 69] Lease to Richard[3] and Elizabeth Monyngton, Elizabeth's son Thomas

---

[1] Richard and Agnes were still tenants in 1546: *L. & P. Hen. VIII*, xxi (1), p. 357.

[2] Now a public right of way leading to the Wye at SO 570306, where a ford gave access to Carey Mill on the opposite bank: *Trans. Woolhope N.F.C.* xxxiv. 71–3; cf. below, **323.**

[3] d. 1557: P.R.O. PROB 11/40, f. 60v. The prior's bailiff at Great Barrington 1535, holder of an additional lease there from 1538, purchaser of Dodd's Mill there 1542 and purchaser of the manor 1553: *Valor Eccl.* (Rec. Com.), ii. 423; *L. & P. Hen. VIII*, xiv (1), p. 608; xvii, p. 634; *Cal. Pat.* 1553, 108.

and [   ] of property in the manor of Great Barrington (*Bernynton Magna*) from next Michaelmas [29 Sept.] as follows.

(a) the *bailyes chambre* with certain rooms (*domibus*) and a servants' kitchen annexed,[1]

(b) buildings and a dovecot[2] situated in the outer court, except two stables,

(c) demesne land, meadow and pasture lately held by Richard Bigge and not let to tenants and

(d) tithes of corn and hay on the above

for 60 years, rendering annually:

(a) £12,

(b) 3 qr. of winnowed wheat, 6 qr. of winnowed malt barley and 3 qr. of winnowed oats,

(c) 2 qr. of oatmeal and 16 cocks and hens to Dudstone hospital,

(d) 2 qr. 1½ bu. of winnowed wheat, 2 qr. 1½ bu. of winnowed barley, 4 bu. of oats and ½ bu. of salt to the prior's shepherd at Little Barrington, [f. 69v.] for which the lessees will have a sheepfold (*faldam bidencium et clausturam simul cum fimo*) there,

(e) victuals and beds for the cellarer, steward and understeward, their servants and horses and the prior's servants when they come to hold courts or are on the way to or from London, Oxford and Henlow [Beds.],

(f) hay and straw for the prior's horses when the prior comes to superintend the manor or for other purposes, with victuals for the prior, his horses and his men on one or two days and nights per year and

(g) an account to the priory exchequer between the feasts of All Saints and St. Andrew [1–30 Nov.].

The lessees will also mow the prior's meadows above and below the bridge and carry the mown hay yearly to the prior's sheephouse (*bercariam*) at Little Barrington;[3] let the prior's sheep use their pasture at shearing time;[4] let the vicar of Great Barrington have an acre of sown wheat and an acre of sown barley yearly;

---

[1] Since the inner court of the manor house is mentioned below as kept in the prior's hand these rooms were peripheral and probably comprised an outer north wing with three chimneys which survived in 1712: Atkyns, *Glos.* pl. 13.

[2] A circular buttressed dovecot W. of the manor farmyard: ibid.

[3] Property which the prior kept in hand in 1515, but which was let to Richard Monyngton in 1535 and 1538 for an additional £12 a year, comprised a sheephouse, Sheephouse Close of 2½ a., Mill Ham of 2 a., meadows of 14 a. above and below the bridge, pasture for 400 sheep on Barrington Downs, two stables in the outer court of the manor and all houses and buildings in the inner court: *Valor Eccl.* (Rec. Com.), ii. 423; P.R.O. E315/211, f. 11 copied in Hockaday Abs. cxiii, 1538 and noted in *L. & P. Hen. VIII*, xiv (1), p. 608. A 'sometime sheephouse' at Little Barrington is recorded as belonging to charity feoffees from 1644 to 1829: Glos. R.O. GDR/V5/37T/3; *21st Report of Commissioners for Charities* (1829), 169. For a second sheephouse at Great Barrington see below, **315** *ad finem*.

[4] The priory's sheep were probably concentrated annually for shearing at Barrington by 1318 when the prior delivered 87 sacks of wool to a purchaser there: *Trans. B.G.A.S.* xviii. 44. In the 16th century nearly 2,000 sheep were sheared there in a year: *V.C.H. Glos.* vi. 21.

provide fuel for entertaining the prior, cellarer etc. as above; carry to Llanthony any of the 3 qr. of wheat, 6 qr. of barley and 3 qr. of oats which is not consumed at the prior's sheep-shearing; grind their corn and barley at the prior's Canon Mill;[1] [f. 70] send a cart, horses and two servants to Llanthony twice a year to take and bring the prior's supplies; maintain ditches, roads, hedges and enclosures and live on site.

They may use the buildings in the inner court[2] whenever the prior, cellarer etc. are not staying or keeping goods there. They may take fuel and timber for carts and ploughs but have no admittance to the wood in the prior's park.[3] The prior will repair buildings but the lessees will carry requisite timber from the prior's park and tiles from the quarries (*tegulas sufficientes de quarruris*).[4] The Nativity of St. John the Baptist 6 Hen. VIII [24 June 1514].

315. [f. 70v.] Stock delivered to the above lessees, to be restored (or its value repaid, at the prior's choice) at the end of the lease. 3 Jan. 6 Hen. VIII [1515].

4 horses worth 8s. each.
A bull worth 4s. 6d.
18 oxen worth 11s. a head.
7 cows worth 7s. a head.
2 calves worth 2s. a head.
A boar worth 3s. 4d.
3 sows worth 2s. 6d. apiece.
10 pigs worth 2s. a head.
14 piglets worth 10d. each.
6 capons, 16 cocks and hens.
16 qr. of wheat, 12 qr. of *pulce*, 54 qr. of barley, 12 qr. of oats.
2 wagons with iron bound wheels worth 16s. each.
4 ploughs worth 12d. each.
4 ploughshares and 4 coulters (*cultros*) worth 6s. 8d.
9 iron chains worth 12d. each.
9 good yokes with bows worth in total 3s.
7 wooden harrows (*herpices ligneos*) worth 4d. apiece.
6 sets of iron tines (*settes tyndes ferri*) worth 13d. *le sett.*
A cart with iron bound wheels worth 16s.
2 strakes (*protractus*) worth 5d. each.
5 leather collars worth 8d. each.
5 leather halters (*capistra*) worth 4d. each.
A cart saddle (*cellam carectalem*) worth 10d.

---

[1] Cf. below, **318**.

[2] Including *an olde halle and a faire parlour*: P.R.O. SC 11/206. David Smith supplied this reference.

[3] The park survives as a square enclosure of 178 a. N. of the manor house: map, Glos. R.O. GDR/T1/17.

[4] Cf. below, **318**.

A tawed hide (*corium dealbatum*) worth 14d.

3 dung pots (*dongpouts*) worth 12d. each.

3 barrows (*ceniov[ectoria]*) worth 6d. each.

2 wagon ropes (*cordas plaustrales*) worth 12d. each.

A dung fork (*furcam fimalem*) worth 4d.

3 corn forks (*furcas garbales*) worth 3d. each.

4 *thressholds* worth 4d.

A great basket (*magnam sportam*) worth 12d.

A winnowing fan (*ventilabrum*) worth 20d.

A seed-lip (*semilionem*) worth 3d.

A wooden bushel (*modium ligneum*) worth 8d.

A tub (*cowle*) worth 8d.

2 *payls* worth 3d. each.

A wooden peck (*peccum ligneum*) worth 2d.

3 sieves (*cribra*) worth 3d. each.

4 hemp vats (*factos canabeos*) worth 8d. each.

2 close vats (*clesefats*) worth 3d. each.

2 bolting sieves (*poltridia*) worth 8d.

2 scythes (*falces*) worth 13d. each.

A sickle (*falsiculam*) worth 3d.

A bucket (*setulam*) worth 6d.

2 hatchets (*hachetts*) worth 3d. each.

A billhook (*falcastrum*) worth 3d.

A haircloth sieve (*cribrum cilicinum*) worth 5d.

A gridiron (*craticulam ferream*) worth 4d.

A haircloth (*pannum cilicinum*) for drying malt upon, worth 12d.

2 bronze candlesticks (*candelabra enea*), 1 salt (*salar*) *de pewter*.

An iron chest (*uccam*) with a lock and key.

A large auger (*terebrum*), 2 small augers.

16 wooden dishes and bowls (*discos et bollas ligneos*).

39 a. of demesne fallow in the field by *le shephouse* of Great Barrington, of which 18 a. are thrice ploughed (*rebinantur*), 12 a. manured by cart and 12 a. manured by folding.

16½ a. of demesne fallow in the fields of Little Barrington and Windrush of which 4 a. are thrice ploughed, 2 a. [f. 71] manured by cart and 5½ a. manured by folding.

14 wagon-loads of hay.

All straw arising from the corn of the demesne lands and 4 stands (*stondes*) to put straw upon.

316. Lease to Richard Monyngton, his wife Elizabeth and his son [   ] of a tithe barn and tithes of corn and hay from land and meadow belonging to the rectory of Great Barrington, including tithes already in the lessees' hands from demesne in

Little Barrington within Great Barrington parish[1] but excluding tithes from demesne in Great Barrington, for 60 years at 20s a year. 3 Jan 6 Hen. VIII [1515].

317. [f. 71v.] Presentation of Thomas Weere[2] to the vicarage of Tytherington (*Tydryngton*) vacant by the death of Thomas Draper. 20 Mar. 1514[/15].

318. Lease to Robert and Margery Peynten[3] of Great Barrington, their son [   ] and Robert's brother Humphrey of a watermill there called *Canon Myll*[4] for 60 years, rendering 30s. a year [f. 72] and suit to Great Barrington court. The prior will find stone and timber for repairs except stone roof tiles and millstones (*exceptis lapidibus tegulinis et molaribus*).[5] When Humphrey takes possession he will pay a fine of 40d. 23 Mar. 6 Hen. VIII [1515].

319. Proxy to William Chadsley canon of Llanthony, David Paynott chaplain, Roger Port[er], Henry ap Thomas and William Laurence[6] to act for the church of Caldicot [Mon.] [as in **130** above], especially in collecting tithes of straw, hay and other crops growing in the park or moors by Caldicot castle (*in vivario sive moris iuxta castrum de Caldecote*) which are now in arrear. [No date.]

320. [f. 72v.] Lease to Nicholas Corbaly, chaplain, and Patrick Ballard, merchant of Drogheda [Louth], of the tithes of corn, hay and thorns (*bladum et fenum decimalia ac rampnos de stagrenan'*) of Stameen (*Stamenes*), of Newtown, of St. James's and of the land held from Furness Abbey by Roger Blake and the said Patrick Ballard,[7] which tithes belong to the rectory of Colp [Meath], for 21 years at £5 a year. 14 Mar. 6 Hen. VIII [1515].

321. [f. 73] Lease to William Arkehill of Aylworth (*Eylworth*) [in Naunton], his wife Agnes[8] and their son William of the manor of Aylworth[9] including arable land

---

[1] Where the parish extended S. of the River Windrush: map, Glos. R.O. GDR/T1/17.

[2] d. 1519, when vicar of Llanwarne (Herefs.) and Tytherington: below, **374–5**.

[3] Alias Peyton, resident in 1522 at Little Barrington owning goods worth 40s.: *Military Survey of Glos. 1522*, 90.

[4] Later called Barrington Mill, at SP 209131: *V.C.H. Glos.* vi. 22–3.

[5] Freestone, ragstone and tilestone are present in the Great Oolite series N. and S. of the Windrush valley at Barrington, although better tilestone occurs elsewhere: L. Richardson, *The Country around Cirencester: Explanation of Sheet 235* (Memoir of the Geological Survey, 1933), 44–5, 104–6 & accompanying map. The prior, who as lord finished rebuilding the nave of Great Barrington church in 1511, possessed a quarry there which was let for 6s. 8d. in 1535: *V.C.H. Glos.* vi. 25; *Valor Eccl.* (Rec. Com.), ii. 423. The present passage suggests that his quarry yielded no tiles.

[6] Auditor of the priory: below, **335**.

[7] Places detailed above, **123**.

[8] Agnes Arkyll survived in 1522 owning goods worth £8: *Military Survey of Glos. 1522*, 121.

[9] Originally of 2½ hides: P.R.O. C 115/75, s. xxii; cf. *V.C.H. Glos.* vi. 80.

there and a ruinous messuage at Harford (*Hertford*)[1] lately held by Richard Lorde (but excluding *Canehey* Close, all the meadows and several and common pasture for the prior's sheep, which are reserved to the prior)[2] for the term of their lives, rendering yearly:

(a) 8s.,

(b) stipend of 3s. 4d. and livery of 9 bu. of wheat, 9 bu. of barley, 2 bu. of oats and 1 peck of salt to the prior's shepherd,

(c) dues to the lord and court of Rendcomb,

(d) 13d. rent to the lord of Guiting and

(e) suit to the prior's court at Turkdean.

They will maintain buildings, walls, hedges and ditches in the manor except for the prior's sheephouse (*bercariam*), [f. 73v.] will mow the prior's meadows and closes, will carry the mown hay to the sheephouse and will provide victuals, a bed, hay and straw for the prior's superintendent of sheep (*supervisori bidencium*) when he visits.[3] They may have *housebote*, *heybote*, *firebote* and *ploughbote* but may not sublet. 10 Apr. 6 Hen. VIII [1515].

322. Title of Dudstone hospital (for the purpose of ordination) granted to William Voyle, clerk [as **132** above]. 26 June 1515.

323. [f. 74] Lease to John and Thomas Looder of two watermills in one tenement, a fish weir and a fishery at Carey Mills[4] in Fawley [then in Fownhope, now in Brockhampton], Herefs., for 20 years, rendering annually £6 13s. 4d. and the first good salmon to be caught or 3s. 4d. at the prior's choice. They will maintain cogs, rungs and buckets [of the machinery], fences [of the weir] and roofing, will meet the costs of other repairs not exceeding 6d. and will make a salmon pipe [i.e. trap] in the weir. 2 Feb. 1515.

Hec indentura facta in festo Purificacionis Beate Marie Virginis anno regni Regis Henrici Octavi sexto inter Edmundum Forest, priorem domus et ecclesie Beate Marie de Lanthonia iuxta Gloucestriam, et eiusdem loci conventus ex parte una et Iohannem Looder et Thomam Looder ex parte altera testatur quod predictus prior et

---

[1] Perhaps in Brockhill Meadow of 5 a. at SP 127229, which ran with the Aylworth estate in 1838: Glos. R.O. P224/IN/3/1; P224/VE/3/1.

[2] When Prior Brockworth let the manor in 1367 he reserved the rents of customary tenants as well as sheep pasture and a sheephouse: Reg. Brockworth, f. 15. Such tenants, gone by 1515, will have inhabited the now deserted medieval village at SP 109217: cf. *V.C.H. Glos.* vi. 77.

[3] By 1535 the priors of Llanthony had lifted these conditions, relet the manor for 36s. 4d. and let the sheep pasture separately for £7 16s., while the priors of St. Oswald's let other property at Aylworth for 31s. 8d.: *Valor Eccl.* (Rec. Com.), ii. 427, 487.

[4] At SO 573307: *Trans. Woolhope N.F.C.* xxxiv. 71–3 (with map). Prior Hart relet the property in 1528 and 1535 to Roger Cockes of Fawley, who also rented Mordiford Mill; the property then included a riverside meadow of 19 a. called the Range and underwood in Carey Wood and the rent was £4. The Cockses remained lessees until 1608 but Sir John Scudamore took possession and built an ironworks there in 1628: *Trans. Woolhope N.F.C.* 1914–17, 170–2; xxxiv. 3–8.

conventus tradiderunt, concesserunt et ad firmam dimiserunt prefato Iohanni Looder et Thome unum tenementum et duo molendina aquatica in eodem tenemento existencia iacencia in Falley vocata Cary Mylls cum gurgite et piscaria dictis molendinis quovismodo pertinentibus sive spectantibus in comitatu Herefordie.

Habendo et tenendo predictum tenementum, duo molendina aquatica, gurgitem et piscariam cum omnibus suis pertinenciis prefatis Iohanni et Thome a die confeccionis presencium usque ad finem termini 20 annorum extunc proxime sequencium et plenarie complendorum, si ipsi tam diu vixerint aut unus eorum tam diu vixerit. Reddendo inde annuatim prefato priori et successoribus suis £6 13s. 4d. sterlingorum ad festa ad vincula[1] Sancti Petri et Purificacionis Beate Marie Virginis per equales porciones solvendas durante termino predicto. Et predictus Iohannes et Thomas dabunt et liberabunt prefato priori et successoribus suis 1 salmonem bonum et habilem cum primum in aqua predicti gurgitis fuerit congruus[2] et seisitus, sive precium eiusdem videlicet 3s. 4d., ad eleccionem et placitum dicti prioris durante termino predicto.

Et predictus Iohannes et Thomas reparabunt, sustentabunt et manutenebunt omnia predicta tenementum, molendina et gurgitem in scariaballis Anglice 'coggs', limonibus Anglice 'ronggs', cocliariis[3] aquaticis Anglice 'ladylls', sepibus et cooperturis, necnon in omnibus aliis reparacionibus existentibus infra valorem 6d. sumptibus suis propriis et expensis tociens quociens necesse fuerit durante termino predicto. Et si reparacio dicti tenementi, molendinorum et gurgitis superonerabit valorem 6d. preter scariaballa, limones, cocliaria aquatica et sepes, ut predictum est, quod tunc predictus prior et successores sui inde facient et supportabunt omnes sumptus et expenca durante termino predicto.

Et si contingat dictum redditum £6 13s. 4d. aut aliquam inde parcellam a retro fore insolutum per unum mensem post aliquem[4] finem festorum predictorum quo solvi debeat aut si contingat prefatum Iohannem et Thomam omnes et singulas convenciones supradictas minime observare et perimplere, quod extunc bene licebit prefato priori et conventui ac successoribus suis in predicta tenementum et molendina aquatica reintrare, rehabere et gaudere et prestinum statum suum possidere, dictosque Iohannem et Thomam inde totaliter expellere et amovere, presenti indentura in aliquo non obstante.

Proviso semper quod predicti Iohannes et Thomas facient unum nomine 'le samon pype' infra dictum gurgitem sumptibus suis propriis et expencis. In cuius rei testimonium presenti indenture partes predicti sigilla sua alternatim apposuerunt. Data in domo nostro capitulari Lanthonie predicte die et anno supradictis.

324. [f. 74v.] Proxy to Thomas Cysseter and John Haresfyld, canons of Llanthony, and William Perott, vicar of Ardcath [Meath], to act for the prior in Ireland [as in **229** above]. [f. 75] 12 June 1515.

---

[1] MS. *vincule.*
[2] MS. *congrua.* The meaning seems to be 'met'.
[3] MS. *cocliaria.*
[4] MS. *aliquid.*

325. [f. 75v.] Lease to Thomas and Alice Lynett[1] of Prestbury and their son [   ] of

(a) The manor of Prestbury with buildings and a dovecot on the manor site and demesne land, meadow and pasture in Prestbury, Cheltenham and Southam,[2] now held by the said Thomas and formerly by William Parks, all for 60 years at annual rents of £4 and 12 geese and 12 capons or 6s., at the prior's choice, and

(b) a tithe barn by the gate of Prestbury rectory or manor, formerly held in a ruinous condition by Parks but now rebuilt, and the tithes and oblations belonging to the rectory for 60 years at £12 a year.

The lessees will render dues, live on site and entertain [as in **78** (a–d) above]. [f. 76] They will perform the office of bailiff there, accounting for rents, issues, fines and amercements at the priory exchequer between the feasts of All Saints and St. Andrew [1–30 Nov.] and receiving an allowance of 10s. a year. They will also receive the tithe of shorn wool for a month after the end of the term. 12 Oct. 7 Hen. VIII [1515].

326. [f. 76v.] The king's exemplification[3] of letters patent of 24 Nov. 12 Hen. VII [1496] confirming letters patent of 26 Oct. 21 Edw. IV [1481][4] excusing the prior's absence from his property in Ireland. [f. 77] Prior Edmund has sought exemplification, as John Straunge[5] has sworn in Chancery that the original letters are lost. Westminster, 10 July 7 Hen. VIII [1515].

327. The king's confirmation of the above letters patent. [f. 77v.] Knole [in Sevenoaks, Kent], 17 July 7 Hen. VIII [1515], [signed] Yong.[6]

328. Proxy to William Chadsley canon of Llanthony, Thomas Myllyng,[7] John Fremantell B.Cn. & C.L., John Laurence,[8] Robert Aylond B.C.L., William Laurence

---

[1] The Lynetts surrendered this lease before Sept. 1520 and moved to Charlton Kings, having acquired freehold land worth 63s. 4d. a year in Cheltenham and its hamlets: below, **430**; *Military Survey of Glos. 1522*, 44–7. Alice d. 1550 or 1551 a widow survived by two daughters, her bequests including 3 cattle, 66 sheep and 4 wagons: P.R.O. PROB 11/34, f. 114.

[2] Cf. above, **78**. Land at Southam was given by Margaret de Bohun and the earls of Hereford and Essex between 1171 and 1277: P.R.O. C 115/77, s. vi nos. 58–61, 65–6.

[3] Calendared in *L. & P. Hen. VIII*, ii, p. 184.

[4] *Cal. Pat. 1494–1509*, 73; *1476–85*, 246.

[5] Clerk of the Peace for Glos. 1516–30: Sir Edgar Stephens, *Clerks of the Counties 1360–1960* (London, 1961), 91.

[6] Calendared in *L. & P. Hen. VIII*, ii, p. 191.

[7] D.Cn.L, B.C.L., d. 1540; fellow of New College, Oxford, 1490–1509 and rector of many churches including Upper Heyford (Oxon.) 1508–35, Bromyard (Herefs.) 1513–35, St. Stephen's, Bristol, from 1513 and Wimbledon (Surrey) 1535–40: Emden, *Biog. Reg. Oxon. to 1500.*

[8] One of the name was B.C.L., d. 1542; fellow of New College, Oxford, 1500–10 and rector of St. John-in-the-Soke, Winchester (Hants.), 1510–42 and Overton (Wilts.) 1515–42: ibid.

and Thomas Salmon to act for the church of Barton S[t]ac[e]y [Hants.]. 12 Oct. 1515. [Abstract in MS.; cf. **130**].

329. [f. 78] Lease to John and Juliana Kenelocke[1] of Colesbourne (*Collisbourne*), their son John and the elder John's son John by his first wife Alice, of property at Colesbourne as follows:

(a) the manor site with its buildings and demesne land, meadow and pasture,[2] except woods, coppices and sufficient summer pasture for the prior's sheep,[3] which are reserved to the prior, and

(b) tithes of corn, hay, wool, lambs, calves, colts, pigeons, piglets, geese, hides, pasturage, milk, cheese, eggs, flax, hemp, apples, pears and other produce except one third of the tithe of corn throughout the parish, the whole tithe of hay and the altarage of other tenants and parishioners, which are reserved to the rector,

for 60 years, rendering £4 13s. 4d. a year and suit of court. The lessees will provide food, drink and protection (*gardam*) for the prior's shepherd when he is there watching sheep. They will serve in the office of bailiff there,[4] [f. 78v.] accounting at the priory exchequer between the feasts of All Saints and St. Andrew [1–30 Nov.] for rents, issues, fines and amercements, especially a rent of 10s. a year from Gothurst (*Gootehurste*) Mill [in Chedworth].[5] They will maintain thatched roofs, the prior maintaining the rest of the property. They may take *housebote, haybote, cartbote, firebote* and *ploughbote* except in woods and coppices, and may use all the pasture in winter when the prior's sheep are not there. The lessees will provide food, drink, beds, hay, straw and provender for the cellarer, steward and understeward, their servants and their horses when they come to hold courts or for other business. They will return live and dead stock at the end of the term or repay its value at the prior's choice. 9 Oct. 7 Hen. VIII [1515].

330. [f. 79] Grant [in English] to Gerald Fitzgerald earl of Kildare, deputy of Ireland, of an annuity of £10 in Irish money *for favours, benevolences & others by the said earle unto the said same prior & hous, ther procurators, servantes & tenants in Irland hertofore shewed & don and herafter duryng the lyfe of the sayd erle to be shewed & don.*[6] If the earl is succeeded by another as deputy the annuity will be reduced to £5. [f. 79v.] In case of default he may distrain on the prior's land there. 24 June 7 Hen. VIII [1515].

---

[1] Alias Keylok, owning goods worth £13 6s. 8d. in 1522: *Military Survey of Glos. 1522*, 109.

[2] Totalling *c.* 385 a. with the excluded land: *V.C.H. Glos.* vii. 187.

[3] Summer pasture for 400 sheep was let to Arthur Porter for 53s. 4d. by 1535: *Valor Eccl.* (Rec. Com.), ii. 425; cf. *L. & P. Hen. VIII*, xvii, pp. 157, 212.

[4] A John Kenelocke still held this office in 1535, collecting rents of 8s. 7d. from free and £3 0s. 1d. from customary tenants: *Valor Eccl.* ii. 425.

[5] Cf. *V.C.H. Glos.* vii. 171.

[6] Cf. below, **344**.

331. Citation from Edward [Vaughan] bishop of St. David's to the prior of Llanthony Prima to attend a prorogued convocation of Canterbury province in St. Paul's cathedral, London, on 13 Nov. next.[1] [f. 80] Lamphey manor (*manerio nostro de Lantesey*) [Pemb.], 4 Sept. 1515.

332. Prior Forest's objection to the citation. 28 Sept. 1515.

Copia littere directe episcopo Menevensi ut revocet[2] citacionem predictam.

Right reverende fader in God, in my most humbliste & hartyste maner I recommend me to you. So it is, as I am credibly informyd, my lorde of Canterbury for dyvers and urgent causis moving his grace hathe decreid all abbotts, priors and othir prelats of his provins to be anew cytid to appere personally in the convocacion proroged to the 13 day of Novembre next cumyng, and according to that decre hathe send forthe citacions, and by the auctoryte of one of them your lordshipp hathe send your citacion under your seale to oure prior of our sell of Lanthony in Wales within your diocese to appere on the said 13 day in the said convocacion. Truly, my lorde, that prior is obediente unto me and one of my chanons and not perpetuall prior ther by eleccion, confirmacion, institucion or any othir wise but alweys removyble at my pleasure as othir of his brethren there be. And that howse with all that belongithe to it is aproperid unto this pore priory wher I am master, and so the nater of that howse is chaungid, and this howse & it now is all one, as your lordeshipp knoweth right well. For the whiche, my goode lorde, as I am informyd by my councell larnyd, it shall not be requisite that our said prior do appere in the said convocacion, and hethurto none of our priors ther in suche convocacions have be so citid or chargid sethe the said howse was unyted to us & the priory here. And this knowne to my lorde of Canterbury, I suppose it is not the mynd of his grace to have our prior in the said convocacion. For the whiche I hartily desyor your good lordshipp to revoke your said citacion and to be goode lorde to me & to that poore howse, as my speciall truste is in you. And so doyng bothe I & my brethren shall daily pray for the preservacion of your good lordeshipp. Writin at Lanthony by Gloucester the 28 day of Septembre.

333. The official of Gloucester's[3] letter supporting the objection. [1515.]

Copia littere officialis Gloucestriensis directe domino priori Lanthonie iuxta Gloucestriam de materia predicta non formidanda.

My lorde, if the bishope will not be intretid butt forhtur loke for intercessions & rewards seying he woll certify, lett hym do it in Goddis name. His doyng therin shall not be prejudiciall to you nowthur your prior; lett not hym be inquietid for this. And [f. 80v.] *I dowte not but suche as be larnyd woll marvell to seyn such a citacyon pas his hande, etc.*

---

[1] Cf. Wilkins, *Concilia*, iii. 658. The prior of Llanthony Prima was cited again in 1529: *L. & P. Hen. VIII*, iv, p. 2700.

[2] MS. *revocat.*

[3] William Burghill: below, **335.**

334. Proxy to William [Parker] abbot of Gloucester[1] and Mr. Thomas Wellis S.T.P.[2] to attend the above convocation. 27 Oct. 1515.

Pateat universis per presentes nos Edmundum, permissione divina priorem monasterii sive prioratus Lanthonie iuxta Gloucesteriam ordinis Sancti Augustini Wigorniensis diocesis, et eiusdem loci conventum constituisse, ordinasse et in loco nostro posuisse reverendos in Christo patres Willelmum abbatem Sancti Petri Gloucestrie ac venerabilem Magistrum Thomam Wellis, Sacre Pagine Professorem, nostros veros et legittimos procuratores ad comparendum coniunctim et divisim pro nobis et monasterio nostro coram reverendissimo in Christo patre et domino Domino Willelmo [Warham] permissione divina Cantuarensi archiepiscopo, tocius Anglie primati et apostolice sedis legato, in convocacione sua generali in ecclesia Sancti Pauli London' et ad tractandum de negociis in eadem convocacione proponendis et statuendis, necnon ad omnia et singula que ibidem circa statum ecclesie Anglicane et defencionem eiusdem aguntur et geruntur consenciendum,[3] causasque absencie nostre allegandum et si opus fuerit probandum, omnibus privilegiis, libertatibus, immunitatibus ac iuribus quibuscumque nobis et monasterio nostro a sede apostolico graciose concessis in omnibus semper salvis.

In quorum omnium testimonium sigillum nostrum commune presentibus est appensum. Date in domo nostra capitulari Lanthonie predicte vicesimo septimo die mensis Octobris anno Domini millesimo quingentesimo quintodecimo.

335. Thomas Bucke's[4] homage for free land in the demesne of Aylburton (*Ailbrighton*) in the Forest of Dean.

He did homage on Friday after Corpus Christi 7 Hen. VIII [8 June 1515] in the prior's inner chamber (*conclavi*) at the Newark near Hempsted in the presence of William Borowehill clerk, official of Worcester diocese,[5] John Gloucester canon of Llanthony, Robert Stinchecumbe B.Cn.L., clerk, William Chadesley canon of Llanthony, William Laurence auditor of Llanthony, Thomas Shoyer gentleman, Philip Buck son of Thomas, Robert Phipport[6] and others. At the same time he paid 27s. 2d. relief for lands and tenements held in fee [f. 81] and seven heriots for seven messuages also held in fee.

[1] S.T.P., d. 1539, abbot 1514–39: Emden, *Biog. Reg. Oxon. 1501–40*; *D.N.B.*

[2] d. 1524; fellow of New College, Oxford, 1485–1500, prebendary of Wells 1506–24, of Tamworth (Warw.) from 1508 and of Chichester 1508–24 and chaplain to Archbishop Warham: Emden, *Biog. Reg. Oxon. to 1500.*

[3] MS. *consensciendum.*

[4] Anthony Bucke had succeeded by 1522, holding land worth 26s. 8d. and goods worth £10: *Military Survey of Glos. 1522*, 67; cf. *V.C.H. Glos.* v. 67.

[5] Alias Burghill, notary public, B.Cn. & C.L. 1512, D.Cn.L. 1516, d. 1526; rector of St. Michael, Gloucester, from 1512, vicar of Brookthorpe from 1513, official and vicar general of the bishop of Hereford from 1516, rector of Eardisley (Herefs.) by the prior's gift 1517–19, treasurer of Hereford 1519–26, prebendary there 1522–6 and vicar of Churcham 1522–5 and Kempsford 1523–6: Emden, *Biog. Reg. Oxon. 1501–40*; below, **347**. J.P. for Herefs. 1522: *L. & P. Hen. VIII*, iii, p. 1017.

[6] Alias Philpott, resident at Hempsted in 1539: Glos. muster roll, P.R.O. E 101/59/9.

336. Edward Cotynton's[1] homage for free land in the demesne of Aylburton in the Forest of Dean.

At the death of his father Morgan, Edward Cotynton owed the prior the homage, heriot and relief for his lands which his ancestors had rendered, as appears in old rolls of the court of Aylburton for various reigns. On an order (*precepto*) from that court the bailiff, Philip Shoyer, sought to distrain and impound Cotynton's animals for such service, and when Cotynton rescued the animals (*fecit rescussum*) the king issued a writ for his arrest (*pro corpore eius habendo*). Afterwards, on 15 Aug. 7 Hen. VIII [1515], Cotynton did homage in the prior's great chamber (*in magna camera domini prioris*) in the presence of Philip Bristow canon of Llanthony, Robert Cun cellarer,[2] William Chadsley canon and prior's chaplain, Henry Bett' undersheriff of Glos., William Laurence auditor, Edward Bryggs gentleman, Philip Shoyer, Philip Buck, Robert Phiport, William Addyse[3] and many others. He also paid 8s. 11¾d. relief for land held in fee. He owed four heriots worth 26s. 8d. for four messuages held in fee, as appears in a rental of 8 Edw. IV [1468–9], but the prior waived payment on his meeting the 8s. cost of the writ.

337. Lease to William and Catherine Hereford and their son Roger, gentry of Sufton[4] [in Mordiford], Herefs., [f. 81v.] of a weir called Ree Mill[5] (*qui quidem gurges ab antiquo vocatur 'le Ree Mill'*) and an adjacent meadow in Mordiford for 60 years, rendering 16s. 8d. a year to the prior and rent and service to the king and the bishop of Hereford. They will maintain the weir with its leat, dam and banks (*cum cursu aque, stagno[6] et ripis*), receiving an allowance of 20d. a year in return. They may not obstruct or divert the common watercourse running to the prior's Mordiford Mill in the parish of Fownhope (*communem cursum aque currentem ad quoddam molendinum predicti prioris et conventus iacens[7] infra parochiam de Fownehope vulgariter vocatum 'Mordefordis Mill'*). Michaelmas 7 Hen. VIII [29 Sept. 1515].

[1] d. 1527: *Hereford Probates 1407–1581*, 236. In 1522 he held land worth £13 6s. 8d. a year and goods worth £10: *Military Survey of Glos. 1522*, 67.
[2] Alias Conne or Conde, holder of this office since at least 1513: *V.C.H. Glos.*ii. 319. Son of a sister of Prior Deane, recommended unsuccessfully in 1514 as replacement for a dissolute prior of St. Oswald's, Gloucester: *L. & P. Hen. VIII*, i, p. 1356. Probably a descendant of Walter Cone who rendered homage to Prior Wyche for land in Aylburton demesne in 1410: Reg. Wyche, f. 11v.
[3] Either a burgess of Gloucester in 1539 or a curate of Oxenhall from 1522 who d. 1559: Glos. muster roll 1539, P.R.O. E 101/59/9; *Military Survey of Glos. 1522*, 62; Glos. R.O., GDR wills 1546/190, 1559/360.
[4] William (1479–1549) m. 1506 Catherine daughter of Thomas ap Harry of Poston and left issue Roger (d. 1561): *Burke's Landed Gentry* (1952 ed.). They were lords of Mordiford and owners of land at Burghill, Cowarne, Littlehope in Fownhope and Preston-on-Wye (all in Herefs.), and Roger also bought chantry land in 1548 thus enlarging his estate in Mordiford from *c.* 400 a. to *c.* 1,300 a.: P.R.O. C 142/42/103; C 142/133/97; Duncumb, *Herefs.* iii. 72.
[5] i.e. a derelict mill, evidently the second mill in Mordiford given to the priory before 1199: above, **135** & n.
[6] MS. *stangno.*
[7] MS. *iacentem.*

338. [f. 82] Extent [of monastic property in Tidenham and Woolaston]. Wednesday after St. Gregory 12 Edw. III [18 Mar. 1338].

Jurors:[1] John Waldyng, Adam of Wirwode, Nigel Borweye, Thomas Waldyng, Henry Pyrke, Howell Philipp, William of Dula and William of Anneford, free tenants, and Richard Cole, Adam son of William, Henry Beche, Adam Cole, Stephen Cole and John White.

The abbot of Tintern [Mon.] holds (a) the manor of Aluredston [in Woolaston], Woolaston, 'Hatheleshall' [and] Madgett,[2] (b) 'Crokwere' and Lancaut in the demesne of Tidenham[3] and (c) Baddings Weir, Wall Weir, Stow Weir, half of Plum Weir[4] and half of Ash Weir [the latter then in Woolaston, now in Hewelsfield].[5] The abbot of Malmesbury holds half of Plum Weir and woods at Plumweir Cliff.[6] The prior of Llanthony in Wales holds half of Ash Weir, 'Kylenham' wood of 20 a., 1 a. of meadow there, a messuage, 60 a. of land and a meadow at Wibdon.[7]

Abbas de Tynterne tenet manerium de Alureston, Wolaston, Hatheleshall, Modesgate, Crokwere et Lancaugt infra dominium de Tudenham et gurgites de Bathingwere, Walwere, Stawere et medietatem de Plomwhere [et] medietatem de Aisshwere, et abbas de Malmesburye tenet medietatem gurgitis de Plomwere et quedam bosca vocata 'Plomweresclyf'. Prior de Lanthonia Wallie tenet medietatem gurgitis de Aisshewere et boscum de Kylenham, videlicet 20 acras, et unam acram prati ibidem, unum[8] messuagium, 60 acras terre et pratum in Wibbedon.

[1] John Waldyng and William of Anneford lived in Tidenham, since they also occur in **339**. Places identified are now in the parish of Tidenham unless specified otherwise.

[2] The abbot of Tintern's manor of Woolaston included land at Madgett from 1131, at Aluredston (i.e. Brookend) from 1302 and at 'Hathelishall' or 'Halishall' by 1535: *Valor Eccl.* (Rec. Com.), iv. 370; *V.C.H. Glos.* x. 103, 106–8, 114. His holding at Madgett was evidently an enclave of 108 a. there transferred from Woolaston to Tidenham parish in 1882: *V.C.H. Glos.* x. 2 (with map), 102.

[3] Cf. *V.C.H. Glos.* x. 50.

[4] All on the Wye and acquired before 1148 when Baddings (not located) and Wall (ST 539979) Weirs belonged to Woolaston and Stow (ST 535985) and half of Plum (ST 538996) Weirs belonged to Penterry (now in Tintern, Mon.): *Cal. Charter R.* 1300–26, 88, 97.

[5] Acquired by 1223, at SO 529003, 500 yd. NW. of the abbey church: Dugdale, *Mon.* v. 268.

[6] Acquired before 1086: *V.C.H. Glos.* x. 107, 113. Let to Tintern Abbey by 1535 for 26s. 8d. a year under the name of Modesgatessponne: *Valor Eccl.* (Rec. Com.), iv. 370.

[7] As given by Hugh de Lacy (d. *c.* 1115) the prior's estate included half of Ash Weir and a hide at Tidenham and Madgett of which half was wood and half plain, the land at Madgett being granted to Tintern Abbey and recovered again before 1169: Dugdale, *Mon.* vi. 137; P.R.O. C 115/75, f. 216v. no. 25; C115/77, s. iv nos. 97, 105 = C115/83, ff. 155–6. After the present entry, however, no property of the prior is recorded there. Thomas duke of Gloucester held half of Ash Weir in 1398 and the abbot of Tintern held the whole weir at the dissolution: *V.C.H. Glos.* x. 113.

[8] MS. *unius.*

339. Record of an inquisition taken at a court [of the manor of Tidenham] on Saturday after Hockday 2 Edw. III [16 Apr. 1328] in pursuance of a letter from the lord[1] brought by the prior of Llanthony Prima in Wales.

Jurors: Roger of Saymore, William of Waleys, John de la Lee, Hugh Duraunt, William of Beudevill, William Adam, Robert of Auste, Stephen of Wirwode, John Waldyng, Nicholas of Betesley, William of Anneforde and Nicholas of Auste.

John le Botyler of Llantwit (*Laimbtwit*)[2] held directly from the prior of Llanthony Prima half a hide of land and a weir with appurtenances in the fee of Tidenham for 36s. a year. They came into the hands of the lord earl for a year and more because John was an adherent of the younger Hugh Despenser (*adherens cum domino Hugone le Spenser filio*).[3]

340. Letter of Richard [Mayew] bishop of Hereford reporting the resignation of Thomas Taylor as rector of Stretton Sugwas [Herefs.]. Whitbourne manor [Herefs.], 14 Dec. 1515.

341. [f. 82v.] Presentation of Thomas Pumfret, chaplain,[4] to the rectory of Stretton Sugwas [Herefs.] vacant as above. 30 Jan. 1515[/16].

342. Lease to Richard[5] and Joan Taylor and their son Robert of

(a) a messuage called Pipper Lace[6] in the suburbs of Hereford lying between land

---

[1] Thomas of Brotherton earl of Norfolk (1300–38), lord of Tidenham 1310–38: *V.C.H. Glos.* x. 62–3.

[2] b. *c.* 1264: *Cal. Pat.* 1334–8, 157. Retainer of Maurice of Berkeley *c.* 1312 and steward of the younger Hugh Despenser 1322–6: N. Saul, *Knights and Esquires* (Oxford, 1981), 65, 271, 277. Commissioner of oyer and terminer in Oxon., Bristol, Herefs. and S. Wales 1322–5: *Cal. Pat.* 1321–4 *passim*; 1324–7, 64, 233. M.P. for Glos. 1324, 1332, 1339: W. R. Williams, *Parliamentary History of Glos.* (Hereford, 1898), 11. Lord of Hardwicke, of Brawn in Sandhurst and of Grimsbury by Banbury (then in Northants., now in Oxon.): *V.C.H. Glos.* x. 181; *Cal. Pat.* 1327–30, 394; *Cal. Inq. p.m.* x. 388.

[3] Botyler, as Despenser's steward, evidently annexed the priory's land to the manor of Tidenham in 1323–6 when Despenser held the manor from the earl: *V.C.H. Glos.* x. 63.

[4] Alias Pumphrey, instituted 12 Feb.: *Reg. Mayew*, 284.

[5] d. 1540, survived by a wife Matilda and a daughter; a miller, owning houses and stables in Hereford by St. Nicholas's church extending to Wroughtall Lane (now the W. corner of King and Aubrey Streets) and barns by 'the Grene Townediche' (now Mill Street): P.R.O. PROB 11/28, f. 152.

[6] Sold in 1542 to the city of Gloucester, which resold it in 1549 to Matilda Taylor: *L. & P. Hen. VIII*, xvii, p. 488; Glos. R.O. GBR/B2/2, f. 65. The abuttals to Greyfriars identify it as a curtilage, mapped in 1919 as an old tanyard, containing the extant timber-framed house no. 1 Barton Road at the W. corner of Greyfriars Avenue: plans, *Trans. Woolhope N.F.C.* 1918–20, 130; Isaac Taylor, *Map of Hereford* (1757).

of the Friars Minor and land lately of John Skydmore, knight,[1] and extending from
the highway to land of the said friars, and

(b) a garden there lying between land of David Groyne and a highway and
extending from a highway to land of David Groyne

for 31 years at 7s. 6d. a year, rendering dues to the king and the bishop of Hereford.
[f. 83] All Saints 7 Hen. VIII [1 Nov. 1515].

343. Lease to John and Joan Theyr alias Heyr and their son Thomas[2] of

(a) the mansion house of Brockworth in which Theyr lives[3] with a great barn,[4] a
pig house, a byre and a dovecot, and a granary on the manor site with right of access
and a garden belonging (*domum mansionis de Brokworth in qua ipse Iohannes modo
inhabitat una cum magna grangia, domu porcorum cum boveria et columbario, ac
granarium infra situm manerii ipsorum prioris et conventus ibidem cum liberis
ingressu et egressu una cum gardino dicto situi pertinente*),

(b) Sally Mead (*Salymede*) meadow,[5]

---

[1] Alias Scudamore, of Kentchurch (Herefs.), J.P. for Herefs. 1443–60 and 1470, M.P. for
the county 1445–6 and 1449, sheriff there 1449 and 1456 and commissioner for oyer and
terminer for Wales and the March 1458–60: *Hist. of Parl., Biographies 1439–1509* corrected
by *Hist. of Parl., Commons 1386–1421*; *Cal. Pat.* 1441–6, 471; 1446–52, 590; 1452–61, 444,
562, 666; 1467–77, 615; *Cal. Fine R.* 1452–61, 175. Keeper of Pembroke castle 1461,
attainted as a Lancastrian 1461 but restored to his possessions 1474 as lord of 'Grove',
Moccas (Herefs.) and 11 other manors in Herefs. and Glos. and owner of 19 messuages in
Hereford and elsewhere: *Cal. Pat.* 1461–7, 77, 372; 1467–77, 454.

[2] Joan d. 1546: Glos. R.O. wills 1546/45. Thomas married a sister of Prior Hart of
Llanthony (d. 1545), became Hart's executor and acquired much of the priory library; he
rented additional land at Brockworth from Joan Cook and in 1545 purchased other land of the
former priory there at Hampen (E. of Droys Court, SO 900151) and Cooper's Hill which
passed with the library to his son John (d. 1631) and his grandson John (1597–1673), M.A.,
lawyer and bibliophile: *Trans. B.G.A.S.* vii. 164–5; lii. 287–8; Austin, *Crypt School*, 160; *L. &
P. Hen. VIII*, xx (2), p. 455; *Inquisitions post mortem for Glos.* 1625–36 (Index Lib. 1893),
173; Irvine Gray, *Antiquaries of Glos. and Bristol* (B.G.A.S. 1981), 43–4; for Hampen cf.
Glos. R.O. GDR/T1/39.

[3] On the manor site beside Brockworth Court: *Valor Eccl.* (Rec. Com.), ii. 424. As
described in this lease, both the manor site and the manorial demesne were divided between
the Theyrs and the prior, a division which was perpetuated in 1540 when the king granted the
prior's title to John Guise subject to a life interest in the manor house for ex-prior Hart: *L. &
P. Hen. VIII*, xv, p. 411; *Trans. B.G.A.S.* lxiii. 142. The division persisted in a modified form
in 1841 when Sir John Guise kept in hand Brockworth Court and 329 a. to the N. while his
lessee Daniel Thayers occupied Park House Farm at the NW. corner of Green Street and
farmed 328 a. in the SW. quarter of the parish including Sally Mead, Crock Mead and Great
Park: Glos. R.O. GDR/T1/39.

[4] Now a stone-slated barn of eight bays, four bays of the roof being dated by dendrochronology
1307–15 until their renewal after a recent fire: inf. from Tim Wiltshire, the present owner,
quoting Ancient Monuments Laboratory Report 46/98.

[5] W. of Golf Club Lane at SO 882159: Glos. R.O. GDR/T1/39.

(c) pasture under *Huntwodd* at *Cheyneleyse* Hill, pasture in *le Hey*[1] and pasture anciently called *Aldewyke*[2] which lies in the lord's outer park[3] by the highway next below *Crokemede*[4] and

(d) demesne land now held by Theyr and formerly by the lessee Richard Hoone, except such demesne land, meadow, pasture, wood and underwood as is anciently reserved to the prior

for 40 years, rendering yearly as follows:

(a) 30 qr. of winnowed wheat, 30 qr. of winnowed barley and 6 qr. of winnowed oats,

(b) 12 geese worth 4d. a head and 12 capons worth 3d. a head or 7s. at the prior's choice,

(c) 8s. for the dovecot, 46s. 8d. for Sally Mead, 14s. for pasture under Hunt Wood and at *Cheynleyse* Hill and 5s. 8d. for pasture in the Hey, amounting altogether to 74s. 4d., less an allowance [f. 83v.] of 13s. 4d. from the farm of Sally Mead for pasture called *le Plashe* which is now in the lord's park,

(d) food, beds, hay, straw and provender for the cellarer, steward and understeward, their servants and their horses when they come to hold courts and leets and for other business,

(e) straw for the lord [prior]'s horses and for the beds of the lord [prior] and his servants when they stay at his Brockworth manor and

(f) victuals, bedding, 20s. and a pair of thigh-boots (*ocrearum*) or 18d. for the prior's servant who carries fuel from Buckholt Wood [in Cranham] to the manor and other places assigned by the prior, for which the lessees are allowed 20s. and 18d. in their account.

The lessees will maintain walls, thatched (but not tiled) roofs, ditches, enclosures and hedges. Because they have received 25 a., nearly amounting to the whole, of the arable land fallow they will restore it so at the end of the term, together with the live and dead stock of the manor or its value at the prior's choice. If the prior builds or rebuilds on the manor site they will help to carry timber, tiles and other stone and will find bread, ale and victuals for craftsmen and labourers, for which they will be allowed half the cost of victuals in their next account. [f. 84] They will carry fuel from the lord's park for the hall and kitchen at Brockworth whenever the prior stays there. They will render annual accounts of money at the Llanthony exchequer before St. Andrew [30 Nov.] and annual accounts of grain before the Purification [2 Feb.] and will live on site. Michaelmas 5 Hen. VIII [29 Sept. 1513].

[1] E. of Brockworth Court at SO 893169. Hunt Wood was probably near Hunt Court on the boundary with Badgeworth.

[2] In the 13th century a grove bounded by Cosley, Crock Mead, Redding and Sally Mead, i.e. straddling Golf Club Lane at SO 884161: *Trans. B.G.A.S.* vii. 152.

[3] The prior's inner park, of 90 a. around SO 880157, was bounded on the W. by the parish boundary, on the NE. by Wotton Brook and on the SE. by the abbot of Gloucester's Abbotswood: Glos. R.O. GDR/T1/39; cf. *Trans. B.G.A.S.* vii. 148.

[4] W. of Golf Club Lane at SO 883164: Glos. R.O. GDR/T1/39, misspelt *Cock Meadow.*

344. The king's warrant[1] to Gerald [Fitzgerald], earl of Kildare, to amend in the prior's favour a bill of resumption before the Irish parliament.

Whereas the king by letters patent at Westminster on 7 Oct. last [1515][2] appointed Kildare as deputy [f. 84v.] to hold a parliament in Ireland within a year in order to agree on certain articles [which are recited in English] as follows:

(a) that the subsidy of 13s. 4d. on every ploughland granted for eight years by the Dublin parliament of 24 Hen. VII [1508] be continued for 10 years and extended to the clergy and

(b) [f. 85] that all licences to persons to absent themselves from their possessions be revoked, so that the king may take two thirds of the revenues of absentees' lands according to an earlier statute,[3]

now the king at Prior Edmund's request forbids the above article to be enacted without a proviso as follows:

Provided alway that this Acte of Resumpcion or any othir acte made or to be made in this present parliament extend nott nor be prejudiciall nother hurtfull to Edmund now prior of the howse & church of Lanthony beside Gloucester in England & the covent of the same ne to ther successors of, for & concernyng a graunte of licence made to Henry Deane, late pryor of the said howse & church of Lanthony beside Gloucester, to be absent oute of Irland by the late kyng of famous memorye Kyng Edward the IVth under his lettres patents dated at Westminster the 26 day of October the 21 yere of his reigne [1481].[4] And by our soveraigne lord the king's grace yt now is confermyd but the said graunte & lettres patent of licence & everything in them conteyned be as good & avaylable to the said now prior & covent & ther successours as they were before the begynnyng of this parliament, this Acte of Resumpcion or eny other acte or actes in this present parliament made or to be made notwithstonding.

Westminster, 12 June 8 Hen. VIII [1516], [signed] Studde, by writ of the privy seal.

345. [f. 85v.] Bond of John Theire *husbandman* of Brockworth, Thomas Theire *husbandman* of (Wood) Hucclecote (*Wodde Huckylcote*)[5] and Richard Rive[6] *husbandman* of Brockworth in £20 to perform the covenants of an indenture of this date.[7] 12 May 8 Hen. VIII [1516].

346. Proxy to Mr. Robert Stynchecombe B.Cn.L., John Phelpys,[8] Richard Hunte chaplain[9] and Thomas Lynett to act for the churches of Prestbury and Brockworth

---

[1] Calendared in *L. & P. Hen. VIII*, ii, p. 603.
[2] Ibid. p. 267.
[3] Cf. above, **216**.
[4] Cf. above, **326**.
[5] i.e. Hucclecote Green, SO 871168: *V.C.H. Glos.* iv. 431.
[6] Alias Reve, bailiff of the manor in 1535: above, p. xxix.
[7] *Recte* dated 29 Sept. 1513: above, **343**; cf. above, p. xl.
[8] Vicar of Prestbury: above, **305**; below, **383**.
[9] Of Brockworth: *Valor Eccl.* (Rec. Com.), ii. 424.

[as in **130** above] [f. 86] provided that they do not harm the priory.[1] 27 May 1516.

347. Presentation of Mr. William Burghill B.Cn.[& C.]L. to the vicarage of Eardisley (*Yardisley*) [Herefs.][2] vacant by the death of Geoffrey Jones,[3] in the form of a letter asking 'Edward' bishop of Hereford[4] to induct. 13 Oct. 1516.

348. Presentation of Richard Butler, chaplain, to the vicarage of Haresfield (*Harysfeld*) vacant by the death of Geoffrey Jones. [f. 86v.] 13 Oct. 1516.

349. [Another version of **347** above in the form of] a letter asking William [Warham] archbishop of Canterbury to induct as the see of Hereford is vacant. 13 Oct. 1516.

350. Manumission of William[5] son of John Bysshop, neif of Quedgeley (*Quedesley*), and his issue [as **164** above]. 13 Oct. 8 Hen. VIII [1516].

351. [f. 87] Presentation of Mr. Robert Stynchecombe B.Cn.L. to the rectory of St. Mary de Crypt (*de Cripta*), Gloucester, vacant by the resignation[6] of Richard Shyer. [ ] Feb. 1516[/17].

352. Title of Dudstone hospital (for the purpose of ordination) granted to William Taylor, clerk. 6 Feb. 1516[/17]. [Abstract in MS.: cf. **132**]

353. Proxy to fellow canons Robert Cun, Richard Hereford and John Haresfyld to act for the prior in Ireland. 4 Mar. 1516[/17]. [Abstract in MS.; cf. **65**]

354. Lease to John and Agnes Hockull of Henlow [Beds.] and their chosen child (*uni proli de corporibus suis legittime procreate et in futuro per ipsos nominande*) of property there already held by John and Agnes as follows:
(a) the manor with buildings on the manor site, demesne land, meadow and pasture, demesne tithes, strays, amercements, view of frankpledge and courts, [f. 87v.] for 40 years at £5 13s. 4d. a year and
(b) a tithe barn on the manor site with tithes of corn belonging to the rectory for 40 years at £8 3s. 4d. a year.

---

[1] Marginal note: See that this clause is always inserted in letters of proxy (*Vide ut ista clausula sit in omnibus aliis litteris procuratoriis semper inserta*).
[2] Eardisley church, with tithes of Willersley, was given to the priory by Ranulph de Baskerville before 1141: P.R.O. C 115/75, f. 214 no. 22.
[3] He held other benefices in the prior's gift, Hempsted in 1498 and Haresfield *c.* 1497–1516: *Reg. Morton*, ii. 137; below, **348**.
[4] Charles Booth was nominated bishop of Hereford as successor to Richard Mayeu on 12 Apr., provided 21 July, consecrated 31 Nov. and granted spiritualities 1 Dec. 1516: Le Neve, *Fasti 1300–1541, Hereford*. He inducted Burghill to Eardisley rectory 23 Mar. 1517: *Reg. Bothe*, 331.
[5] Owner of goods worth £3: *Military Survey of Glos. 1522*, 192.
[6] On a pension out of the living: Fosbrooke, *Glouc.* 163. Cf. above, **177**, **191**.

The lessees will

    (a) pay an annual fee of 13s. 4d. to the prior's chief steward,

    (b) scour ditches and maintain hedges, enclosure walls and bridges,

    (c) provide lodging, victuals, beds and other necessary things for the cellarer, steward and understeward, their servants and their horses for four days and nights a year when they come to hold courts and leets or for other business and

    (d) live on site.

Michaelmas 8 Hen. VIII [29 Sept. 1516]. [Cancelled]

355. [f. 88] Stock delivered to the above lessees by William Chadisley, subcellarer, to be restored (or its value repaid, at the prior's choice) at the end of the lease. Michaelmas 8 Hen. VIII [29 Sept. 1516].

    6 carthorses (*equos carectales*) together worth £3 13s. 4d.

    9 cows and a bullock (*bovectum*) together worth £4 10s.

    9 younger bullocks (*boviculos*) together worth 38s.

    A boar, a sow and 5 piglets together worth 9s.

    A gander, 4 old geese and 20 young geese together worth 5s.

    A cock and 4 hens together worth 10d.

    A cart with iron bound wheels worth 20s.

    A cart saddle (*sellam carectalem*), 5 leather collars, a pair of *boditraces*, 5 other pairs of traces and 5 leather halters together worth 5s. 6d.

    A plough with a share and a coulter, 2 iron chains and other accessories together worth 5s.

    Hay worth 6s. 8d.

    2 small *bacouns* worth 3s. 4d.

    A pelt (*peluc'*) and 3 wool-fells (*lanar'*) together worth 3s. 4d.

    A cradle (*cunam*) worth 8d.

    A lead *fornace*[1] holding about 50 gallons.

    An iron anvil (*incudem*).

    A *bokett* for the well with 3 iron hoops, an iron handle and an iron chain.

    A windlass (*cardinem*) for the well.

    A brass pot (*ollam*) holding 6 gallons, superficially damaged (*defractam in superficie*).

    A worn brass pan (*patellam*) holding 6 gallons, with a iron hoop.

    An iron *tripod.*

    A gridiron (*craticlam ferream*).

    2 worn table boards (*tabulas mensales debiles*).

    A pair of trestles (*trestellorum*).

    2 forms (*formulas*).

    2 oak *plankes* in the hall.

    A pewter salt (*salarium de pewter*).

[1] i.e. cauldron: *O.E.D.*

A bench with a stone for pressing cheese (*scabellum cum petra pro caseo deprimendo*).

2 tables for holding cheese (*pro caseo supponendo*).

A ladder (*scalam*) of 18 steps (*passuum*).

A coop for keeping poultry in the hall (*coobe in aula pro pultria imponenda*).

A worn chest (*archam debilem*).

A *setill* and a board making 2 beds (*tabulam in 2 lectos factam*) in the cellarer's chamber.

6 locks and keys (*seras cum clavibus*) fitted to doors.
[Cancelled]

356. [f. 88v.] Bond of John Hockull of Henlow, Beds., and Robert Hockull of Cardington (*Caryngton*), Beds., *husbandmen*, in £20 that John will observe the terms of his lease [above, **354**]. 20 Oct. 8 Hen. VIII [1516]. [Cancelled]

357. Lease to Christopher and Marion Wryght and their son [   ] of Lynford Mill in Henlow, Beds. 29 Sept. 1516.

This indenture made in the feste of Seynt Michaell tharchangell in the 8 yere of the reigne of Kyng Henry the VIII betwene Edmunde Forest prior of the howse & churche of our Lady of Lanthony besyde Gloucester & covent of the same of the oon parte and Cristofer Wryght, miller, Marion his wyf and [   ] ther son uppon the other parte witnesseth that the said prior & covent have grauntyd, dimisid & to ferme lett to the forsaide Cristofer, Marion and [   ] oon watermill callid Lynforde Mill lying in Henlowe in the countie of Bedforde with other parcells of land to the same mill belongynge or apperteynyng late in the holdyng of John Sherman. To have & to holde all the said mill with other parcells of land to the said Cristofyr, Marion his wif and [   ] ther son frome the day of makyng of these presents to thende & terme of 31 yeres, yf that they lyve so longe or oon of them lyve so long, yeldyng therefore yerely to the seid prior & his successors 66s. 8d. of lawfull money of Englande at 2 termes of the yere, that is to say att the fests of thannunciacion of our Lady the Virgyn and Seynt Michaell tharchangell by evyn porcions to be paid duryng the terme aforesaid.

And the seid Cristofer, Marion and [   ] shall well & sufficiently repare, susteyne & maynteyne all the seid mill, excepte that the said prior & his successors shall make & repare all the mill howse, waterwarkes & waterwhels of the said mill duryng the terme aforesaid and the seid prior & his successors shall fynd to the said Cristofer, Marion & [   ] tymber to the reparacions of the said mill duryng the said terme.

And if it happyn the seid rent of 66s. 8d. to be behynd nott paid in parte or in all after eny of the said fests by the space of oon monyth, that then it shal be lawfull to the seid prior, covent & to ther successors into the said mill & other the premises to reentre, to enjoye & the said mill with thappurtinances into ther hands to reassume and the forsaid Cristofer, Marion & [   ] to expell & to put oute, these presente indentures [f. 89] in anything notwithstanding. In witnes whereof to oon party of thes indenturs remaynyng with the seid Cristofer, Marion & [   ] the seid prior & covent have put to ther comyn seele, and to the other parte of the same endenturs remaynyng with the same prior & covent the seid Cristofer, Marion & [   ] have put to ther seales. Yevyn the day & yere abovesaid.

358. Lease to John and Agnes Griffith[1] of Mordiford [Herefs.] and their son [   ] of a watermill there lately held by William Lewson, with the buildings, land and watercourse belonging to it, for 40 years at 8s. a year [on the same conditions as in **135** above]. 20 Oct. 8 Hen. VIII [1516].

359. [f. 89v.] Lease to Walter[2] and Matilda Cocks of Okle [in the parish of Newent] and their son John of the manor of Okle [Clifford][3] with demesne land, meadow and pasture lately held by Walter's father Giles, all for 50 years at £8 a year and suit to the prior's court. The prior will pay rent to the chief lords of the fee.[4] The lessees will maintain the buildings on the manor site and pay for work on stone tiled roofs, the prior paying for the stone tiles and the great timbers and for work on the latter. They will supply victuals and other necessaries to the cellarer and subcellarer, their servants and their horses once a year when they come to hold courts and to superintend. The lessees may take *housebote, haybote, firebote* and *ploughbote* without touching the prior's *Aschelowys Grove, Hasill Grove, Markill Grove* and *Granenhill*[5] Wood, including parcels of woodland lying outside the fence. They will receive six wagon-loads of fuel a year from the woodland for watching and keeping it. The prior reserves a right of access to build on the manor site. Michaelmas 8 Hen. VIII [29 Sept. 1516].

[ff. 90–3 were the middle of a quire and are lost. Nos. **360–8** and part of **369** are supplied from the MS. index.]

360. [f. 90] Indenture with Edward Shyer, bailiff of Alvington.[6]

361. Indenture with Philip Hye[7] of Prior's Court [probably in Dormington],[8] Herefs.

---

[1] Still tenants in 1546: *L. & P. Hen. VIII*, xxi (1), p. 357.

[2] d. 1530: *Hereford Probates 1407–1581*, 249. Bailiff of the manor in 1535: *Valor Eccl.* (Rec. Com.), ii. 425.

[3] Cf. above, **217**.

[4] 23s. a year to Fotheringhay College (Northants.) as successor to the alien priory of Newent: *Valor Eccl.* ii. 425; cf. *V.C.H. Glos.* ii. 106.

[5] Grinnell's Hill ½ mile E. of the manor house: A. H. Smith, *Place-Names of Glos.* (Eng. Place-Name Soc.), iii. 178.

[6] Recipient in 1535 of 53s. 4d. yearly wage for this office and 26s. 8d. yearly fee for life as bailiff of Aylburton: *Valor Eccl.* (Rec. Com.), ii. 425–6.

[7] A clerk of this name preceded Thomas Berinton as tenant of a messuage and 36 a. from the prior's manor of Widemarsh Moor (Hereford), including land at Holmer: P.R.O. C 142/71/107.

[8] A property of St. Guthlac's Priory, Hereford: Duncumb, *Herefs.* ii. 335. Prior's Court in Aylton and Prior's Court in Wellington Heath are more remote from the Llanthony Priory estates.

362–3. Titles of Dudstone hospital (for the purpose of ordination) granted to John Garden and [f. 91] Thomas ap Ieuan.

364. Indenture with Thomas Smith[1] of Ashleworth for property at Staunton, Worcs. [now in Glos.] and [at Oridge Street in Corse] Glos.[2]

365. Indenture with Thomas Meryott of Matson.[3]

366. [f. 92] Indenture[4] with William Mathowe[5] of Gloucester.

367. Grant of wardship and marriage of the Bentham family[6] of Brockworth [and Badgeworth] (*Brockworthe*: *copia concessionis warde et maritagii Bentham*).

368. [f. 93] Presentation of Roger Brayne[7] to the vicarage of Kenchester, Herefs.

369. Lease to Thomas[8] and Alice Symes and their children Thomas and Margery of

---

[1] Owner of goods worth £15 and freehold land worth 5s. a year: *Military Survey of Glos. 1522*, 140.

[2] The prior owned a messuage at Staunton by 1303 with land including 2½ yardlands in 'Hathemare's Crofts', 3 a. extending from a wood to a highway at Newland (?SO 795290), 4 a. in Birchley (around SO 769292), 15 selions in 'Rudynges Field' by Henfield (around SO 770283), 6 selions in Staunton Field (around SO 787287) abutting 'Long Mead', 1½ a. in 'Long Mead', 2 a. on the Glos. side of the Glynch Brook by a bridge at Stanbridge Mead (SO 778281) and rents from more than 5 cottages: P.R.O. C 115/77, s. xi nos. 3, 26–31; map, Glos. R.O. P309/SD/2/1. The lessee was John Smyth in 1544 when Thomas Bell bought the prior's title: *L. & P. Hen. VIII*, xix (2), p. 82.

[3] A lease, dated 1517, of the prior's manor of Matson and 2 a. of meadow in Hempsted for 60 years: *V.C.H. Glos.* iv. 443, cf. 441.

[4] Probably a lease of a tenement within the block nos. 205–9 Westgate Street, which Mathowe rented from the priory for 10s. in 1535, said to be the tannery formerly held by the elder John Hayward: Glos. R.O. GBR/J5/4; cf. P.R.O. C 115/73, f. 48 (46)v. nos. 95–6.

[5] d. 1539 or 1540, a tanner resident in St. Nicholas's parish: P.R.O. PROB 11/26, f. 150v. copied in Hockaday Abs. ccxx, 1540. Sheriff of Gloucester 1516 and 1524, alderman from 1527–8 and mayor 1532 and 1538: Fosbrooke, *Glouc.* 208; *V.C.H. Glos.* iv. 376.

[6] On the death of William Bentham, merchant of the Staple, whose son Anthony succeeded before 1529 to the manor of Bentham in Badgeworth including land at Buckholt in Cranham, Kimsbury in Upton St. Leonards, Colesborne and Brockworth: *Glouc. Corp. Rec.* p. 428, cf. pp. 377–8. Of their predecessors John Draper alias Bentham of Bristol rendered homage to Prior Wyche in 1425 and Robert Draper alias Bentham of Gloucester in 1434 for Bentham's Place and 4½ virgates of land, 4 a. of meadow, 3 a. of wood and 13s. 4d. rent in Brockworth and Badgeworth: Reg. Wyche, ff. 184–6 and 245.

[7] B.Cn.L., d. 1527; vicar of Lydney 1488–1527, prebendary of Hereford 1509–27, rector of Staunton-on-Wye (Herefs.) 1513–27 and of Taynton 1524–7: Emden, *Biog. Reg. Oxon. to 1500*.

[8] Resident at Quedgeley in 1522 owning goods worth £24: *Military Survey of Glos. 1522*, 191; cf. below, **415**.

property at Hempsted[1] [f. 94] comprising a site, buildings, land, meadow, pasture and tithes. They will

(a) maintain a byre and a piggery (*domos boverie et porcorum*) and other buildings with thatched roofs there,

(b) scour ditches and repair adjacent hedges and bridges except *Wayn Brige*[2] which lies in the demesne of Quedgeley at the north end of Quedgeley township,

(c) collect amercements on such estreats of the court of Quedgeley as are supplied to them, rendering account accordingly and receiving 4s. a year for the collection and

(d) restore at the end of the term the live and dead stock which is delivered to them at the beginning or repay its value, at the prior's choice.
[Cancelled]

370. Lease to Thomas and Alice Symys of a messuage at Rea (*le Ree*) [in Hempsted] formerly held by Richard Peere and previously by William Baron, for Thomas's faithful service (*pro bono et fideli servicio dicti Thome prefato domino Edmundo priori impenco et imposterum impendendo*), to hold for life at a yearly rent of a red rose, suit to the court of Llanthony and other customary service.[3] They may live elsewhere and sublet. [f. 94v.] The prior's attorneys William Lawrens and Richard Partriche will deliver seisin. Easter 4 Hen. VIII [27 Mar. 1513].

371. Presentation of John Yayden,[4] chaplain, to the vicarage of Eardisley (*Yerdisley*) [Herefs.] vacant by the resignation of Mr. William Burghyll D.Cn.L. 5 May 1519.

372. [f. 95] Bond of William Burghyll to the prior in £40. 13 Apr. 10 Hen. VIII [1519]. [In Latin except as follows:]
The condicion of this obligacion is suche, that if the within bounden William Burghill save & harmles keepe the within named prior & his successors of and for any suyte for any agmentacion to be hadde by any prist or chapleyn which in the lyf of the within bounden William Bourghill shall happen to be vicary of the parisshe churche of Erdesley in the diocese of Hereford, that then this present obligacion to be voyd, or ells to stand in his full streynth & vertue.

373. Lease to John Mors of Pencoyd (*Pencoyte*) [Herefs.] of demesne land, meadow, moor and pasture in Llanwarne (*Lanwaren*) [Herefs.] lately held by John ap

---

[1] Although f. 93 which gave fuller details is missing, the MS. index locates the property in Hempsted and the reference to Wain Bridge on f. 93 identifies it as Sims Farm in the S. extremity of the parish, then or later based on a farmstead at SO 810155 in Sims Lane E. of Sims bridge on the later canal: *V.C.H. Glos.* iv. 422.

[2] A bridge of wood in 1675 carrying the Bristol road over Qued (or Daniel's) Brook at SO 813153: *V.C.H. Glos.* x. 216.

[3] The reference to customary service is underlined in the MS. and indicated by a pointing hand in the margin.

[4] Instituted 9 May, vicar 1519–31: *Reg. Bothe*, 332, 345.

G[wi]ll[y]m extending from the prior's meadow lately held by John and Thomas Hoskyns on the north to the prior's *Woltonessith* meadow lately held by David Gethyn on the south, and lying between the Hereford–Monmouth road on the west and the *Milgrene* of a watermill called *New Mill*[1] on the east, and also bounded on the south by *Keuendenam* close and a small meadow, all for 60 years at 15s. 4d. a year, suit of court and heriot. The lessee may take *housebote* and *haybote*, may remove brambles and thorns (*vepres et spinas*) and may assign the lease to his son Solomon. Eve of St. Matthew 10 Hen. VIII [20 Sept. 1518].

374. [f. 95v.] Presentation of Mr. Henry Marten B.[Cn. & C.L.] to the rectory of Llanwarne [Herefs.][2] vacant by the death of Thomas Weere. 13 Aug. 1519. [Abstract in MS.; cf. **39**]

375. Presentation of Richard Broode B.A.[3] to the vicarage of Tytherington (*Tydrington*) vacant by the death of Thomas Weere. 13 Aug. 1519. [Abstract in MS.; cf. **39**]

376. Letter from Cardinal Thomas [Wolsey] to the general chapter of the Augustinian order on building a college.[4] Nothing is more conducive to the Christian faith than the humanities (*bonas litteras*),[5] and nothing is more important to the vicars of Christ than learning what to seek and what to avoid. It distresses the cardinal, and is a disgrace to the order, that few or none of its members enjoy true scholarship (*bonarum litterarum vereque discipline studio oblectentur*). To help the order, which is in peril and threatens speedy ruin (*periclitanti ac ruinam brevi comminanti*), the cardinal has determined to erect and construct (*erigere construereque*) a college where its canons may apply themselves solely to study.[6] He urges the order to make common cause with him, to contribute its wealth as was decreed at a synod of Canterbury [province],[7] and to deliberate this in chapter. It will

---

[1] If this is Lower Mill on the Gamber at SO 501264 it locates the property at Hendre in the township of Monkton: cf. *Herefs. Field-Name Survey, Llanwarne*, 9 & map.

[2] Llanwarne church with its chapels of [Much] Birch, Ballingham and Carey was given to the priory by Hugh de Lacy (d. *c*. 1115): P.R.O. C 115/75, f. 217 no. 26. The rectory was called a prebendal portion when the prior of Llanthony in Wales presented to it in 1308: *Reg. Swinfield*, 538.

[3] d. 1523; M.A. 1520, vicar of Tytherington 1519–23 and schoolmaster at Westbury(-on-Trym) College 1521–3: Emden, *Biog. Reg. Oxon. 1501–40*; for his school, *V.C.H. Glos.* ii. 313–4.

[4] Read on 14 June at a chapter which sat at Leicester Abbey from 12 to 16 June 1518. Printed in full in the original Latin proceedings: Salter, *Chapt. Augustin.* 134–5.

[5] For the meaning, Knowles, *Religious Orders*, iii. 148.

[6] Discussed above, p. xxiii.

[7] In 1502, by a levy of 2d. in the £: Salter, *Chapt. Augustin.* pp. xxxiv, 128, 179; cf. above, **114**.

soon gather the fruits of its labour. Beaconsfield (*Ex villa de Bekensfeld*) [Bucks.], 12 June[1] 1518.

377. [f. 96] The chapter's reply to the above.[2] The chapter promises to admit Wolsey to confraternity and puts the Augustinian order under his protection. It submits to his mandate for building its (nay, his) college, begs him to be called the founder, hopes that the college may be incorporated by royal charter and puts its existing college buildings and statutes into his hands. Its visitors would welcome discretion to vary the taxes in Wolsey's schedule. Some ill-disposed persons have rendered the order powerless by claiming that its disciplinary fines may attract a writ of *Praemunire*.[3] The chapter asks Wolsey not to let such a writ pass his Chancery, or preferably to decree otherwise. 16 June 1518.

Littera responsiva predicte littere domini cardinalis.

Quociens amplissime dignitatis tue racionem habemus (habemus enim quam cepissime nimisque, profecto si ad tam excellentis virum authoritatis et doctrine litterarum aliquid dare vereamur), perurgens tamen nostre tocius ipsa religionis utilitas singularisque ille tuus (quem et vere scribis ingenitum) eiusdem affectus tuas nobis perquam iucundissimas silencio litteras preterire minusve responsas obire[4] non sinunt, sed quum hoc a nobis incultum tuaque dominacione satis indignum de innata tibi pietate omni pene seculo cognita facillime nobis ignoscendum speramus, id attentare et exarare vehementer impellunt. Habemus igitur quas agere non valemus gracias incredibiles, ipsasque ne tam epistolarum modum egredi quam regiis tocius regni assiduis occupatum negociis detinere perturbareque videamus (etsi brevi complecti nequeant) compendiosissimas fore decrevimus, et (quod nostre est paupertatis et potencie totum) tocius te nostre fratrem religionis omniumque eiusdem meritorum participem constitumus, quam tue totam defensioni conservandam tuendamque committimus. Cuius si conservatorem defensoremque (quod optamus humillimeque rogamus) te prebueris, quam felices atque beatos nos esse dicemus.

Ceteraque tua tam ad ad virtutes quam ad nostri (immo tui) edificacionem collegii consummacionemque hortamenta pro tuo ipsius (uti decet) mandato subeunda duximus et promittimus, teque eiusdem fundatorem dici et esse velle, tuisque ad inclitissimum[5] regem nostrum mediis illud incorporari posse et debere quam humillime petimus et obtestamur in domino, omnia illius edificia et statuta plene tue ordinacioni et reformacioni in omnibus tradi unanimiter pollicentes. Taxis tum tuas per s[c]edulas novissimis gravatos quosdam, aliosque alleviatos nimium nostrorum iudicio visitatorum moderari licere amplissima tua concedat dominacio.

---

[1] MS. *die xii Iulii*, corrected in Salter's edition by authority of his MSS.
[2] Calendared briefly in *L. & P. Hen. VIII*, ii, p. 1311. Summarised with variant detail in the original proceedings: Salter, *Chapt. Augustin.* 141–2.
[3] Disciplinary fines were prescribed for the order by Pope Benedict XII in 1339: Salter, *Chapt. Augustin.* 214–67. The statute of *Praemunire* limited papal authority: 16 Ric. II c. 5.
[4] MS. *abire.*
[5] MS. *inditissimum.*

Id quod pre omnibus restat unum (quod nil te dicente et faciente impetraverimus), nostre totam religionis rem publicam quam brevi perituram cum lacrimis fateri oportet. A quibusdam namque iniquitatis filiis a sua (immo nostra) religione degenerantibus, quum ad levandum in delinquencium penam multas per nostre presidentes religionis legittime et more solito sub censuris ecclesiastics processum fuerit, scripti seu brevis regii 'Premunire' nuncupati ita terror obicitur, ut nedum delicta remaneant impunita sed et tocius religionis authoritas cassa reddatur, inanis et vacua. Huic igitur morbo mederi tua est sola que valet (si dignetur) charitas amplissima, vel scriptum illud a tua exire cancellaria in hoc casu prohibens, vel melius aliud pro tui ineffabili animi iudicio in eodem decernens. Et nullam de tuis laudibus ampliorem fore quam quum hec feceris consecuturus es, nosque tibi (ut par est) dedi[ca]tissimos continuosque habebis ad Altissimum tua de salute interpellatores, in quo pientissima tua valeat dominacio, qui et te conservet in eundem. E sacra Virginis ede Laycestrie, 16 Kalendas [Iulias]¹ H[en]. 8. 10.[2]

378. [f. 96v.] Letter of fraternity from William [Spires][3] prior of Guisborough (*Gisborn*) [Yorks.], William [Salyng][4] prior of Merton [Surrey] and Edmund prior of Llanthony, presidents of the general chapter of the Augustinian order held at St. Mary's church, Leicester, in the quindene of Trinity [i.e. June] 1518, to Thomas Wolsey cardinal [archbishop] of York, papal legate and Chancellor of England. *16 Kalendas Iulias anno Domini prelibati* [16 June 1518].

379. Letter to [William Barton][5] abbot of Osney [Oxon.] on replacing [Hugh Witwicke][6] as prior of St. Mary's College, Oxford. [Great] Barrington, 3 Aug. [1519].[7]

Littera prioris Lanthonie directa abbati de Oseney circa priorem et studentes in collegio Beate Marie Oxonie.

Right reverent fader in God, in my moost lovyng maner I hartely recommend me to you. So it is, as I am credibli enformed by our brethrne the students of Seynt Mary

---

[1] Month supplied from **378** below.

[2] MS. *8* and *10* in arabic, with *Φ* representing 0.

[3] Prior of Guisborough alias Gisburne 1511–19: *V.C.H. Yorks.* iii. 212, cf. 208.

[4] d. 1520; S.T.P. (Cantab.) 1505–6, S.T.P. (Oxon.) 1509, prior of Merton 1502–20: Emden, *Biog. Reg. Oxon. to 1500.* Collector and bursar for building work at St. Mary's College, Oxford, 1504–9, and past president of the order 1506–9: Salter, *Chapt. Augustin.* 122, 128, 132, 138.

[5] B.Cn.L., abbot of Osney 1505–24: Emden, *Biog. Reg. Oxon. to 1500.* President elect but absent though illness from the general chapter 1518: Salter, *Chapt. Augustin.* 131. His rôle here is that of the 'neighbouring prelate' to whom, under Pope Benedict's constitutions of 1339, the presidents were required to depute the choice of a prior of students: ibid. 237.

[6] Student from 1506, suppliant for B.Th. 1514–15 and prior of students by 1518 but not recorded as a graduate: Emden, *Biog. Reg. Oxon. 1501–40.*

[7] Year taken from the mandate **386** below, which follows closely upon the sequence of letters **379–82** and **385**.

College in Oxenford, that the reverent fader in God the abbot of Leycester hath
sende home for his brother the prior of studens, nott likely to retorn agayn to the
sayd universite, as he hath of late wrote unto them to use his office & rome ther.
Whereuppon the bretherne of the seid college hath dyrectid a letter unto me as ther
next [i.e. nearest] *presydent subscribyd with their singuler names according to the*
olde statuts & laudable customs, desiring me in the same of myn advise & councell
what is best to be don in the premisses, and my lycens to procede to a new eleccon.
And forasmoche as ye are oon of the honorable faders of our religion & a very
nyghe neybour adjoynyng to the said college, I therefore desire & hartly pray you to
take the payn & labour to make the most diligent serche amongst the said [f. 97]
brederyn as ye kan, to know who is moost apte in good maners, vertu & connyng to
occupy & use the said rome.

And theruppon it may ferther please you to send a servand of yours with a discrete
letter frome you dyrected in my name & yours also unto the reverent fader in God
the prior of Marten shewing hym in what case & condicion our sayd college standith
& how it is at this owre destitute of an hedd, ruler & governer ther, desiring hym
farther in the same in like maner of his best advice & councell for a new prior to be
electe & substitutyd in the old prioris rome. The wise man saith 'Fac omnia cum
consilio et postea non penitebis'.[1] *Insomoche therefore that the reverent father in*
God the prior of Marten aforsaid is nott wonly won of our presidents butt also a
Doctor of Divinite & a man of quyte grett & good experience, I think itt very good &
expedient that his opynyon & mynd be felyd [i.e. felt] *& knowyn in the premissis. In*
this doyng I dowte nott, my good reverent father, butt that ye shall please God & do
a meritorious dede & a thing that shal be honorable both to our seid college & to all
our religion and ferther deserve herein our both right harty thanks, as knoweth our
blessyd Savyour, to whose mercy I fully committ you. Written at Barrington in
Cotteswold the 3 day of the present August.

380. Letter from [William Salyng] prior of Merton [Surrey] on reforming the
Augustinian order and on calling to account [Canon Witwicke] late prior of St.
Mary's College. Merton, 3 Aug. [1519].

Littera prioris de Marton directa priori Lanthonie circa nostre religionis
reformacionem.

Reverend & my singlar belovyd father in God, my duties don, I hartly commaunde
me to you, beyng glad of your good prosperite, which our Lorde preserve. Amen.
Fayn have I bee meny a day since our last departing, & yett am, to speke with your
good fatherhode to have your good advyse & councell in all suche dyreccions as of
very grete nede must be takyn for the welthe of our hoole religion, which, as it hathe
be thogte & also said, hathe ron into this grete decay & ruyne, most chefly because
the presidents, the which owghte to be heds & rulers of it, hathe be men of noo
lernyng. Wherefore yf ye & I shulde noo notherwise looke upon itt then it hathe be
now in tymes of late past, truly as be sume of the leeste of [i.e. lowest in the history

---

[1] 'Do everything with advice and you will not regret it later.'

of] *the relygyon, it hathe be sayd to me of late it wolde be nott wonly in grete blame & rebuke of us bothe in long tyme to cum, but also in grete derogacion & obloquy of all clerks.*[1]

Wherfore, good father, hartly I besech you to take sume labour that other before Michelmas or sone uppon, att your best leysure, we myghte mete together att Oxford[2] *or els sumwhere nyghe therabowte. At the which tyme & place by you assygnyd, as my good father & lord of Bruton* [Som.][3] *hathe advysed me for to doo, I shall cause the prior of students to wayte on you, that now unwisly withoute eny discharge, withoute eny acowmpte yevyng as priors of students in tyme past hathe be used to doo, is departyd, and the beste juells of the howse, as I am informyd, loste in his tyme. If your fatherhode have don enything for the ordering of the howse I am well contente therewith, butt* [i.e. save that] *att our metyng this prior then, as I have said, lawfully the howse aunswerde. I trust thorow this mynde & councell that we shall provyde another maner of pryor then there is now eny to be. If I were able to geve you cowncell I wold advise you to send your* [f. 97v.] *scolar thether as sone as ye myghte* (*Noscis, scio, bene Catonem: Patere legem quam ipse tuleris*)[4] *and also to make up the sume of your colleccion to the prior of Elssing Spityll,*[5] *or els I am insuryd that ye shall have other letters shortly. In everything I pray you geve credens to this brynger. And our Lorde for his infinith mercy evermore preserve you in good helth, longe lyve & grett honowre. Att Meryton in haste the 3 day of Auguste.*

381. Prior Forest's reply to the above. [Great] Barrington, 8 Aug. [1519].

Littera prioris Lanthonie responsiva littere suprascripte.

Right reverent fader in God, in my most loving maner I hartly recommend me to you, ascerteynyng you the same that I have recevyd by the hands of your servand your sadde and discrete letters, the contents whereof I do right well perceve, and where amoungst all other things your good fatherhod's desire is that you & I att sume convenyent tyme bytwene this & the fest of Migelmas next approching or soone

---

[1] Despite his professed zeal Salyng was reproved in 1509–10 for consorting with disreputable people of both sexes, for absence from choir and for failing to take counsel, to keep accounts, to remedy dilapidations or to maintain the statutory number of canons at Merton: Knowles, *Religious Orders*, iii. 81.

[2] Owing to Salyng's continual absence at Oxford in 1509–10 his bishop forbade him to return to the university without permission: Emden, *Biog. Reg. Oxon. to 1500.*

[3] William Gilbert S.T.P. (d. 1532–3), prior of Bruton 1496–1511, abbot there 1511–32, bishop *'Majorensis' in partibus infidelium* and suffragan to the bishops of Bath and Wells 1519–26: Emden, *Biog. Reg. Oxon. to 1500.*

[4] 'You are acquainted, I know, with the saying of Cato: Submit to the law which you yourself proposed'. The general chapter of 1518, at which Forest and Salyng presided, imposed fines on houses which defaulted on their obligation to keep students at the universities: Salter, *Chapt. Augustin.* 141; cf. above, **231.**

[5] Collector of the levy described in **382** below: *Oxoniensia*, xliii. 68. Elsing was a hospital under Augustinian rule in Aldermanbury, London, later used in part as the parish church of St. Alphage: *V.C.H. London*, i. 539.

theruppon shuld have sume metyng, other att the universite of Oxenford or in sum other place ther nyge adjoynyng, to have sume communicacion concernyng the welthe of our hoole religion. Father, I am very well contente & plesyd with your good mocyon hereyn. I think it in my conciens a merytorious & a rygte charytable dede for us to take sume paynes & labours uppon us to helpe reforme suche enormytes and abusyons as be comprised & twygte [i.e. censured] *in your seyd dyscrete letters. Therefore for the place & tyme of our nexte metyng, as towching the place first, I thenke none soo convenyent a place, with your better advyce, as Oxford is. And as for the tyme, I desyre your good fatherhod to appoynte any tyme att your best lesure bytwix this & the forsaid feste of Migelmas, & your plesure herein knowyn, I shal be glad ther to wayte uppon you & to geve you my best attendaunce, and then & ther to have farther communycacion with you in other artycles bysyds the premisses specifyed in your seid letters.*

Father, as towching the prior of studens, I have doo sumwhatt theryn alredy. So is itt of late that all our brethrene & students there have wrote unto me a letter subscribid with ther singuler names as to won of there nexte presidents, to have my licence to procede to eleccion of a new prior accordyng to ther olde statuts & lawdable customs there, as they sayth, insomoche the olde prior is callid home agayn by his master & nott to retorne to Oxford to use his rome ther, as they have instructed me by ther said letters. But forasmoche as I suppose that ther is few or none of the faders of our relygyon that know [Pope] *Benedict's statuts & also the rule of Seynt Austen's ordor better than ye know, I have therfore uppon ther peticion wrote a letter to the reverent fader the abbott of Osney, that incontynent uppon the sieght of my letter it mygte please hym to send a servant of his with sume letter from hym to you directyd shewing you in the same in what case our college now standyth in, & to have your best advice & cownsell what is best to be don for the eleccion of a new prior ther, and in the mene tyme that it wolde ferther please hym to cause sume sadd brother of our religion to see to the good rule & order of our college unto such tyme that he know ferther of your pleasure, as your servant this berer on my behalf can more* [f. 98] *at large declare to you by mowth, so I pray you to geve credence. And this almygty God have you in his blessed governaunce, my good lovyng father, with long lyff & good helthe bodely & gostely. Amen. Writen att Barryngton in Coteswold the 8 day of this present August.*

382. Order from Cardinal [Wolsey] to collect arrears of contributions for rebuilding St. Mary's College. Waltham Abbey [Essex], 29 Aug. [1519].

Littera domini cardinalis directa presidentibus religionis canonicorum.

Ryght welbelovyd in God, we gret you wel. And forasmoche as hertofore we uppon sundrie good & substanciall growndes & auctorites directyd our speciall letters unto dyveres fathers of your religion for to levye & gedre up certan sommes of money taxid uppon the places of the same by the incumbenttes of the said places or ther predecessors, long afore graunted for the buyldyng & reedifying of Saint Maryes

College in Oxforth,[1] *and tho all the saide sommes for this tyme of ther payments wer by us taxide to moche lesse then their duties wer to have paid, yet sundry of them hedirtoward* [i.e. hitherto], *as we be informyd, haith denyyde & yet doith to content & paie the said sommes; we therfore considering our ample auctorite in this your religion, not oonlye grauntide unto us by the hool body of the same but also by the popis holines, and furthermore remembring that ye two*[2] *be presidents of your said religion, will & commaunde you that with all convenient spede ye in our name strathe charge and commaunde all suche collectors as wer specifiede in our said formor lettres that they endevor themself for to arrere & gedre up all & everye of the forsaide sommes dependyng uppon their accomptes & yet unpaide, and whosoever of the said incumbents that doth denye to content & paye the saide sommes soo taxid uppon ther monasteriis unto the saide collectors, we will that in all goodlie hast ye do see us advertiside of ther names and aunswers in that behalf, to thentent that we may looke uppon them oursylf as apperteynythe. And so fare ye well. Yeven under our signett in this our progresse at thabbey of Waltham the 29 day of August.*

383. Presentation of William Etkins to the vicarage of Prestbury vacant by the resignation of John Phelpis. 22 Oct. 1519.

384. Lease to Richard Tuppe, yeoman of the guard (*valectum domini regis de gardo*), of a tenement in Eastgate Street (*vico orientali*), Gloucester,[3] under the wall of St. Michael's church between a tenement belonging to St. Nicholas's church on the east and a tenement belonging to the said St. Michael's church[4] [f. 98v.] on the west, containing in front 4 yd. with inches between and extending from the highway to the wall of the church, namely a tenement lately inhabited by William Mauncell, *scryvener*, and now held by John Bawell, *hosyer*, to hold for 39 years at 13s. 4d. a year and suit to the prior's court in the church of St. Owen. The Nativity of St. John the Baptist 11 Hen. VIII [24 June 1519].

385. Letter from Prior [Salyng] of Merton accompanying Cardinal Wolsey's commission [below, **386**] to summon a general chapter. Merton, 3 Dec. [1519].

To hys reverende fadre in God the prior of Lanthony, presydent of our religion, this be delyveryd.

Ryght honorable fader in God, I hartly commaunde me to you evermore, very glad of your good prosperite, the which our Lorde preserve, and hartly thankyng you

---

[1] Above, **376**.

[2] The third president, Prior Spires of Guisborough, was evidently dead: cf. below, **386**.

[3] The second tenement E. of the church entrance, held by Thomas Hert in 1442, by John Pole in 1455 and by Thomas Ashorth in 1535 at the same rent, of which the prior forwarded 12d. to the town bailiffs: above, **33**(g) & n.; Glos. R.O. GBR/J5/3; J5/4.

[4] Belonging in 1455 to Hailes Abbey: *Glouc. Rental 1455*, 103b.

for your good Lanthony chese[1] and for your grete chere at our last being togedir in Oxford. Newys I have none to send but suche as I thinke ye knowe right well, how and as my lorde cardinal's commission, the which I sent to you in a box, will plainly shew you. I know nott what cowncell ye have to make owte mandatums to the visitors in your coo[a]sts, and therfore I am bolde to sende a copy of suche mandatum as I sende to the visitors in this co[a]ste. If I presume farther than nedith, as I know well I doo, I pray you pardon me, for it cummyth nott of males. And faille nott, for the love of God & blessyd Seynt Austyn, to be here at the day appoyntyd, for be you sure, all the religion shall have grete nede of you. Fathir, if eny howsis of the saide religion or observance be within the diocese of Seynt Davi[d]s or eny othir diocese in that coo[a]ste of the province of Canterbury they must be cytyd, thow ye have noo visitors for them, as God knoweth; whoo ever have you in his blessid keping. At Merton in gret haste the 3 day of December by your owne assured whyle lyf duryth, William prior of Merton.

386. [f. 99] Cardinal Wolsey's commission to William [Salyng] prior of Merton, Edmund prior of Llanthony and James [Cockerill][2] prior of Guisborough [Yorks.] of the order of St. Augustine. In pursuance of powers granted to him by the pope,[3] Wolsey has already conferred with some of the commissioners and others of their order at his usual residence [York Place] near Westminster[4] and given them written articles of reform for further deliberation. Seeking a wider consensus he now bids them to cite all abbots and priors of their order, with those of the orders of Arrouaise and St. Victor, to appear on 26 Feb. next[5] in the chapter house of St. Bartholomew in West Smithfield [London] in order to have the articles explained, to give a final answer on them[6] and to do what seems best. Meanwhile all members of the order are to be asked to observe the articles, and the commissioners are to certify the names of those cited. From Wolsey's house aforesaid, 29 Nov. 1519.

Thomas [whose titles are here recited] *dilectis nobis in Christo religiosis viris Willelmo domus sive prioratus de Merton, Edmundo domus sive prioratus de*

---

[1] '[There is] very goodly meadowe ground about Lantony, for cheese there made is in great price': John Leland in *Trans. B.G.A.S.* xiv. 245. Prior Hart gave Llanthony cheeses to the king in 1530 and 1532: *L. & P. Hen. VIII*, v, pp. 750, 758.

[2] S.T.P., prior of Guisborough 1519–36: Emden, *Biog. Reg. Oxon. 1501–40*, App. p. 669. Addressed here as successor to the late William Spires who was also president of the order: cf. above, **378**.

[3] By bulls of Aug. 1518 and 10 June 1519: *L. & P. Hen. VIII*, ii, p. 1354; iii, pp. 167, 231.

[4] A conference on 12 Nov. 1519 attended also by Benedictines and Cistercians: Pantin, *Chapters of Black Monks*, iii. 117–19; *L. & P. Hen. VIII*, iii, p. 167. York Place was later called Whitehall: John Stow, *Survey of London* (Everyman edn., 1956), 401.

[5] Timed to precede seasonal plague in London and to coincide with a chapter of the Benedictine order at York Place : Wilkins, *Concilia*, iii. 661; Pantin, *Chapters of Black Monks*, iii. 119–24. (A legatine council in Westminster Abbey, dated to the same day through a misreading in *Reg. Bothe*, 74, actually met the previous year: Wilkins, ibid.)

[6] Which they failed to do: above, pp. xxiv–xxv.

Lanthony et Iacobo domus sive prioratus de Gysborn ordinis Sancti Augustini prioribus salutem, graciam et benediccionem. Cum nos Thomas, cardinalis et legatus de latere antedictus, tam ex iuris communis disposicione pretextu huiusmodi legacionis nostre de latere quam ex speciali prefati sanctissimi [pape] domini nostri commissione omnia et singula huius regni Anglie et locorum predictorum monasteria et loca religiosa exempta et non exempta eorumque prelatos, presidentes et ministros visitandi, corrigendi et reformandi potestatem habentes, super huiusmodi reformacione (quatenus vos et ordinem vestrum concernit) cum quibusdam ex vobis et nonnullis aliis vestre religionis abbatibus et prioribus in edibus nostre solite residencie prope Westmonasterium intra Londoniensem diocesim ad hoc dudum convenientibus et congregatis tractaverimus, contulerimus et communicaverimus, ac eciam quosdam articulos sive quedam capitula huiusmodi reformacionem concernencia (ad plenius super eisdem deliberandum et consultandum) vobis ac illis in scriptis dederimus, cupientes tamen ut dicta reformacio pleniorem et firmiorem sorciatur effectum quo maturiore et saniore complurium vestri ordinis abbatum et prelatorum insimul congregatorum deliberato consensu admissa, recepta et comprobata fuerit, vobis coniunctim et divisim committimus et mandamus quatenus omnes et singulos dicti religionis vestre abbates et priores abbates non habentes, eciam sub observancia Sancti Nichloai de Arrusia necnon sub observancia Sancti Victoris constitutos, citetis peremptorie et moneatis seu per visitatores ordinis vestri sic citari et moneri faciatis (quos eciam nos tenore presencium auctoritate predicta et qua fungimur in hac parte simili modo citamus et monemus) quod die Lune ebdomade prime Quadragesime proxime future in domo capitulari monasterii Sancti Bartholemei in West Smythfeld Londoniensis diocesis cum prorogacione dierum et locorum si et quatenus oporteat personaliter conveniatis et compareatis ac conveniant et compareant super dictis articulis sive capitulis ac aliis tunc ibidem fortassis proponendis et exponendis reformacionem predictam, honorem Dei, religionis vestre augmentum et ipsam religionem profitensium honestatem ac vivendi modum concernentibus plenius tractaturi, nobisque sive nostris in ea parte commissariis finaliter et resolutive super eisdem responsuri, ulteriusque facturi et perimpleturi quod iustum videbitur et iuri ac racioni necnon religionis nostre regulari observancie [f. 99v.] congruum et consentaneum.

Vos insuper hortamur et nichillominus vobis firmiter iniungendo mandamus, ac per vos ceteris abbatibus et prioribus locorum per priores regi solitorum vestre religionis omnibus et singulis auctoritate et nomine nostris iniungi et mandari volumus quod interim et medio temporis intervallo vestris et suis subditis regularibus sive obedienciariis dictos articulos sive dicta capitula (que videlicet illos concernunt) exponatis et declaretis, exponantque et declarent, ac super eisdem illorum mentes et vota solerter investigetis et investigent, ac ipsos ad huiusmodi articulorum sive capitulorum debitam observanciam (quantum racionis ordo et regularis observancie honestas id exposcit) sollicite moneatis et inducatis ac moneant et inducant. Et quid in premissis feceritis ac de modo execucionis presencium, deque nominibus omnium et singulorum per vos et unumquemque vestrum in hac parte monitorum et citatorum, nos aut nostros in hac parte commissarios citra dictam diem Lune debite certificetis litteris vestris patentibus sigillis vestris [sigillatis], seu quilibet vestrum sic certificet litteris suis patentibus harum seriem ac nomina et cognomina omnium et singulorum per vos aut illos respective citatorum et monitorum in se continentibus sigillo suo sigillatis. Data sub sigillo nostro in edibus nostris predictis penultimo die mensis Novembris anno Domini millesimo quingentesimo decimo nono.

387. Mandate from Prior Forest, as Cardinal Wolsey's commissioner, to the priors of Taunton [Som.] and Bodmin (*Bodemyn*) [Cornw.], visitors of the Augustinian order in the dioceses of Exeter and Bath and Wells, [f. 100] to cite the abbots and priors of the Augustinian, Arrouaisian and Victorine orders within the limits of their visitations to appear at the time and place appointed by the cardinal. The visitors are to certify to Prior Forest the names of those cited. 10 Jan.[1] 1519[/20].

388. Similar mandate to the priors of Studley (*Stoodeley*) [Warws.] and St. Oswald, Gloucester, visitors in the dioceses of Worcester, Hereford and St. David's. [Abstract in MS.]

389. Similar mandate to the abbot of Darley [Derb.] and the prior of Repton (*Repingdon*) [Derb.], visitors in the diocese of Coventry and Lichfield. [Abstract in MS.]

390. Certificate from Nicholas [Peper][2] prior of Taunton acknowledging a mandate [**387** above]. 9 Jan. [1520].
Right reverent and my good lorde, I mekely commaunde me unto your good lordeshipp, and glad as any man of so little aquayntance to here of your good prosperite etc. Moreover, for defaute of tyme convenient, I ascerten your lordeshipp by this my rude letters that I have recevyd your mandatum & perceve by the contents of the same my lorde legate's mandatum to you directid. I shall as nye as I can performe every article in the same conteynyd. Howbeit, my lorde, it is nott only laborious but also chargeable, namly this tyme of the yere in this west partes. This I hartly desire you, bycause the tyme is shortt, and as your servant can shew, Y from home, to take my letters for a certificat for this tyme, and at London, with Godd's grace, I shal be byfore tyme of your apparence & to ascerten you of [f. 100v.] the speede in this byhalff, God helping, who preserve your honour. By your assured bedeman the 9 day of Januarii, Nicholas pryor of Taunton.

391. The prior of Repton's certificate acknowledging a mandate [**389** above]. 12 Jan. [1520].
Right reverend father in God, after all dewe recommendacion I recommend me unto

---

[1] Evidentlly an error: cf. above, p. xl.
[2] d. 1523; suppliant for B.Th. and D.Th. at Oxford 1519, prior of Taunton 1514–23: Emden, *Biog. Reg. Oxon. to 1500*.

your good lorshipp, ascerteynyng you the same I have recevyd your letter with your mandate and the booke of my lorde cardinal's acts & new statutes. Whereuppon, according to your commandement, I have takyn a copye of the seide booke & also of your commission, and so send the booke with your commission unto our father the abbott of Darley, and as shortly as I can er may conveniently I shal be glad to perform your forther commaundement, as in citing our fathers & heeds within our said progresse. Besekyng your good lordshipp of your good assistance & cowncell in thes newe acts & statutes, as we may all have cause to pray for you & shall, with grace of Jesus, who ever preserve you to his pleasure. Amen. Writt at Repingdon the 12 day of Januarii by your beidman & assured lover John Yong, prior ther.

392. Letter from William Burghill D.Cn.L., vicar general of Charles [Booth] bishop of Hereford, reporting the resignation of William Harbarte as rector of Cusop [Herefs.] in hope of a pension. 17 Nov. 1519.

393. Presentation of [f. 101] John ap John to the rectory of Cusop [Herefs.] vacant as above, saving the priory's rights including an annual due of 6s. 8d. 28 Apr. 1520.

394. Lease to Thomas Salmon of Barton S[t]ac[e]y, Hants., and his son John[1] of the rectory there with greater and lesser tithes and emoluments of the glebe, for 40 years at £17 a year [f. 101v.] [on the same terms as in **185** above]. Michaelmas 11 Hen. VIII [29 Sept. 1519].

395. [f. 102] [Duplicate of **264** above.]

396. Record of an Exchequer court discharging the prior from 15s. 10½d. poundage at the port of Bristol. 12 Nov. [1515].[2]

The Pipe Roll for 6 Hen. VIII [1514–15] shows that poundage of 15s. 10½d. was exacted from the prior of Llanthony on goods and merchandise brought to the port of Bristol[3] [f. 102v.] valued at £15 17s. 6d., according to the accounts of John Bartilmew and John Grene, collectors of subsidy, for the year to Michaelmas 6 Hen. VIII [1514]. On the morrow [12 Nov.] of St. Martin the prior appeared by his attorney William Grauntineson and claimed discharge, reciting the king's grant of exemption dated 1 May 4 Hen. VIII [above, **264**] as enrolled in the King's Remembrancer's roll no. 11 of Hilary 4 Hen. VIII [1512]. He said that the sum of

[1] John (d. 1551) had succeeded Thomas by 1535 and renewed the lease in his own name and that of his sons, to whom he bequeathed a wheat barn adjoining the parsonage, local landed property, livestock and a mill: *Valor Eccl.* (Rec. Com.), ii. 428; P.R.O. PROB 11/34, f. 253v. He bought half the manor of Barton Stacey in 1538: *V.C.H. Hants.* iv. 419.

[2] For the year cf. below, **476**.

[3] Probably landed at Gloucester or another of the 59 quays, creeks, pills and havens then included in the port of Bristol: Jean Vanes, *Documents illustrating the Overseas Trade of Bristol in the 16th Century* (Bristol Record Soc. xxxi, 1979), 9, 35, 39, 41–2.

15s. 10½d. was subsidy on salmon worth £6 15s. and 2,500 salt fish worth £9 2s. 6d. [f. 103] brought by him to the port from Ireland on 26 Sept. 6 Hen. VIII [1514] in the boat Caden of St. David's (*in bato vocato le Caden de Seynt Daves*), as is contained in the collectors' detailed account book in the King's Remembrancer's keeping. The prior had previously possessed the goods in Ireland, as his men Richard Spencer and Richard Coke declared on oath on 26 Sept. to the collectors. He brought before the court a writ under the Great Seal addressed to the Treasurer and the Barons of the Exchequer and enrolled in Easter term 7 Hen. VIII [1515]. Having seen and discussed the evidence the barons gave judgement that the prior should be discharged and quit of the 15s. 10½d.

397. [f. 103v.] Lease to Thomas Staunton of Burford (*Boureford*) [Oxon.] of tithes of corn and hay of Little Barrington (*Parva Berynton*) except the hay of *Cutles Mede*, tithes formerly held by the late vicar William Harden and lately by William Forthey, to hold for 60 years at £3 a year. 4 Jan. 6 Hen. VIII [1515].

398. Bond of Thomas Staunton of Burford, *yoman*, in £10 to perform the covenants of the above lease. 4 Jan. 6 Hen. VIII [1515].

399. [f. 104] Lease to Thomas Smyth of Ashleworth (*Asshilworthe*) of 6 a. of meadow lying in two parcels at *Wydenham*[1] in the demesne of Hasfield, viz.

(a) 4 a. belonging to the almoner of Llanthony, lying between meadow of St. Augustine's Abbey, Bristol, on the south and that of Deerhurst Priory on the north and extending from that of the lord of Hasfield on the west to that of Deerhurst Priory held by John Williams on the east and

(b) 2 a. formerly belonging to the refectorer of Llanthony, lying between meadow of the lord of Hasfield on the south and that of Guy Wyttington held by John Bele on the north and extending from the Severn on the east to the meadow of Nicholas Apperley held by Nicholas Stanshawe on the west

for 30 years at 14s. 4d. a year to be paid to the prior or his officer. The lessee will bear all expenses arising there, except annual rent to the lord of Hasfield and grants to the king, regardless of inundations of rainwater, destruction of beasts or other misfortunes. The Annunciation 8 Hen. VIII [25 Mar. 1516].

400. Lease[2] to Thomas ap Philippe, vicar of Llantrisant [Mon.], of a tithe barn with the tithes of corn of Llantrisant [f. 104v.] for 30 years, if he remains vicar for so long, rendering 5 marks a year and 4 salmon in season whenever they can

---

[1] Flanking the Severn at the S. limit of Hasfield parish between SO 829259 and SO 846259: Glos. R.O. D6/E4, map 6. The priory, like two Gloucester hospitals, acquired parcels there in the early 13th century: P.R.O. C 115/77, s. xi nos. 32–5; *Glouc. Corp. Rec.* pp. 79, 142.

[2] The initial *H* of *Hec indentura* is ornamented with four interlaced flourishes one of which terminates in a figure of a fish.

conveniently be caught in the river there. He will maintain the barn with its walls and stone-tiled roof and collect rents, heriots, fines and amercements from the prior's free and customary tenants, rendering accounts at the Llanthony exchequer when required and receiving 4s. a year for his trouble.[1] The Annunciation 11 Hen. VIII [25 Mar. 1520].

401. Bond of Thomas ap Philippe of Llantrisant, clerk, and Henry ap Thomas of Caldicot [Mon.], *gentilman*, in £10 to perform the covenants of the above lease. The Annunciation 11 Hen. VIII [25 Mar. 1520].

[ff. 105–114 were a separate quire and are lost. Nos. **402–16** and part of **417** are supplied from the original index.]

402. [f. 105] Lease to John Malet[2] of property at Alvington (*Alvynton*: *copia indenture Iohannis Malet pro firma ibidem*).

403. [f. 106] Stock at Alvington delivered by indenture to the above lessee.

404. Indenture with Robert Wye of Over Lypiatt [in Stroud] for land at Redgrove [in Cheltenham].

405. [ff. 107–9] Inquisition held at Winchcombe in the abbot of Winchcombe's[3] court concerning the priory's land in Westbury[-on-Severn] (*Wynchelcombe*: *copia inquisicionis capte ibidem pro terris nostris in Wesbury in iudicio de predicto [abbate]*).[4]

406. [f. 110] Letter from [George de Athequa] bishop of Llandaff on paying tenths.

407. Letter from Mr. Leyland[5] about 2s. unpaid for tithes[6] at Ballingham (*Balyniam*), Herefs.

---

[1] Thomas ap Phelip was still vicar, lessee and bailiff in 1535: *Valor Eccl.* (Rec. Com.), ii. 429.
[2] The richest inhabitant of Alvington, owning goods worth £20: *Military Survey of Glos. 1522*, 63. His was evidently one of sundry leases of demesne there which yielded 110s. 4d. to the priory in 1535: *Valor Eccl.* (Rec. Com.), 426. By 1535 he was also head lessee of the prior's manor of Quedgeley: *V.C.H. Glos.* x. 217.
[3] As arbitrator or judge delegate, since he had no regular jurisdiction in Westbury.
[4] *abbate* supplied from the previous index entry, which is for **254** above.
[5] A servant of the Hospitallers who wrote on this matter at about this time to the Hospitallers' bailiff at Bolstone, Herefs.: below, **453**.
[6] Arising at Bolstone by the Ballingham boundary: below, **424–5**.

408–9. Letters of Robert Wye and Mr. Chamberlain on discharging a debt of 13s. 4d. at Great Barrington (*Bernynton Magna*: *copia littere Roberti Wye de exoneracione 13s. 4d. ibidem*; *copia littere Magistri Chamberlayn de predictis 13s. 4d. ibidem*).

410. Letter of Robert Wye about tenths at Caldicot and Llantrisant [Mon.].

411. [f. 111] Letter of Robert Wye about 13s. 4d. rent at Chearsley, Bucks.[1] (*Chardessey in comitatu Buck.*: *copia littere Roberti Wye pro redditu 13s. 4d. ibidem*).

412. [f. 112] Schedule of a half tenth of the spiritualities and temporalities of the priory.

413. Resignation of Roger Brayne as vicar of Kenchester, Herefs.

414. Lease to Morgan Lowes of the manor of Alvington[2] (*Alvynton*: *copia indenture Morgani Lowes pro manerio ibidem*).

415. [f. 113] Lease to Thomas Symes of the Pools in Quedgeley (*Queddesley*: *copia indenture Thome Symes pro 'le Pooles' ibidem*).

416. Indenture with John Webbe[3] of Tytherington.

417. [f. 114] Certificate of [Thomas Atwood] prior of Studley, Worcs. [*recte* Warws.], testifying that he received a mandate [**388** above] [and accordingly cited the following prelates in the diocese of Worcester on the following dates, together with others whose names were on f. 114 and are lost]:
 [f. 115] 29 Jan. John Hackbone abbot of Cirencester.
 31 Jan. Robert Elyot, Victorine[4] abbot of St. Augustine's, Bristol.

418. Certificate of Nicholas Cheltnam prior of St. Oswald's, Gloucester, visitor of the Augustinian order in the dioceses of Hereford and St. David's, testifying that he

---

[1] Comprising 5s. 4d. from Lescot's holding, 7s. 7d. from Richard Digun's holding and 5d. from Peter Spirewit's holding, as given by Roger of Cressy and confirmed in 1308: P.R.O. C 115/77, s. x nos. 129–30.

[2] For £10: *Valor Eccl.* ii. 426, where *xl s.* is a misreading of *x l.* as corrected in a copy in Gloucester library and as confirmed by the total shown.

[3] Owner of goods worth £10: *Military Survey of Glos. 1522*, 31. Bailiff of the manor in 1535: *Valor Eccl.* ii. 427.

[4] The kindred orders of Arrouaise and St. Victor are included in this and the following citations as required in **386** above.

received a mandate [**388** above] and accordingly cited the following abbots and priors[1] on the following dates by his mandatory Robert Towkysbury, sub-prior of St. Oswald's. Given at St. Oswald's Priory, Gloucester, 18 Feb. 1519[/20].

17 Jan. John Malverne prior of Wormsley [Herefs.].

28 Jan. Thomas [Morice][2] prior of Carmarthen (*Carmarien*).

31 Jan. Thomas prior of Haverfordwest (*Herefordwest*) [Pembs.].

31 Jan. The claustral prior of Talley Priory [*recte* Abbey, Carms.],[3] a monastery which is now without a prior [*recte* abbot] (*dominum priorem claustralem domus sive prioratus de Talley Meneviensis diocesis, prioratu sive monasterio ibidem prioris solacio et regimine iam destituto*).

419. [f. 115v.] Certificate of Thomas [Vivian][4] prior of Bodmin [Cornw.] and Nicholas [Peper] prior of Taunton [Som.] testifying that they received a mandate [**387** above] on 9 Jan. [f. 116] and accordingly cited the following abbots and priors on the following dates. Sealed at Bodmin on 1 Feb. and at Taunton on 10 Feb. 1519[/20].

In the diocese of Exeter:

29 Jan. Thomas Parre, Arrouaisian prior of Frithelstock [Devon].

30 Jan. John Pruste, Arrouaisian abbot of Hartland [Devon].

30 Jan. John Davyd prior of Plympton [Devon].

30 Jan. John Carlyon prior of Launceston [Cornw.].

30 Jan. Robert Swymmer prior of St. Germans [Cornw.].

In the diocese of Bath and Wells:

13 Jan. William Gilbert abbot of Bruton [Som.].

14 Jan. William Rolf, Victorine abbot of Keynsham [Som.].

14 Jan. Richard Crewce, Victorine prior of Stavordale [Som.].

17 Jan. Richard Sprynge, Victorine prior of Woodspring (*Worlspringe*) [Som.].

20 Jan. Thomas Byrde prior of Barlinch (*Berleche*) [Som.].

420. [f. 116v.] Certificate of Henry [Wyndeley][5] abbot of Darley [Derb.] and [John Young] prior of Repton (*Repyngdon*) [Derb.], visitors of the Augustinian order in the dioceses of Coventry and Lichfield and St. Asaph, testifying that they received a

---

[1] Apparently omitting the priors of Flanesford (Herefs.) and Chirbury (Salop.) and the Victorine abbot of Wigmore (Herefs.).

[2] Replaced 1524: *L. & P. Hen. VIII*, iv., p. 173.

[3] A Premonstratensian house: *Archaeologia Cambrensis*, xcvi. 69–91. Evidently its prior met the Augustinian visitor at Haverfordwest and sought a citation in case his own order failed to cite him.

[4] d. 1533, prior of Bodmin 1507–33, bishop of Megara (Greece) and suffragan to the bishop of Exeter 1517–33, buried under an effigy in Bodmin parish church: Emden, *Biog. Reg. Oxon. 1501–40*, where he is distinguished from a graduate namesake; Dugdale, *Mon.* ii. 460.

[5] Abbot 1518–24: *V.C.H. Derb.* ii. 53.

mandate [**389** above] on 13 Jan. and that the following abbots and priors will appear before the cardinal. 12 Feb. 1519[/20].

Of the diocese of Coventry and Lichfield:

The abbot of Norton [Ches.].

The abbot of Rocester (*Rowcetur*) [Staffs.].

The prior of Burscough (*Brystowe*) [Lancs.].

The abbot of Kenilworth [Warws.].

The abbot of Ha[ugh]mond [Salop.].

The abbot of Lilleshall (*Lilleshull*) [Salop.].

The prior of Trent[h]am [Staffs.].

The prior of Stone [Staffs.].

The prior of St. Thomas [by Stafford].

The prior of Wombridge (*Wembryge*) [Salop.].

The prior of Ranton (*Rounton*) [Staffs.].

The prior of Maxstoke (*Maystocke*) [Warws.].

The prior of Arbury [Warws.].

The prior of [Church] Gresley [Derb.].

The prior of Breadsall (*Braydesall Parke*) [Derb.].

421. [f. 117] Certificate addressed to Cardinal Wolsey attesting that Prior Forest received a commission [**386** above] on 21 Dec., that he speedily told six visitors of the Augustinian order to cite prelates accordingly in six dioceses, [f. 117v.] that he asked his canons to observe Wolsey's articles of reform in the meantime and that the visitors have returned their certificates, which are annexed to this certificate with the names of those cited. Sealed (*Data quoad sigillacionem*) on 20 Feb. 1519[/20].

422. [f. 118] Lease to John Sysell of Monkton [in Llanwarne, Herefs.] and his sons Robert and John of property there for 40 years at 24s. 6d. a year as follows.

A newly built messuage[1] with orchards and appurtenances.

Long Croft lying between *Leygrene* Way and the *Mochetre*[*e*] and extending from *Stony Lane* to *Colverhouse Forlong.*[2]

The *Over Heyfeld* between *Longe Croft* and *Withgus Broke* together with *Withgicbroke Medowe* adjacent extending from the *Holwey* to land of Roger Jonys.

Le close beyonde the Holway extending from land of Richard Pyers to land of the same Richard and lying between the Holway and land of Richard Pyers which extends to *Sandays Well.*

---

[1] Probably Lower Monkton Farm at SO 490268, now a 16th-century house of sandstone rubble with later additions: *Inventory of Herefs.* (Royal Commission on Historical Monuments, 1931), i, 178. It lies among the fields identified and ran with them in 1840: *Herefs. Field-Name Survey, Llanwarne*, 8.

[2] Alias Pigeonhouse Field, around SO 492268: *Herefs. Field-Name Survey, Llanwarne*, 8.

Land and *Brokynglate* meadow lying between the Holway and Richard Pyers's *Sandayswall Felde* and extending to *Wilmosslade Cliv* [i.e. cliff] and a parcel of Richard Pyers's land by *Brokynglate*.

½ a. of *Curns Acre* extending from *Rusheturfe*[1] to *Parrock Feld* and lying between land formerly held by Walter Coytiff.

Parrock Field extending from Sandayswall Field to *Wilfaderes Hill* and lying between *Stany Dell* and a new ditch between Parrock Field and *Muche Hill*.

Adam Cockes Hill alias *Aracocks Hill* extending [f. 118v.] from Wilfadres Hill to *More Hill* and lying between Stony Dell and the *Ruggewey* leading from *Harpe Acre* to *Orcopes Pole*.[2]

Le Hill above the Towne[3] extending from the Holway to *le Greneway* and lying between Richard Perce's land and the Holway.

½ a. of Pendiggott's Yard (*Pendegotes Yord*) extending from land formerly of David Goode to *le Groveway*.

Land called *Holokeston* extending from Stony Lane to *Gagges Yord*.

Land called *John Adamc Yord* extending from Richard Perce's close to *Muctys Yord* and lying between Stony Lane and *Hobyes Hill*.

Wilfadereshill pasture extending from Parrock Field to the Ridgeway and lying between Adam Cocks Hill and land held by Hugh alias Howell ap G[wi]ll[y]m.

A day-work (*dietam*) of land called *David Goodes Orcheyard* extending from *le Tuppe* to *Saundres Pitte* and lying between *Saundres Lane* and a close held by John Hoskyns.

The lessees will render suit of court and heriot of a best animal. They may take *housebote*, *heybote*, *firebote* and *ploughbote*. Michaelmas 12 Hen. VIII [29 Sept. 1520]. [Finishes on f. 119]

423. [f. 119v.] Letter of fraternity to John Cun[4] the king's servant (*valecti*) and his wife Joan. 15 Dec. 1520.

424. Agreement between Robert the Treasurer, prior of the Hospitallers in England [c. 1230],[5] and the prior of Llanthony in Wales concerning tithes [in Bolstone, Herefs.] claimed by the latter as belonging to his church of Llanwarne [Herefs.] and arising from land of John Bollyng and Wrono of Holme [Lacy], viz.

(a) tithes which John Bollyng previously gave to the Hospitallers arising from his land,

[1] Alias Rush Close, around SO 487272: ibid. 4.
[2] The ridgeway, now metalled, follows the parish boundary from Harp Acre (now Homelands) at SO 483263 to Orcop's Pool (now Poolfield Farm) at 479272, so the demised land is part of Hill Field around SO 482270: ibid. 8–9.
[3] MS. *le hill acove heth towne*.
[4] Entered in the original index as John Conne of London. Evidently a kinsman of Robert Cun alias Cone the cellarer: cf. above, **109** n., **336**.
[5] Date inferred from Dugdale, *Mon.* vi. 799.

(b) tithes from a new assart at Abertarader and

(c) tithes from land which lies between the Wye and the road from Holme [Lacy] to Ballingham and extends to the Hospitallers' mill from the brook which runs from Bolstone to the Wye.[1]

In satisfaction of this claim the Hospitallers' proctor in Herefordshire will pay to Llanthony Priory 2s. a year.

Hec transactio facta fuit inter fratrem Robertum Th[esaur]ar[iu]m, tunc priorem, et fratres Hospitalis Iherosolom in Anglia ex una parte et conventum canonicorum de Lanthonia in Wallia ex alia parte super quibusdam decimis provenientibus de terra Iohannis Bollyng et de terra Wronoi de Hama quas dicti prior et canonici Lanthonie petebant quasi pertinentes ad ecclesiam suam de Lanwaren versus predictum priorem et fratres Hospitalis Iherosolom, videlicet quod predictus prior et canonici clamaverunt quietas predictis priori Hospitalis et fratribus omnes decimas de terra Iohannis Bollyng quas idem prior et fratres Hospitalis prius habebant de dono eiusdem Iohannis, et insuper decimas de novo assarto de Abertared, et preterea decimas illius terre que est inter[2] Vagam fluvium et viam que ducit ab Hama usque ad Balyniam in latitudine, et a rivulo qui descendit a Boliston in Vagam usque ad molendinum [f. 120] predicti prioris et fratrum in longitudine; ita quidem quod pro bono pacis et pro hac quieta clamancia quicumque fuerit pro tempore procurator domus Hospitalis Iherosolom in Herefordsir solvet annuatim predictis priori et conventui Lanthonie duos solidos, scilicet medietatem ad Pascham et medietatem ad festum Sancti Michaelis. Hiis testibus, fratre H. abbate etc.

425. Letter from Thomas Docwra, Kt.,[3] prior of the Hospitallers in England, on the above. 6 Feb. 1521.

To the prior of the Black Freres in Hereforde and to Thomas L[lywely]n, fermer at Bolston[4] in Irchenfeld [i.e. Bolstone in Archenfield, Herefs.] *& to aither of them, etc.*

I grete yow well. And forasmoche as I perceyve & undrestonde that there is a composicion betwene my religion & the prior of Lanthony in Gloucester for an

---

[1] The Taratyr Brook (formerly so called) leaves Bolstone village, follows the boundary between Bolstone and Holme Lacy and enters the Wye at Abertarader (SO 565328) near the site of Abertarader mill, mentioned here, which lay beside the Wye in Bolstone and was among property of the Hospitallers sold to John Scudamore in 1544: *Trans. Woolhope N.F.C.* 1914–17, 166, 170; xxxiv. 71–2 (with map); cf. *L. & P. Hen. VIII*, xix (2), p. 472. The tithed land (b) and (c) evidently flanked the adjacent road in Bolstone near the boundary of Ballingham, a chapelry of Llanwarne where the priory collected tithes similarly: cf. above, **113**.

[2] MS. *infar.*

[3] d. 1527, prior of the Hospitallers 1502–27, holder of many royal commissions, ambassador to Flanders 1507 and 1521 and to France 1510, 1514, 1517–9 and 1521: *D.N.B.*

[4] A demesne of 200 arable acres: L. B. Larkin, *The Knights Hospitallers in England A.D. 1338* (Camden Soc. 1857), 31, where *Bolston* is misread as *Rolston*. Llewelyn was also tenant of the Hospitallers' manor house there: *L. &. P. Hen. VIII*, xix (2), p. 472.

annual pension of 2s. due unto the said prior goyng owt of Bolston whereof ye have
the charche & occupacion with the profitts betwene you, and the seid 2s. is unpaid
be the space of 2 yeres past at the fest of Seynt Michell last, and the seid prior hathe
made sute unto me for the same; therefor I will ye se the seyd pension unto hym or
his officers contentyd & payd, so that he may have no cause hereafter to complayne,
and as ye entende to avoyde the daunger off the lawe. Thus fare ye well. Frome
London the 6 day off February the 12 yere of the reinge of Kynge Henry the VIII.

Be the prior of Seynt John's, T. Docwra.

[Gloss:] *Require aliam litteram de eodem in folio 15 subsequente.*[1]

426. [f. 120v.] Letter from John Belle D.Cn.[& C.]L.,[2] vicar general of Silvestro [de'
Gigli] bishop of Worcester, to the Treasurer and Barons of the Exchequer.

Considering the imminent ruin of Llanthony Priory church and the great expense
of rebuilding and maintaining it (*imminentem*[3] *ruinam ecclesie conventualis*
prioratus de Lanthonia . . . ac magnas et sumptuosas expensas circa
reedificacionem, sustentacionem et manutencionem eiusdem ecclesie conventualis
per dictos priorem et conventum expositas), whereby the prior and canons cannot
easily bear the burdens incumbent upon them, Belle has exercised the authority
granted to the ordinary at the last convocation and has exempted them from
paying or levying the second half of the first tenth and the whole of the second
tenth that were granted to the king at that convocation[4] subject to such
exemptions. He asks the Treasurer and Barons to accept that the abbot of Pershore
(*Parshore*), as collector, is discharged from collecting these dues. Worcester, 12 July
1518.

427. [f. 121] Citation to a visitation of the priory on 17 May by John Breton D.Cn. &
C.L., commissary general and principal sequestrator of William [Moore][5] prior
of Worcester and William [Warham] archbishop of Canterbury in the diocese of
Worcester *sede vacante.* Given under the prior's seal at Worcester, 5 May 1521.

428. [f. 121v.] Certificate acknowledging that the above was received on 8 May. 11
May 1521.

---

[1] 'See another letter on the same on the 15th [*recte* 13th] leaf following', i.e. **453** below.
[2] d. 1556; dean of the Arches 1517, vicar general and chancellor of the bishop of Worcester
1518–35, archdeacon of Gloucester 1518–39, chaplain to the king and counsel concerning the
royal divorce from 1526, prebendary of Lichfield 1526–9, of Lincoln 1528–39, of Southwell
(Notts.) 1528–48 and of Westbury-on-Trym *c.* 1532–9, contributor to the Bishops' Book of
doctrine 1537 and bishop of Worcester 1539–43: Emden, *Biog. Reg. Oxon. 1501–40; D.N.B.;*
Hockaday Abs. xxv, 1532 subsidy.
[3] MS. *iminentam.*
[4] Granted on 20 Dec. 1514 at a convocation which also sat on 22 June 1514 and 13 Nov.
1515: Wilkins, *Concilia*, iii. 658; cf. above, **302, 331–4, 406, 412.**
[5] Prior 1518–36: Le Neve, *Fasti 1300–1541, Monastic Cathedrals.*

429. Lease to Olive widow of Alderman William Coole[1] and her daughter Dorothy of *Hyde Crofte*[2] lying outside the north gate of Gloucester towards Newland (*Newlonde*), measuring 84 yd. (with inches between) on the side next to a garden of the Carmelite friars, 112½ yd 4 in. (with inches between) from the Carmelites' garden to land of St. Oswald's Priory and 76 yd. (with inches between) on the side next to the land of St. Oswald's,[3] [f. 122] to hold for 40 years, rendering 6s. 8d. a year to the collector of rents for Hempsted and suit to the court of St. Owen. They will make a hawthorn hedge and a ditch (*sepem vivum de spinis albis cum fosso*) on the boundary with the land of St. Oswald's Priory and will maintain all buildings constructed or to be constructed on the croft. The Annunciation 12 Hen. VIII (25 Mar. 1521).

430. [f. 122v.] Lease to Robert[4] and Alice Atwell of Prestbry and their son John of

(a) The manor of Prestbury with buildings and a dovecot on the manor site and demesne land, meadow and pasture in Prestbury, Cheltenham and Southam, lately held by Thomas Lynet,[5] to hold for 50 years at annual rents of £4 and 12 geese and 12 capons or 6s., at the prior's choice, and

(b) a tithe barn by the gate of Prestbury rectory or manor, lately held by Lynet and lately ruinous but now rebuilt, and the tithes and oblations belonging to the rectory [f. 123] for 50 years at £12 a year.

The lessees will render dues, live on site and entertain [as in **78**(a–d) above] and will serve in the office of bailiff [as in **325** above].[6] [f. 123v.] They will receive the tithe of shorn wool for one month after the end of the term. Michaelmas 12 Hen. VIII [29 Sep. 1520].

---

[1] Alias Cole (d. 1517), sheriff 1486 and mayor 1494 and 1504: Fosbrooke, *Glouc.* 208. Resident at nos. 45–9 Northgate Street on the W. side of the inner N. gate, where he rented a tenement from the Bisley family and constructed buildings before 1509 on land under the town wall rented from the borough: Glos. R.O. GBR/J5/3; for the tenement, *Glouc. Rental 1455*, 78b; cf. P.R.O. C 115/73, f. 71 (69)v. no. 131; plan in Carolyn Heighway, *The East and North Gates of Gloucester* (Bristol, 1983), 12. He bequeathed this dwelling to Olive with two other tenements and a malthouse in the same street and a lease from St. Oswald's Priory of tithes in Twigworth: P.R.O. PROB 11/19, f. 41, copied in Hockaday Abs. ccxv, 1518.

[2] Although Hyde Croft also included the site of nos. 14–16 London Road in 1282–1350, the parcel here demised is that behind nos. 6–16 London Road now occupied by railway premises and bounded by George Street on the SW., a subway under the railway station on the SE. and Great Western Road on the NE.: P.R.O. C 115/75, ff. 108–9, 119; cf. C 115/73, f. 83 (81) no. 163; R. Hall and T. Pinnell, *Map of Gloucester* (1780). It was bought by Thomas Bell in 1543 and by the Gloucester and Dean Forest Railway Co. in 1846–50: *L. & P. Hen. VIII*, xviii (2), p. 52; Glos. R.O. Q/RUm/203.

[3] i.e. 259 ft. on the SW., 347 ft. on the SE. and 234 ft. on the NE.

[4] The richest or second richest inhabitant of Prestbury, owning goods worth £40: *Military Survey of Glos. 1522*, 175.

[5] As in **325** above.

[6] Robert was still bailiff in 1535: *Valor Eccl.* (Rec. Com.), ii. 425.

431. Bond of Robert Atwell *husbandman* of Prestbury, John Man *wever* of Prestbury and John Hoggs *husbandman* of Prestbury[1] in £40 to perform the covenants of the above lease. 9 Jan. 12 Hen. VIII [1521].

432. [f. 124] Lease to Thomas Flewmynge, vicar of Windrush (*Wynryche*), of the tithe corn of the rectory there (reserving to the prior the tithes of hay) for 20 years at yearly rents of 7 marks [f. 124v.] and a wagon-load of straw for the prior's sheep. Michaelmas 12 Hen. VIII [29 Sept. 1520].

433. Thomas Flewmyng's bond in £10 [f. 125] to perform the covenants of the above lease. 14 Oct. 12 Hen. VIII [1520].

434. General proxy to William Chaddesley canon of Llanthony, William Burghill D.Cn.L., Robert Stynchcombe B.Cn.L. and Masters John Hyde,[2] William Clayton,[3] John Talkar,[4] Andrew Smythe, John Neele, Zachariah Dawtry, Thomas Stacy, Simon Longe and John Bothe[5] notaries public of the court [of the archbishop] of Canterbury (*notarios publicos curie Cantuariensis*). [ff. 125v., 126] 14 July 1521.

435. Citation to a visitation of the priory by John Bell D.Cn.[& C.]L., vicar general of Cardinal Giulio de' Medici perpetual administrator of the see of Worcester,[6] on 9 Oct. [f. 126v.] Worcester, 26 Aug. 1521.

436. Certificate acknowledging that the above was received on 31 Aug. [f. 127] 7 Sept. 1521.

437. Lease to John and Joan Hunt[7] of Quedgeley and their son William of an acre of meadow in *Clippes Mede* [in Hempsted][8] with trees and hedges upon it (formerly held by Roger Barun of Hempsted by deed with bounds and lately held by William

---

[1] Man owned goods worth £13 6s. 8d. and Hoggs goods worth £10: *Military Survey of Glos. 1522*, 175.

[2] B.Cn.L. 1522: Emden, *Biog. Reg. Oxon. 1501–40.*

[3] d. 1532; B.Cn.L. 1515, D.Cn.L. 1528, chaplain to the king, vicar of many churches including Kempsford 1526–30 and canon of York 1530–2: ibid.

[4] B.Cn. & C.L., proctor in the court of the chancellor of Oxford University 1510–13 and counsel to Queen Catherine 1528: Emden, *Biog. Reg. Oxon. to 1500.*

[5] M.A., d. 1542; fellow of Brasenose College, Oxford, 1516–21, senior proctor of the university 1520–1, archdeacon of Hereford 1523–42 and prebendary there 1524–42: Emden, *Biog. Reg. Oxon. 1501–40.*

[6] de' Medici (d. 1534) held this office in lieu of the bishopric 7 June 1521–26 Sept. 1522: Le Neve, *Fasti 1300–1541, Monastic Cathedrals.* He was elected as Pope Clement VII on 19 Nov. 1523: *L. & P. Hen VIII*, iii, p. 1477.

[7] Alias Hut, owners of goods worth £9 6s.: *Military Survey of Glos. 1522*, 191. John was bailiff of Llanthony demesne in 1535: above, p. xxix.

[8] Below Hempsted village by Horsepool, i.e. on the Severn bank above Upper Rea: P.R.O. C 115/83, s. i nos. 75, 78, 82; cf. above, **253**.

Whiteby[1] at term) to hold for 20 years at 4s. 6d. a year payable to the almoner. The lessees will nurture the trees and hedges growing around the meadow and will plant and maintain trees in any gaps, but may crop branches and take prunings for their own use without committing waste (*arbores et haicias circumcrescentes nutrient aliasque in locis vacuis inde debite plantabunt illasque custodient bene et honeste, ac sine vasto et destruccione sarment[aciones] et frondes inde ad usum suum proprium metent, scindent et asportabunt*). They will clean ditches and make fences adjacent. The Assumption 13 Hen. VIII [15 Aug. 1521].

438. [f. 127v.] Presentation of Richard Frett[2] to the vicarage of Yazor (*Yasor*) [Herefs.][3] vacant by the resignation of John Goghe. 12 Feb. 1521[/2]. [Abstract in MS.; cf. **39**]

439. Nomination by Edward Mille, lord of Harescombe, of William Okey to the chaplaincy of Harescombe and Pitchcombe. [Apr. 1522.]

Be yt knowen unto you, my lorde, by this presente that I Edward Mille, squyer, hathe gyvyn the benyfice of Harescombe and Pynchencombe to one Sir William Okey berer hereoff, that you wyl be so gracious lorde unto hym as to gyve hym the presencacion of the bothe, & he shall do his deuty unto you as yt becomythe hym to do. My lorde, I pray you for Master Kyngeston[4] sake & my ladyes & sumwhat for myne to se that this be shortly done, for the tyme is nye.[5] No more to you at this tyme but Jesus preserve you. Edward Mylle.

440. Presentation of William Okey, chaplain, nominated as above, to the chapel or chantry of Harescombe [f. 128] with the chapel of Pitchcombe (*Pynchencombe*)

[1] Of Longney, owner of goods worth £15: *Military Survey of Glos. 1522*, 192.

[2] Instituted 18 Mar.: *Reg. Bothe*, 334.

[3] Yazor church was given to the priory by Ranulph de Baskerville before 1141: P.R.O. C 115/75, f. 214 no. 22.

[4] William Kingston, Kt., of Elmore and of the Blackfriars in London (d. 1540), yeoman of the chamber from 1497, holder of many other offices at court from 1504, under-marshal 1512, knighted after Flodden 1513, J.P. for Glos. 1506–40, sheriff there 1514, steward of the Duchy of Lancaster in Glos. and Herefs. 1521–40, chief steward of the duchy in S. England and Wales 1525–40, constable of Thornbury and St. Briavels 1522–40, captain of the guard 1523–40, constable of the Tower 1524–40, M.P. for Glos. 1529 and 1539, Privy Councillor 1533–40, K.G. and comptroller of the Household 1539–40: *Hist. of Parl., Commons 1509–58* correcting *D.N.B.*; *L. & P. Hen. VIII*, i, p. 552; *V.C.H. Glos.* v. 415. Chief steward by 1535 of Gloucester Abbey, Keynsham Abbey (Som.), Deerhurst Priory and Great Malvern Priory (Worcs.): *Valor Eccl.* (Rec. Com.), i. 182; ii. 418, 484; iii. 241. Lord of Haresfield from 1522, of Rendcomb from 1531, of manors lately of Flaxley Abbey in Glos. and Som. from 1537, of Painswick from 1540 and ultimately of Rush in Wallingford (Berks.): *V.C.H. Glos.* vii. 220; x.191; xi. 66; *L. & P. Hen. VIII*, xii (1), p. 353; *Hist. of Parl.* ibid. He evidently recommended Okey.

[5] i.e. the right of presentation is about to lapse as the vacancy has lasted for nearly six months: cf. Richard Burn, *Ecclesiastical Law* (London, 1781), i. 131.

annexed, vacant by the resignation of William Nycolls, reserving the portion due to the priory. 16 Apr. 1522.

441. Grant to John Horne, chaplain,[1] of the service of Elmore chapel with the usual tithes and oblations (*servicium annuale pertinens capelle predicti prioris et conventus de Elmore Wigorniensis diocesis antedicte cum omnibus decimis et oblacionibus prout capellani dictum servicium occupantes ab antiquo habere et percipere consueverunt*), provided he sees that divine service is celebrated there and the cure of souls is not neglected. 7 Oct. 1522.

442. Presentation of Mr. Richard Wente B.Cn.L.[2] to the rectory of Llanwarne [Herefs.] vacant by the death of Mr. Henry Marten. 16 Apr. 1524. [Abstract in MS.; cf. **39**]

443. Presentation of John Skydmore[3] to the same rectory vacant by the resignation of Mr. Wente.[4] 1 May 1524. [Abstract in MS.]

444. [f. 128v.] Lease to John and Elizabeth Howell (Elizabeth being daughter of Ieuan ap David) and their daughter Margaret of property in the demesne of Monkton [in Llanwarne, Herefs.], viz. a messuage, land, woodland and closes by the Cold Brook (*Col Broke*), the Hereford–Monmouth road and the branch road to Pendiggott (*Pendeugoyd*) [in St. Weonards] [as described in **278** above] to hold for 60 years at 16s. a year, suit of court and heriot of a best animal. [f. 129] If all the lessees die within the term the next blood relation may have the property if he offers as large an entry fine as anyone else. 27 May 14 Hen. VIII [1522].

445. [f. 129v.] The king's order to levy and equip ten archers ready to serve at a day's notice. Woking [Surrey], 20 Aug. [1521].[5]

---

[1] Still in office in 1534 when Prior Hart granted the advowson to Anthony Kingston for 60 years: John Rylands library, Rylands Charter 1762.

[2] Alias Gwent (d. 1543), D.C.L. 1525, fellow of All Souls' College, Oxford, 1515–28, principal of the canon law school there 1525–8, rector of many churches including Doynton (in the prior's gift) to 1531 and Leckhampton 1529–31, counsel to Queen Catherine 1529, dean of Arches and chaplain to the king 1532–43, prebendary of Lichfield 1531–43, Lincoln 1534–43, St. David's and Llandaff 1534–43, archdeacon of London 1534–43, Brecon 1539–43 and Huntingdon 1542–3: Emden, *Biog. Reg. Oxon. 1501–40*; *D.N.B.* Instituted to Llanwarne rectory 7 Apr. (sic): *Reg. Bothe*, 337.

[3] Instituted 17 May, rector 1524–32: *Reg. Bothe*, 337, 346.

[4] Possibly the prior had allowed the presentation to lapse, offered it belatedly to Skydmore in ignorance that the bishop had instituted Wente, and persuaded Wente to resign in return for recognition and compensation. Wente indeed claimed a pension of £4 payable at Llanthony until he received a benefice worth £20 a year: *Reg. Bothe*, 337. He received another pension from 1531 on resigning the rectory of Leckhampton and an annuity of £4 from 1533 for advice rendered (*pro bono consilio impenso*) to Prior Hart of Llanthony: Hockaday Abs. xxv, 1532 subsidy; P.R.O. E315/92, f. 60v.

[5] Part of a levy of 6,000 archers ordered to stand by for the defence of Calais: *L. & P. Hen. VIII*, iii, p. 611.

To our trusty and welbelovyd in God the prior of oure monastery of Lanthonye. By the kynge.

Trusty and welbelovyd in God, we grete yow well. And forasmuche as to good policie it appertenyth in tyme of peace to provyde agenst warres, we therfore intendyng to have a good nombre of archers prepared and put in aredynes as well for the defence of us and this realme as for the furniture of oure other dominions and garnisons in outwarde parties, woll and desire you and nevertheles commaunde you that furthwith upon the sight of these our lettures ye endevoure yourselfe with all diligence possible to put the nombre of 10 good, hable and sufficient bowemen and archers in suche aredines sufficiently furnished for the warres, so that they may be furthcummyng upon a day's warning at any tyme whan ye shal be by us hereaftur required, not failing in theffectuell preparacion and puttyng in aredines of the seide nombre of archers in maner and forme above mencioned, as our trust and confidence is in you and as ye tender our honor and suertie. And these oure lettres shal be as sufficient warraunt and discharge unto you for youre indempnite in the reteignyng, levieng and preparyng of the seid nombre, as though ample auctorite were yeven unto you for that porpose undre our great seale, any acte, statute or ordinaunce made to the contrey notwithstondyng. Yeven under our signet at oure maner of Okynge the 20 day of August.

446. *These be the names of the sowdears sende to oure soverayne lorde the kynge Henry the VIII.*

Jamys Crede, Lewes Morgen, Jamys Barly, Jhon Knolys,[1] Philip More, Richard Scull, Brion Bruton, William Golde, Richarde Atkyns, Jhon Ledbury.

447. [f. 130] The king's order to levy ten men within the prior's lands, equip them and send them by 5 June to Southampton for the defence of Calais. Greenwich [Kent], 18 May [1522].[2]

To our trusty and welbelovyd in God the prior of oure monastery of Lanthony. By the kynge.

Trusty and welbelovyd in God, we grete you well. And albeit that we, tenderyng the tranquillite, quiet and restfulnes of Cristendome, have employd oure mynde and study to the pacificacion of the discordis and variaunce dependyng betwene oure derest brother, cosyn and good nephieu themperor on thone partie and the Frenche kynge on thother partie, by whose warres all Cristen regions be troubled and vexid, yet nevertheles we cannot as yet perceyve or see any towardnes or lykelyhode of unite betwene them, and forasmuche as in this tyme of the warres the frontiers & confines of Pycardy and other places nere to our marches of Calais be replenished with sondry bands and companyes of men of warre, by meane whereof our towne of Calais and oure seide marches myght be in daungier in caase we shulde not in tyme sufficiently provyde for the suertie and conservacion of the same, we therfor by

---

[1] Probably of Newent, still an archer in 1539: Glos. muster roll, P.R.O. E 101/59/9.

[2] Variant of a letter sent from Richmond (Surrey) on 3 May ordering Sir William Sandys to levy and lead 200 men: *L. & P. Hen. VIII,* iii, p. 951.

deliberate advise of our councell have determyned and appoynted to sende to our seide towne and marches with convenient diligence a crewe of men, amonge whome we have appoynted you to furnishe the nombre of 10 able men to be by you levied and had withyn any your lands and patrymony.

Wherfor we woll & commaunde you that incontynently upon the recepte hereof ye cause to be prepared and put in aredynes the seid nombre sufficiently harnessed with other requisits so that they may be at our towne of Southampton the 5 day of June next ensuwyng, where shippyng and passage shal be redy for theire transportyng to oure seide towne and marches. Fayle ye not taccomplish diligently the premises as ye tender our honor & pleasur and the suertie of this our realme. And these our lettres shal be as well unto you for levieng, musteryng, sendyng & gaderyng of the seide persones, as also to every of the same persones so levyed and had sufficient auctorite and discharge in this behalfe at all tymes hereaftur, any acte, statute, ordinaunce or proclamacion had or passed to the contrary notwithstonding. Yeven under our signet at our maner of Grenewyche the 18 day of May.

448. [f. 130v.] Lease to John Watkyns of Yazor (*Yasor*) [Herefs.], his wife Margery and his son John of tithes of corn and hay at Yarsop (*Yarsope*) and Foxley [both in Yazor] lately held by John's father Thomas, to hold at a yearly rent of 8 qr. of threshed and winnowed wheat with one bushel heaped in every qr., 2 bu. of green peas and 2 bu. of *grey* peas, all to be rendered between All Saints [1 Nov.] and the Annunciation [25 Mar.] They will

(a) provide victuals, hay, straw, provender, beds and stabling for the prior's servants and their horses when they come to carry the wheat and peas and

(b) repair the chancel of Yazor parish church whenever necessary and whenever given notice (*premunicio*) by the bishop of Hereford, by the archdeacon or by the bishop's officials at a visitation.
The Nativity of St. John the Baptist 14 Hen. VIII [24 June 1522].

449. [f. 131] Lease to Thomas and Agnes Gardyner and their son William of tithes of corn, hay, flax and hemp with other revenues, emoluments and tithes both great and small belonging to the prior as rector of Brookthorpe and Harescombe (*racione rectorie sue de Brockethroppe et Harscombe*) to hold for 60 years at 56s. 8d. a year. 14 July 12 Hen. VIII [1520].

450. [f. 131v.] Memorandum of [tithes demised above, namely] the first tithe (*totam primam decimam*) in each of the following places.[1]

[1] All the fields identified below lie near or were farmed in 1842 from Webb's Farm, now Wynstones, on the N. side of Whaddon church: Glos. R.O. GDR/T1/195. The demised tithes are probably those of Walter of Gloucester's demesne in Whaddon and Brookthorpe as given to St. Owen's church before 1095 and to Llanthony Priory in 1137, together with tithes of Miles of Gloucester's villeins in Brookthorpe as added to the latter gift: *Camden Misc.* xxii. 38; Dugdale, *Mon.* vi. 136.

Estudige field except 2 a.

Tydestan field.

Lone Crofte now or lately held by Roger Comper.

Wode Felde[1] except 1 a. by the highway to Gloucester and 1 a. in a corner by a small meadow at the *Harsse Broke.*[2]

Boden field.

A fore-earth (*una forerde*) held by Richard de Ponte.

Hedley field.

8 selions adjacent held by Philip of Quedgeley.

Wythurne field.[3]

Brodecroft field[4] held by the monk of Tuffley,[5] except 2 crofts.

Mora Acra held by Roger Comper.

Sengesforlonge field.

2 selions and 3 fore-earths in *Dodin Furlonge* conveyed by Sir Nicholas of Whaddon[6] to Mistress Ymenye (*traditi Domine Ymenye de Domino Nicholao de Wad'*) and held by Henry Comper.

The upper furlong of *Godwora* field.

Piragapha field.

Land of Philip of Quedgeley on the other, front, side of *Piragapha.*

5a. above Whaddon held by the monk of Tuffley.

Another acre at Tuffley called *Ascworth* which [the monk] ploughs.

Blagefurlonge field except 3 fore-earths.

Clegarst field except 3 fore-earths.

16 selions of *Atholphus Croft.*

Atturlynge Furlonge[7] in *Wode Felde* abutting Whaddon church.

Bruglond piece[8] extending to Whaddon bridge on the south.

A piece in *Godworthe* field extending to *Holowlond.*

451. [f. 132] Resignation of Thomas Powmfray as rector of Stretton Sugwas [Herefs.] delivered in the great hall of the college of the vicars choral at Hereford in

---

[1] In Whaddon around SO 831135: Glos. R.O. GDR/T1/195.

[2] Daniel's Brook, identified from Hasbrook field adjacent: ibid.

[3] In Whaddon at SO 824134: ibid.

[4] Either Broad Croft around SO 845126 in Whaddon and Brookthorpe or Broad Croft around SO 830138 NW. of Whaddon church in the hamlet of Tuffley and the parish of St. Mary de Lode: Glos. R.O. GDR/T1/41, 86, 195.

[5] Superintendent of the abbot of Gloucester's manor there: cf. *V.C.H. Glos.* iv. 394; A. H. Smith, *Place-Names of Glos.* (Eng. Place-Name Soc.), ii. 140.

[6] Probably a priest, since the medieval lords of Whaddon were absentees: Rudder, *Glos.* 812–3.

[7] In Whaddon at SO 834137: Glos. R.O. GDR/T1/195.

[8] Alias Whaddon Bridge Ground in Tuffley at SO 831141: Glos. R.O. Q/RI/70. Whaddon bridge, immediately NE., carries the Gloucester–Stroud road at the corner of Grange Road.

the presence of William Burghill D.Cn.L. and John Walker notary public of Hereford diocese, recorded by John Blaxtun notary public of Hereford diocese. 24 Dec. 1522.

452. [f. 132v.] Bond of John Davys[1] rector of Stretton Sugwas and William Davys *husbondeman* of Lyde, Herefs., in £20. 9 Jan. 14 Hen. VIII [1523]. [In Latin except as follows.]

The condicion of this obligacion is suche, that if the above bounden Sir Jhon Davys do repare or cause to be repared sufficiently the mansion place of the parsonage of Stretton beforeseid within 5 yeres next after that the seid parsone is in peassable possession of the seid parsonage, and also content & pay yerely 2s. to the seid prior and his successors in name of a pencion, and 12 bu. of whete to the prior & convent of Lanthony in Walys for the tyme beyng, that then this obligacion to stonde voyde, or els to stonde in full strength and vertu.

453. Letter from Thomas Docwra, Kt., prior of the Hospitallers in England, on tithes owed at Bolstone in Archenfield [Herefs.]. London, 24 Jan. 1522[/3].

To my trusty and welbelovyd Thomas Ll[ywely]n, fermer and bayliffe at Bolston in Irchenfeld.

Thomas Ll[ywely]n, I grete you well. And forasmuche as ther is a composicion betwene me and my religion uppon the one partie and the priour of Lanthony and his brethern uppon the other partie for 2s. of pension yerely to be paid unto the seide priour, wherof I have writon to you affore this tyme and also sende you worde but late by my servaunt Thomas Leyland[2] to se it contentid and paid accordyng to the seid composicion, and so eftsones I will in any wise that ye so do, as ye entend my favour, so that the seid priour have no cause hereafter to compleyn, or els he wil cause the fruts of the church to be sequestred as reason will & accordyng to the lawe. And therefore in eschewynge and avoidyng the daunger of the premisses I will that ye accomplishe this my mynde in payeng of the same etc. Writton in hast at London the 24 day of Januarii 1522.[3]

By the prioure of Seynt John's, T. Docwra.

454. [f. 133] Lease to William Heynes, *yoman* of Stanton Lacy (*Staunton Lacy*), Salop., his wife Margaret and their sons Richard and Oliver of the rectory of Stanton Lacy with the glebe, tithes, oblations, profits and emoluments belonging to it, reserving to the prior

(a) the advowson, fines, heriots, rents and the vicar's portion and

(b) a moiety of waif and stray cattle above the value of 3s. 4d., the other moiety being retained by the lessees in return for their good and faithful service, for 41 years at £16 a year. The lessees will

---

[1] Instituted 9 June, rector 1523–9: *Reg. Bothe*, 335, 343.
[2] Above, **407, 425**.
[3] MS. *1522* in arabic.

(a) [f. 133v.] pay 20s. towards the expenses of the prior and convent once a year when they come to Ludlow [Salop.] to hold court at Stanton or to transact business at Ludlow,

(b) provide food, beds, hay, straw, provender and other necessities at Stanton for the cellarer, steward and understeward, their servants and their horses twice a year or at other times when they come to hold courts and leets and to superintend the manor,

(c) collect rents of assize there and render account of the rents and of the rectory to the prior's auditor at the Llanthony exchequer yearly within two months of the feast of St. John the Baptist [24 June], paying the sums due on their account as determined by the auditor and receiving an allowance of 3s. 4d. for collecting such rents and other profits and for serving in the office of bailiff[1] and

(d) supply oil and other expenses to keep a lamp burning in Stanton church at the usual times.

12 Sept. 11 Hen. VIII [1519].

[The following entry is inserted here on an extra half leaf.]

455. William Heynes's bond in £40. 6 Nov. 14 Hen. VIII [1522]. [In Latin except as follows.]

The condicion of this obligacion is suche, that if the within bounden William Heynes brynge and fynde 2 sufficient men any day within this 2 yeres next comyng aftur the date within writton to be bounden by obligacion in £40 sterlinge for hym & Margaret his wife [and] Richard and Olyver the children of them, so that they and everych of them shall holde, performe & kepe all and singler covenaunts and condicions specified in a peire of indentures made betweixt the within named prior, convent and there successors, the date of which indenture ben the 12th day of Septembr in the 11th yere of the reinge of Kynge Henry the VIIIth, that this present obligacion to be voyde, otherwise to stande in his full strength and vertu.

[f. 134, which contained the greater part of entry **456**, was a half sheet retained by a stub in the binding and is lost. Only a default clause of the entry survives on f. 135 but the parties, the property and the date are supplied from **457**.]

456. [f. 135] Lease [to Thomas and Alice Symes and their children Thomas, William, John, Elizabeth, Margery and Joan of the site of Quedgeley manor.[2] 28 Sept. 1522].

457. Stock delivered to Thomas and Alice Symes and their children Thomas, William, John, Elizabeth, Margery and Joan as lessees of the site of Quedgeley

---

[1] William was still bailiff in 1535: *Valor Eccl.* ii. 429.

[2] The lease probably marks the completion of a newly built house called the farmer's place which was mentioned in 1538 and may partly survive in Quedgeley Manor Farm: above, pp. xxii–xxiii.

manor (*firmariis de scitu manerii de Queddisley*). The stock is to be restored or its value repaid, at the prior's choice, at the end of the lease. 28 Sept. 14 Hen. VIII [1522].

12 qr. of wheat, 12 qr. of pulse and 12 qr. of barley, not valued.

12 oxen worth 15s. each.

2 corn wagons with iron bound wheels and 6 chains and 6 yokes with bows belonging to the wagons (*plaustra garbalia*[1] *cum rotis ferreis ligatis unacum 6 cathenis [et] 6 iugis cum arcubus eisdem plaustris*[2] *pertinentibus*) worth 14s. each.

10 wagon-loads of hay, [not] valued.

12 a. of demesne fallow, thrice ploughed (*warecte et rebinate*).

4 a. manured (*compostate*).[3]

[Cancelled]

458. Lease to John son of John Hoskyns and to his mother Margaret Jones of

(a) two messuages[4] with land and meadow at Monkton [in Llanwarne, Herefs.] for 60 years at 52s. 2d. a year and

(b) tithes of the prior's demesne in Monkton and Llanwarne[5] for 60 years at 26s. 8d. a year.

29 Sept. 1522.

This indentur made in the fest of Seint Michel tharchaungel the 14 yere of the reinge of Kynge Henry the VIII betwix Edmonde, lorde priour of Lanthony beside Gloucester & the convent of the same of that one partie and John Hoskyns late of the parish of Mounketon and Lanwaren and Margaret Jones mother to the said John of that other partie witnessyth that the seide Edmonde, priour, and convent by theis presents have covenaunted, grauntid, dimised and to ferme lette to the seide John and Margaret all there tenements and mes[suag]es that one Thomas Hoskyns and John Hoskyns, father to the seid John Hoskyns, late hilde and occupied in the [f. 135v.] *towne of Mounketon with dyverse parcels of lande, that is to sey*

2 clouses lyenge to the forseide mes[suag]es,

one medowe callid Seint John's Walle medowe,

3 acres of arrable lande called the Bery Croft,

one felde lyeng betwixt Bery Croft and Portwey called Myll Furlonge,[6]

one closse called Colverhouse Furlonge,[7]

---

[1] MS. *plaustratas grarbiles.*

[2] MS. *plaustratis.*

[3] MS. *composcantis.*

[4] The messuages are distinguished at the end of the penultimate paragraph. One of them, probably Upper Monkton Farm, had been let in 1510 to the elder John Hoskyns with Mone Hill, Gorste Close and 11 plots as listed here from Wilmaston to Hunt Hill inclusive: above, **202**.

[5] *Recte* in Monkton only, as described in 1535 when Hoskyns still held them: *Valor Eccl.* (Rec. Com.), ii. 426.

[6] Probably named from a mill site at SO 493266 among earthworks of a deserted village plotted by the Ordnance Survey.

[7] Alias Pigeonhouse Field around SO 492268: *Herefs. Field-Name Survey, Llanwarne*, 8.

another croft callid Yate Furlonge,
a felde lyeng betwixt Yate Furlonge & Portwey callid Hey Felde,[1]
a closse callid Watt's Furlonge,
an acre of lande lyenge beside the crosse callid Adam's Crosse and
one feld lyenge betwixt Pendecoyt and Caudenas Broke callid Nether Felde,[2]
one closse callid Daygoodis Hill,
another felde lyenge betwixt Holowey and Ruggewey callid Mone Hill,
a closse callid Gorste Closse,
an acre of lande callid Harpe Acre[3] *lyenge beside Gorste Closse,*
one acre of mede callid Meredithes Yarde,
halfe an acre of medowe callid Hampton's Mede,
halfe an acre of lande belongyng to the seid half acre mede and
one acre of mede callid Wilmaston,
one feld lying betwixt the mes[suag]e and the Portwey callid Litle Felde,
one acre of mede lying at Decon's Crosse,
2 acres of mede callid the Littlefelde Medowe,
one felde callid Henry Felde and one acre of mede lying to the same,
one crofte callid Parke Furlonge,
one closse callid Wente Closse,
one closse callid Caudinans and extendyth to the crosse callid Merywalle Crosse,
one felde callid Wethibed Feld lying betwixt Harold's Wey and Caudinans Broke,
halfe an acre mede lyinge in the same felde,
one felde callid Hunt Hill [and] one acre lande lying above the Hunt Hill
with all there appurtynaunces.

And also the seid priour & convent by theis presents covenauntith, grauntith, dimisith and to ferme lettith to the forseid John and Margaret all there tuthynge [i.e. tithes] of all there demayns in the lordeshippe of Monketon and Lanwaren as one Sir Thomas Weere there late hadde and occupied.

To have and to holde the forseid tenements, lands, mes[suag]es, medowes, crofts and the tuthynge afforeseide with the premisses to the forseide Jhon and Margaret for the terme of 60 yeres if they live so longe or one of them 2 lyve so longe, yeldyng and payng yerely for the seide tenements, mes[suag]es, lands, medowes [and] crofts with thappurtenaunces to the seid priour and convent and to there successors 52s. 2d. sterlynge at 2 termes in the yere, that is to sey at the fest of thannunciacion of Oure Lady 26s. 1d. and at the fest of Seint Michell tharchaungell 26s. 1d. by equall porcions; and also payng yerely for the forseide tuthynge at the fest of Seint Michel tharchaungel 26s. 8d.

And also the seid John & Margaret covenauntith and grauntith by theis presents to kepe all maner of reparacions of the seid tenements and mes[suag]es with other

---

[1] Around SO 492271: ibid.
[2] Around SO 491259 E. of *Pendecoyt* alias Pendiggott: ibid.
[3] Now Homelands at SO 483263: ibid. p. 9.

the premisses on there owne proper costs & charge duryng the forseid terme. And the seid Jhon & Margaret or one of them being occupier of the premisses shall make sute to the courte of the seid priour & convent at Monketon & Lanwaren as often as it shall chaunce any courte there to be holden duryng the terme afforeseid. And the seid John & Margaret the occupier or occupiers of the premisses to pay at his or there dicesse for the one mes[suag]e the best beest and for the other 6s. 8d. of lawfull money of Englonde.

Also the seid Edmonde, priour, and convent by theis presents covenauntith & grauntith to the seid John and Margaret that if it fortune the forseid John to take [a wife] and to have a childe, that then the forseid prior and convent by theis presents covenauntith & grauntith the seid John & Margaret uppon there resonable request made to the forseid priour & convent or to there successors for an indenture under [f. 136] the covent sele to be hade to hym, hys wyfe and chylde after the purporte & effecte of this present indenture, that the seyde prior, covent & ther successurs within a quarter of a yere nexte after the seyde request made shal make a grante by there indentore under the covent s[e]ale to the seyde Jhon, his wyfe & childe by there ryght names suche as the seyde John shall name, & lymite al the premisses for the ende and terme that then shal be of the seyde 60 yeres yf they lyve so longe or on of them 3 lyve so longe, or else the rent reservyd on this present lese to cesse tyll the tyme that the seyde indenture under there covent seale to be made & delyverid accordynge to the premisses, and at the delyverance of the newe indenture to delyvere the arrerage of the rent and also this present indenture to the handdys of the seyde prioure & covent or to there successurs. And also the seayde Johon & Margaret to be at the costs and

[Space is left in the MS. for the missing final clauses.]

459. [f. 136v.] Grant to Richard Warnecombe,[1] for good counsel and faithful service[2] (*pro bono consilio et fideli servicio suo nobis et monasterio nostro impensis et postea impendendis*), of 20s. yearly rent for life from land and tenements at Widemarsh Moor in Hereford, with payment of 1d. as livery of seisin (*nomine possessionis et seisine*). 15 Feb. 15 Hen. VIII [1524].

---

[1] d. 1547; commissioner for subsidy in Herefs. 1515, town clerk of Hereford by 1518, mayor there 1525 and 1540, M.P. for Herefs. 1529–42, escheator of Herefs. and the marches 1532–3 and 1543–5 and J.P. for Herefs. 1538–47: *Hist. of Parl., Commons 1509–58*. By 1535 understeward to the bishop of Hereford, steward to the dean and chapter and nine prebendaries there, steward of Wigmore Abbey and Aconbury Priory (both Herefs.) and the Herefs. properties of Great Malvern Priory (Worcs.), and auditor of Dore Abbey and Clifford and Wormsley Priories (all Herefs.): *Valor Eccl.* (Rec. Com.), iii, *passim.* Parishioner of All Saints in Hereford, lord of Ivington (in Leominster), Canon Bridge (in Madeley), Yatton and Pixley and from 1540 of Lugwardine and owner of land in Hereford, Ledbury, Coddington, Colwall, Eastnor, Yarkhill, Weston Beggard, Mordiford, Bullingham, Credenhill and Kingstone (all Herefs.): *Hist. of Parl., Commons 1509–58*; P.R.O. PROB 11/32, f. 19v.
[2] As bailiff of the prior's Widemarshmoor manor: *Valor Eccl.* ii. 428.

460. Appointment of the priory's servant John Asten to the offices of refectorer and launderer, viz. launderer of the refectorer's linen cloths and of articles of clothing, both of linen and other, belonging to the convent (*lavatoris pannorum liniorum pertinencium refectorio nostro predicto ac omnium et singulorum ornamentorum vestimentorum pannorum liniorum et aliorum ornamentorum pertinencium conventui nostro monasterii predicti*),[1] these being offices formerly held by William Paty. In case of illness he may serve by deputy if the prior approves. He will receive

(a) 20s. a year paid half-yearly,

(b) a priory yeoman's gown whenever the prior gives livery and

(c) broken bread and victuals left in the refectory after dinner.

[f. 137] In case of default he may distrain upon the prior's tenement in Southgate Street, Gloucester, where Thomas Bell lives now (*modo inhabitat*) and John Fawkener lived formerly.[2] 12 Mar. 15 Hen. VIII [1524].

461. Appointment of the priory's servant John Crosse as keeper of a rabbit warren[3] at Newark in the parish of Hempsted, receiving

(a) 26s. 8d. a year paid quarterly,

(b) a priory yeoman's gown and tunic whenever the prior gives livery,

(c) meals to be taken outside the monastery, viz. a dish of meat, fish or dairy produce daily according to the day, like that served to the shepherd and others, seven small loaves weekly, like those served to yeomen[4] in the monastery hall, 2 gal. of better ale and 5 gal. of middling ale weekly and victuals at meal times, like those received by yeomen waiters in the monastery hall, and

(d) tithes of Arland meadow by the Severn [in Hempsted][5] now held by John Sysemore, to hold for 5s. a year.

He will not pasture draught-animals in the warren. The prior reserves pasture there for his own sheep and beasts and also reserves apples, pears, other fruit and wood, including large firewood except rotten sticks. The appointee, by self or deputy, will

---

[1] As prescribed in Cardinal Wolsey's rules, which forbade employment of a laundress: Wilkins, *Concilia*, iii. 685.

[2] Cf. below, **462**.

[3] Surveyed in 1535 as *Conyngarth orchard* and in 1630 as a conyger of 6 a.: *Valor Eccl.* (Rec. Com.), ii. 430; *Inquisitions post mortem for Glos.* 1625–36 (Index Lib. 1893), 128. Mapped *c.* 1790 as occupying a high plateau at Newark and in 1882 as a sub-rectangular banked enclosure of 13 a. containing 7 long mounds irregularly disposed: Glos. R.O. D134/P8; Ordnance Survey 1:2500, Glos. xxx. 2 (all edns.).

[4] The writer of the register may have put *serviuntur* twice in error for *servientes*, in which case the dish was received by the shepherd and other servants and the loaves were received by yeomen waiters.

[5] Around SO 809168: Glos. R.O. GDR/T1/99.

(a) plant hedges, both quick and dead, and scour ditches as necessary at the warren,

(b) sweep and keep clean yards and walks there,

(c) make and maintain gins to catch weasels, birds of prey, dogs, cats and other wild animals,

(d) not give away rabbits without permission and

(e) work faithfully to increase the rabbits.

[No date]

Omnibus Christo fidelibus ad quos presens scriptum pervenerit Edmundus Forest Dei paciencia prior domus et ecclesie Beate Marie Lanthonie iuxta Gloucestriam et eiusdem loci conventus salutem in Domino sempiternam. Sciatis nos prefatum priorem et conventum unanimi nostro assensu et concensu dedisse, concessisse et hoc presenti scripto confirmasse Iohanni Crosse servienti nostro pro suo bono, fideli et laudabili servicio nobis impenso et postea impendendo quoddam officium custodis warenni cunicularii nostri apud Novum Edificium nostrum situatum infra parochiam de Hemstyd in comitatu ville Gloucestrie predicte. Habendo, tenendo, occupando et exercendo officium predictum prefato Iohanni Crosse a data presencium ad terminum vite sue temporalis, et recipiendo annuatim de nobis prefato priori et successoribus nostris pro exercicio, occupacione ac diligenti custodia officii predicti, necnon pro fideli servicio suo (ad terminum vite sue) nobis impendendo, viz. summam 26s. 8d. legalis monete Anglie ad 4 anni terminos, scilicet ad festa Sancti Iohannis Baptiste, Sancti Michaelis Archangeli, Nativitatis Domini et Annunciacionis Beate Marie per equales porciones solvendam, ac unam togam et unam tunicam de liberatura nostra, viz. de secta valectorum nostrorum, quociens aliquam liberaturam generalem servientibus nostris nos dare et distribuere contingit.

Concessimus eciam prefato Iohanni Crosse unum corradium, scilicet victus, panis et cervisie, septimanatim per annum extra monasterium nostrum capiendum et recipiendum in forma sequente, viz. qualibet die unum ferculum victuale, viz. carnis vel piscis vel lacticinii sicut dies requirit et sicut bercarius et alii serviuntur, et qualibet septimana septem minores panes prout valecti nostri serviuntur in aula monasterii nostri, ac septem lagenas cervisie, viz. duas de meliore et quinque de [f. 137v.] mediocri[1] cervisia, ac victum tociens quociens ad debitas horas venerit sicut alii valecti nostri in aula monasterii nostri predicti servientes percipere solent, habendo et percipiendo dictum corrodium panis et cervisie ac victum prefato Iohanni Crosse a data precencium usque ad terminum vite sue temporalis. Concessimus eciam dicto Iohanni Crosse totam decimam nostram unius prati iacentis in quodam campo vocato Ardelond prope Sabrinam modo in tenura Iohannis Sysemore sub redditu per annum 5s. ad terminum vite sue temporalis duraturam.

---

[1] MS. *mediocre.*

Proviso semper quod [nec] dictus Iohannes Crosse nec aliquis alius nomine suo adducet seu intromittet aliquam averiam suam infra septa et limites dicti cunicularii ad pascendum ibidem, sed pasturam tocius cunicularii nostri nobis et successoribus nostris pro bidentibus et aliis averibus nostris ibidem pascendam omnino excipimus et reservamus, exceptis eciam et nobis ac successoribus nostris omnino reservatis omnibus pomis, piris ac omnimodis generibus fructuum infra et extra dictum cunicularium crescencium. Preterea excipimus et ad usum nostrum semper reservamus omnimoda ligna ibidem crescencia, necnon et omnia focalia maiora tam viva quam mortua, exceptis minoribus focalibus vocatis 'le rottyn sticks', que dicto Iohanni Crosse per presentes damus et concedimus.

Et pro omnibus predictis dicto Iohanni Crosse in forma predicta a nobis concessis prefatus Iohannes Crosse concedit dicto priori, conventui et successoribus suis quod per se vel per sufficientem deputatum suum plantabit et faciet omnes sepes tam vivas quam mortuas tociens quociens opus fuerit, necnon et fossas eiusdem cunicularii escurabit et mundabit quandocumque necesse fuerit, scopabit eciam ac munde et honeste servabit omnes areas et deambulatoria infra dictum cunicularium existencia. Concedit eciam per presentes quod per se vel per sufficientem deputatum suum faciet et reparabit singulis anni temporibus quociens necesse fuerit infra et extra dictum cunicularium existentes omnes muscipulas viz. 'le gynnis' ad capiendum mustelas, miluos, canes, murilegos et alias feras. Nec dabit alicui persone aliquem cuniculum de dicto cuniculario absque licencia dictorum prioris et conventus prius petita et obtenta, sed cuniculos ibidem existentes et postea existuros[1] fideliter pro posse suo semper augmentare studebit et laborabit, et hoc sub pena forisfaciendi hunc statum suum. In cuius rei testimonium [etc.].

462. [f. 138] Lease to Thomas Bell of Gloucester, capper,[2] and his wife Joan of two

---

[1] MS. *existendos.*

[2] Later Sir Thomas (1486–1566); sheriff of Gloucester 1523, 1527 and 1530, alderman from 1531, mayor 1536, 1544 and 1554, M.P. for the borough 1539, 1545–53 and 1554, knighted 1547, J.P. for Glos. 1554: *Hist. of Parl., Commons 1509–58*; *V.C.H. Glos.* iv. 376. Employer of 300 workers in 1538: *L. & P. Hen. VIII*, xiii (1), p. 548. In 1539–44 he paid £1,113 for former monastic property in Gloucester, Staunton-by-Corse, Leigh, Norton, Ulting (Essex) and Hatfield Peverell (Essex) including Gloucester Blackfriars, which he took as his dwelling and drapery house, and 123 properties in Gloucester from the estate of Llanthony Priory: *L. & P. Hen. VIII*, xiv (1), p. 590; xvii, p. 265; xviii (2), pp. 51–2; xix (2), pp. 82–3; *V.C.H. Glos.* iv. 290. In 1548 he contributed to a purchase of chantry property in seven counties for £1,297: *Cal. Pat.* 1548–9, 40–4. He gave in trust four local properties in 1542 for repairing Westgate bridge and Over causeway and another 29 in 1562 for repairing Lower Southgate Street, relieving the poor and supporting his foundation of St. Kyneburgh's hospital: Glos. R.O. GBR/B2/2, ff. 24–5; *14th Rep. Com. Char.* (1826), 17–21.

newly built tenements[1] in which John Fawkener[2] formerly lived opposite the pillory [in Southgate Street, Gloucester], by the tenement of John Locksmyth, *corveser* [i.e. cordwainer] on one side and the lane leading to *Gorre Lane*[3] on the other, for 41 years at £3 2s. 8d. a year. The lessees will maintain the tenements and the pavement opposite them[4] and will surrender at the end of the term as standards the fittings which they have bought from John Fawkener, namely glass windows, a buttery with shelves, tables and embroidered cloths and paving in the wool house (*fenestras vitriatas ibidem iam existentes et promptuarium, Anglice 'a botery', cum 'shelves', 'bourdes' et pannis pictis cum omnibus rebus dicto promptuario pertinentibus, ac eciam dimittent omnia et singula paviamenta iam existencia in 'le wollehouse'*). The Annunciation 15 Hen. VIII [25 Mar. 1524].

463. [f. 138v.] Manumission of John Bishope,[5] neif of Quedgeley (*Quedesley*), and his issue [as **164** above]. 18 May 16 Hen. VIII [1524].

464. Lease to Thomas ap Yeuan, chaplain, of tithes of corn and hay with revenues, emoluments, oblations and other tithes both great and small belonging to the prior as rector of Ro[w]lston[e] and Llancillo [Herefs.], to hold for life at 13s. 4d. a year. He or his deputy will administer sacraments and celebrate divine service and masses in the two churches, [f. 139] pay dues and maintain the chancels.[6] If he neglects priestly duties and is so reported to the bishop of St. David's (*sic quod publica vox et fama coram domino episcopo Menevensi seu ministris suis inde fiant*) the prior may evict him. The lease takes effect only on the death of Philip [   ] the present incumbent. 9 June 16 Hen. VIII [1524].

---

[1] Nos. 16–18 Southgate Street, built in 1442–55 and used as Bell's residence: *Glouc. Rental 1455*, 7; cf. P.R.O. C 115/73, f. 44 (42) no. 91; above, **460**. Bell entertained there in 1536 the alderman of the Steelyard and other merchants from London and the Baltic: *L. & P. Hen. VIII*, xii (1), p. 139. He owned the freehold from 1539 to 1555 and let the property to Thomas Pury, mercer and mayor 1550 and 1560: *L. & P. Hen. VIII*, xiv (1), p. 590; *Cal. Pat. 1555–7*, 211; cf. Fosbooke, *Glouc.* 208–9. Later residents included Luke Garnons, draper and mayor 1570, 1586 and 1600 and Luke Nourse, mercer and mayor 1644 and 1646: *Glouc. Rental 1455*, 126; P.R.O. PROB 11/342, f. 72v.; cf. Fosbrooke, *Glouc.* 209; *V.C.H. Glos.* iv. 376–7.

[2] Alias Falconer (d. 1545), likewise a capper and a major employer, resident in the parish since 1513, sheriff 1515, alderman from 1519 and mayor 1525, 1534 and 1542: *V.C.H. Glos.* iv. 53, 375; Glos. R.O. GBR/B2/1, f. 226v.; Fosbrooke, *Glouc.* 208. He moved to nos. 20–4 Eastgate Street where he bought the freehold in 1543 and bequeathed it to the city together with half the suburban manor of Wotton Court, his cash bequests including £90 for repairing roads and bridges in Gloucester and Chepstow: Glos. R.O. GBR/J1/1940–3; GBR/B2/2, f. 128v., cf. GBR/ J4/12, plans 42–4; *V.C.H. Glos.* iv. 398; *Glouc. Corp. Rec.* pp. 435–7.

[3] i.e. Cross Keys Lane leading to Bull Lane: *V.C.H. Glos.* iv. 365.

[4] From the frontage to the middle of the street, as required by an order of 1473: ibid. 265.

[5] Owner of goods worth £13 15s.: *Military Survey of Glos 1522*, 191.

[6] The wording (cf. above, **113**, **274**) shows that the cure was a chaplaincy and the churches were chapels, probably dependent on the prior's adjacent rectory of Clodock (Herefs.).

465. [f. 139v.] Anthony Welsshe's homage for the manor of Netheridge in Quedgeley, rendered at Quedgeley manor house on 31 May 1524.

Memorandum that Anthoni Welsshe gentilmon, son & heire off William Welsshe[1] late off Queddisley in [the] counte off the towne off Gloucester gentilmon, the Tewseday next before the fest off Corpus Christi in the yere off the raigne off Kynge Henry the VIIIth the 16th came in his propere person before lord Edmunde prior off Lanthony besidis Gloucester to the scite place of his manner off Queddisley in the parlour above the hall off the scite and there made his homage to the foreseid lorde prior for his manor lands and tenements callid Netherrugge in manner and forme as hereafter folowithe. First the seid prior sate in his cheyar in the foreseid parlour and the said Anthony kneled bytwixe the leggs of the foresaid lorde prior and held his hands wyntely[2] upp betwixt the hands of the said prior and said thes wordes subscribid.

> *I become your mon from this day fortheward off lyff and off member and off orthely honour and to you and your successours shal be feythefull and troue, and feythe to you and your successours I shall bere for my manor of Netherrugge lyenge within your lordischipp off Queddisley in the foresaid counte off the towne off Gloucester wiche I knowlege to hold off you in fee as parcell of your foresaid maner of Queddisley by service off one hoole knyghtes fee saving the ferthe [i.e. fealty] that I owe to the kynge oure soveraigne lorde and other lordis that I hold certen lands off as well as off you.*

And then the said Antony rose upp and kyssed his lorde and then and there paid to the lorde prior an 100s. for his relif and to his chamburleyn 6s. 8d. accordinge to an old custom used. And after this so done the said Antony made and didd his fealte to his lorde leynge and settinge his hand uppon a booke seynge in this maner this.

> *Here ye, my lorde, that I shal be to you feythfull and true, and feithe to you shall I bere for my maner lands and tenements lyenge in Queddisley aforesaid in the counte off the towne off Gloucester called Netherrugge, and truly to pay to you and to your successours al customes, duties and fines at times assigned that I owght to doo, & a lb. of peper yerly to be paid, so Godde me helpe & al seints.*

And then the said Anthony kissed the booke. And al this was done in the parlor aforesaid the day and yere abovesaid in the presence of Sir John Gloucester, Sir William Baryngton,[3] Henry Frensche gentilmon, Edwardus Brugge, Thomas Toothe, Thomas Nurce,[4] Johannes Reynolds & Thomas Symys with diverse other.

---

[1] Lords of Woolstrop in Quedgeley: *V.C.H. Glos.* x. 218–9.

[2] Probably for *wynely* or *winly*, 'pleasantly': *O.E.D.*

[3] Two canons of Llanthony: above, **335**; *Trans. B.G.A.S.* lxiii. 136.

[4] One of the name lived in St. Michael's parish, Gloucester, and another at Quedgeley owning goods worth £6: Glos. R.O. GBR/B2/1, f. 226v.; Glos. muster roll 1539, P.R.O. E 101/59/9; *Military Survey of Glos. 1522*, 192.

466. [f. 140] Lease to John Perman, chaplain, of Tillington chapel [in Burghill, Herefs.] with the lands, tenements, meadow and pasture belonging to it and the pasturage of Burghill churchyard for life at 20s. a year [on the same terms as in **147** above]. 16 June 15 Hen. VIII [1523].

467. Bond of John Perman late of Gloucester, clerk, in £100. 1 Aug. 16 Hen. VIII [1524]. [In Latin except as follows.]

[f. 140v.] *The condicion of this obligacion ys suche, that yef the within bounden Sir John Perman surrender all his lesse & title that he hathe off certen lands & tenements & tihies[1] that he hathe in Tyllyngton in the parisshe of Boroughill in the counte of Yereford with the covent seale whiche he hathe of the within named prior & covent for termes of yeres, at suche tyme as the seid Sir John Perman shal be required by the within named priour or [any] of his successours if any variaunces, strives or debets shall chaunce hereafter for the seid lesse, so that the seyde stryves, debats or variaunces shulde be in any wyse prejudiciall or hurfell to the house of our Lady of Lanthony wythein specifyede in tyme to cum, that then this presente obligacion be had for nought, otherwyse to stonde in full strengt & affecte.*

468. Letter from John Babington [Knight Commander of the Hospitallers] on 2s. owed at Dinmore [*recte* Bolstone, Herefs.].[2] London, 19 Nov. [1523].

Littera Iohannis Babington pro 2s. in Dynmore.
    Mastres Locherd,[3] I commende me to yow, and here is the priour of Lanthony that shulde have yerely 2s. paid by yere out of Dynmore, which is unpaid dyverse yeres. Ye be bound, and soo was your husband, to discharge all out rents, and if ye pay not at syghte of this same without any farther delay I can no lesse do but put your obligacion in sute. And I marvell ye sende not uppe as muche money as ye were bounde & promest to doo at your last beynge in London. Faile ye not to sende this same at this Candulmas as ye entende to avoide farther displeysure, & Jhesus kepe yow. By your lover Jhon Babyngton, Jhe. maria iiire,[4] die vero Novembris 19[5] att London.

469. Another letter from the same on the same. London, 23 Nov. [1523].

To my luffynge frende Alexander Haworth, fermor of Dynmore, this be delivered.
    Alysaunder, I grete you well, marvelinge gretely ye pay not the prior of Lanthony 2s. wich hath ben acustomed to be paide forthe of Dynmore. Moreover ye say that ye

---

[1] i.e. *tyes*, 'closes': *O.E.D.*
[2] Cf. above, **424–5**, **453**; on Babyngton, below, **469**.
[3] Eleanor Lochard (d. 1527) of Dinmore: *Hereford Probates 1407–1581*, 209, 231. She and Alexander Haworth evidently preceded Margaret Rotsey who held the manors of Dinmore and Garway from the Hospitallers for £96 a year at the Dissolution: W. Rees, *History of the Order of St. John of Jerusalem in Wales and the Welsh Border* (Cardiff, 1947), 89.
[4] Unexplained.
[5] MS. *19* in arabic.

have made counte with me, which is contrarie. Wherefore in any wise se ye faile not to be here at Candlemas nexte & bringe your accompte with you, otherwise ye shall farther ocupie [i.e. be busied]. *And so fare ye well. Frome London the 23 day of Novembre, your frende John Babyngton, Knight Commander.*

Ye reste every yere in debts, & therefore cum uppe and make a clere rekonyng. Faile not of the same.

[There is no f. 141, and f. 142 recto is blank.]

470. [f. 142v.] *The copy of the supplicacion made by the priour of Lanthony to the king's commissioners in Irlande agenst the priour of Molyngar* [i.e. Mullingar, Westmeath] *for the pension of Donboyne* [i.e. Dunboyne, Meath].[1] [1521.]

Grevously complanyth unto youre discrete wisdomes youre daily oratour Edmonde Forest, priour of the house of oure Blessid Lady of Lanthony besidis Gloucestur in Englande, that whereas your complaynante and all his predecessors priours of the seide house hath ben seisid of an annuell rente of 20 mark yerely goynge out of the parsonage of Seint Petur of Donboyne by the handis of the priours of God of Molingar, parsones of the seide Seint Petur's of Donboyne, fro the tyme that no mannys mynde can remembre to the contrary, til now of late one Jhon Petytte, now priour of the seide house of God of Molingar, and one Melioris Petytte and Sir Thomas Dillon, predecessours of the seide Jhon and priouris of the seide house, never paide the seide anuell rente of 20 mark fully nor truly frome the seconde yere of the reinge of our sovereinge lorde Kynge Henry that now is [1510–11] *unto this day, and so restyth behynde to your forseide complaynant 200 marks of laufull money of Irland of the arrerage of the seide anuell rente of 20 mark, and oftentymes syns your forseide complaynant by his proctours in Irland did require the seid Jhon Petytte, now priour of the seid house, to pay youre forseide complaynante the seide 200 mark with the seide yerely rente of 20 mark; he that to do utturly refusith, contrary to all ryghte and goode consciens.*

The premisses therfor tendurly considerid, pleasith it your discrete wisdomes to take suche ordre and direccion in the premisses so that your forseid complaynante for lack of payment of the seide 200 mark with the seide rente have no cause farther to complayne. And your seide complaynante shall pray to God for your discrete wisdomes longe to endure.

471. *The answere of the priour of Molingar to the seide complaynte.*

Thereunto the seide priour seith that the mater comprised within the seide bill is mater determinable by wey of accion of the commyn lawe, whereunto he prayith that he may be remitted etc. And if he be put to answer, he seith that the seide Edmonde, priour of Lanthony, ne all his predecessours priours of the same have not be seasid

---

[1] A benefice without cure (*beneficium simplex*) awarded by arbitration in 1233 to the priors of Llanthony in Wales, who obtained judgement against the priors of Mullingar for arrears in 1402 and *c.* 1406: *Irish Cart. Llanth.* pp. 72, 135–8.

of the same anuell rente of 20 mark [f. 143] *goynge out of the parsonage of Donboyne by the hands of the seid priour of Molyngar out of tyme of mynde of any man to the contrary in maner and forme as he hath alegid in his seyd bill of complaynte, the which mater he will prove as your discrete wisdomes will awarde.*

And for the declaracion of the concernynge an anuell rente of 20 mark yerely whiche the prioures of Lanthony before this tyme clamyth to have out of the seide parsonage, [it] is by composicion and not by prescripcion, which mater is not complayned of by his seid byll. But as to that, the seid priour of Molyngar seith that by a frendly agrement made betwene the seid parties, considerynge there povertie and for other dyverse consideracions, it was agreed that the seid priour of Lanthony shulde have no more but 10 mark yerely, [which] they have payde and be redy to pay any arrerage thereof. And suche evidences and wryghtyngs as they had concernynge the premisses was burnyd whan the seide house was burnyd by Irishemen. And this is the true mater which shal be proved as your discrete wisdomes shall thynk goode.

472. *The replicacion of the priour of Lanthony to the seide answere.*

[He reiterates his claim to 20 marks a year and denies] *that the seid priour of Lanthony or any of his predecessours made any agrement with the seid priour of Molyngar or with any of his predecessours for any lesse sum. Which mater the seid priour is redy to prove as youre discrete wisdomes shall thynke necessary. Wherefore he prayith yow of remedy.*

473. The prior of Mullingar's recognizance, given *coram rege* in the Irish chancery, to implement the following decree or pay £100 to the prior of Llanthony and the latter's proctor of Duleek. 29 July 16 Hen. VIII [1524].

474. [f. 143v.] *The decre.* [29 July 1524.]

Memorandum that the 29 day of July in the 16 yere of the reinge of Kynge Henry the VIII before James Denton clerk, Sir Raufe Eggerton knyght and Anthony Fitzherberte, commissioners of our sovereinge lorde the kynge within this his lande of Irlande,[1] *and the hoole counseyl of the same, for the mater in variaunce betwene the priour of the house of our Blessid Lady of Lanthony in Englande, playntif, and the priour of the house of God of Molyngar in Irlande, defendant, hit is ordred and decreed by the seid commissioners & counseil that the seid prior of Molyngar & his successors shall pay yerely unto the seid prior of Lanthony and to his successors one yerely anuel rente of 20 marke of lauful money of Irlande goynge out of the parsonage of Seint Petur's of Donboyne as by the same priour of Lanthony before us*

---

[1] Commissioned in 1524 to pacify Ireland and to reconcile the earls of Kildare and Ormond, whose differences they composed on 28 July: *L. & P. Hen. VIII*, iv, p. 244. Denton (d. 1533) was dean of Lichfield, Fitzherbert, Kt. (1470–1538) justice of Common Pleas in England and Egerton the king's standard-bearer and constable of Chester: ibid. ii, pp. 141, 874; iv, p. 309; *D.N.B.*

*is duly proved, that is to sey 10 mark at the fest of All Seints nexte cummynge
[1 Nov.] and other 10 mark at the fest of Seint Peter ad vincula [1 Aug.] by evin
porcions to be paid at the hy aulter in the seide churche of Seint Peter of Donboyne
betwix the houres of 9 of the clock & 12 of the clock before noon of the seide days.*

*And also we decre that the seid priour of Molyngar & his successors shall pay
unto the seid priour of Lanthony for arrerage of the seid anuel rente leynge behynde
unpaid £40 of lauful money of Irland in maner & forme folowynge, that is to wit at
the seid fests of All Seints & Seint Peter 10 mark in the seid place & betwix the seid
houres by evin porcions until the seid sume of £40 be fully satisfied and paid. And
moreover we decre that whereas the seid priour of Lanthony hath forgevyn unto the
seid priour of Molyngar all the other arrerage amountynge unto the somme of £120,
that the seid priour of Molyngar shal be therof acquetyd & dischargid.*

Nomina commissionariorum et consiliariorum domini regis in Hibernia:[1] *H[ugh
Inge archbishop of] Dublin, G[eorge Cromer archbishop of] Armachan,*[2] *G[erald
Fitzgerald earl] of Kyldare, James Denton, Raufe Eggerton, Anthony Fitzherberte,
[John] Rawson priour,*[3] *P[atrick] Bremyngham justice,*[4] *Patrick White baron,
Richard Delahide justice, Sir B[artholomew] Dillon justice, Thomas Netturvile
justice.*[5]

475. *The decre made by the seid commissioners agenst Laurence Balarde of
Drogheda [Louth]. [6 Aug. 1524.]*

*Memorandum the 6 day of August in the 16 yere of the reinge of Kynge Henry the
VIII, we James Denton clerk, Sir Rauf Eggerton knyghte [and] Anthony Fitzherberte,
commissioners of our seid sovereinge lorde within his lande of* [f. 144] *Irlande, and
the king's councel of the same, for the mater in variaunce betwix Edmonde, prior of
the house of our Blessid Lady of Lanthony beside Gloucester, playntif, and Laurence
Balarde of Drogheda, defendant, for the ryghte, title and interest of an anuel rente of
19s. goynge out of a tenement with thappurtynances in Drogheda aforeseide.*

*It is decreed by us the seid commissioners and counsel that forasmuche as the seid
priour by goode substanciall evidence hath proved before us his ryght and [title] of
the seide anuel rente of 19s., that the seide Laurence & his [successors] shall yerly
pay or cause to be paid unto the seid priour and his successors the seide rente of
19s. at suche like days and fests as ben accustomed, unlesse the seid Laurence
brynge in before the seid counseil [or] 6, 5, 4 or 3 of them a sufficient discharge of*

---

[1] 'Names of the king's commissioners and councillors in Ireland.'
[2] i.e. Armagh.
[3] MS. *Mawson*. Rawson (d. 1547), created Viscount Clontarff 1541, prior of Hospitallers in
Ireland from 1511 and Treasurer of Ireland 1517–18, 1522–4 and from 1530: *D.N.B.*
[4] *Recte* Bermingham (d. 1532), chief justice of the King's Bench in Ireland 1513–32:
D.N.B.
[5] White was Baron of the Exchequer in Ireland, Delahide and Netturvile justices (and
Delahide later chief justice) of Common Pleas there and Dillon (d. 1533) justice (later chief
justice) of the King's Bench and chief remembrancer of the Exchequer there: *L. & P. Hen.
VIII*, iii, pp. 965–6; iv, pp. 244, 2357; vi, p. 411.

the predecessours of the seid priour under there covent seall before the fest of the
Nativite of Our Lorde nexte cummynge.

   Also we decre that the seid Laurence shall pay for the arrerage of the same rent
9s. of lauful Irish money to be paide this present day, and that the seid Laurence shal
be dischargid of al other arrerage due before the date hereof amountynge to the
somme of £28, and that this our decre be observed & kepte in every of the premisses
by the seid Laurence Balard uppon payne of £40 to be forfetid to the seid priour and
his successors.

   Nomina commissionariorum [*et consiliariorum*] *domini regis in Hibernia*:
H[*ugh Inge archbishop of*] *Dublin, James Denton, Raufe Eggerton, Anthony*
Fitzherberte, Sir N[*icholas St. Lawrence*] *lorde of Houth,*[1] *Sir Jo*[*hn*] *B*[*arnewall*]
lorde of T[*rimleston*],[2] *W*[*illiam Preston*] *vi*[*s*]*c*[*ount*] *of Gormanston,*[3] *P*[*atrick*]
Bermyngham justice, Richard [*Nugent*] *b*[*aron*] *of Delvyn,*[4] *Sir B*[*artholomew*]
Dillon justice, P[*atrick*] *Fynglas baron,*[5] *T*[*homas*] *Neturvile justice.*

476. Extracts from the Pipe Roll for 15 Hen. VIII [1523–4] under Gloucester
concerning discharge of poundage at the port of Bristol.[6]

   The prior of Llanthony owes 28s. 4d. poundage on goods and merchandise worth
£28 7s. 8d., viz. 287 yd. of Irish linen narrow cloth (*panni stricti*), ¾ of a linen *brode*
cloth, 14 hogsheads of salmon containing 10 pipes, 24 barrels of herring, 25 dozen
hake, 74 *lynge*, 2 red cloaks (*mantella rubea*) and 17 salt fish brought to the port of
Bristol in the year to Michaelmas 5 Hen. VIII [1513], [f. 144v.] but is discharged and
quit by a decision of the barons in a similar case noted by the Treasurer's
Remembrancer on roll no. 5 of the records of Michaelmas term 7 Hen. VIII [1515].[7]

   Similarly for 29s. poundage on imports [worth £29] in the year to Michaelmas 8
Hen. VIII [1516].

   Similarly for 43s. 4d. poundage on imports worth £43 6s. 8d. in the year to
Michaelmas 10 Hen. VIII [1518].

   Similarly for 48s. 4½d. poundage on imports worth £48 7s. 1½d. in the year to
Michaelmas 11 Hen. VIII [1519].

   Similarly for 23s. 9d. poundage on imports worth £23 15s. in the year to
Michaelmas 12 Hen. VIII [1520].

   [f. 145] Similarly for 43s. 10½d. poundage on imports worth £49 17s. 6d. [sic] in
the year to Michaelmas 13 Hen. VIII [1521].

---

[1] d. 1526, Lord Chancellor of Ireland 1509–13: *D.N.B.*

[2] d. 1538; justice of the King's Bench in Ireland from 1509, Vice-Treasurer there 1522–4,
Treasurer 1524–30 and Lord Chancellor 1534–8: *D.N.B.*

[3] d. 1532; Lord Deputy 1493 and Lord Justice of Ireland 1515: *Complete Peerage.*

[4] d. 1538; Lord Justice 1527 and acting Deputy of Ireland 1534: *D.N.B.*

[5] Alias Finglas, Chief Baron of the Exchequer of Ireland 1521–34 and chief justice of the
King's Bench there 1534–5: *L. & P. Hen. VIII*, iii, pp. 801, 888; *D.N.B.*

[6] i.e. poundage on imports unloaded at Gloucester, which was then included in the port of
Bristol: above, **396** n.

[7] A discharge for the year to Michaelmas 1514: above, **396**.

Similarly for 24s. poundage on imports worth £24 in the year to Michaelmas 14 Hen. VIII [1522].

[Signed] *per T. Warton.*

Continued [at **483**] below (*Require plus de hac materia scilicet pro anno 14 et 15 in quarto folio sequente ad tale signum +*).

477. [f. 145v.] Grant to Robert Wye Esq., for faithful service, and to his sons Thomas, Robert, William, Giles, Richard, John and Francis of the reversion of property at South Cerney now held for a term of 48 years by Richard and Joan Tryndar and their son William,[1] viz.

(a) the manor buildings with demesne land, meadow and pasture and

(b) great and small tithes on the premises

together with

(c) tithes of customary tenants,

(d) the *steward's chambre* on the manor site with a stable adjacent and

(e) rents of free and customary tenants

to hold for 60 years from the reversion at £8 13s. 4d. a year. The prior reserves to himself fines of lands and tenements, penalties, forfeits of chattels, heriots, *infangethefe, outefangethefe,* waifs, strays, amercements and other profits of the courts there. The lessees will

(a) provide food, beds, hay, straw and provender for the cellarer, steward and understeward, their servants and their horses when they come to hold courts and courts leet there and to transact business at Chirton [Wilts.] and Barton Stacey [Hants.],

(b) entertain the prior, his men and his horses overnight once a year when he comes to superintend his manors in the same three places and

(c) [f. 146] observe other conditions listed [as in **292** above].

13 Jan. 16 Hen. VIII [1525].

478. [f. 146v.] Presentation of Ralph Wenysley to the vicarage of Windrush vacant by the death of Thomas Flemynge. 31 Mar. 1525. [Abstact in MS.; cf. **39**]

479. Citation by Cardinal Wolsey in pursuance of powers granted him by papal bull.[2] Wolsey is reliably informed that, as recent priors of Llanthony have relaxed the rule, members of the community have put aside the fear of God and, both in dress and in conduct, are behaving less honourably than they should to the ruin of their souls, the horror of the church, the disgrace of their order, the dishonour of clerks and the derogation and scandal of all (*in animarum suarum perniciem, divine* [f. 147] *maiestatis offensam, religionis opprobrium ac clericorum inhonestatem malumque exemplum et scandalum plurimorum*). He therefore cites

[1] Cf. above, **292**.
[2] Cf. above, **386** n.

the prior, canons, clerks and servants (*ministros*) of the house to a visitation of the priory by his commissary general, chaplain and councillor John Alen, D.Cn. & C.L.,[1] canon and prebendary of Lincoln, on 28 March or within seven days before or after at Wolsey's convenience. Copies of their foundation charter and of grants of chantries, benefices, appropriations and privileges, with inventories of movable and immovable goods, are to be supplied to Wolsey's registrar. From Wolsey's house at Westminster, 5 Mar. 1524[/5].

480. [f. 147v.] Certificate acknowledging that the above was received on 7 March. 15 Mar. 1524[/5].

481. Grant to Thomas Berinton, gentleman,[2] John and Humphrey Parker of Barnwood, laymen, and their assigns of the advowson of Weobley (*Webley*) [Herefs.] for one turn. [f. 148] 9 Apr. 1525.

482. *The tityll of the prior of Lanthony to Jordanys Crofte* [Gloucester][3] *to be shewyd to my lorde* [abbot] *of Seynte Petor's of Gloucestor and Sir Edmonde Tame, knyghte.*[4]

Memorandum that there is a certen parcell of lande lyinge in the suburbs of Gloucester in the parische of Seinte Audoen of the same callid Jordanis Crofte, qui

---

[1] 1476–1534; fellow of Peterhouse, Cambridge, 1495–1503, proctor of Archbishop Warham at the Roman curia c. 1503–c. 1514, prebendary of Lincoln 1503–28, of Westbury-on-Trym from 1505 and of Southwell 1526–8, chancellor of Ireland 1528–32 and archbishop of Dublin 1529–34: Emden, *Biog. Reg. Oxon. to 1500.* For his service to Wolsey and a discussion of this entry cf. above, p. xxv.

[2] d. 1544; free tenant of a messuage and 160 a. from the prior's manor of Widemarsh Moor (Hereford), including land at Holmer, and owner of 4 burgages in Hereford, 84 a. at Larport in Mordiford and 58 a. in Bartestree (all Herefs.): P.R.O. C 142/71/107; cf. *Visit. Herefs. 1569,* 10.

[3] Of 4 acres, now Brunswick Square: P.R.O. C 115/73, f. 17 (15)v. Approached by a private entrance way, now Albion Street: ibid. f. 8 (6). Purchased in 1539 by Thomas Bell, who gave it to the borough in 1542 (for repairing Westgate bridge) as *Jorden's Close otherwise Gawdy Grene*: *L. & P. Hen. VIII,* xiv (1), p. 590; Glos. R.O. GBR/B2/2, f. 24v. Mapped as borough property 1731: ibid. GBR/J4/1, map 18. Developed as the site of Brunswick Square from 1822: *V.C.H. Glos.* iv. 165.

[4] 1470–1534; J.P. for Glos. 1499–34 and Wilts. 1525–34, sheriff of Glos. 1506 and 1524 and Knight of the Body from 1516; *List of Sheriffs* (List & Index Soc. ix); *Cal. Pat.* 1494–1506, 641; *L. & P. Hen. VIII,* i, p. 1537; ii, pp. 190, 299, 872; iii–v, *passim*; vii, p. 558. Bailiff of the seven hundreds of Cirencester, resident beside the bridge in Fairford, where he finished the church and in 1520 entertained the king: J. G. Joyce, *The Fairford Windows* (London, 1872), 17, 27, 30–2. Lessee of Fairford manor, lord of Harnhill and of Winson in Bibury and purchaser of the manors of Dowdeswell, Rendcomb (where he rebuilt the church), Nympsfield, Upton in Tetbury and Paunton's Court in Eastleach Turville: Joyce, op. cit. 39–40; *V.C.H. Glos.* vii. 31, 64, 75, 221, 227; xi. 265; Rudder, *Glos.* 414, 476, 576.

eam tenuit,[1] *whiche lande one Mile[s] de Bohun*[2] *somtyme erle of Hereforde and originall founder of the house of Lanthony gave unto the seide house in the firste foundacion off the same, what doth appere in matter of recorde by the charter or dede of the seide Milis gifte.*[3] *Whiche lande one Roger Tockenam and Richard [the] chappelen,*[4] *sonne of one Ernalde, hilde of the seide Mile[s] before his seide gift to the house of Lanthony. By colour whereof one Stephyne [the] taylor as nexte of kynde to the seide Richarde [the] chappelen pretendid a titull to the seide lande, as it is supposid. Howbeit in conclusion he relesid his titull of the seide parcell of lande unto the house of Lanthony as doth evidently appere by his dede of releese in parvo albo registro Ricardi Steymor folio 3.*[5]

   Whereupon the priour and convent of Lanthony beynge in peaseable possession of the seide lande put it out by leese or indentour to one Walter Glede[6] *for terme of his life for 12s. 10d. of yerely rente as it apperith by an indentour made the yere of our Lorde 1312 and in the black register of Richard Aure*[7] *folio 7. And after the time of the seide Walter Glede the seide lande was put to ferme at the same rente to one Roberte Brocthorpe, burges of Gloucester, for terme of 40 yere the 16 yere of Kynge Edwarde the III [1342–3] as it apperith by another indentour in the seide regestur folio 44 and also in the register of [Prior] William Pynbury folio 120. And after his terme and yeris the seide lande was put out by lease to one John Dagette, burges of Gloucester, for terme of 49 yere at the same rente as it apperith by another indentour made the 22 yere of Kynge Edwarde the III [1348–9] in the redde register of William Pynbury folio 168. And after the seide John Dagette it was dimised and put to ferme to one William Griffith, burges of Gloucester, for terme of 49 yeris at the seide rente of 12s. 10d. as it apperith by another indentour made the 37 yere of Kynge Edwarde the III [1363] feyre wrete in the grete white feodary of Lanthony the*

---

[1] '[called after] him who held it'.

[2] *Recte* Miles of Gloucester: cf. above, **7**.

[3] Dugdale, *Mon.* vi. 136, where the croft is not mentioned specifically but is presumed to be included in the parish (*parochia*) or parish land (*parochia terra*) previously given to St. Owen's church by Miles's ancestors, i.e. included among the plots (*terrule*) which St. Owen's held from Walter of Gloucester before 1095: *Camd. Misc.* xxii. 38.

[4] Prebendaries of St. Owen: above, **7**.

[5] 'in f. 3 of Richard Steymor's little white register' (a cartulary of property in Gloucester dated 1441), i.e. P.R.O. C 115/84, f. 3v., deed no. 12; also in C 115/75, f. 24v., deed no. 125. Canon Richard Steymor of Awre, who compiled that register in collaboration with the town renter Canon Robert Cole, may be the same person as Canon Richard Aure who was town renter shortly before: C 115/84, title page; C 115/73, f. 68 (66). He or another Richard Aure was cellarer in 1408–12: *Trans. B.G.A.S.* lxiii. 109–11. Stephen the tailor's deed is for 4 a. of arable land between land of William son of Jordan on both sides and is dated *c.* 1230 by the presence of Robert Pouleseye and William of the More as witnesses: cf. *Glouc. Corp. Rec.* pp. 123, 128, 152.

[6] Cf. Glede's Croft, a strip of land N. of Jordan's Croft and S. of the Butts: P.R.O. C 115/73, ff. 16–17 (14–15).

[7] This and the next two registers cited here are lost.

firste volume signo primo et folio 31.[1] *And after the seide William Griffith's terme the seide lande was put to ferme to one Water Sawndurs of Gloucester, bruer, for terme of 49 yeris,* [f. 148v.] *rente by yere 12s. 10d., as it apperith by another indenture made the 6 yere of Kynge Henry the V* [1418] *feyre registred in the register of Richard Aure folio 59 and also in the register of* [Prior] *John Wiche folio 126.*[2]

And after the seide Water Saundurs one John Ferrour and after hym one John Cooke[3] *father to Marget Fynche mother to Edwarde Fynche hilde the seide lande at will without indentour as it apperith by Robert Cole's register folio* [. . .][4] *in the time of Henry Dene prior of Lanthony. And then many yeris after the terme of the seide Walter Saunders one Thomas Smythe otherwise callid Thomas Fynche of Gloucester hilde the seide lande of the prior and covent of Lanthony at will without any writynge and his wife Marget after hym, payinge therefore yerly 6s. 8d., as it apperith by the seide priour's* [. . .]*rell*[5] *booke of parcells, and 16d. to the rentegetherer of Hempsted beside the tale of her gardens. Ferther to shewe that the priour and covent of the house of our Blessid Lady of Lanthony have be in peseable possession of the seide lande callid Jordanis Crofte and of the yerely rente of 12s. goyng out of the same, it doth evidently appere by dyverse books of accompte made in the accompts of the baly of Podismede in the reigne of Kynge Edward the III.*

[Signed:] *Willelmus abbas prefatus vidit et ultro prestabit ut vera testatur;*[6] *Edmundus Tame.*

483. [Extracts from the Pipe Rolls, continued from **476** above.]

(+) The prior of Llanthony owes 27s. 8d. poundage on goods and merchandise worth £27 13s. 4d. brought to the port of Bristol in the year to Michaelmas 15 Hen. VIII [1523] but is discharged and quit [as in **476**].

He also owes 21s. 10d. poundage on imports worth £21 17s. 4d. according to the account of John Bartilmewe, William Wyse and William Gudwyn, collectors of customs and subsidy in the port of Bristol, for the year to Michaelmas 16 Hen. VIII [1524] but is discharged and quit similarly.

---

[1] i.e. P.R.O. C 115/77, s. i no. 151. The croft then lay between land of Walter Glede and land of Agnes Glede and the rent was 12s. for the croft and 10d. for the entrance.

[2] Extant at the latter reference as a lease of the croft and the entrance, together with the second tenement in Southgate Street S. of the corner of Parliament Street, at rents of 27s 6d. payable to the town renter and 12s., reducing after four years to 10s., to the rent collector of Hempsted: cf. P.R.O. C 115/73, f. 16 (14)v. Walter Saunders later held a tenement within the block nos. 75–7 Southgate Street and was succeeded as brewer by William Saunders: ibid. f. 8 (6)v.; cf. above, **3(f)** n.

[3] Not John Cooke the mercer (d. 1528), who died childless: above, **239** & n., **290**.

[4] Number lost in torn margin.

[5] Word partly lost in torn margin.

[6] 'William [Parker], abbot, saw this and will willingly vouch that it may be taken as a true record'.

APPENDIX I:
ACCOUNTS OF THE PRIOR'S LESSEE AND BAILIFF AT PRESTBURY, 1481–2, 1482–3 AND 1485–6

Gloucestershire Record Office D1637/M26

484. Account of William Parkys, lessee of the demesne and parsonage of Prestbury (*Prestbery*), for the year to Michaelmas 22 Edw. IV [1482].

	£	s.	d.
Arrears from the last account	17	15	4
Farm of the demesne[1] as demised to Parkys 11 years ago for 20 years, including 6s. in lieu of 12 geese and 12 capons	4	6	0
Farm of the parsonage[2] as demised to Parkys 11 years ago for 19 years, together with 40s. for the portion of the dean and precentor of Hereford[3]	12	0	0
Sum due	34	0	16

Allowances	£	s.	d.
Storage of hay and corn while the tithe barn is ruined (*loco grangie decimalis in decasu existente*)		10	0
Assigned by the prior to John Comber from the dean's and precentor's portion		33	4
Repairs to a tenement lately Thomas Teynton's		9	6
8 wagon-loads of stone from Brockhampton quarry (*de quarera de Brokehampton*)[4] including carriage to *Sandeforde brug*[5] [in Cheltenham]		8	0
Tiling the church chancel, 2 days at 6d.			12
A gown		5	0
Parchment for writing the account			4
Sum allowed		67	2

---

[1] In Prestbury, Cheltenham and Southam, with a manor house and a dovecot: above, **325**; cf. **78** n.

[2] Cf. above, **77** nn., **325**.

[3] The dean and chapter of Hereford already owned two thirds of the tithes of the bishop of Hereford's demesne in Prestbury by 1136 when the other third was given with the parsonage to Llanthony Priory: Barrow, *Hereford Episcopal Acta 1079–1234*, no. 35. The demesne thus tithed was surveyed in the 14th century and again in 1838 when it amounted to 525 a. including 144 a. at Hyde Farm: P.R.O. C 115/77, s. vi no. 73; Glos. R.O. GDR/T1/143, schedule 4. The third and the two thirds were still farmed together in 1851: Glos. R.O. D855/T9.

[4] A quarry rented by the prior: *V.C.H. Glos.* ix. 182.

[5] Sandford bridge carrying Old Bath Road over the River Chelt: James Hodsdon, *An Historical Gazetteer of Cheltenham* (B.G.A.S. 1997), 161.

Paid to the prior and John Carwent in the year, including payments
by the hands of Richard Chapman, William Wayte, the granger
(*granitoris*) and William Skrevener   16   0   0
Paid to John Carwent at the accounting   7   6
Arrears remaining including £12 from the year's harvest   14   6   8
                                                                                                       [34   1   4]

485. Account of William Halle, bailiff and rent collector in Prestbury, Ham [in
Charlton Kings], Charlton [Kings], Southam and Leckhampton (*Prestebery, Hamme,
Charleton, Southam, Lekehampton*) for the year to Michaelmas 22 Edw. IV [1482].

	£	s.	d.
Arrears from the last account	70	3	2
Prestbury: rents of assize as in a rental of 24 Mar. 20 Edw. IV [1480][1]	4	2	7
Ham: rents as in the same rental		24	0
Charlton [Kings]: rents as in the same rental[2]		6	8
Southam: farm of the parsonage as demised to Robert Stevenes two years ago for 12 years		53	4
Leckhampton: corn tithes demised to the rector[3]		3	4
Court perquisite: heriot of Thomas Teynton deceased by court roll of 29 Mar., apart from amercements and mortuaries which belong to the farmer		8	0
Sum due	**79**	**0**	**13**

Allowances   £   s.   d.
(a) Out rent to the king for land at Southam formerly of the earl of
Hereford[4]   12
(b) Out rent of 4s. 6d. to the lord of Charlton, paid by the tenant at Ham[5]   nil
(c) Reduction in rent of a messuage and land in Prestbury, lately
Robert Lokyer's, which is now let to John Walter for 10s. by
court roll of 14 Mar. 21 Edw. IV [1481] but will yield 14s. 3d.
again after rebuilding   4   3
(d) Reduction in rent of a messuage in Prestbury, lately Richard
Arland's, now let to John Frere the vicar for 6s. 8d. by court roll
of one year ago for 20 years   4
(e) Rebate of Robert Stevenes's farm at Southam, for his good service   3   4

[1] Including rent from Brockhampton and 10s. a year from Southam: below, **486**; P.R.O.
C 115/77, s. vi no. 64.
[2] The yield of 6s. 8d. was as in the 12th century: *Charlton Kings Local Hist. Soc. Bulletin*,
xlv. 2. It here included rents of 12d. for 'Geybreche' and 9d. elsewhere: below, **486**.
[3] Tithes of Simon Despenser's demesne as given to the priory before 1158: P.R.O.
C 115/75, f. 216 no. 25; C 115/77, s. v no. 90. The tithed land comprised 96 selions and 4
furlongs extending at intervals from the town hedge in Leckhampton village to Salter's Well
hedge in Salterley: ibid. C 115/77, f. 314.
[4] For land 'by the way to Benthone hill' given in 1277: ibid. C 115/77, s. vi nos. 65–6.
[5] For 2 half-yardlands given in the 12th century, including 6d. in lieu of gilt spurs: *Charlton
Kings Local Hist. Soc. Bulletin*, xlv. 2.

(f) Reduction in rent of customary tenements and land lately of John
    Baderon and John Forke, now let to John Hogges for 21s. by court roll   2   4

(g) Rebate of arrears owed by Elizabeth widow of Thomas Teynton   30   0

(h) Rebate of John Brerage's[1] surety, at the instance of William Bette
    of [Bishop's] Cle[e]ve, for arrears on the farm of Southam parsonage   20

(i) Default of rent of the late Thomas Teynton's messuage and
    customary and demesne land, of which *Salyhegge* close is let to John
    Hogges for 4s. this year but will yield 11s. hereafter   9   4

Sum allowed   52   3

Paid to the prior and John Carwent, including payments by the hands
    of John Clyfford, William Bette and John Porter and rents of 6s.
    8d. from John Frere vicar of Prestbury, 3s. 8d. from John Nasshe
    of Prestbury, 10s. from John Walter of Prestbury, 2s. 6d. from
    Margaret Hale of Charlton [Kings] and 2s. 5d. from Thomas
    Huntley of Charlton [Kings]   8   8   3

Arrears remaining   68   0   7

         [79   1   1]

486. Schedule of arrears to the bailiff of Prestbury's account as at Michaelmas
22 Edw. IV [1482]. (Arrears at Michaelmas 1 Ric. III [1483] and Michaelmas 2 Hen.
VII [1486] are the same unless specified otherwise.)   £   s.   d.

Heirs of John Grevyle,[2] of Walter Frenssh[3] and of Walter Boroghill,
    for Charlton Kings   49   8

Tenants holding *Geybreche*[4] in Charlton Kings, for rent of 12d.
    a year from 1479 (in 1483 2s. 6d. and in 1486, when it was
    lately John Throckmorton's,[5] 3s. 3d.)   3   0

Heirs of Walter Frenssh, for rent of 9d. a year in Charlton [Kings]
    (in 1483 35s. 3d., in 1486 37s. 6d.)   34   6

---

[1] Bailiff of Sir Ralph Boteler as farmer of Cheltenham manor and hundred 1459–60: P.R.O.
SC6/853/2.

[2] Cf. above, **79** & n.

[3] d. 1476, owner of 1½ burgages and a messuage called 'Plofeldes' in Cheltenham with
land there in the tithing of Naunton: P.R.O. PROB 11/6, f. 201v. copied in Hockaday Abs.
cxlvii, 1476. About 1450 he and his namesake father, who was bailiff to successive lords of
Cheltenham 1422–49, held from the chief lord (Syon Abbey, Mdx.) a messuage, a furlong
and 13 a. in Cheltenham and a tenement, 3 messuages, 1¼ yardlands and 9 a. at Bafford in
Charlton Kings, with Lordsleyn also in Charlton: P.R.O. SC 6/852/10–23; Glos. R.O.
D855/M68, ff. 40–2.

[4] At SO 962189 N. of Mountain Knoll: *Charlton Kings Local Hist. Soc. Bulletin* xlv. 4.

[5] d. 1472; commissioner for mustering archers in Worcs. 1457: *Cal. Pat.* 1452–61, 409;
Visit. Glos. 1623, 162. Woodward of Dean Forest, lord of Apperley (in Deerhurst) and
Tirley and owner of land at Staunton (then Worcs., now Glos.), Eldersfield and Pendock
(Worcs.) and Baysham Gate (in Sellack, Herefs.): *V.C.H. Glos.* viii. 38, 98; *Calendarium
Inquisitionum post mortem* (Rec. Com.), iv. 361. He also held from the abbess of Syon a
messuage and 2 yardlands at Bafford in Charlton Kings and 2 burgages, 4 messuages and 3
yardlands in the tithings of Cheltenham: Glos. R.O. D855/M68, ff. 39, 42–3.

John Chapman as surety of Adam Carpenter, with tenants of Brock-			
hampton and executors of John Hawfield and of John Machyn		24	3
Executors of John Purce, for corn tithes in Leckhampton, and			
executors of Thomas Fosse and Robert Lokyer, for fines		18	8
Executors of John Andreux of Gloucester,[1] for Southam parsonage	13	6	8
Executors of John Hogges for the same		12	0
Executors of Catherine Burgeys for the same		23	5
Executors of William Goderugge,[2] for rent of 24s. a year in Ham			
(in 1483 £17 17s., in 1486 £21 9s.)	16	13	0
The rector of Leckhampton, for corn tithes of 3s. 4d. a year less			
3s. 4d. paid each year		10	0
John Smyth, William Gosehorn, Thomas Arlond and John Webbe,			
for Prestbury		66	7
Tenants at Charlton Kings		28	8
The rector of [Bishop's] Cleeve, for Southam parsonage		110	0
Hugh Huntley, for rent of 10s. a year in Southam from 1478 (in			
1483 50s., in 1486 £4)		40	0
Robert Whitehed of Prestbury, for rent of 9s. 8d. a year from 1473			
to 1482 apart from 12d. a year paid by him to Southam manor	4	7	0
Henry Lewyn		4	0
Richard Arlond, for rent of 7s. a year		35	0
The same, for heriot at his surrender		3	4
Elizabeth widow of Thomas Teynton, for the residue of the late			
Thomas's arrears by plea of John Vynour (in 1483 and 1486 nil)		16	8
John Hogges, rent of 32s. a year for tenements and land including			
those formerly of John Baderon and Thomas Teynton (in 1483			
74s. 8d., in 1486 53s. 4d.)		74	8
Thomas Westlond,[3] for Southam parsonage		13	4
John Brereage, for the same		46	8
Robert Stevenes, for the same (in 1483 56s. 8d., in 1486 £6 16s.)		53	4
Robert Newman (6d.), John Walter (12d.) and Thomas Champyon			
(12d.), for land lately Robert Lokyer's (in 1483 22d., in 1486 nil)			22
John Nassh, for a tenement in Prestbury lately Elizabeth Reve's (in			
1483 2s., in 1486 nil)		4	4
Elizabeth Wylkyns (in 1483 nil, in 1486 2s.)			nil
William Halle, accountant			nil
	68	**0**	**7**

[1] Cf. above, **40** n.

[2] He or a namesake was bailiff of Sir John Cornwall at Cheltenham 1417–22: P.R.O. SC 6/852/7–9. The Goodriches owned Ham Court at SO 974212 until 1574; *c.* 1450 William also held from the abbess of Syon 3 messuages, a half yardland and 17 a. at Charlton Kings together with a half yardland at Westal in Cheltenham: Glos. R.O. D855/M68, ff. 41v., 43; cf. *Charlton Kings Local Hist. Soc. Bulletin*, xx, 16; cf. xv. 12, 16.

[3] He or a namesake held a messuage and a yardland at Alstone in Cheltenham *c.* 1450: Glos. R.O. D855/M68, f. 42v.

487. Account of William Parkys, lessee of Prestbury [as above] for the year to
Michaelmas 1 Ric. III [1483].

	£	s.	d.
Arrears from the last account	14	6	8
Farm of the demesne [as before]	4	6	0
Farm of the parsonage [as before]	12	0	0
Sum due	**30**	**12**	**8**

Allowances	£	s.	d.
Storage of hay and corn while the tithe barn is ruined		10	0
3 bundles of shingles for the demesne barn (*bundellis assularum pro orreo dominicali reparando*)			18
1000 pegs (*clavis assulinis*)			13
Tiling of three bays (*tegulanti 3 spacia*) of the above barn by Hugh the *sclatter*		9	0
Repairs to the tenement lately Thomas Teynton's, now Elizabeth Wilkins's, including 4d. for a lock			10
A gown		5	0
Parchment for writing the account			4
Sum allowed		27	9

	£	s.	d.
Paid to the prior and John Carwent in the year, including payments by the hands of William Somerford, William *de stabulo* and John Newarke and payments at Newark by Hempsted (*apud Novum Edificium apud Hempsted*)	13	6	0
Paid to John Carwent at the accounting on Friday [23 Jan. 1484] before the Conversion of St. Paul		40	0
Arrears remaining including £12 for the year's harvest	13	18	11
	[**30**	**12**	**8**]

488. Account of William Halle, bailiff of Prestbury [as above] for the year to
Michaelmas 1 Ric. III [1483].

	£	s.	d.
Arrears from the last account	68	0	7
Prestbury, Ham and Charlton [Kings]: rents [as before]	5	13	3
Southam and Leckhampton: farms of spiritualities [as before]	2	16	8
Sum due	**76**	**10**	**6**

Allowances

	£	s.	d.
(a–f) [as before]		11	3
(g) Default of rent of the late Thomas Teynton's tenement in Prestbury		2	4
(h) Default of rent of land in Prestbury and Southam, lately Robert Whitehed's, let to John Walter for 4s. in this year		6	8
(i) Roofing, wattling and daubing (*pro coopertura, plectacione et dawbacione*) by John Nassh of the late Thomas Teynton's house in Prestbury		3	4
Sum allowed		23	7

	£	s.	d.
Paid to the prior and John Carwent, including payments by the hands of William Scrivener		107	10
Arrears remaining	69	19	2
	[**76**	**10**	**7**]

489. Account of William Parkys, lessee of Prestbury [as above] for the year to
Michaelmas 2 Hen. VII [1486].

	£	s.	d.
Arrears from the last account	11	2	9
Farm of the demesne [as before]	4	6	0
Farm of the parsonage [as before]	12	0	0
Sum due	**27**	**8**	**9**

Allowances

	£	s.	d.
Storage of hay and corn while the tithe barn is ruined		10	0
Repairs to the demesne barn including 10s. for 3 bays (*spacia*) repaired by Hugh the *tyler* of Bishop's Cleeve		13	8
A gown		5	0
Parchment for writing the account			4
Sum allowed		29	0

	£	s.	d.
Paid to the prior and John Carwent in the year, including a payment by Parkys's servant William Blower, payments to Thomas Clement at Cheltenham and to John Frenssh at Sevenhampton and 62s. 8d. as the price of 28 hoggs bought for the prior	13	2	8
Paid to the prior at the accounting		17	1
Arrears remaining, i.e. £12 for the year's harvest	12	0	0
	[**27**	**8**	**9**]

490. Account of William Halle, bailiff of Prestbury [as above] for the year to
Michaelmas 2 Hen. VII [1486].

	£	s.	d.
Arrears from the last account	73	7	2
Prestbury, Ham and Charlton [Kings]: rents [as before]	5	13	3
Southam and Leckhampton: farms of spiritualities [as before]	2	16	8
Sum due	**81**	**17**	**1**

Allowances	£	s.	d.
(a–e) as before		8	11
(f) Reduction in rent of customary tenements and land lately of John Baderon and John Forke, now held by John Hogges and yielding 17s. 8d. through Richard Hogges		5	8
(g) Reduction in rent of *le Sterte*,[1] a croft under Southam wood and other land, lately Robert Whitehede's, now let to John Walter for 8s. a year by court roll		2	8
Sum allowed		17	3
Paid to the prior and John Carwent, including payments by the hands of Thomas Rykarde and William Parkys		79	6
Arrears remaining	77	0	4
	[**81**	**17**	**1**]

---

[1] Meadow and arable land given in 1245 and 1289 extending N. to 'Ley brook' near Prestbury village: P.R.O. C 115/77, s. vi, f. 124.

APPENDIX II:
APPOINTMENT OF A MUSIC MASTER, 1533

From a decree of the Court of Augmentations
Public Record Office E 315/93, ff. 231v.–232[1]

The following indenture was submitted by John Hogges on 20 Nov. 33 Hen. VIII [1541]. The court ordered the receiver of revenues of the dissolved priory to pay him compensation of 106s. 8d. a year for life, with arrears since the dissolution.

491. *This indenture made the 29th day of the moneth of Marche the yere of the rayng of Kyng Henry the Eight the 24th* [1533] *betwene Richard* [Hart], *by the grace of God prior of the howse and churche of our Blessed Lady of Lanthony by Gloucester, and the covent of the same place of the one partie and John Hogges late of Coventre* [Warws.], *syngyng man,[2] of that other partie, witnesseth that the seid John Hoggys of hys meare mynde, not coacted, hath covenaunted, graunted and bargayned and by these presents doyth covenaunte, graunte and bargayn to and wyth the seid Richard, prior, and covent that the said John Hogges wyth foure childerne well and suffycyently enstructed, that is to say too meanys[3] and too trebles, shall serve the seid pryor and covent and their successou*[r]*s in the science of musycke, that is to say personally in syngyng and playeng at organs, and to kepe Our Lady masse and antheym dayly, and further well and truely to kepe all other massys and antheyms, evensonges and matens as of olde tyme hath byn accustomed to be kepte, and further as* [the] *pryor and his successours shall appoynte hym to kepe.[4]*

Also the seid John Hoggys by theise presents dooth covenaunte to and wyth the seid prior and covent that he in his owne proper person shall ryde wyth the seid prior and his successors and wayte at his table at suche tymes and seasons as he shal be appoynted and commaunded by the seid prior and his successors from the day of the makyng of these presents duryng the naturall lyf [of] *the seid John Hoggys.*

[1] Prof. Nicholas Orme and Michael Greet supplied this and supporting references.

[2] Alias Hodges, instructor of choristers at Hereford cathedral 1538–43, organist there 1538–*c.* 1582 and verger 1551–*c.* 1582: John Harper and Nicholas Orme in *Hereford Cathedral: a History*, ed. G. Aylmer and J. Tiller (London, 2000), 391 & n., 393 n., 395, 573.

[3] Boys taking the alto part in five-part polyphony (with two tenor parts) as practised by the choirs of monastic Lady chapels from *c.* 1470: Roger Bowers, *English Church Polyphony* (Ashgate Publishing, 1999), s. iii pp. 54, 56. Boy singers, called *childerne of* [the Lady] *chappull* here in the penultimate paragraph, were prohibited from the canons' choir under Cardinal Wolsey's rules: Wilkins, *Concilia*, iii. 686.

[4] The abbot of Gloucester assigned similar duties in 1515 to a music master who was also grammar master: *Hist. & Cart. Mon. Glouc.* (Rolls Ser.), iii. 290–1.

Also the seid John Hoggys shall well and suffycyently enstructe and teche in the seid science of musike, syngyng and playing at organs as well all suche chanons[1] as other childerne as shall playce [i.e. please] the seid prior and his successours to have enstructed and taught in the seid sciyence duryng the terme aforeseid; and that the seid John Hoggys shall see that the seid foure chyldren be suffycyent arayed in their vesture, and further shall dyscarge the seid prior and his successours as well for their seid vestures and apperell as for logyng, wasshyng and wryngyng wyth all other necessares to them apperteynyng, as well in syckneys as in helthe, excepte mete and drynke whyche the seid prior and his successours shall fynd them upon their owne proper costs and charges duryng the terme aforeseid.

For all whiche covenaunts, grauntys, bargayns and aggreaments befor specyfyed of the seid John Hoggs' behalfe to be well and truely performed and kepte, the seid prior and covent covenauntyth and grauntyth to and wyth the seid John that he shall have yerely duryng the seid terme for his wagys eight poundes three shyllyngs foure pence sterling to be paid to the seid John at [the] foure termes in the yere moost usuall by equall porcions. Also the seid John shall have wykely duryng the terme aforeseid syx caste[2] of whyte brede of the same [kind] that the lordys gentylmen shall ete in the lord's hall, and syx gallons of good ale wykely duryng the seid terme. Also the seid John Hoggys to have yerely the grasse for a cowe all the sommer goyng wyth the seid prior's kene and his successours', and a lode of hey agaynst the wynter to be caryed wyth the lordes wayne home to his howse yerely duryng the seid terme.

And yf it happen the seid John Hoggys herafter by [f. 232] reason of syknes or age that he be not able to doo his servyce in maner and forme above rehersyd, that then the seid John Hoggys shall fynde an able and suffycyent person to do the seid servyce whiche he is bounde to do, or ells to abate half his wagys and halfe all other thyngs to him graunted by these presents towarde the wagys of the seid person untyll suche tyme the seid John Hoggys be able to do his servyce in hys owne proper person. And also the seid prior and covent and their successours shall fynde the seid foure childerne meate, drynke, wasshyng, wryngyng, lodgeyng wyth all other maner necessaryes to them apperteynyng upon their owne costys and charges duryng the terme that the seid John Hoggs shall not be able to do his servyce hymselfe.

Also it shal be lawfull to the seid John Hoggys to absent hymselfe yerely by the space of foure wykes, requyryng lycence of the seid prior and his successours, so that he be not absent at noo solempe feast in the yere duryng the terme aforeseid. Also the seid prior and his successours shall assigne or appoynt too of the seid childerne to be of chapull at all tymes duryng the seid terme, and the seid John Hoggs to admyt and appoint the too other childerne at his pleysure duryng the seid terme.

In witnes wherof the parteis aforeseid to theise present indentures inter-

---

[1] Wolsey allowed canons to sing polyphony in their own choir on Sundays and holidays but prohibited canons other than a celebrant from singing with a Lady chapel choir: Wilkins, *Concilia*, iii. 686. The latter rule may have been ignored at Llanthony since the indenture does not mention clerks as supplying the men's parts.

[2] i.e. bakings: *O.E.D.*

chaungeably have put to their saylles. Yoven in our chapyter howse of Lanthony aforeseid the day and yere above seid. Also it is covenaunted that the seid John Hoggys shall have mete and drynke wythin the monastery of Lanthony aforeseid for hymselfe duryng the terme aforeseid.

INDEX OF PERSONS AND PLACES

References are normally to the serial numbers of the entries; those in roman figures are to the pages of the introduction. Welsh patronymics beginning with 'ap' are indexed as surnames. The unqualified title 'prior' or 'canon' refers to a prior or a canon of Llanthony-by-Gloucester. The footnotes have not been systematically indexed.

Buckinghamshire, *see* Beaconsfield; Chearsley; Ravenstone

Bucknell, William, 174

Buckwold, *see* Cranham

Bullock (Bullocke, Bulloke), Thomas the younger, 270

— William, 69

Burford (Oxon.), man of (*named*), 397–8

Burforde, William, refectorer of Ciren., 236

Burgeys, Catherine, 486

Burggis, *see* Bridges

Burghill (Herefs.), 226 (p. 93)

— bailiff (*named*), xxx

— church, 226 (p. 92)

— churchyard, 147, 466–7

— manor, xxx

— Tillington chapel, xxvi, 147, 226, 466–7

Burghill (Boroghill, Borowehill), Walter, 486

— William, notary public, xxvi, 333 *n*, 335, 347, 349, 371–2, 392, 434, 451

Burnell, Thomas, 91–3

— William, 91–3

Burscough (Lancs.), priory, 231, 420

Burton, William, canon of Ciren., 236

Bushmead (Beds.), priory, 231

Butler (Botiler, Botyler), John le, of Llantwit, 339

— Richard, chaplain, 348

— William, bailiff of Glouc., 84

Butley (Suff.), priory, 231

Butor, William, 7 (p. 6)

Butte, John, coroner of Glouc., 23

— Robert, bailiff of Glouc., 74

Byconyll, *see* Bicknell

Byrde, *see* Bird

Bysshop (Bysshoppe), *see* Bishop

Cady, James, prior's bailiff at Glouc., xxix

Caernarvonshire, *see* Bangor; Bardsey; Beddgelert; St. Tudwal's

Calais (France), 445 *n*, 447

Caldicot (Mon.), xiv

— bailiff (*named*), xxix

— castle, 319

— church, proctors of, xxv–xxvi, xxviii, 131, 214, 319

— man of (*named*), 266, 401

— park, 319

— rectory, 248, 266–7, 410

— vicarage, 140

Caldwell (Beds.), priory, 231

Calowe, Humphrey, bailiff of Westbury-on-Severn, xxix

Cambridgeshire, *see* Anglesey

Canon Frome, *see* Frome

Canons Ashby, *see* Ashby

Canterbury, province, archbishops of, *see* Bourgchier, Thomas; Deane, Henry; Warham, William; Winchelsey, Robert

— convocations (1460–1), xxvi, 58–9, 63, 67; (1497), 204 *n*; (1502), xxiii, xxvi, 114, 376; (1514–15), xxvi, 302, 331–4, 426

— court, 75

— — notaries public at (*named*), 434

— — proctors at (*named*), 3 (p. 2), 4

Canton, Richard, 123

Capel, John, alderman of Glouc., 117

— Richard, clerk, 172

Cardington (Beds.), man of (*named*), 356

Carew, Richard of, bishop of St. David's, 284

Carey, *see* Fownhope

Carlisle (Cumb.), priory, 231

Carlyon, John, prior of Launceston, 419

Carmarthen, prior of (*named*), 418

Carmarthenshire, *see* Talley

Carpenter (Carpentar), Adam, 486

— John, bishop of Worcester, 1–2, 3 (pp.1–3), 5–6, 39, 58, 63, 71

— John, refectorer of Llanthony, 3 (p. 2)

— Rees, 170

Carwent (Carewent), John, of Newent, xxviii, 117, 119, 143, 225, 484–5, 487–90

Castello, Adrian de, bishop of Hereford, 132

Celestine III, pope, 29

Cely, Alexander, clerk of the Admiralty, 68–9

Cerney, South, bailiff of (*named*), xxix

— — Cerney Wick mill, 294

— — manor and tithes, xxvii, xxix–xxx, 292, 477

Cerney (Cernay, Serney, Serynen), —, 220

— William, precentor of Ciren., 236

Chaddesley (Chaddysley, Chadesley, Chadisley, Chadsley), William, canon, 300, 319, 328, 335, 434

— — prior's chaplain, xxv, 336

— — subcellarer of Llanthony, 355

Chadwell, John, of Stow-on-the-Wold, xxvii–xxviii, 117, 120, 142–3, 218

Champyon, Thomas, 486

Chandos (Chaundos), John, prior, 36

SELECTIVE INDEX OF SUBJECTS

References are normally to the serial numbers of the entries; those in roman figures are to the pages of the introduction.

229